MISS TEENAGE AMERICA
Tells How to
MAKE THE GOOD
THINGS HAPPEN

*A potpourri of ideas
from many of your friends
who have survived the teenage years—
and who hope to help make good
things happen for you*

MISS TEENAGE AMERICA
Tells How to
MAKE THE GOOD THINGS HAPPEN

COMPILED AND EDITED BY
Judith D. Houghton
Executive Vice President, MISS TEENAGE AMERICA

Associate Editors
BONNIE PIEDMONTE
JUDY THOMAS

Special Illustrations by Mac Martin

ABELARD-SCHUMAN
NEW YORK

Photograph Acknowledgments

OFFICIAL PAGEANT PHOTOGRAPHERS

1976 Pageant:
    John McCormack, Tulsa, Oklahoma
    Bob McCormack, Tulsa, Oklahoma

1975 Pageant:
    Rod Dungan, Little Rock, Arkansas
    David Conrad, Little Rock, Arkansas

1974 Pageant:
    Bud Fichte, Fort Worth, Texas

1973 Pageant:
    Smiley Irvin, Fort Worth, Texas

1972, 1971, 1970 Pageants:
    Jarrold Cabluck, Fort Worth, Texas

Pageants prior to 1970:
    Don Barnett, Fort Worth, Texas
    John Mazziotta, Dallas, Texas

1961 Pageant:
    Charles Neblett, Dallas, Texas

PHOTOGRAPHY FOR "EXERCISE" CHAPTER
    Terry Wier, Dallas, Texas

OTHER PHOTOGRAPHS
    Ed Findley, Braniff International, Dallas, Texas
    Peter Hogg, Honolulu, Hawaii
    Robert Lubell, Toledo, Ohio
    David Sinkler, Arlington, Texas
    Ken White, Dallas, Texas

Copyright © 1976 by MISS TEENAGE AMERICA
1165 Empire Central Place, Suite 101, Dallas, Tex. 75247
All Rights Reserved

The mark MISS TEENAGE AMERICA® is registered in the United States Patent Office. Use of this mark without written permission from MISS TEENAGE AMERICA, Dallas, Texas, is prohibited.

MISS TEENAGE AMERICA is an operating division of the Dr Pepper Company, Dallas, Texas.

Published simultaneously in Canada by Fitzhenry & Whiteside Limited, Toronto.

Designed by S. S. Drate

Manufactured in the United States of America

Library of Congress Cataloging in Publication Data
Main entry under title:

Miss Teenage America tells how to make the good
  things happen.

   1. Adolescent girls—Addresses, essays, lectures.
I. Miss Teenage America (Corporate body)
HQ798.M57   301.43'15   76-12407
ISBN 0-200-04037-5
ISBN 0-200-04038-3 (special pbk. ed.)

2 3 4 5 6 7 8 9 10

DEDICATION

There was a man who was unique among men. He spent forty years of his working life in the business of the theater and during that time, created innovations that changed the face of theater in America.

Integrity was his byword and everyone who knew him associated his name with honesty and a passion for high principles.

Because he was one of them, all of the show business greats were his friends and they could always count on his friendship in return. But though he was respected by America's idols, he was perhaps the best friend a teenager ever had. He was a rare man, of great stature, who never knew there was such a thing as a generation gap.

He touched the lives of young people by the thousands each year. He counseled them. He taught them. He listened to them. He guided them. He defended them. But most of all, he believed in them.

This was the man who breathed the first breath of life into the MISS TEENAGE AMERICA Program. He served as its President and Executive Producer of the national telecast. He built the Program into the national entity it is today, carefully protecting it from those who sought to exploit it and guarding its integrity every inch of the way. He was the very heartbeat of MISS TEENAGE AMERICA and the very special person who could always bring a smile to the faces of the MISS TEENAGE AMERICA Candidates. He was the man who gave them wonderful memories and a new belief in themselves.

This unique man passed away suddenly and unexpectedly soon after this book was completed. Those who had an opportunity to share part of his life were the fortunate ones. It is our fondest hope that this book will continue his devotion to helping and encouraging teenagers.

With love and respect we dedicate this book to the memory of

CHARLES R. MEEKER, JR.

BOB HOPE—ADMIRED AND RESPECTED BY TEENS FOR HIS LIFETIME OF SERVICE TO OTHERS.

Bob Hope, at the top of teenagers' list of great Americans, says, "I'm very high on today's teenagers. That's why I am so confident that our future is in good hands."

No single individual in American life is more esteemed or held in greater affection than Bob Hope.

His devotion to the welfare of our nation and his belief in the well-being and happiness of people of all ages has been exemplified by an outpouring of his energies, his time, and his talents to bring sunshine where there was darkness, smiles where there were frowns, and optimism where there was gloom.

A virtual idol of teenagers around the globe, he has demonstrated by his life that serving others is one of the greatest and most enduring achievements. Chosen by MISS TEENAGE AMERICA Candidates as their "Favorite American," Mr. Hope was our first and only choice to write the introduction for this book.

Where there is Bob Hope—there is also hope for all of us that life may widen our horizons, while granting each one of us its richest blessings.

CHARLES R. MEEKER, Jr.
President
MISS TEENAGE AMERICA

Introduction

BY
BOB HOPE

Asking me to write an introduction to a book for teenagers is like requesting Alice Cooper to write a book about Grand Opera. However, I'm notorious for biting off more than I can chew . . . and chewing it, so here goes.

If my memory can be trusted, I vaguely recall a time in the distant past when I was a teenager. And regardless of what you may have read, I was not Betsy Ross's date at her senior prom. Of course, the country was vastly different when I was a teenager. In those dear bygone days, a "hippie" was a girl who was overweight . . . a drop-out was a kid with loose knickers . . . when you looked for grass, you were planning a picnic . . . and if you wanted to take a "trip" you called Hertz-Rent-a-Horse!

How things have changed. We had no television, no hotcombs, no Dippity-Do, no "Big Macs," no Lady Remingtons, no Certs, no rock festivals . . . how we survived is one of the mysteries of the world.

Today, a teenager without a sports car, or at least a Honda, an eight-track stereo rig, a credit card, and a roomful of tapes is considered underprivileged.

But really, I am somewhat qualified to express my views on today's youth because I have two daughters, who not so long ago were teenagers, and they were constantly coming to me with their earth-shaking problems. And I'm proud to say I invariably had the answers to every one of them. It was "Go ask your mother!"

Could that be one reason why I was never voted "Father of the Year"?

I may not have known the answers but this timely book compiled by the sponsors of MISS TEENAGE AMERICA certainly does. Indeed, there isn't an area of interest to young people that is not covered in great detail by experts in their fields. In fact, this book might accurately have been titled "Everything Every Teenager Needs to Know."

For instance, the chapter on make-up and skin care was so engrossing, I rushed out and bought some acne cream. Actually, I don't do my own make-up. I'm fortunate in having the finest make-up man in show business. You may have seen the film based on his association with me—*The Miracle Worker!*

I was especially interested in the chapter dealing with the importance of a sense of humor. A sense of humor is vital to any youngster regardless of the field of endeavor he or she eventually chooses. The importance of humor cannot be overestimated. Look what it's done for "Laverne and Shirley."

I consider this book *must* reading for every teenager who wants to reach his or her full potential, especially since there are now more career opportunities for women than ever before.

The advice in this book is extremely useful whether you choose a profession or marriage, or for that matter both. In short, it can make you a happier, healthier, more fulfilled human being.

I'm very high on today's teenagers because they are the most aware, the best informed, and the most concerned in our history.

That is why I am so confident that our future is in good hands.

Contents

INTRODUCTION   vii
    by Bob Hope

FOREWORD   xvii
    by Charles R. Meeker, Jr.

ADVENTURE I
Making the "Beautiful" Things Happen

FEATURING FABULOUS FACES (Make-up and Skin Care)   3
    by Julie Bell, Bonne Bell Cosmetics

YOUR CROWNING GLORY (Hair Care)   20
    by Susan Bigler, Model

TO SEE OURSELVES AS OTHERS SEE US
    (Dressing to the Best Advantage)   25
    by Donna Miller, Designer, PBJ Fashions

THE FIGURE FACTORY   31
    by Karen Petersen, MISS TEENAGE AMERICA 1975 and Judith Houghton
    EXERCISES—DEMONSTRATED   34
    DRAT THAT FAT   55
    BASIC FOODS FOR HEALTH   56
    SOME SUGGESTIONS   56

TWENTY QUESTIONS
    (The Twenty Most Often-asked Questions)   59
    by Beauty Editor, Teen Magazine

ADVENTURE II
Making Good Things Happen with Others

INNER BEAUTY (Personal Values)   67
    by Colleen Fitzpatrick, MISS TEENAGE AMERICA 1972;
    Melissa Galbraith, MISS TEENAGE AMERICA 1973;
    Lori Matsukawa, MISS TEENAGE AMERICA 1974

A SURVEY OF HIGH ACHIEVERS   74
    by Paul Krouse, Publisher, Who's Who Among American High School Students

HOME IS WHERE THE HEART IS
    (Family and Parental Relationships)   77
    by Bonnie Piedmonte, Special Education Teacher

I'LL TELL THEM   82
    by Erma Bombeck, Nationally Syndicated Columnist

A FRIEND IN DEED OR A FRIEND IN NEED?
    (The Art of Being a Good Friend)   84
    by Marvin Porter, Youth Worker

ATTITUDE—YOUR APPROACH TO LIFE, LOVE AND BEAUTIFUL FRIENDSHIPS   87
    by Elizabeth Lacey, Oklahoma Association for Mental Health

THE COMMON SENSE (A Sense of Humor)   91
    by Dick Hitt, Feature Columnist, Dallas Times Herald

HEY, LOOK ME OVER
    (What Guys Look for in the Girls They Date)   96
    by The Gary Moore Singers, National Pageant Escorts

QUESTIONS TEENAGERS ASK THE MOST— AND THE ANSWERS   101
    by Jean Adams, Nationally Syndicated Teen Columnist

ADVENTURE III

Making Your Femininity a Beautiful Part of Your Life

HOW TO SURVIVE ADOLESCENCE   120
    by The Editors

HUMAN SEXUALITY: MORE THAN ONLY NATURAL   124
    by Eric W. Johnson, Author and Teacher

ADVENTURE IV

Making Your Own Success Story Happen

IT'S YOUR CHOICE   136
    by Margaret Epps, Author, Encyclopedia of Careers and Vocational Guidance

A SAMPLING OF OPPORTUNITIES IN COMMUNICATIONS 143
   JOURNALISM 143
      by Nikki Nixon, Women's Page Editor, Michigan City, Indiana, News Dispatch
   TELEVISION—ON CAMERA 145
      by Tina Coleman Loy, Assistant Promotion Director, KCST-TV, San Diego, California
   TELEVISION—BEHIND THE SCENES 149
      by Doris Williams, Manager, Practices, NBC Television Network

A SAMPLING OF OPPORTUNITIES IN EDUCATION 151
   CLASSROOM TEACHING 151
      by Suzanne Meadows Taylor, Teacher
   COUNSELING 153
      by Diane Morisato, Counselor, University of Hawaii
   EDUCATIONAL TELEVISION 156
      by Jan Paulich Jones, Teacher/Performer, "Telewave Reports," Cleveland, Ohio

A SAMPLING OF OPPORTUNITIES IN FASHION 159
   MODELING 159
      by Jayne Modean, Teenage Model
   FASHION RETAILING AND PROMOTION 162
      by Jeanine Zavrel Fearns, Fashion Coordinator, MISS TEENAGE AMERICA *1964*
   MORE ABOUT FASHION 165
      by Mary Kernan and Ester Bogart, Lord & Taylor

A SAMPLING OF OPPORTUNITIES IN GOVERNMENT 166
   WOMEN IN GOVERNMENT 166
      by U.S. Representative and Mrs. Dale Milford
   WOMEN IN THE ARMED FORCES 168
      by Anne Taubeneck, Editor, LadyCom *Magazine*
   ACTION PROGRAMS—THE PEACE CORPS AND VISTA 171
      by Betty Murphy, Office of Public Affairs

A SAMPLING OF OPPORTUNITIES IN MEDICINE 174
   HEALTH INDUSTRY CAREERS 174
      by Texas Hospital Association
   MEDICINE 178
      by Judy Harvey, Medical Student

NURSING   182
    by Nancy Meek Taylor, Surgical Nurse
DENTAL HYGIENE   183
    by Karen P. Hughes, Dental Hygienist

A SAMPLING OF OPPORTUNITIES IN THEATRICAL
    AND PERFORMING ARTS   186
  THE THEATER—A PRODUCER'S VIEW   187
    by Charles R. Meeker, Jr., President and Executive Producer, MISS TEENAGE AMERICA *Pageant and Telecast*
  THE THEATER—A VIEW FROM THE STAGE   193
    by Barbara Sigel, Actress
  A CAREER IN MUSIC   197
    by Lehman Engel, Conductor, Composer, Author, and Lecturer

A SAMPLING OF OPPORTUNITIES IN TRANSPORTATION   201
  AIRLINE OPPORTUNITIES   201
    by John E. Raymond, Airline Executive
  LADY AT THE THROTTLE   206
    by George T. Grader, Santa Fe Railroad

A SAMPLING OF OTHER PROFESSIONAL AND
    TECHNICAL OPPORTUNITIES   210
  TAX AUDITOR   210
    by Johnnie Nell Young, Auditor
  A CAREER IN ELECTRONIC DATA PROCESSING   212
    by Jim Battistoni, Electronic Data Systems, Inc.
  ENGINEERING   215
    by Anita Columbo Morgan, Electrical Engineer
  THE FLORAL INDUSTRY   216
    by J. M. Schmidt, President, Florafax International, Inc.
  HOTEL SALES AND PROMOTION   219
    by Anastasia Rene Kostoff, Director of Sales, Beverly Wilshire Hotel
  INTERIOR DECORATION   221
    by Felicia Hebert Kaplan, Interior Decorator
  PUBLIC RELATIONS—MEDIA BUYING   222
    by Beverly A. Martin, Media Director, Hal Lawrence Agency
  SALESMANSHIP   224
    by Ebby Halliday, Realtor

URBAN AND REGIONAL PLANNING 226
by Jeannie Gruber, Senior Planner, East Central Regional Planning Council

YOUNG WOMEN AND PRIVATE ENTERPRISE 229
by John Benjamin, President, Youth Enterprise Foundation, Inc.

HOW TO APPLY FOR A JOB 231
by S. Robert Freede, author, Cash for College *and President, Scholarship Search*

PERSONAL GUIDELINES FOR SUCCESS IN YOUR CAREER 241
by Western Temporary Services

ADVENTURE V
Making Your Education a Lifetime Experience

LET'S TALK ABOUT YOU—YOUR ABILITIES, YOUR GOALS, AND YOUR FUTURE 247
by O'Neil Harris, Director of Vocational Education, Arlington Public Schools, Texas

MOVIN' ON UP 250
by Whitmer High School Guidance Department, Toledo, Ohio

COLLEGE PROSPECTING 254
by Admissions Office, University of Rochester

"I WISH I'D KNOWN THAT BEFORE I CAME TO COLLEGE" 259
by Rochester University Freshmen

TO THE CLASS OF 1979 265
by Jacob Neusner, Professor of Religious Studies, Brown University

EXCERPTS FROM FINANCIAL AIDS 270
by Oreon Keeslar, Financial Aids for Higher Education

EXCERPTS FROM CASH FOR COLLEGE 281
by S. Robert Freede, President, Scholarship Search

THE MISS TEENAGE AMERICA SCHOLARSHIP PROGRAM 291
by Cathy Durden, MISS TEENAGE AMERICA *1976*

HOW TO BE A SUPER STUDENT 292
by Dr. William Nault, World Book Encyclopedia

STUDYING ABROAD 298
by Council on International Educational Exchange

ADVENTURE VI
Making the Experiences of Others a Bridge over Troubled Waters

HOW TO BE A WINNER WHEN YOU FEEL LIKE A LOSER
(Teens vs Alcohol and Drugs) 305
by Mary Swensen, Drug Education Consultant

THE TRUTH BEHIND THE V.D. SCARE 312
by Kathy McCoy, Teen Magazine

ABORTION—YES, NO, AND WHY? 320
by Kathy McCoy, Teen Magazine

ADVENTURE VII
Making the Most of Your Youth

MAKING THE MOST OF FUN 333
  PERFECT PARTIES AND ENCORE ENTERTAINING 333
by Judy Due, Director, Consumer Service, Dr Pepper Company
  TRAVELING ABROAD 345
by Council on International Educational Exchange

MAKING AN OUNCE OF PREVENTION WORTH A POUND OF CURE 355
  AVOIDING DANGEROUS SITUATIONS 355
by Clarence M. Kelley, Director, Federal Bureau of Investigation
  SAFETY ON THE STREETS 361
by Officer Gay Fisher and Lt. Gary Fisher, Law Enforcement Officers

MAKING "I CAN" A PART OF BEING AMERICAN 374
  WHY YOUNG PEOPLE SHOULD TAKE AN INTEREST IN THE GOVERNMENT 375
by John B. Connally, Statesman and National Leader

I AM PROUD TO BE AN AMERICAN 378
    by W. W. Clements, Chairman of the Board and
    President, Dr Pepper Company
I SPEAK FOR DEMOCRACY 382
    by Susan Huskisson, Miss Teenage Knoxville,
    Tennessee 1967
INVOLVEMENT FOR ENVIRONMENT 384
    by Karen Petersen, MISS TEENAGE AMERICA *1975*
INVOLVEMENT TO HELP OTHERS 386
    by Cathy Durden, MISS TEENAGE AMERICA *1976*

ADVENTURE VIII
MISS TEENAGE AMERICA *Makes the Good Things Happen*

THE MISS TEENAGE AMERICA EXPERIENCE 391
    NOT A BEAUTY CONTEST 392
    NATIONAL AWARDS 392

HOW TO ENTER THE MISS TEENAGE AMERICA PAGEANT 395
    THE LOCAL PAGEANT 396
    THE CANDIDATE-AT-LARGE PROGRAM 396
    THE OVERSEAS CANDIDATE-AT-LARGE PROGRAM 396
    OFFICIAL RULES 397
    ABOUT THE JUDGING 398
    HOW CAN I PREPARE? 398
    STOP! LOOK! LISTEN! 399

WHAT IT'S LIKE TO BE MISS TEENAGE AMERICA 402
    by Colleen Fitzpatrick, MISS TEENAGE AMERICA *1972;*
    Melissa Galbraith, MISS TEENAGE AMERICA *1973;*
    Lori Matsukawa, MISS TEENAGE AMERICA *1974*

VIEW FROM BEHIND THE POTTED PALM 409
    by Irma Petersen, Mother of MISS TEENAGE AMERICA *1975*

BEING A WINNER—EVEN IF YOU DON'T GET FIRST PRIZE 413
    by Patti Larkin, Miss Teenage San Diego 1974

FROM THE PRESIDENT'S FILE
    (A Sharing of Special Thoughts) 417
    by Charles R. Meeker, Jr., President, MISS TEENAGE
    AMERICA

MISS TEENAGE AMERICA
This Was Your Special Year

KAREN PETERSEN
1975

CATHY DURDEN
1976

DIANE COX
1962

DARLA BANKS
1963

LORI MATSUKAWA
1974

MELISSA GALBRAITH
1973

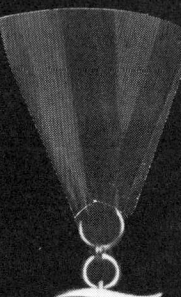

JEANINE ZAVREL
1964

COLLEEN FITZPATRICK
1972

CAROLYN MIGNINI
1965

REWA WALSH
1971

COLETTE DAIUTE
1966

DEBORAH
(DEBBIE) PATTON
1970

MELISSA BABISH
1969

STEPHANIE CRANE
1968

SANDY ROBERTS
1967

Foreword

BY

CHARLES R. MEEKER, Jr.
President, MISS TEENAGE AMERICA

More than a generation has passed since I created a miracle by making it through my teenage years. The pains are only dimly remembered, but I still carry some of the scars.

Now, my work year is spent almost entirely with men and women who are considerably younger. Some are in their teens. I consider this to be one of the richest blessings of my career.

While claiming no special wisdom as it relates to youth, I do believe that I am kept aware of current problems with which young women and men must cope.

I do not believe the values have changed, but I quickly acknowledge that our present society has multiplied the complexities of the problems. The answers are harder to find and the solutions are more difficult to achieve.

I continue to believe deeply in the eternal truths. Love. Honor. Integrity. Individual Achievement. To Be at Peace with One's Self. I also believe in the eternal opportunities to make these truths a part of our lives, which is the ultimate triumph.

It seems exceedingly wasteful to personally experience the normal and easily available disasters just to prove that they are correctly labeled. To ignore the warning lamps lighted by those who have "been there once before" is like driving on the wrong side of the street in heavy traffic just to see what will happen.

You are certain to have a special experience during the drive. It may take some time to determine whether it was worth the cost.

If there were no other benefits of experienced information and good advice, the time spent enjoying the multitude of available pleasures instead of recuperating from an accident would be enough.

That's what this book hopes to accomplish.
Like all good road maps, it will guarantee a desired destination when honestly followed. It will also bring you there in the shortest possible

time, but in direct proportion to the number of side-trips you feel you must make.

It is also another opportunity for MISS TEENAGE AMERICA to serve its own generation.

"There is only one MISS TEENAGE AMERICA" and we continue to believe that the steady and continuing growth of our organization is due solely to our determination to be meaningful to a very special age in a very special world in a very special way.

Others have attempted to imitate our name and our methods of operation, but never our integrity or our purpose.

If by this book we continue to touch the lives of young women in a positive way, and in the same manner as the MISS TEENAGE AMERICA program has been able to do, then such an achievement shall serve to widen our horizons and strengthen our determination to press forward.

We remain dedicated in our belief that we shall have a better world in which to live when each one of us shall have determined that it be so.

We believe there is action, excitement and even drama on many of the pages, yet no story line is intended. Can there be more excitement or drama than discovering even a single fact that will change your life?

Expertise is indeed hard to come by and is the result of years of diligence and superior workmanship. We, at MISS TEENAGE AMERICA, consider ourselves rich indeed to have been favored so generously by so many experts who deserve their titles.

We will remain deeply and happily indebted to all of those exceptional people who have elected to be a part of this endeavor and who have signified their willingness to share our objectives by generous contributions of their time, their expertise and their wisdom.

Our gratitude to each one of them shall abide and it is our dream that many lives will be touched in a positive and rewarding way.

This book presupposes that good things can and do happen. We want them to happen to you.

ADVENTURE I

Making the "Beautiful" Things Happen

YOUTH

You see youth as a joyous thing
About which love and laughter cling
You see youth as a joyous elf
Who sings sweet songs to please himself
You see his laughing sparkling eyes
To take earth's wonders with surprise
You think him free from cares and woes
And naught of fear you think he knows
You see him tall, naively bold
You glimpse these things, for you are old

But I—I see him otherwise
An unknown fear within his eyes
He works and plays and never knows
Where he is called or why he goes
Each youth sustains within his breast
A vague, infinite unrest
He goes about in still alarm
With shrouded future at his arm
With longings that can find no tongue
I see him thus—for I am young

Chas. Brown

Featuring Fabulous Faces

**BY
JULIE BELL**

Julie Bell, a teenager herself, has a reason for being the expert she is on skin care and cosmetics. Her father, Jess Bell, is the President of the well-known Bonne Bell, Inc., known for its outstanding line of cosmetics for "young women of all ages." Her aunt, Bonnie Bell, is the company's namesake and Julie (featured in dozens of magazine ads), its image.

If you are the kind of girl who wants to be able to look in the mirror and see a reflection of the All-American natural look, there is a place for you.

You don't have to resort to following crazy fads or relying on artificial gimmicks because your own natural, good looks are the real attention-getters. You really care about having clean, clear, honest skin and soft shiny hair so you don't mind spending a few minutes daily to keep both in the best shape possible. You're so good at applying make-up that no one even knows you wear it at all.

Because you're natural, fresh and vital, you have that kind of beauty which never grows old. You're the kind of young woman who will get up at sunrise for the first run just for the thrill of making tracks in the snow. On the tennis court, you can afford to play as hard as any man because you can still be as soft as any woman. Well, even if you just dream about it, you still look as if you could hang ten, win 6-0 at Forest Hills, or teach the instructors a thing or two on the slopes.

The foundation of the All-American natural look is clean, clear honest skin. A face that can strip down to its birthday suit and never be ashamed is the face to have. Modern cosmetics and make-up techniques can do wonders for any girl but even the most skillful application of make-up can't conceal a bad complexion.

"Beauty is more than skin deep" but there is no reason why a girl shouldn't put her best face forward along with a great personality. The combination is unbeatable!

Your skin condition depends partly on heredity—whether you are dark or fair, whether your skin texture is fine or coarse, whether it is sun-sensitive or sun-resistant, oily or dry. You can't change your genes. But you can maintain and even improve most skin conditions through proper care and by following common sense rules for overall good health.

Eating sensibly, getting enough sleep, and outdoor exercise are good for your skin as well as your general health.

WHAT ABOUT SKIN PROBLEMS

During the teens and twenties, even the smoothest complexion can run into trouble; an "oily" shine that comes right through your make-up, a sprinkling of blackheads, or a flock of red blemishes that won't budge.

The explanation for this is easier than the cure. Beneath the surface of your skin are tiny "sebaceous" glands which secrete the natural oil "sebum" that lubricates your skin and hair. While you're young, certain body changes speed up this oil secretion, and your pores can't throw off the excess oil fast enough. The result is hard little plugs called blackheads or whiteheads.

The worst thing you can do is pick-and-squeeze a blackhead or whitehead. Squeezing will only puncture skin tissue, leave the pore wide open for infection, and cause irritations, bruises, or possibly, scars.

KEEP YOUR COMPLEXION SUPER CLEAN

The smart way to handle your complexion problems, then, is to keep your skin clean, but ordinary soap and water can clean only the skin surface; it can't sink down to where your troubles begin. That's why I recommend a good deep-cleansing lotion that seeps into pores to loosen and lift up excess oil, soil and stale make-up.

Moisten a cotton pad with deep-cleansing lotion; then start at the neck and scrub upward: around the mouth, up and across the cheeks, up the nose, across the forehead, up into the hairline. Use upward, outward strokes that are brisk, but not rough, to get it deep into pores.

Follow this procedure at least twice a day. First thing in the morning to refresh your skin and prevent mid-morning "shine." And last thing at night to remove all traces of make-up.

A medicated deep-cleansing lotion will help clear up any blemishes you already have, and keep your complexion well-protected. If you want to suds-away surface oil and make-up first, choose a complexion bar with a matching medicated formula. Make sure the cleansing bar is non-alkaline, so it won't leave a drying, irritating "soapy" film.

KEEP YOUR SKIN IN-THE-PINK WITH A STIMULANT

When anything stops up, it becomes sluggish. When your pores clog up with excess oil, your complexion may turn "murky" or "pale." Now's the time for a creamy facial masque to help speed up the blood flow that makes you glow. A medicated masque works best because it helps heal blemishes and draws out impurities as it dries on your skin.

Three times a week, spread the medicated masque on your face and throat. Let your pores tighten and your skin tingle for ten minutes. Wash off with tepid water and rinse with cool. You'll actually feel your skin being stimulated. That's why your complexion looks brighter and clearer.

Use your masque as a quick spot treatment to draw out the excess inside a bad bump, and to help heal up those real stubborn blemishes. Before you go to bed, dab the masque on affected areas. Let it work overnight. Then remove in the morning with deep cleansing lotion.

GET A HEAD START ON BEAUTY

Your hair can be your crowning glory or your worst enemy, looking stringy and flaky and causing blemishes.

That's right—blemishes. Excess oil can also build up in your scalp, trap dead flakes of skin, attract dirt and eventually turn to dandruff. This condition can spread through your bangs and cheek curls to cause facial blemishes (as well as looking very unattractive.)

To help clear up your scalp and your complexion, I recommend using a good medicated shampoo to remove that excess dirt and oil. For best results, always lather up twice; once to remove the heavy dirt and again to let the medication take action.

Another way to shake dandruff: keep your comb and brush clean, and keep them to yourself!

If dandruff isn't your problem, but split ends and fly-away hair are, make yours a protein shampoo to give your hair nourishment plus the body and bounce you want.

It's a good idea to use a conditioner after you shampoo to help make your hair soft and shiny and to ease out tangles.

ENJOY A FRAGRANT BATH EVERY DAY

I can't stress enough the importance of a daily bath or shower in your beauty routine. Fresh, clean skin makes you feel prettier and more confident, and a daily moisturizing helps your skin actually stay prettier.

Be sure to add a few drops of bath emollients to your water to soften skin and help smooth roughness on heels, knees and elbows. If you prefer to shower, why not use a fragrant liquid cleanser that moisturizes as it bubbles.

We'll talk about manicures and pedicures later. However, do take a few minutes before your bath to do any clipping or filing. Once nails are softened by water, trimming can cause them to shred or flake.

KEEP FRESH AND POISED WITH AN ANTI-PERSPIRANT

A normal flow of perspiration is healthy, helping to regulate your body temperature and purify your skin by eliminating waste. But once perspiration has a chance to linger, it attracts bacteria that cause body odor and clothing stains. That's why it's important to take a daily bath or shower, and follow up with an anti-perspirant deodorant. As an anti-perspirant, it controls the actual flow of perspiration by contracting your skin pores. As a deodorant, it helps prevent body odor by destroying skin bacteria.

Always apply anti-perspirant to dry skin that's fresh, clean and free of hair. To keep up your fresh, clean appearance, be sure to change your lingerie daily, and give your clothes a good "airing" between trips to the cleaners.

PUT YOUR SKIN ON A BALANCED DIET

Now that you've cleansed and cared for your skin, don't feed your complexion the wrong kind of food. When you crave chocolates, nuts, popcorn, potato chips. . . , nibble on a fresh carrot! Stay away from fried, fatty and highly spiced foods. Stick with the foods that keep your skin clear: eggs, cheese, lean meat, broiled fish, bread, cereal, leafy greens, fresh fruit and vegetables. Substitute milk, or a milk shake, for candy and other sweets. Watch your diet, and just watch your skin get prettier. Healthy skin and a healthy body go hand in hand.

About Your Complexion

There are four basic skin types: oily, dry, combination, and normal. Remember—the T-Zone is the oiliest on every complexion. The T-Zone area includes the forehead, nose and chin. Regardless of skin color, all women have one of these four skin types.

OILY SKIN

Oily skin begins to occur during the early teen years and in many cases is the cause of problem skin. This skin type needs constant attention with frequent cleansings and protective, medicated make-up. Oily skin usually disappears after the teen years, but for a few women the skin will tend to remain oily.

The problem of OILY SKIN exists, if . . .

- Pores are enlarged, particularly about the nose
- Occasional skin blemishes appear on face and across shoulders
- Skin has morning shine due to oil accumulation during sleep
- Skin often appears shiny during the day as natural oil breaks through make-up
- There is a tendency to perspire freely

DRY SKIN

The problem of dry skin occurs most frequently with the over-thirty woman. It is not uncommon, however, for younger women to have dry skin, especially if they work in buildings with dry heat or are exposed to

extreme temperatures. Dry skin needs emollients and moisturizers to prevent a dry, flaky appearance and keep it supple and young looking.
The problem of DRY SKIN exists if . . .

- Skin reacts readily to heat, cold, and wind; therefore chaps easily
- Face powder flakes
- Skin feels drawn and tight after washing
- There is a feeling of tightness—a lack of "give" or elasticity

COMBINATION SKIN

Women in their twenties usually have a complexion that has both oily and dry areas. This complexion is therefore called a combination skin type. The T-Zone oily areas, forehead, nose, and chin, need the frequent cleansing and medication of oily skin, but the remaining areas need the emollients and moisture necessary for dry skin. To give both these areas the care they need requires special attention.
The problem of COMBINATION SKIN exists if . . .

- Middle parts of the face—forehead, nose, and chin—show shine, have enlarged pores
- Sides of the face have dry, flaky skin
- Skin around eyes and on throat may be dry, feel tight, and show tiny lines

NORMAL SKIN

Few women have normal skin throughout their lives, but those fortunate women who do, need to give their skin special care in order to maintain and protect their normal complexion.
You have NORMAL SKIN IF . . .

- In a magnifying mirror skin texture appears smooth with no perceptibly enlarged pores
- Skin oils are imperceptible—the skin appears luminous but not shiny
- Surface is clear with no blackheads, whiteheads, or pimples
- Skin is elastic—springs back readily when pinched or depressed

Beauty Is Clear, Smooth and Naturally Pretty

GO LIGHT ON MAKE-UP

Whether your complexion is troubled, fair-weather or flawless, your make-up should look natural, not noticeable. Remember, your pores must stay clear of excess oil, soil and stale make-up. That's why it's so important to choose make-up that covers up lightly, without caking or clogging up pores.

If you have troubled skin, you need a medicated make-up to bring out your best and help conceal and heal the rest. If you have flawless skin, you still need medicated make-up to keep it protected from sudden problems.

A make-up expert from Bonnie Bell gives pointers on television make-up to MISS TEENAGE AMERICA National Candidates.

CHOOSE A MAKE-UP SHADE TO MATCH YOUR SKIN TONE

To find your true skin tone, remove any make-up and hold a sheet of dull white paper along the side of your face and under your chin. This will eliminate any reflections of color from the room or your clothing which would distort your coloring. Now decide. If your skin is too sallow, too olive, then perk it up with a warm rosy shade.

Black girls can add a healthy glow to light or nude-toned skin with a natural ivory or faintly pink tint. Olive or beige browns will brighten up with light coffee, dark beige or suntan shades. Tone down bronze or red browns with deep coffee or yellow bronze tints. If your skin is too gray, perk it up with a suntan or red brown foundation. And the very darkest skins look most attractive with colorless transparent make-up.

HOW TO APPLY MAKE-UP
SO IT LOOKS SMOOTH AND NATURAL

1. First, deep-cleanse your skin.
2. Smooth on a protective base of moisture lotion to soften your skin and keep make-up out of pores. Make-up glides on easily, blends quickly, over a base of moisture lotion. And best of all, you'll have that moist, glow-y look the models have—without an oily shine!
3. Before you apply make-up foundation, hide any dark circles or shadows with a white cover-up make-up or a lighter shade of foundation. Dab the white right under your eyes; press gently to cover dark areas. Always work from the outer corner of the eye to avoid stretching delicate skin tissue. Let the white set to a soft, matte finish.
4. Dab make-up foundation on forehead, cheeks, nose, mouth, chin. Blend quickly, smoothly, covering one area at a time. (If you've applied white make-up under the eyes, be sure to cover that area, too.) End with sweeping, downward strokes to prevent make-up from being forced into pores, and to smooth down any tiny facial hairs.
5. Put a smooth finish on make-up, and prevent extra-oily areas from shining through, with a medicated compressed powder in a matching shade. Stroke powder over forehead, nose and chin. Blot off any excess with tissue.

On the days when you want to go really light or look a little brighter, smooth on a moisturizing gloss with a delicate pink tint. This looks great alone, or under or over your regular foundation for just a touch of sparkle.

GO AHEAD, BLUSH A LITTLE

Now that your skin looks clean and smooth, put a fresh bloom on your cheeks with just a touch of blush. Pick a transparent gel to give a lasting, natural glow in the daytime, a sparkling blushing cream for evening.

Smile. The area that swells into a mound is where you start, blending the blusher up and out toward the hairline. Keep the color high on your cheeks to highlight your cheekbones and make your eyes sparkle.

HIGHLIGHT LIPS WITH COLOR AND GLOSS

A young face needs just a touch of lipstick—to brighten your skin, highlight your lips and bring out the colors you're wearing. Shades will be determined by the general complexion tone and the current make-up fashions. Be in style—but more important, choose what looks best on you. If you aren't comfortable with very light or very dark lipsticks, avoid them. And if you find that any shade changes color on your lips (that's due to your skin "chemistry"), try a little white make-up as a lipstick foundation, to lighten the shade and make it last longer.

For the smoothest look, apply lipstick with a lip brush. Steady your hand by resting your little finger on your chin. Outline both lips, then fill in with color. If your lips are too full, draw an outline just inside your natural curve and fill in with soft, light color. If your lips are too thin, outline with bright color and fill in with a lighter shade.

Add a moist, romantic glow with a clear lip gloss. Use it under your lip color for a soft, see-through sheen. Or use it over lipstick to make lips glisten and help prevent color from changing. Always use short, vertical strokes when applying gloss to prevent the lip-color outline from smearing.

More lip tips. Never put new lipstick over old—this causes caking. Never wet lips before applying—this causes the color to slide off. And never press lips together to blot—let lipstick set for a minute, then blot lightly with tissue.

MAKE YOUR EYES BIGGER AND BRIGHTER

Raise your brows by plucking the stragglers underneath your brow. Never, never touch the top line, and always tweeze in the direction the hairs grow. (Try doing this after your bath; the hairs are softest then.)

Color and shape your brows with a brush-on cake or pencil. Use short, feathery strokes to fill in any voids. If you want to extend your brows, keep the line level with or higher than the brow's starting point to avoid a "droopy" look.

Shadow your lids with soft, soft colors. Try a beige shade or white highlighter for daytime to "light up" your eyes, and "open up" the space between your lashes and brow bone. For evening, try pale green or blue. Keep the depth of color near your lashes, then sweep the color up toward the brow to create delicate shadings of the same color.

Shape your eyes with liner, but keep the line fine, right near the roots of your lashes. I recommend a cake eyeliner, since it stays on better and looks more natural than liquid or pencil. Here are some hints to help you "draw the line."

Tilt your head back. With your lids half-lowered, start at the center of your lid and draw a thin line to the outer corner. Then come back to the inner corner and draw a line back to the center. Be sure the line tapers at both the inner and outer corners of the eye. Drawing the line in short strokes allows for better control and fewer mistakes. Another hint: steady your hand by resting your little finger on your cheekbone.

Make your lashes thicker with mascara. I recommend the "spiral brush" mascara wand that curves, colors and separates lashes with just a few quick strokes. Start at the roots of your lashes and brush under and up. To make lashes appear longer: dust loose powder on your lashes, add another coat of mascara. (Make sure mascara dries between dustings of powder.)

EVENING-OUT MAKE-UP

Those special evenings out call for a little extra glamor, make-up that highlights your special good features and helps soften your skin. There is one kind that will do this, a white cream make-up to wear with or without your regular make-up.

Use it to highlight eyes and cheekbones. Stroke it right under your eyebrows to make your eyes look bigger and brighter. Sweep it across your cheekbones for that "high-cheekbones" look models have.

For a misty, romantic glow, stroke a pearl-dipped cream across your cheekbones, under your eyebrows, on the tip of your chin, your nose, even on the tips of mascara'd lashes. Or use it as "frosting" for lid shadow or lipstick.

Whatever "special effects" your choose, ask yourself: Does it really make me look more beautiful, or just more made-up? I hope your answer is the first, for that's what make-up is all about.

Especially for Dark-skinned Young Women

The pigment that creates a dark skin tone is called melanin. The amount of melanin in the skin determines the depth of color. In dark skin there are often undertones of yellow, ruddy-red, gray, or olive.

Darker complexions tend to retain oil longer, which in turn, helps the complexion to remain younger-looking (longer). The concentration of melanin can vary, causing "dark patches" in some areas of the skin.

There are five general complexion categories. The chart below lists these five categories, how to determine each and what foundations Bonne Bell recommends for each skin tone.

COMPLEXION COLORING	DESCRIPTION	FOUNDATION SELECTION
Light or nude brown	Hints of pale cream, faint pink	Toast or coffee medicated make-up
Bronze or red brown	Hints of red, rose, bronze	Coffee medicated make-up
Olive or beige brown	Hints of yellow, deep ivory, green	Deep tan medicated make-up
Gray brown	Hints of gray, blue	A little beige translucent make-up or toast or coffee medicated make-up
Black brown	Good deep black with some warm brown overtones	A little beige translucent make-up, beige or deep tan medicated make-up or bronzing gel— depending on depth of skin tone

Things to Remember When Selecting Your Make-up

The most important thing is to select shades that aren't too red or too dark, or shades that are too light which will leave a gray cast. Choose a shade that blends with your skin tone.

Deep-tone skin often tends to oil and needs a non-oily make-up.

If the skin is free from blemishes, the "no color" transparent foundations are best for a shining, healthy look.

A beige tone (without a pink or red base) is best for the skin with underlying color tones (yellow, ruddy, gray, etc.). To mask an undertone, a blusher or frosty blush can be applied over make-up to create a "natural glow."

Make-up can and should be used to "even out" a complexion tone—especially for toning down heavily pigmented areas.

To mask all but a ruddy-red undertone, a medium make-up shade is perfect.

Medium to light-dark skin can use a light beige translucent make-up for summer—a heavier (but not darker) tone for winter. Tawny-tone blushers are good for winter while strawberry shades are best for summer days.

Translucent loose powder is preferred over any colored compressed powders. It helps set make-up and prevent caking and streaking on oily skin while it adds no more color and eliminates shine to create a soft as silk finish.

YOUR LIPS

Pigmentation can cause uneven tones in the lips (from pink to dark brown). Often one (or both) lips will have a variety of tones. To even out spotted or uneven lip tones, use make-up or a cover cream under lipstick.

Some women have a heavy, dark purple cast on the edge of their upper lip. A make-up base will help de-emphasize this line. Always remember to apply lipstick inside this line.)

If your lips are too full, a lip brush is helpful. Stay inside the natural lip line and use a lighter color on the top lip. Often very full lips should not use lipstick at all. A lip gloss alone provides a moist, attractive finish.

If you prefer to de-emphasize your lips, try using lip gloss on upper lip and lipstick only on the bottom.

YOUR EYES

The depth of shadow colors should be determined by skin tones—the deeper the skin tone, the deeper the shadow.

If your eye area is oily, use translucent loose powder as a base before applying shadow.

Lighter skin tones can use white highlighter directly below the brow to draw attention to the eyes.

If you have a problem with shadow holding, try using an eye cover cream as a shadow base. It helps the shadow cling longer and also helps keep it from accumulating in the crease of the lid.

Eye liner should be dark enough to subtly contrast with your skin tone. Most effective shades are soft black, medium to dark browns.

If you wish to use an eyebrow pencil, soft black or brown shades are recommended.

Step by Step Make-up for Black Women

Cleanse your complexion thoroughly. It is essential that your skin is "deep-down" clean before applying any make-up.

Moisturize your complexion before applying make-up. A good moisturizer helps keep the make-up from sinking into the pores. Even if you do not wear make-up every day, your favorite moisturizer is an absolute necessity. Whether your skin is oily or dry or anywhere in-between, a good lotion (or cream) keeps your skin softer and more pliable while helping to protect it against the drying elements of the environment.

Apply make-up, using the shade and texture recommended for your skin type and shade. In applying make-up, always cover one area of the face at a time; apply several dots to the area and blend for a smooth, even cover. Use light, feathery strokes blending under the jaw line and end by brushing cheeks lightly in a downward movement to smooth down any tiny facial hairs. Also, smooth a little make-up over the eyelids to even out the skin tone and create an ideal base for your shadow.

A blush is rather hard to maintain all day without a little help from your make-up kit, but no one has to know that! A transparent, non-greasy blusher is easy to apply and adds a soft, natural blush to your complexion for a healthy, glowing look.

Start under the center of the eye, and dot color along the cheek bone. Then quickly sweep the color upward and outward. Always keep the blusher high on the cheeks.

Powder should always be applied to set your make-up and prevent natural oils from breaking through and creating a heavy shine. Pat it over the T-Zone—forehead, nose and chin. Do not powder the cheeks. Finish with light, downward strokes to smooth out facial hair.

Accent your eyes with shadow shades that blend with your skin tone. Use deepest shadow shade on eyelid, lightest closest to brow. Gently blend shades to create a soft, flowing look. If you wish, add a soft, narrow line no further than the outer corner of the eye with eyeliner. Eyebrows are best cared for when they are left as natural as possible. We suggest they be shaped carefully, then simply brushed and glossed.

Lipstick, when applied properly, can create an illusion of perfect contour, the final touch to enhance the total look of a woman who cares about her appearance.

To minimize very full lips, keep the color slightly within the natural lip line. If one lip is slightly lighter than the other, use a darker shade of lipstick on the light lip to even out the tone.

Lip gloss will moisturize lips, provide an even base and help mask heavily pigmented areas. It also helps keep the lipstick color-true.

Now we follow with some special hints that make any girl look prettier—no matter what her face shape, coloring, or skin type is.

Beauty Is Bright, Lively and Well-protected

CARRY COMPLEXION CARE WHEREVER YOU GO

Have you ever been caught in the middle . . . like this ? You've just finished a long ski run, or a long day of classes, or a long stretch on the beach. And someone special pops up you've been wanting to date. How you'd love to give your face a real quick refresher! Be prepared for times like these. Tuck away a few cleansing towelettes that are saturated with a good medicated lotion. In minutes your face will be off to a cool, fresh start, and your skin will stay clear of new blemishes.

Look for cleansing tissues that are folded smaller than a hanky, sealed inside a tiny foil pack. You can slip one right into your parka, purse, beach bag, tennis racquet cover—even your tiny evening purse.

SMOOTH OUT THE ROUGH SPOTS

Skin needs plenty of moisture to stay smooth, firm and dewy-fresh. But sun, wind and cold have a way of robbing natural moisture and letting skin run dry. You'll find that a daily application of moisture lotion removes dry, flaky skin from ankles, elbows, knees, and soothes the taut feeling of newly shaved legs. After you've been in the sun, follow your shower or bath with an all-over application of moisture lotion or a special after-sun lotion. The moisture keeps your tan intact, gives it a lovely glow and makes it last far longer.

COME OUT WITH THE SUN

Fresh air and exercise are essential under any conditions. Sports like tennis, swimming, golfing, bicycling, skating and skiing keep your figure trim, your muscles toned, your skin firm and your spirits up! Daily exercise also helps you develop good posture and poise, and keeps your complexion clear and bright. However, you must give your skin a sporting chance by protecting it from the great outdoors.

PLAN YOUR TAN!

The sun supplies essential vitamins, develops strong bones and teeth, and gives your complexion a healthy glow. However, too much sun—too soon—will only darken the top layer of skin, causing you to burn, blister and peel. Whether you're sunning, swimming, or conquering the ski slopes, protect yourself with a good sunscreen lotion . . . one that filters out just the ultraviolet rays that burn your skin. A sunscreen lotion lets your skin darken gradually, evenly, starting with the lower layer. And that's the whole secret to a smooth, golden tan.

HOW TO PLAY SMART WHILE THE SUN SHINES

Be careful between the hours of ten and two. That's when the sun is the strongest—especially at the beach or right on the water.

Apply your sunscreen lotion all over. Re-apply frequently on extra-sensitive areas: nose, ears, tummy, back of your thighs, knees, shoulders, nape of your neck, tops of your feet. And always re-apply after swimming, since salt and chlorine can "steal" some of the lotion.

When you're lying under the sun, protect your lids with moistened cotton pads. Otherwise you'd have to wear sunglasses, which cause those "raccoon" rim marks around your eyes. Never let one part of you get too much sun. Shift around, turn over, take a walk on the beach.

KEEP YOUR LIPS WELL-PROTECTED

When you're facing the winds on the ski slope, or the sun on the beach, be sure to wear a lipstick, or lip gloss, or anti-chap stick to protect lips from chapping, cracking and peeling. Also, choose lip treatments that actually seal in moisture while they make your lips shine, to prevent color from caking, flaking or fading in the sun.

Beauty Is Everything Nice About You

POSTURE TO BE PROUD OF

Don't be a slouch. Stand tall and be counted! The prettiest clothes, face and figure are overlooked if you don't hold up your head, tuck in your tummy, and pull back your shoulders. Many young women tell me:

"When I do stand up perfectly straight, I don't feel relaxed or look natural." Why? Because you haven't made posture an everyday habit. You have to practice until your posture makes every movement more graceful and becomes a real part of you. Here are some suggestions:

When you brush your teeth, bend from the waist, bend from the knees, but break the habit of slouching your shoulders. When you put on your socks or stockings, sit on the bed with your back straightened up. Then draw your legs up toward you. When you're walking to school, balance your books so you're not stooping over. And look straight ahead, not down at the sidewalk. Practice your posture in the classroom, too. Keep your hips tucked against the back of your chair. Your spine will straighten up, and you'll be sitting pretty. When you get up from your seat, stretch "tall." Make a "long neck" to relieve tension, and to put your head on top of your spine—where it belongs!

Pleasingly plump? During your teens, there's a tendency to get a little hippy, or a little rounder and fuller than you were last year. But please remember this: the reason you're suddenly becoming wider, rounder and fuller is that you're suddenly becoming a woman. In time, your proportions will balance out nicely for a pretty figure. But for now, do stay away from fatty, fried and highly spiced foods. (Follow the same diet suggested for complexion care.) And never go to school with an empty stomach. You're not apt to snack and munch all the time when you have the keep-alert nourishment of a well-balanced breakfast.

PRETTY SHOW OF HANDS AND FEET

Well-groomed nails need a once-a-week manicure and lots of moisturizing. Take time before a bath to trim and file nails. Always shape them to an oval, never to a point. This is what causes quick cracks and tears. If your nail is split or torn, remove the damage with a straight-across clip, then smooth the top into a squarish shape. Always use an emery board for filing, brushing across the nail tip in one direction only.

After your bath, make it a habit to push back softened cuticle with the tip of your towel to remove those loose bits of skin. Follow-up with a good moisturizing. Also, whenever you're cleaning or painting, apply a little moisture lotion under nail tips to avoid discoloration.

Don't forget toenails. Especially when you wear sandals or go barefoot on the beach. Before the bath, clip toenails straight across, and keep them rather short. During the bath, smooth off the nail edges with a little brush (this prevents stocking snags later) and push back the cuticle with a warm washcloth. After the bath, moisturize the entire foot to remove any dry, flaky skin.

PERFUMERY—ONE OF THE JOYS OF BEING A GIRL

When you want to feel extra-pretty, apply a light touch of fragrance anywhere a pulse beats: the arm, at the temples or base of the throat. During summer, go extra light, for the heat can make a little dab go a long way. Do match up your dusting powder, cologne and perfume. After all, your fragrance lingers after you leave. Make it nice to remember.

YOUR TRUE-YOU BEAUTY

Beauty is not just a glowing complexion, or a pretty figure, or a perfect tan. Beauty is also charm. Natural charm. The ability to delight and please and put others at ease.

Charm is a pleasant smile, a thoughtful gesture. A genuine desire to listen and learn. To be charming is to be gracious, sincere, unselfish. The big difference between being "pretty" and "pretty wonderful."

Your Crowning Glory

BY
SUSAN BIGLER
Miss Teenage Green Brook,
New Jersey 1974

A MISS TEENAGE AMERICA *Finalist in 1974, Susan is appearing in commercials and magazines all over the world, including Japan, England, Italy, and the United States. She has offered to share a few tips on hair care that have helped her to create and maintain a fresh and well-groomed appearance.*

Basic steps for clean, bouncy hair include:

1. *A good cut to start with.* A trim every six or eight weeks will eliminate split ends and keep your style in shape.
2. *Clean hair.* This means washing as often as necessary for your own particular hair type, from every day or two for oily hair to once a week for dry hair. Most hairdressers now recommend a pH balanced shampoo.
3. *Manageable hair with thickness and body.* This can be aided by using a "conditioning" or "protein" shampoo. If you need to add temporary fullness to your hair, use a conditioner. Be selective for your individual hair needs since there are many different formulas from which to choose.

4. *A good style.* Decide upon a hair style that is flattering to your face shape and fits in with the "look" you would like to present to others. Choose a hair style suitable for your lifestyle—one that will last, not require too much time for care, and one that is you. Don't try to copy what you see in magazines or what your friends do just to be "with it." Make sure that the style fits you and your personality.

5. *A good set.* This is necessary for most styles and if you are not one of those lucky enough to be able to just dry your hair and be on your way, be sure to use care in combing, brushing, and setting your hair. When your hair is wet, be very careful to comb slowly to remove tangles; do not brush when wet, since wet hair tends to tangle more easily and be more fragile than dry hair—brushing can break it. If you are using eletric rollers for your set, be sure that your hair is dry, as wet hair will not take the set and hot rollers could damage the hair strands.

Following these basic steps and making them a part of your beauty routine should put you well on your way to making your hair an asset to your overall appearance. However, there are probably many questions that you might still need to ask. Let's touch on just a few common problems concerning your hair.

1. What does pH mean when talking about shampoo?

According to the World Book Encyclopedia, pH is a number used by chemists to indicate the strength of an acid or a base. The number is usually on a scale ranging from 0 to 14. A pH that is below 7 indicates that a solution is acidic, and a pH above 7 indicates that a solution is basic. A neutral solution such as pure water, is neither acidic nor basic—its pH is 7.

So when shampoo manufacturers advertise their product as "pH balanced" this simply means that their shampoo is proportionately balanced acidic/basic so as not to be too harsh.

2. Are all of the new hair appliances harmful to my hair?

Curling irons, electric rollers, and high-powered dryers are fast becoming a beauty necessity these days with the busy schedules that many young girls keep. The heat from these is in itself not necessarily damaging to one's hair, but the combination of this along with many other stresses, including weather factors and your diet, over a period of time can cause damage, especially in the form of split ends. Always be extremely careful when using any form of heat on your hair, and compensate for its effect by pampering your scalp and hair. Replenish oils by giving yourself a scalp treatment at least once a month and using a hair conditioner each time you wash your hair.

3. What is dandruff and can shampoo help?

Dandruff is a condition in which dead skin cells on the scalp cause uncomfortable itching and flaking. Dandruff can be caused by a poor diet, poor health or an emotional state, and even people with oily hair may inherit the condition. A good dandruff shampoo can help since it remains on your scalp to fight the flakes. If you have a severe dandruff condition, you may need to consult a dermatologist (a skin specialist).

4. Why do I lose so much hair after shampooing?

Everyone loses some hair with normal washing and setting—fifty to one hundred hairs a day is considered a normal loss. The oldest hairs on your head are three to five years of age. When they mature, they drop out and are replaced by new ones. If you are losing a great many hairs, you should consult your doctor. Excessive hair loss can be a sign of a more serious medical problem, perhaps glandular in nature. Any change in the body can affect the hair, even something as simple as a cold. If you feel that your hair fallout is really abnormal, don't hesitate to ask your doctor about it.

It seems that all women feel that they have problem hair no matter how lovely the texture and appearance may be. You shouldn't be too rough a critic on yourself and how your hair looks—remember everyone has those "bad days" when your hair (or even a model's hair!) just won't do anything that you want it to. On the other side of the coin, you should be aware of troublesome hair conditions that do exist and remedies or adjustments that can be made.

Here's a simplified list of some of the most frequently asked questions about hair problems, along with some suggested solutions.

PROBLEM	SOLUTION
Split Ends	Trim frequently.
Dandruff	Wash often with dandruff shampoo, rinse extraordinarily well, massage your scalp before each shampoo.
Dull Hair	Be sure to rinse well after a shampoo. Use a conditioner. Highlighting, streaking or shading can sometimes help add life to dull hair. This is usually best done by a professional. If, however, you choose to do this yourself, be sure you completely understand all instructions.

Damaged Hair	To have shiny, healthy hair you really need to wait until it all grows out, but you can give damaged hair some protection by using a conditioner, texturizer, or bodybuilder. Do not bleach, permanent, or straighten it.
Slow-growing Hair	Keep the ends of your hair trimmed. This doesn't really make your hair grow faster—it just seems that way because the hair doesn't break off at the ends.
Dry Hair	Don't wash your hair more often than absolutely necessary. Choose a shampoo designed for dry hair. Try a scalp treatment and use a conditioner designed to lubricate the hair.
Fine Hair	A blunt cut may help to hold a style. A body permanent or an "extra hold" setting lotion usually helps to add body. Experiment to see what works best for you.
Oily Hair	Wash every day or as often as possible. Use a shampoo designed for oily hair and between shampoos use a dry shampoo. Wash your comb and brush frequently and keep your skin as clean as possible to avoid any excess oil from getting in your hair. Also watch your diet, which sometimes has a lot to do with the oiliness of your hair.

Since modeling is a field in which one's personal appearance is of the utmost importance and is really one of the products being sold to the consumer, I have learned several "tricks" to help me in the care and appearance of my hair, which is the first feature many people notice.

I hope they will be helpful to you.

1. Keep the emphasis on simplicity in cut, style, and care.
2. Any drastic change in style or hair procedure, such as cuts, permanents, streaking, or frosting, should be done by a professional.
3. After washing hair, let it dry naturally for a while before setting or blowing dry.
4. When using a high-powered blow dryer, dry with hot air, but finish with cold air to make the set hold longer.

Rewa Walsh, MISS TEENAGE AMERICA 1971, had hip length brown hair at the time she won her medallion.

5. When brushing your hair or blowing dry, brush or blow in the opposite direction to give hair fullness.

6. If using electric rollers, use tissue or end papers before rolling to keep hair from being damaged.

7. If you are using electric curlers and don't want to leave them in too long, because of a too tight curl, try this. Unroll the curlers after a short time, rewind them with your finger, then use pins to hold them in place until you are ready to brush out.

8. For a quick set between shampoos, spray on water with a spray bottle and blow dry. If necessary, then set hair on hot curlers or with a curling iron.

To See Ourselves as Others See Us

BY
DONNA MILLER

Ms. Miller is the PBJ designer of Jerell, Inc., a National Associate of MISS TEENAGE AMERICA. *Jerell designs and creates each official* MISS TEENAGE AMERICA *wardrobe.*

One of the first and basic needs of civilized man is clothing. There were actually two reasons for covering the body. One was for protection from the elements and the other was for adornment. Because man is more vain than practical, most of his covering of the body was for adornment. Even the most primitive of men wore beads or elaborate headdresses. During the periods of great royalty rank was sometimes displayed by the wearing of elaborate garments.

Fashion as everything else has changed with the times according to lifestyle. To consider fashion as it relates to you, you need to know yourself better and what is needed to help you look your best.

First, you should determine what type of silhouette you have. Tape a large sheet of brown wrapping paper on the wall and have a friend trace around the outline of your body or study your shadow to see which silhouette on Chart I (page 28) suits you best. Remember that in reading the chart everyone's aim should be the well-proportioned figure. You should emphasize your good features and minimize those less desirable by drawing attention elsewhere.

Remember to always keep your total look in good proportion. For instance, don't wear high shoes with very short skirts, and consider all your accessories in relation to the overall look.

A few other little helpful hints on shapes should be noted. If you have a very square face be careful of square necklines—V necks or scoop necklines are much more flattering to you as they minimize the sharpness

Cathy Durden, MISS TEENAGE AMERICA 1976, models some of Ms. Miller's designs.

"Remember to always keep your total look in good proportion and consider all your accessories in relation to the over-all look."

of the jaws. The opposite is true of course with a very long pointed jaw line—square necks are great. Those of you with long necks can wear scarves and ruffles or big collars at the neck—avoid plunging necklines without breaking the line. Girls with short necks can wear V necks and should avoid bulky neck treatments.

After you have determined your silhouette and know what lines and types of clothes make you look your best, you can now decide what colors are best for you.

Everyone is different but generally color types can be classified as blonde, black, brunette or redhead. Pick from Chart II (page 30) the type that you feel comes closest to being you and work from there. Color is such an individual thing that it is almost a trial-and-error process. Try different colors, using the chart as a guide and make your own decision.

Now that you know your individual style and color, you can begin to build your wardrobe. First, consider your lifestyle. Make a list of your activities such as dating, school, active sports participation such as tennis, or spectator sports like football. Decide what your wardrobe needs are for each one and make a chart of items you have that you can work with and items you need to add.

Remember that accessories are a part of your wardrobe also. Try to pick shoes or other footwear like boots in colors that will coordinate with more than one item in your wardrobe. It is important to remember, also, that they are accessories and should make your look complete—not be so bold that they overpower the rest of you. This should apply to all of your accessories like jewelry, bags and belts.

When shopping and adding pieces that you need, be practical by coordinating colors where possible. For instance, if you are shopping for a shirt that will go with your pink suit, try to see if you can also wear that shirt with your green skirt. Look for quality in your selections. You will be more pleased with one garment that does not come apart after only a few wearings than with two garments that do not last.

Now that you have planned your wardrobe in the best styles and colors for you, you will want to know how to take good care of it.

It is a federal law that every garment must have a label sewn in that tells you how to care for that garment. Follow those instructions carefully for the longest life of your garment. It also helps the life of the garment to keep it from becoming too soiled between launderings. Be neat.

All of these things are to help you look and be your best you. Most of all, have fun with your wardrobe. Let it reflect your personality—not be your personality. It is better to be underdressed than overdressed, and let your personality shine through. Remember also that comfort is very important. If you feel good and feel like you look good—you do.

CHART I—BASIC FIGURE TYPES

Triangle shaped
Full hips and
Small bust

1. Keep the emphasis above the waist.

2. High waisted trousers are good.

3. Long jackets are best.

4. Big collars or bows at neckline would be good for you.

5. Be careful of tight fitting tops with full skirts.

6. Try to create a fuller look for above the waist.

Upside down Triangle
Full Bust and
Slender hips

1. The emphasis should be below the waist.

2. You have a great pants figure.

3. Fullness below waist will give more fullness to your hips.

4. Simple shirts and tops with no ruffles or shirring across the bustline will look best on you.

Well proportioned
Lucky Gal!

1. You are also a good height, not too short or too tall.

2. You can wear almost anything well.

Tall girl
Slender

1. You can be dramatic in your dress and look great.

2. Wear wide belts.

3. Big skirts look great on you.

4. You're one of the few figure types that can wear large accessories well.

5. If you are tall, wide bands of color horizontally will minimize height.

6. Avoid "cutesy" look.

7. Bold prints are great.

Short girl
Slender

1. Babydoll looks are good, as long as not juvenile.

2. Wear pants with simple shirt top to give your legs a longer look.

3. Be careful of bulky jackets and coats and large accessories such as purses, belts and big shoes as they are overpowering.

4. Vertical lines give you length.

5. Avoid wide horizontal lines. They break you and make you appear shorter.

Well-rounded girl

1. Choose small, muted prints.

2. Small belts are best.

3. Avoid large bands of color horizontally.

4. Narrow stripes vertically will slenderize.

5. Avoid bulky jackets and coats. They make you look fuller.

CHART II—YOUR COLOR TYPE

Choose the coloring category closest to your own. Listed below in each category, are the colors you wear best.

Blonde-blue eyed Rosy pink skin Brown-eyed blondes	Brunette—brown or hazel eyes Skin tones of orange, red	Red hair— Blue eyes Rosy cheeks	Black hair— Dark skin, Brown or black eyes
Blue, greens, rosy pinks—excellent	Browns, yellows, oranges and reds —excellent	White, blue, greens, yellows— excellent	Beige and soft colors, like pastels are excellent
White—fair If you have a nice tan and it does not wash your skin out Red—fair	Blues—blue greens—excellent Bright greens— very good	With brown eyes, browns, yellows, and greens are excellent	Muted colors are good—for instance, cranberry
Blue eyes be careful of yellows. Bright yellow may make skin purplish Browns in light tones only—beige With brown eyes, browns can be really good—try	Be careful of purples and rosy pinks, may make skin look sallow	Red and pinks are also fine if they do not make the hair color too harsh	Avoid black and strong, harsh colors such as purple and orange

The Figure Factory

BY
KAREN PETERSEN,
MISS TEENAGE AMERICA 1975
AND JUDITH HOUGHTON

One of Karen Petersen's favorite hobbies is ballet. Her Individual Accomplishment presentation at the MISS TEENAGE AMERICA *National Pageant Finals was an original dance. She uses dance workouts and school sports, like track, to keep in shape.*

Judith Houghton is the Executive Vice President of MISS TEENAGE AMERICA, *Producer of the national telecast, and former faculty member of the Department of Dance at Southern Methodist University.*

Karen demonstrates the exercises that follow.

Very few of us are blessed with perfect figures. Even those who are must put out an effort to keep them that way. The fact is—you have to *work* at it, but you will reap the rewards.

How Do You Measure Up?

Do you have a few unwanted bulges in the wrong places? Or are you one of those skinny mini's that can't seem to gain weight?

Either way, a good nutritional diet and plenty of exercise are the keys to a healthy and beautiful figure. If you're just where you want to be, the same two basics will keep you at your ideal.

If you have a serious weight problem, go immediately and consult with your doctor. Putting it off won't make it go away.

If you're like most girls and just need to lose or add a pound (or inch) here or there, familiarize yourself with the following information and put it into practice.

A slice of apple pie can be consumed in five minutes. It is 350 calories.

In five minutes, your body will burn 50 calories if you are swimming,

THE FIGURE FACTORY

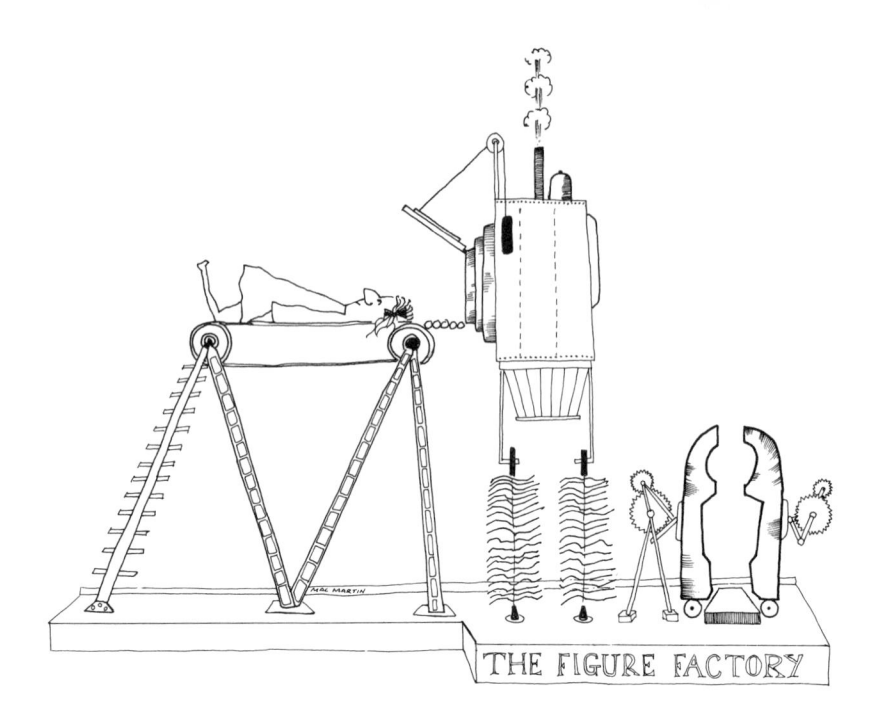

33 if you're playing tennis, 30 if you're riding a bicycle, 97 if you're running and (oops!) 6 if you're sitting.

Exercise goes hand in hand with a good diet and tightens and firms your muscles. It's that tightening and firming that helps you lose inches. Since it improves circulation, exercise is also great for your hair, skin and eyes.

If the thought of doing calisthenics doesn't sound like your cup of tea, think of the active things you enjoy. Skiing (water or snow), skating, dancing, participant sports, and even (would you believe!) cleaning up your room all require physical action. Jumping rope and swimming are fantastic.

You can even get a little exercise as you practice ecology by bending over and picking up paper, candy wrappers, and pop cans in the school yard—one at a time!—until you have a whole sack full.

The above are all good forms of basic exercise, but what if you have a problem area that needs special attention—tummy? (ugh!) hips!

There are several important things to keep in mind as you begin your exercise program.

First, don't try to make up for all your lost time the first session. If you have been relatively inactive, the *worst* thing you can do is to *overdo*. This will result mostly in body strains and pulled muscles. Start off with a few exercises at a time and add a couple each few days, as your body begins to limber up and strengthen itself.

Secondly, once a month (or even once a week) won't do it. And cheating shows. You need a *regular daily schedule* of exercise.

A third thing to remember is that some exercises performed improperly can do more harm than good. The most common example is an exercise intended to flatten stomachs, but which can cause harm to your back if you're not careful to make sure you're putting the "work load" on the right set of muscles.

If you're unsure, ask your gym teacher to check on some of the exercises you think you may be doing wrong.

Exercise need not be "ugh-cercise." It can be pleasant and relaxing—and it's more fun with music. So grab your favorite record or flip the dial to your favorite radio station, and join Karen Petersen, MISS TEENAGE AMERICA 1975 and shape up!

I. BOUNCES—To loosen up

Good for relaxing and stretching muscles, especially in the legs and waistline.

Start in a standing position with feet about eighteen inches apart, knees straight.

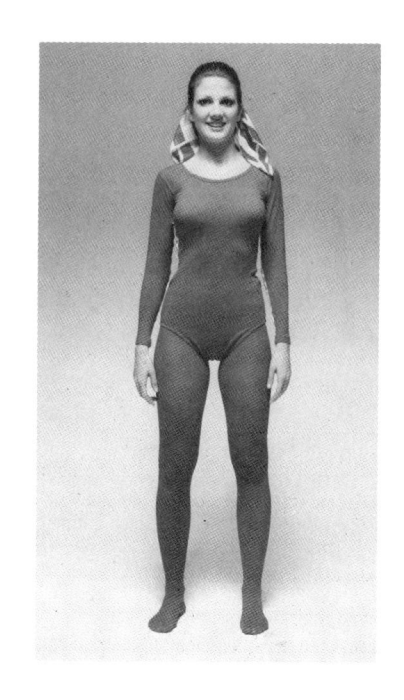

1.) *Forward*

Drop your head forward first, then let the body and arms fall forward and completely relax in a "rolling down" movement. Bounce in an easy rhythm eight times. Do not force or jerk.

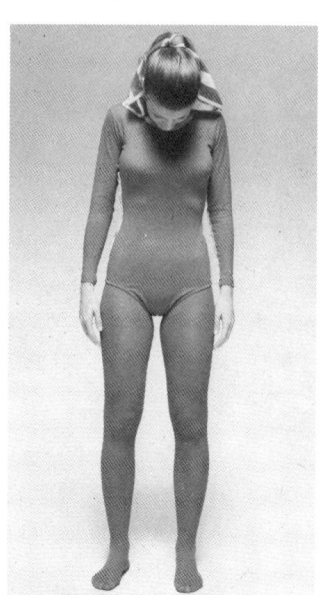

2.) *Right Side*

Return to starting position, bring straight arms up by your ears, lean right and bounce eight times. Make sure your legs stay straight and don't let your derriere stick out. You should feel this in your waist and sides.

3.) *Back*

Keeping arms up and straight, drop your head back and lean backwards as far as possible. Bounce gently eight times.

4.) *Left Side*

Repeat the side bounce to the left side eight times.

Do this series once through to loosen up. This is a good one to begin with.

WRONG   RIGHT

Watch: Your Back!

If you feel it there, you are "swaying" your back on the side bounces. Make sure you "tuck under" your hips. Lean sideways in front of a mirror to check.

II. SHOULDER STRETCH

Good for tension in the shoulder and neck area. Also a good waistline exercise.

1.) Stand with feet apart. Clasp hands overhead as far behind your head as possible. Keep arms straight, and press palms of hands toward ceiling.

2.) Keeping knees straight, lean right, pressing palms toward right wall. Keep hands behind your head. Keep stretching arms as far as you can away from your body.

3.) "Sweep" forward, keeping knees straight. Keeping arms straight, and pressing palms of hands forward, keep pulling arms as far as possible behind head.

4.) Continue sweep to left side and up to center.
Lower arms to sides and let shoulders relax.

Reverse, beginning with the left side and sweeping across the front to the right side and up.

Watch: to make sure your derierre is tucked under each time you return to the starting position.
Start with four times (RLRL) and work up to eight times.

III. EXERCISE FOR BUST AND UPPER ARMS

If you are not as well endowed as you would like to be in the bustline, no exercise is going to achieve that for you. Exercise *will* help achieve good muscle tone. This one is also good for firming the upper arms, too.

1.) Hold your bent arms at chest level, grasping below each wrist with the other hand. Push your hands vigorously toward your elbows. Do this twenty times.

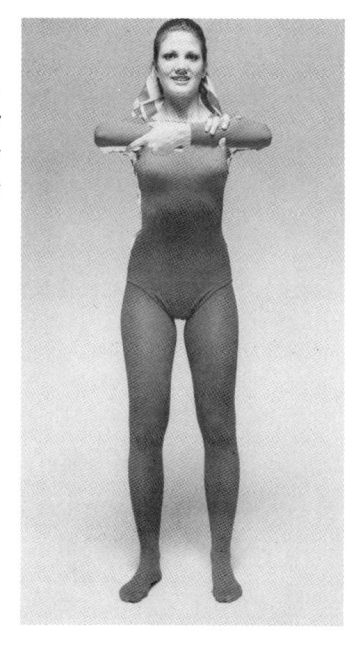

Based on the questions Karen was asked by teenagers during her year of travel, girls are most concerned with hip, tummy and thigh problems.

The next five exercise series take care of all three at once—and even help out a little on the waistline.

These are strenuous and should be "worked up to." Start with two of each. Add two more each week, until you can do eight of each series.

If you feel the strain in your back instead of your leg and stomach muscles, do fewer until you gain the strength in your stomach muscles.

These are all done lying on the floor, in order to help you hold your back in the proper position. At all times, keep your lower back (the small of your back) pressed as close to the floor as possible.

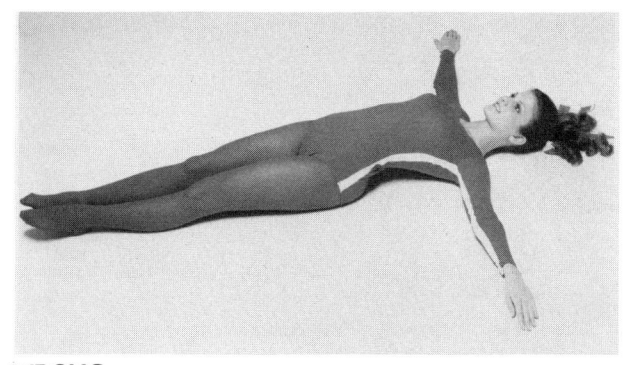

WRONG

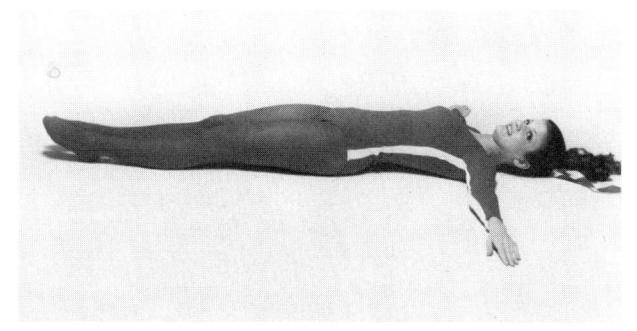

RIGHT

IV. EXERCISE FOR STOMACH AND LEGS

1.) Begin lying on your back, legs stretched straight in front of you, arms to the side.

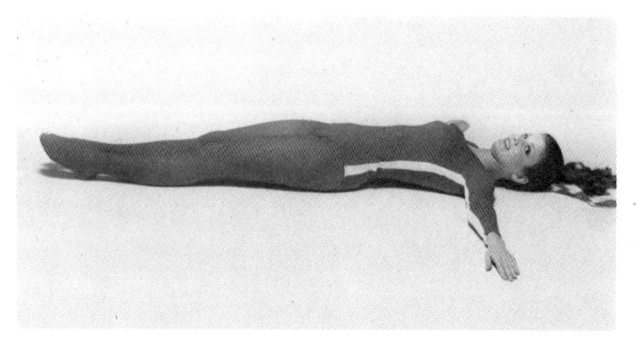

2.) Bend you left leg.

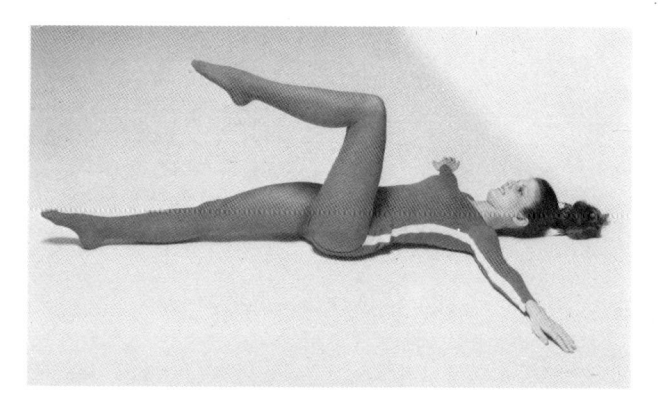

3.) Straighten it, pressing heel (flexed foot) to ceiling.

4.) Bend, point toe.

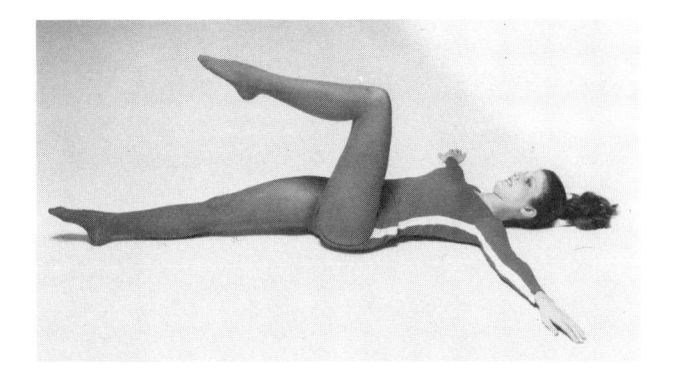

5.) Straighten leg one inch off floor and lower at last possible moment.

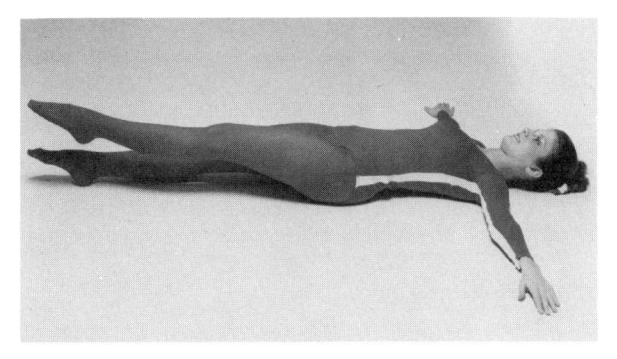

Reverse same on right leg.

Repeat the same move with both legs at the same time

1.) Bend both legs.

41

2.) Flex feet and straighten legs, pressing heels toward the ceiling.

3.) Bend legs, bringing knees as close to chest as possible, point toes.

4.) Bring toes to position one inch off floor and straighten legs entirely before you let your feet touch the floor.

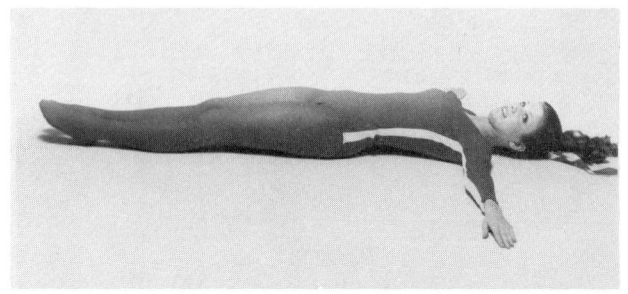

Repeat the entire series. As you begin to get in shape, add one more of the double leg exercise every few days until you can do eight in a row.

V. EXERCISE FOR HIPS, WAIST, STOMACH, AND THIGHS

Begin lying on your back (as in exercise IV) with your arms out to the sides. In this series, both shoulders must touch the floor at *all* times. If you allow one shoulder to leave the floor at any time, you lose the benefit to your waist.

1.) Lift your right leg as high in the air as you can without bending either knee.

2.) Keeping both shoulders on the floor, cross right leg over your body touching the floor with your toe. Try to touch it by your shoulder. Your waist will twist and your right hip will come off the floor.

3.) Return to position one with both hips on the floor and right leg raised in the air.

4.) Lower leg and return to beginning position.

Begin by doing this series eight times, alternating legs. Work up to sixteen, eight on each side.

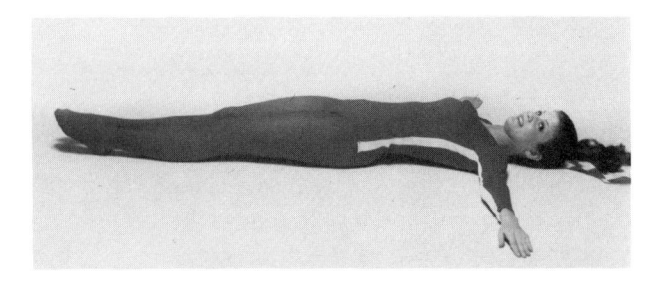

VI. LEG CIRCLES—FOR HIPS, WAIST, STOMACH, AND THIGHS

In this exercise, the leg circles from the hip in one continuous movement. The leg stays slightly off the floor the whole time.

Begin lying on your back, legs extended in front of you and arms to the side. Again, both shoulders always remain on the floor.

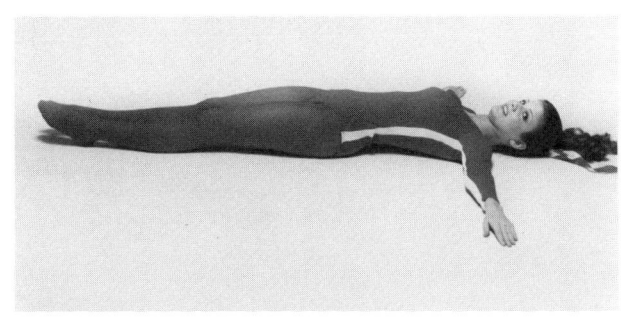

1.) Keep both legs straight. Cross your right leg, over toward your left shoulder, letting your right hip come off the floor.

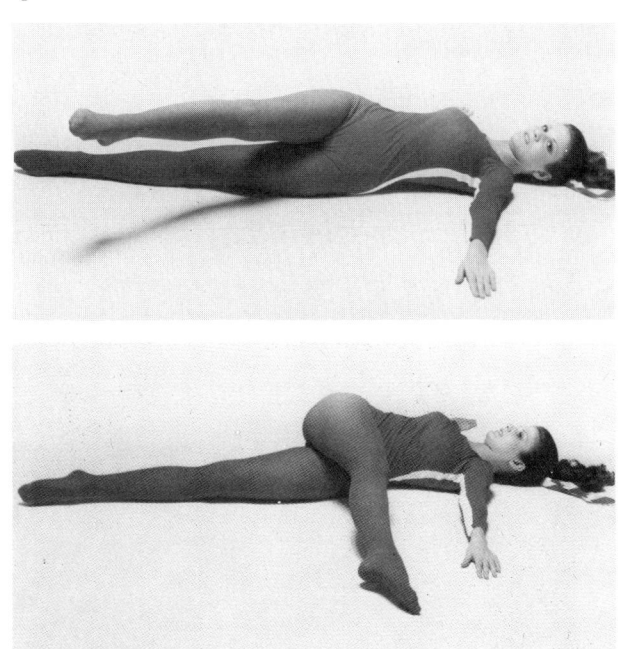

45

2.) Circle the leg straight up over your body, bringing your right hip back down on the floor. Keep the movement continuous.

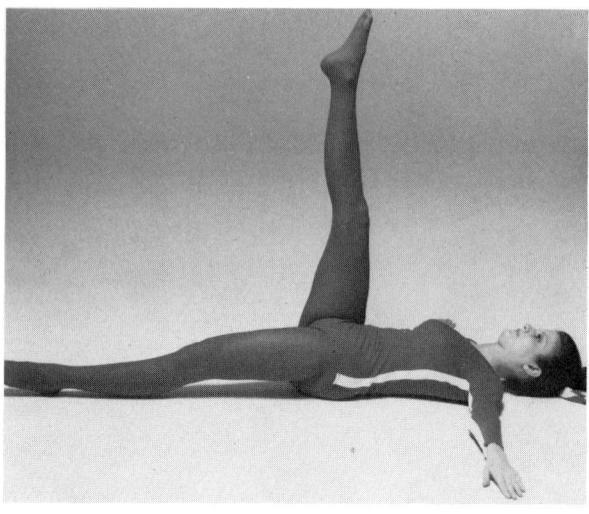

3.) Open right leg out to the right side, as near your right shoulder as possible, sweeping across the floor. *Keep both hips and shoulders on the floor.*

4.) Return to starting position. Now reverse the circle with same leg.

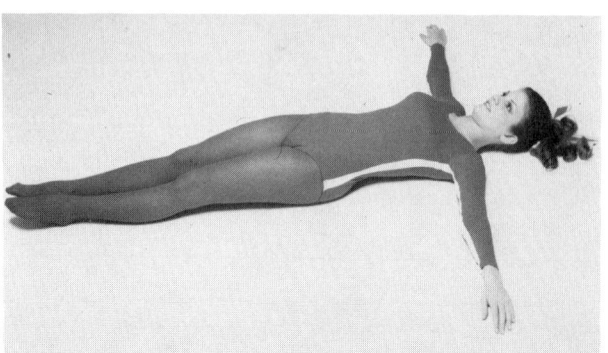

5.) Open your leg to the right side.

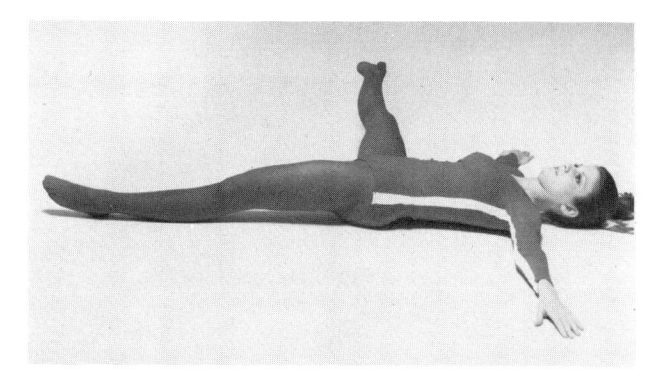

6.) Bring it straight up.

7.) Swing the leg across the body, as before. The hip comes off the floor.

8.) Bring leg back to beginning position. Bring the hip back down to the floor.

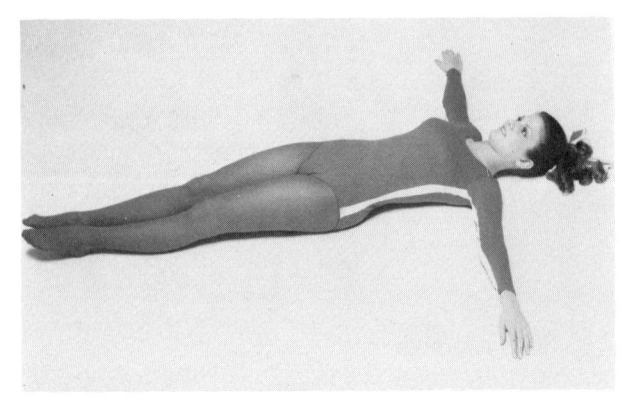

Repeat the inside and outside circle on the left. Start with two sets on each side and work up to eight on each side.

The next two exercises will make you very much aware of which muscles are working. These you should definitely feel in your stomach muscles. If you feel it in your back, you are letting your lower back arch up instead of holding it on the floor where it properly belongs.

In that case, lift your head off the floor and tuck your chin down to your chest. This will make it a little easier to hold your back in position.

VII. EXERCISES FOR LEGS AND STOMACH

The beginning position is the same as in the three previous exercises.

1.) Bend both legs as close to the chest as possible.

2.) Flex your feet and press your heels toward the ceiling until your legs are completely straight. (By flexing your feet instead of pointing your toes, you work your calf muscles more.)

3.) S-L-O-W-L-Y (and probably painfully!) lower your legs to the floor. Keep feet flexed and *keep pressing the small of your back down toward the floor.*

Now reverse the exercise.

4.) Lift both legs up as high as you can, keeping feet flexed and knees straight.

5.) Bend knees and pull your legs in close to your chest, pointing toes.

6.) Bring toes down to about an inch above the floor and straighten legs all the way, keeping them barely off the floor until the last second.

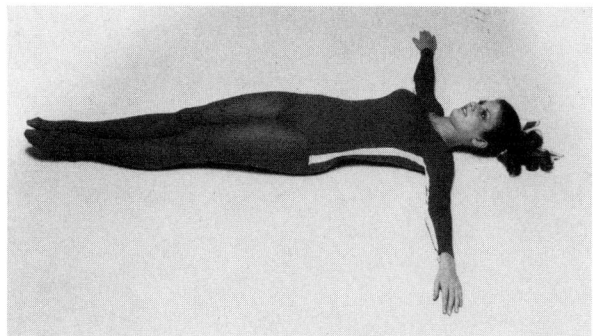

Start with two sets of these and work up to eight sets.

VIII. EXERCISE ESPECIALLY FOR INNER AND OUTSIDE THIGHS AND STOMACH

This exercise should be done with completely parallel legs. In other words, your knees should always be on top rather than turned toward the sides. This way you work the outside of your thighs, where those lumps tend to bulge.

If you don't feel the exercise at all on the sides of your legs, turn your toes more inward. The starting position is the same as before. Again, work with your feet flexed to *stretch* the leg muscles, not build them up. This is another leg circle exercise.

1.) Lift both legs straight up.

2.) Open legs as far wide as you can, keeping knees turned toward the ceiling.

3.) Lower legs to one inch above floor. Keep your back pressed to the floor.

4.) Pull legs together and lower to floor. Reverse the exercise.

5.) Lift heels barely off the floor and open your legs as far to side as you can, making sure your legs are parallel and not "turned out."

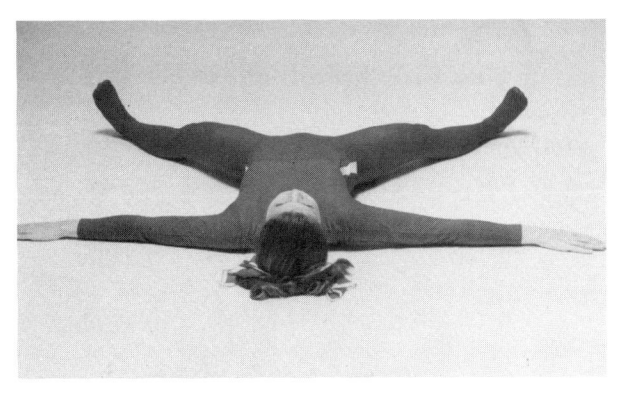

6.) In that position, feet still flexed, lift legs straight up, and together.

7.) Lower legs slowly to the floor.
Begin with two sets and work up to eight.

A FEW GENERAL NOTES

If you are having trouble keeping your lower back in proper position on the stomach exercises, do this exercise each time before you start those series.

Lie on your back, knees bent, feet on the floor.
Press your entire back to the floor until even the small of your back is touching.

Slowly straighten your legs and try to hold your back in that position. This will help acquaint you with the muscles that control your back and stomach and you'll learn to "get the feel" of the proper positions.

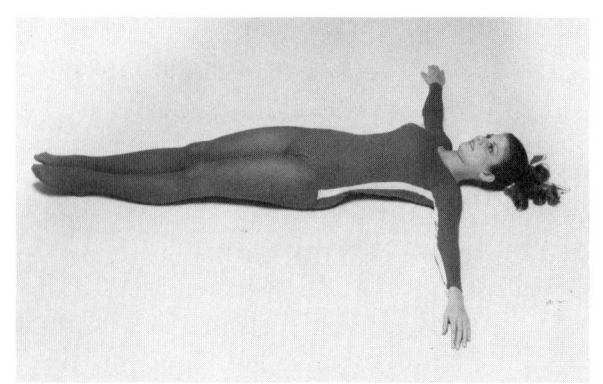

All of the exercises described here are designed to stretch the muscles, which in turn firm and tone your body, while making it more flexible.

While some people recommend such exercises as deep knee bends and sit ups, these can be harmful to the knees (in the case of knee bends) and back (in the case of sit ups) unless the person doing them is well trained and knows what she is doing. Knee bends done improperly can build your legs up instead of slimming and trimming them.

These can be good exercises, but if you are not a trained dancer as Karen is, or an experienced athlete, make sure you are properly supervised until you are sure you're doing them the right way.

If your weight has all "sunk to the bottom," try this.

Before you "work out" each time, wrap your thighs and around hips and tummy with plastic food wrap that comes on a roll. Over that, wear a pair of wool slacks or tights if you have them.

Yes, it sounds ridiculous, but the plastic holds in the heat and makes you perspire heavily right where you want to melt off a few inches. It works—and unlike fad diets, is not harmful to your health. Do remove the plastic at the end of your exercise session. Your skin does need to breathe, so don't leave it on for more than an hour or so at a time.

While you're watching T.V., sitting at your desk, or walking across the campus, try the isometric approach. Hold your stomach in as hard as you can for a count of ten. Then relax for a count of ten. Do this three or four times, several times a day.

At the end of each exercise session, do a few kicks or runs in place to "shake out" your muscles. It's good for your circulation, too.

DRAT THAT FAT

Annually, hundred of letters reach the offices of MISS TEENAGE AMERICA asking for solutions to the problems of overweight.

Any serious diet should be undertaken under the care of a doctor because what may serve one person would be ineffective, or even harmful, for another.

What follows are the replies to these queries. They are general suggestions for developing good eating habits as well as some diet tips for those who are not seriously overweight.

Now that you've decided on a good exercise program, add plenty of rest and a healthy diet, and you're well on your way to making beautiful things happen.

BASIC FOODS FOR HEALTH

The foods you need every day are divided into four categories. At least one serving from each category daily will assure you of the nutrients so vital for health and beauty.

1. *Meat and Meat Substitutes*—all meats, poultry, fish, eggs, dried beans, peas and nuts. These are high protein which build body tissue and give you protection against disease. They are good for energy and contain important vitamins and minerals.

2. *Fruits and Vegetables*—especially don't forget citrus fruits and green and yellow vegetables (loaded with vitamins and minerals). Vitamin A found in green vegetables is super for your skin. The C in citrus fruits does good things for your teeth and gums (your pretty smile) and helps proper functioning in your glands. Your hair will benefit from Vitamin B. The B Vitamin also helps your nervous system and helps prevent fatigue.

3. *Dairy Products*—milk in any form—whole, skimmed, powdered—cheese, yogurt. These contain protein, vitamins, and that very important mineral, calcium. They may not give you those delicious high cheekbones like some models have, but they will assure you of strong bones and teeth.

4. *Cereals*—Check the package for nutrients. This category includes wheat, oats, and whole grain breads. These contain carbohydrates, vitamins and minerals.

Meats and dairy products contain enough fats to be adequate for your daily diet.

You'll note that sugar or sweets are not among those foods *necessary* for good nutrition.

A little more about vitamins. See page 57 for what they do for you.

SOME SUGGESTIONS

1. French fries are not friendly. Avoid fried foods. There are many other ways to prepare the same foods—broiling, for example.

2. Watch the sweets. Anything that contains lots of fats, sugar, and flour is less nutritious than many less caloric foods, and will really put the pounds on—not to mention the damage to your complexion.

A switch in snack habits from "junk" foods to healthy things like fresh raw vegetables and fruit, juices, and hard boiled eggs (remember how

VITAMIN	WHAT IT DOES	SOURCES
A	Helps maintain skin, eyes, urinary tract, and linings of the nervous, respiratory, and digestive systems. Needed for normal growth of bones and teeth, and for good night vision.	Sweet potatoes, milk, liver, fish liver oils, eggs, butter, green and yellow vegetables.
B_1 (thiamin)	Needed for carbohydrate metabolism and release of energy from food. Helps heart and nervous system function properly.	Yeast, meat, whole-grain cereals, nuts, soybeans, peas, potatoes, most vegetables.
B_2 (riboflavin)	Helps body cells use oxygen. Promotes tissue repair and healthy skin.	Milk, cheese, liver, heart, fish, poultry.
Niacin	Essential for cell metabolism and absorption of carbohydrates. Helps maintain healthy skin.	Liver, yeast, lean meat
B_6	Needed for healthy teeth and gums, blood vessels, nervous system, and red blood cells.	Yeast, whole-grain cereals, meat, wheat germ, most vegetables.
B_{12}	Essential for proper development of red blood cells. Helps proper function of nervous system.	Eggs, meat, milk, milk products.
Biotin	Needed for healthy circulatory system and for maintaining healthy skin.	Eggs, liver, kidney, most fresh vegetables.
Folic Acid	Needed for production of red blood cells.	Green leafy vegetables, yeast, meat.
C (ascorbic acid)	Essential for sound bones and teeth. Needed for tissue metabolism and wound healing.	Citrus fruits, tomatoes, raw cabbage, potatoes, strawberries, cantaloupe.
D	Essential for calcium and phosphorus metabolism.	Fish liver oils, fortified milk, eggs, tuna, salmon, sunlight.
E	Helps maintain heart and skeletal muscles, and may help maintain reproductive system.	Whole-grain cereals, lettuce, vegetable oils.
K	Needed for normal blood clotting.	Leafy vegetables; made by intestinal bacteria.

good they used to taste at Easter?) will make your figure happy—and your dentist!

Even if you are trying to *gain* weight, choose healthy, body-building foods like cheese, creamed soups and baked potatoes with sour cream—no pies and candy bars.

3. If you're trying to lose weight, as much as possible avoid starchy foods. Leave off breads, pastas and desserts. Substitute larger portions of

low calorie foods and cut down on high calorie foods. If you just have to have something sweet, stick to diet products like a sugar free soft drink.

4. Get yourself a book on nutrition and a calorie counter. Learn good eating habits.

5. Whether you're trying to gain or lose weight, protein is a very important part of any healthy diet. Proper vitamins are important, too.

6. AVOID FAD DIETS! AVOID FAD DIETS! AVOID FAD DIETS!

Twenty Questions

Your Most Often-Asked Beauty Questions—Solved

Did you find an eyelash on your pillow this morning and feel a surge of panic? If so, you may have written *Teen* Magazine for help.

Teen's Beauty Editor answers thousands of questions each year. We asked her to compile a list of the beauty questions their readers most often ask. Perhaps one of these will shed some light on something you've been wondering about.

1. Q. How can I get my hair to grow faster?
   A. Hair growth depends on age, diet, emotional state and blood circulation. However, hair only grows about a half an inch a month or six to seven inches a year. If you want your hair to grow as fast as possible, you should eat right, exercise daily and get plenty of sleep.
2. Q. Every time I brush my hair, I seem to be losing more and more. I don't want to be bald! How can I get my hair to stop falling out?
   A. Hair loss is normal. Each hair you have stays on the head for an average of two to six years and is then replaced by a new one. We have approximately 90,000 to 140,000 hairs with a daily fall-out rate of 40 to 100 hairs. When you think about it, that's really not a lot to lose! But, if you think your hair is coming out in clumps or fistfuls, see a doctor. Sudden and significant hair loss could be the result of illness, medication or diet deficiency.
3. Q. What should I do about split ends?
   A. The ends of your hair can sometimes be almost six years old and they need special conditioning to stay healthy. Split ends

are very common in long hair. The ends split when the outside (cuticle) layer of the hair shaft has worn away and left the inner (cortex) layer unprotected. If you don't trim the ends, the split will continue to travel up the hair shaft almost like a run in a stocking. Nothing will completely rid your hair of split ends except a good cut. And then to help the problem from recurring again, try treating your hair gently and using a deep-penetrating conditioner at least once a month.

4. Q. My hair is very oily and I wash it every day. Am I hurting it?
   A. Hair that is extremely oily needs to be washed every day. You won't hurt it if you're sure to use a gentle shampoo or one that is specially formulated for oily hair.

5. Q. I colored my hair and now the roots are starting to show. I don't want to color it anymore, since I would rather have my old color back. What should I do?
   A. When it comes to hair coloring, it's very difficult to diagnose a case without seeing the person first. Depending on your natural hair color, the exact product you used and the type of hair you have, will determine what you should do to get you back to your natural hair color. Consult a hair coloring specialist or a good hairdresser.

6. Q. What should I do about pimples?
   A. The most important factor in keeping pimples to a minimum is a good cleansing routine. Clean your face at least twice a day, three times if your skin is exceptionally oily. Keep your hands away from your face, eat well-balanced meals with lots of fruit, skim milk and vitamin A enriched foods.

7. Q. I don't have just a few pimples, I have a bad case of acne. My skin is so awful, what should I do?
   A. Acne sufferers should always be under the care and guidance of a doctor. See a dermatologist about your problem and he'll be able to advise you on eating habits, cleansing routine, and controlling the flow of oil from both the scalp and complexion. There are antibiotics now that can help.

8. Q. What causes dark circles under the eyes?
   A. If they're just temporary, they could be from a lack of sleep, nervousness, or any illness. But if you seem to have them all the time, they could be hereditary. Your skin tissue may be very fine and the underlying blood vessel is showing through, which causes the area to appear dark.

9. Q. What's a good way to cover them up?
   A. Any one of the many cover-up creams or sticks would be good. Try to get a cream that matches your skin tone so you won't have an obvious cover-up.
10. Q. I want long nails, but they're always splitting and breaking even before they have a chance to grow!
    A. Strong nails are a result of a good diet—lots of protein and plenty of calcium. Don't file the corners of your nails or file them to a point because they'll break easily. A blunt rounded shape is better. Also, be sure to use a nail strengthening polish before applying your usual color.
11. Q. Will shaving my legs make the hair grow back thicker and longer?
    A. No, shaving your legs doesn't make the hair grow thicker.
12. Q. I plucked my eyebrows for the first time and now I have black stubbles. How can I get those out?
    A. The best time to pluck your brows is after a hot bath or shower when your pores are open. Be sure to use a sharp tweezer and to pull in the direction in which the hair is growing. If you don't pluck the entire hair out you'll be left with the root or black stubble.
13. Q. Is it okay to bleach facial hair?
    A. Sure it is, just as long as you use a product made specifically for the face. Never use a hair bleach that's meant to dye the hair on your head for your face. Use special precaution if you have sensitive skin. Also, never bleach your eyebrows or lashes.
14. Q. When I wake up in the morning, I always find a few eyelashes on my pillow case. Am I going to lose all my lashes?
    A. No, this is very normal. Be sure to remove all your eye make-up before going to sleep and lubricate your lashes with a bit of petroleum jelly to help stop too many lashes from falling out.
15. Q. I just found out I have to wear glasses. Are there any rules I should follow when picking out frames?
    A. These are the standard rules but remember, there's always a chance that a certain style will do something special for you even though it doesn't fit into those categories. Ask a friend or your mother to come along with you, and help you to choose a style that's best.
    Round faces: Choose a square, rectangle or octagon frame. Narrow ovals may also look good on some.

Narrow faces: Pick a rectangle or long oval which will stretch the horizontal line of the face. Big circles also look good.
Heart faces: Ovals and aviators are best.
Square faces: Soften the sharp angles of your face with circles. Never wear any squares or rectangles.
Diamond and triangle faces: Your glasses should be wider on the top than on the bottom. Heavy cheeks need glasses that slant upwards.

16. Q. I'm about ten pounds overweight. I'd like to rid myself of the extra weight, but I can't seem to control myself. Is there any easy diet I could follow?
    A. Sorry, but no diet is really easy. It takes will power to stick to a diet and you really have to make up your mind that you're going to stay with it and lose that weight. Try to cut down on snacks and avoid eating between meals. Keep active with a sport and get a good exercise routine together. Stay with your diet for at least a month and you'll surely see results.

17. Q. I'm pretty active in sports at school. A friend told me that I'm building muscles and that they're going to look awful after a few years. Is she right?
    A. Sports and extracurricular activities won't hurt your figure at all. They will firm and tighten muscles which is a whole lot better than fat and flab and they won't build huge, ugly muscles. It's good for you.

18. Q. How should I go about picking out a fragrance for myself?
    A. With so many fragrances around today, we can easily see where there might be some confusion. Go to a drug or department store where they let you try on a scent for size. Place it on any of your pulse points—wrist or behind the ear is good. Now don't go by the first whiff, wait awhile and let it sink in. A scent will change because of your body chemistry, and it will smell different on each individual. Don't rely on picking the same fragrance a friend has. It may smell great on her, but be disastrous for you. Experiment until you find one *you* really like.

19. Q. How can I get my teeth to look whiter?
    A. Be sure to brush after each meal and use dental floss at least once a day. Have your dentist clean your teeth twice a year to remove any build up of tartar and plaque. Avoid smoking and drinking too much tea and coffee.

20. Q. How can I look like a *Teen* model?
    A. All of the models we use at *Teen* agree that it takes lots of hard work to keep looking great. They exercise regularly, eat right, and work on their particular problem area every day. One way of improving yourself is to write down all your good and bad points. Decide on what you have to do to improve on the bad points and play up the good ones. Remember that each individual is beautiful in her own way and should work to her fullest capacity to realize and perfect herself.

ADVENTURE II

Making Good Things Happen with Others

Attitude and Relationships

Three Former MISS TEENAGE AMERICAs Speak Up

Your Inner Beauty

Three former MISS TEENAGE AMERICAS, three attractive women who have mastered all those aspects of beauty and grooming we've just discussed, talk about what goes on beneath the lovely facades they present to the world. Each one of them knows that being attractive is important, but she also knows there is more to life than being pretty. If she hadn't known that, she would never have become MISS TEENAGE AMERICA, for it was her values and attitudes, her concern for others and approach to life as much as her pretty face and graceful figure, that convinced the judges each of these girls exemplified what is best in America's young women.

Each girl has her own set of values, her own special attitude toward the world, her own sense of strength and defeat, and her own poise and perspective in victory. These girls are winners—that's for sure—but what makes them extraordinary is that they are as sure of themselves and their values in defeat as in triumph. They have inner strength, and, more important, inner beauty. They know themselves. Now let's get to know them.

BY
MELISSA GALBRAITH
MISS TEENAGE AMERICA 1973

Melissa: "Pretending to be something or somebody other than yourself can only lead to hypocrisy and unhappiness."

At the time of this writing, Melissa is a sophomore at the University of Pittsburgh, majoring in communications. Her interest in the many people she met during her years as MISS TEENAGE AMERICA *greatly affected her choice of college major. But because Melissa has always exhibited those qualities she describes here, we believe she will be successful no matter what she chooses to do.*

In society today, a woman's prominence is no longer contingent upon her physical appearance. The ideals behind the MISS TEENAGE AMERICA Pageant exemplify this assertion. The Pageant itself is not a beauty contest, but morever focuses upon five basic virtues: honor, integrity, leadership, knowledge, and achievement. These five words, which are engraved on the Medallion of MISS TEENAGE AMERICA, represent the basic values she strives to fulfill. But most importantly, these are virtues every young woman should try to incorporate into her character.

Honor may be regarded as respect and esteem, especially from one's own peer group. Although exceptional merit is not requisite for obtaining honor, open and honest communication is most certainly fundamental. Integrity, in the form of trustworthiness to one's family and friends, is undoubtedly essential for success. By taking the initiative and maintaining one's own individuality, a person gains a quality of leadership.

Knowledge obtained from books and classrooms is essential, but practical knowledge gathered in daily living is equally vital. And lastly, one should never be satisfied with her achievements to date, but, moreover, should continually strive for greater excellence in all pursuits. With perseverance and determination, one can feel extreme self-satisfaction upon achieving higher goals. Whatever a young woman's goal in life, these qualities can prove invaluable.

Aside from these virtues, a woman must be herself! Pretending to be something or somebody other than yourself can only lead to hypocrisy and unhappiness. By maintaining one's own individuality, honor, integrity, leadership, knowledge, and achievement will become habitual. Within each of us, these virtues are inherent, and with only a little effort to cultivate them, each of us may become a happier and more successful student, citizen, and person.

BY
COLLEEN FITZPATRICK
MISS TEENAGE AMERICA 1972

Colleen: "Whatever you believe, the important thing to remember is to have the courage and strength to believe in *yourself*."

Colleen's major interest has been music and the theatre, a career goal that will take much effort and determination. Like Melissa, we asked Colleen to share with you her thoughts on goals and personal values, and as you read what she has to say see if you don't agree with us that her talent, combined with these ideas and a generous amount of hard work, are a good recipe for success.

I believe that the attainment of success as a person is a task that anyone can handle if she is willing to practice and really work at being a fine person.

For myself, I think a very basic value that a person should develop is LOVE. I feel that love can handle anything—it's fulfilling and can heal all wounds. There is no way for me to tell you how to learn to be a loving person . . . I don't even think that anyone knows how to define it, let alone teach it! What I do know is that if a person is a loving individual, she will also possess the attributes of kindness, charity, integrity, trust, and honor. I feel that they come under the heading of love.

Whatever you belive, the important thing to remember is to have the courage and strength to believe in *yourself*.

____Learn to trust your judgments
____Learn to trust your intellectual capacities
____Learn to trust your emotional reactions
____Learn to live not as others want to perceive you, but as you are.

Many times in your life a person is pressured into molding himself in the current mores and ideals. Don't let it happen. You alone should be the "captain of your seas." This is not easy. To live for yourself takes practice and sometimes age . . . this I, myself, am finding out. The going is slow . . .

But just because I think a person should live for himself, doesn't mean to be uncaring. One should be alert to the needs of others. When you believe in yourself, you can then extend your values to other people and if they are receptive to the loving person you should be, then they'll extend those values again to others. Idealistically, see what a nice little chain we've got going?

BY
LORI MATSUKAWA
MISS TEENAGE AMERICA 1974

Lori: "When life gives you lemons, make lemonade!"

The first thing the MISS TEENAGE AMERICA *Staff noticed about Lori, and perhaps the quality we will remember the longest, was her positive attitude. She even found something good to say about the earthquake she encountered in Peru! Being around a person like Lori is a delight. With that marvelous attitude, she gives you the feeling that she will accomplish great things, and that everyone she meets will be better off for knowing her.*

Values are those principles that a person learns from his parents, his peers and his society. These principles guide him through life and help him to make decisions which will benefit himself and his fellow man. Each person has different sets of values. Each person holds certain values higher than others. By holding the right values close to your heart, you will find that life, with its many surprises, can be coped with. You will find that life is interesting and that each day holds something new for you. I cannot tell you which values are right for you. Neither can I tell you that the values I mention in this article will change your life and make you happy. Each person must discover and know his own set of values.

The values you hold are based upon your philosophy of life. Everyone, no matter how young, has a philosophy. During the early years, it is subject to change. But by the time a person reaches his late teens, he has a pretty definite idea about his view towards life. For myself, I have what I call a two-point philosophy. First, I believe that we should live life a little bit at a time each day, because time and life is all we have. And second, I believe that life is an eternal learning process. We should always be learning and growing within ourselves.

The reason I feel so strongly about making wise use of time is because there is so much to experience and do. If we don't do things a little every day, we won't have lived like we could have. We are young and we don't think about how long we have to live. It is quite amazing how years fly by. Before we know it, a decade or two will have passed, and we will look back and question ourselves as to what we have done in that twenty years. It is our hope that when we look back, we can smile and say, "I've done a lot. I've lived a useful life."

The most important thing about life and success is to face both situations with a positive attitude. We should wake up each morning saying "I will" instead of "I won't"; "I can" instead of "I can't." By being optimistic, you are that much closer to having a fulfilling day. Being pessimistic is self-defeating, not to mention a waste of time.

Along with a positive attitude, it is important to be flexible. A change in the weather may alter your plans for the day, like a change in your life may alter your plans for the future. Persevere when striving to meet your goals, but be able to adapt to changes that may arise.

Self-discipline is very important. Whether it means sticking to a study schedule, a diet, or piano practice, it plays an important role in doing something well and completely. Many activities can be accomplished each day through careful planning and self-discipline. Again, time is precious, and we must make the best use of it.

Philosophy point two: Life is an eternal learning process. This philosophy has guided me well during my teen years. I know it will follow me through my adult years. My parents are the type of people who encourage their youngsters to experience and learn by doing. They took my sisters and me to museums, aquariums, zoos, movies, plays and parades. They took us out to eat and made us taste various foods. We learned our social graces and how to get along with people. From these varied experiences, my sisters and I learned to appreciate life all around us. Little did we know that we were building good, strong backgrounds.

Each morning, wake up with that positive attitude. Tell yourself that you will learn something today that may make you a better person. It needn't be a major thing. Learn a new word, a new way to wax your car or meet a new friend.

Get various experiences under your belt. The more you see and expose yourself to, the more you will understand people and society. You will see why people act the way they do by seeing how they live. All of the impressions you collect will profit your understanding of people.

While books and schools can give you a lot of academic information, people can teach you about life. People are a boundless source of knowledge and wisdom. Talk to them willingly and *listen* when they speak. Everyone, no matter what their station in life is, can enrich your background.

When I was being judged by the MISS TEENAGE AMERICA judges, they asked me what sort of role I would play should I receive the title. I told them that I would like to express the opinions of youth to all groups of people, but more importantly, I would like to listen to what others had to say to me! Communication is a two-way street. You have to listen as well as speak. During the year, I tried to ask people more questions than they asked me. I found to my delight that they were more than ready to speak about their life, interests and experiences.

Because we are dependent on others to give us the knowledge we crave, it is a good idea to practice some good, old-fashioned courtesy. Treat others as you would have them treat you. Don't take yourself too seriously. Be respectful and considerate. Listen with your whole mind and heart. Be understanding. Don't jump to conclusions about a person too quickly . . . it's passing judgment. Be patient and if you have to leave, be polite. The way you behave reflects on your character and upbringing.

We must also keep our responsibilities. Whether they be home, school or social responsibilities, we should do them promptly and well. By taking on certain responsibilities, we show others that we can be depended upon.

One might ask what all this philosophizing is about. How can all this "talk" provide you with a job, money to live, with success and recognition? A philosophy of life will guide you in your life's endeavors. It will give you the confidence and spirit to make your life what you want it to be.

Sometimes, despite our positive attitude and optimism, life can deliver some hard blows. Hopefully, your philosophy of life will be such that you can pick yourself up and continue to live, telling yourself that soon things will be all right. As someone once said . . . When life gives you lemons, make lemonade! Live so that in retrospect, you can honestly say, "I've lived a good life!"

A Survey of High Achievers

BY
PAUL KROUSE
President,
Educational Communications, Inc.
Publisher,
Who's Who Among American High School Students,
Who's Who Among Black Americans

> *Mr. Krouse's organization sponsors over $35,000 in scholarship awards annually and helps fund numerous youth programs at the secondary school level.* Who's Who *also contributes to the* MISS TEENAGE AMERICA *scholarship program.*

Through the publication of *Who's Who Among American High School Students,* we have recognized and honored over 1,000,000 students since 1967. As a result of our exposure to this unique and select group of distinguished young adults, we have developed an almost fanatical interest in the qualities of leadership. It is interesting to observe the common denominators and characteristics shared by high achievers. What turns them on, what turns them off, what motivates them and why?

Probably one of the more revealing projects sponsored by *Who's Who* is our annual "Survey of High Achievers" which measures the attitudes and opinions of *Who's Who* students on the major issues of the day. There are no sacred cows in this frank and candid survey. Everything from "pot to politics" is covered with a great deal of data in between. Religion. Family relationships. Educational evaluations, etc. It is through this survey that we are able to learn the most about student leaders.

We know that 96 percent of *Who's Who*'ers are college-bound and 97 percent have attained a "B" grade point average or better (68 percent "A", 29 percent "B"). The "average" biographee has participated in eight school- or community-sponsored activities. Obviously, we now know that these students are high achievers academically and generous with their time. They are involved. Not surprising.

When it comes to their attitudes and opinions, there are some surprises. For example, most polls regarding student use of marijuana and other drugs suggest rather wide usage among today's teenagers. Yet, 73 percent of *Who's Who* students have never even tried marijuana and over 90 percent have never tried other drugs. Are they sheltered or "out of the mainstream"? Apparently not, since 47 percent indicate that they associate with friends who do use drugs and 78 percent state that drugs are readily available in or around their schools. We must therefore conclude that these students have determined that while they would not condemn others (like some of their friends) for using drugs, it is not something they deem as positive or desirable for themselves.

Similarly surprising, at a time when "old" standards and values seem to be crumbling and "the new morality" is spreading, we find that 80 percent of the *Who's Who* students consider themselves to be members of an organized religion, 86 percent believe religion is relevant in today's society and 78 percent believe there is a personal God or supreme being. Over 68,000 students in the 1974-75 edition informed us that they participated in church-related activities and programs.

In a limited amount of space it is not possible to totally characterize *Who's Who* students. From the data we collect and compile each year and from the thousands of personal letters we have received over the years, let me assure you that as a group, these young men and women display a sensitivity to the world around them, an awareness of the social and moral problems that confront us all and enough doubt and uncertainty to confirm their basic vulnerability as human beings.

Yet, in spite of their doubts, they are involved in their total universe and committed to excellence in whatever they undertake. In their schools as well as communities, they take responsibility and seem to handle it rather well. While they obviously know that their relative inexperience will result in errors and mistakes, they seem willing to learn and grow from these opportunities.

It is my opinion that *Who's Who* students are similar to leaders in most other fields. They have maximized the benefits of their total educational experience—home, school and church—and developed a sense of values which guides them in their short-range as well as long-range objectives. When obstacles appear, as they do for all of us, it is easier to respond when you have certain moral commitments (or rules) to rely on. These commitments frequently eliminate certain choices while making other opportunities more clear.

For the youthful student as well as the polished and elder statesmen, the learning experience never stops. Values are refined and even redefined as exposure to problems increases. New experiences cause reflection, adjustment causes growth and enough of both generally bring maturity and wisdom.

The cycle never stops. When growth, thinking and self-appraisal slow down, values have a tendency to slide and the consequences can be devastating. On a more positive note, when high individual standards exist and sound values are maintained, the results are generally rewarding and satisfying.

You've decided who you are and the kind of person you want to be. Now add the people whose lives touch yours—your special relationships.

In the next few chapters, some good friends of MISS TEENAGE AMERICA *discuss how to make the good things happen—with your family, your friends and that very special person who, if he is not yet in your life, is on his way.*

Home Is Where the Heart Is
Your Relationship with Your Family

BY
BONNIE PIEDMONTE

> *One of the editors, Ms. Piedmonte is a cum laude graduate of the University of Toledo and did her masters work in Special Education at the University of Miami. Through her work with exceptional children, emotionally disturbed and physically handicapped, she has had a firsthand opportunity to observe the importance of personal relationships as they affected her young students. She tells the story of one of them—a teenager named Sunshine.*

It has been said that the person who can claim six close friends in a lifetime has indeed led a rich and full life. Since you are in command of the direction in which your own life unfolds, why not get involved and strive to fill your life with true friends.

What better place to begin than right in your home with your parents? A closer association than with the two people that you live with would be difficult to find.

Though we often tend to place our family in a different role than our friends, it is important and potentially very rewarding to see relatives as friends too.

When you think of your parents, what is the first role they represent that comes to mind? It would probably be pretty safe to say the disciplinary function is your immediate response. It might seem to you that Mom and Dad are always saying "Don't do that" or "No, you can't go," and your reaction may be negative.

You feel that you should have a right to do what you want and to go where you like. But, before you become angry with them, stop and think why the situation is as it is.

First of all, when your parents decided to raise a child, they assumed full responsibility of caring for and helping you to grow into a responsible, worthwhile adult and an acceptable human being. The job they accepted of guiding and teaching you to become the best person possible, by necessity, carries with it a certain degree of discipline and selection of opportunities and directions for you which they view as best or the right way.

Rules and restrictions are as necessary to individuals as they are to our society, which is an interrelated and interdependent whole made up of millions of individuals. Chaos would indeed prevail if our society, as well as all the others which form our world, did not have laws to govern their people.

Since we as individuals are ultimately only a result of the disciplines we can bring to ourselves, the instillment of "right" and "wrong" early in our growth process is necessary.

Secondly, try and put yourself in your parents' position and think of how you would react to various occurrences. It is sometimes very easy for a teenager to automatically reject what her parents say simply because they are older and could not possibly understand how she is feeling.

Another common complaint is that society has changed so drastically that Mom and Dad have no up-to-date frame of reference, consequently, no ability to understand.

In some cases it may be difficult for parents to relate to experiences that their children are facing. It is much more often the case that they have at some time in their lives experienced the very same feelings. Try to understand your parents' viewpoint and refrain from being too harsh in your judgment. The young and idealistic sometimes lose out on much wisdom and insight which their parents have gained through experience.

Finally, another point to seriously consider when weighing your own opinions and those of your parents is how you evaluate your position in the family unit or in what role you see yourself. It is very easy to take from others and not always as simple to give something in return.

If you were to look objectively at the part you play in your family would you see yourself as a receiver rather than a contributor? An atmosphere of interrelating, sharing, and loving is much healthier than a parent-child relationship that is completely one-sided. Being prepared to give more than you expect to get from a situation is a worthwhile thought to keep in mind.

Remember, the opportunity of building a meaningful relationship with your parents is open to you. It is up to you, as well as them, to take responsibility for your actions and make an effort to give of yourself while trying to understand their point of view.

All your life you will be faced with "another point of view" and an inability to acknowledge another opinion is pure bigotry and can only lead to isolation. There are no relationships where "give" is less important than "take."

An elementary fact which is often forgotten or ignored is that you must take the time to communicate with your family and develop that sought-after closeness. The understanding will not come without an effort on your part as well as your parents.

The family gathering together at dinner time used to provide an atmosphere conducive to talking and sharing feelings, but, as we are all aware, busy schedules and eating on the run have to a great extent eliminated the family being brought together in this way. So it is up to you and your parents to make time available and perhaps set aside a special time each day to sit and talk. Resolving problems and voicing opinions leave you both more receptive to the other's feelings and able to begin the next day with a better understanding.

Meaningful discussions with reinforcing feedback for both parties as well as lighthearted talks and the sharing of day-to-day experiences are all part of establishing and developing that very special closeness with your family which can become a most rewarding facet of your life.

To help you to know your parents better, talk to some of their friends and associates. Sometimes others' opinions and insights can offer a viewpoint which you have overlooked.

What is it in your parents that others notice and admire? In discussions with their friends your parents have probably stated their feelings on subjects which concern you, and to learn of these can be helpful in growing closer to them.

Familiarize yourself with the outlook of your parents' contemporaries and see if you can't understand why they see something a little differently than you do. These opportunities readily present themselves since you frequently come in contact at school with teachers and counselors, at your friends' homes with their parents, and at your job with men and women of your parents' age.

Through my experiences working with teenage girls and boys I have often run across those who are unable to talk with or confide in their parents. The degree to which this lack of personal closeness affects people is a very individual thing.

"Sunshine's" story is obviously an extreme example, but is related in order to point out what can happen when people feel as though they are alone and that no one is interested in them.

Sunshine, as she is known by her friends, is a pretty and quiet teenage girl. She has that blond California look about her that magazine advertisers seem to search for.

Her special love for outdoor activities gives her that healthy golden glow sought by all anemic-looking sun worshippers.

In school Sunshine gets by, but her attention is usually on subjects other than academics. Math, geography, and English seem of little importance compared to the thoughts that occupy her mind and generally take precedence.

Movie stars, dating, and fashion news seem much more interesting to her. Listening to music, sometimes at unbearable volumes, is a time-consuming pastime. Her list of favorite artists range from John Denver and Chicago to Bach and Bernstein. Pizza, hamburgers, and ice cream are an enjoyable part of Sunshine's diet.

If this portrait of Sunshine sounds to you like the description of a typical teenage girl, continue reading. You will see she is not quite so conventional as it may appear from this brief and superficial portrait that has been presented.

Unfortunately, Sunshine is an emotionally disturbed girl with a history of repeated suicide attempts.

There is no simple explanation why Sunshine is unhappy with her life or no easy solution to the problem that she would rather die than try to cope with it. As is generally the case in what we've come to refer to as emotional disturbance, there is not one isolated factor that can be readily identified and cured.

Numerous interrelated aspects of a person's background and experiences combine to form their inability to handle everyday situations.

In Sunshine's case, her lack of communication with her parents is a key factor which has developed her acute feelings of rejection and aloneness. She is unable to reach her parents at all, much less confide in them and trust their advice.

She has tried the "in" solution to find happiness by turning to the use of drugs, but this has worsened her problems rather than served as a remedy. Heavy drinking and "hanging out" with an older crowd of friends were other attempts for her to find herself.

When all else failed, Sunshine resorted to the best solution she knew—slitting her wrists.

We are all guilty at times of taking our families for granted or failing to share our inner feelings with them—feelings of happiness and joy as well as feelings of discontent or unhappiness.

Open communication must be honest in that you are capable of sharing positive as well as negative emotions. Since our happiness in large measure comes from worthwhile relationships with others it seems almost unnecessary to reiterate that without communication there can be no bonds or friendships formed.

We sometimes forget or become so involved in other things that we pass over basic feelings that make us what we are—vulnerable and sensitive human beings who need each other.

Communication is indeed necessary for understanding. Strive for developing a solid relationship with your parents, and it will serve as a stepping stone to other opportunities for worthwhile associations and friendships outside of your home.

I'll Tell Them

BY
ERMA BOMBECK

From *At Wits End*, courtesy of
Field Newspaper Syndicate,
Copyright 1975

"You don't love me!"

How many times have your kids laid that one on you?

And how many times have you as a parent, resisted the urge to tell them how much?

Someday, when my children are old enough to understand the logic that motivates a mother, I'll tell them.

I loved you enough to bug you about where you were going, with whom, and what time you would get home.

I love you enough to insist you buy a bike with your own money that we could afford and you couldn't.

I loved you enough to be silent and let you discover your handpicked friend was a creep.

I loved you enough to make you return a Milky Way with a bite out of it to a drugstore and confess, "I stole this."

I loved you enough to stand over you for two hours while you cleaned your bedroom, a job that would have taken me fifteen minutes.

I loved you enough to say, "Yes, you can go to Disney World on Mother's Day."

I loved you enough to let you see anger, disappointment, disgust and tears in my eyes.

I loved you enough to not make excuses for your lack of respect or your bad manners.

I loved you enough to admit I was wrong and ask your forgiveness.

I loved you enough to ignore "what every other mother" did or said.

I loved you enough to let you stumble, fall, hurt, and fail.

I loved you enough to let you assume the responsibility for your own actions, at six, ten or sixteen.

I loved you enough to figure you would lie about the party being chaperoned, but forgive you for it . . . after discovering I was right.

I loved you enough to shove you off my lap, let go of your hand, be mute to your pleas, and insensitive to your demands . . . so that you had to stand alone.

I loved you enough to accept you for what you are, not what I wanted you to be.

But most of all, I loved you enough to say no when you hated me for it. That was the hardest of all.

A Friend in Deed or a Friend in Need?

BY
MARVIN PORTER

> Mr. Porter has spent much of his adult life working, professionally and as a volunteer, with young people. Not just any young people, but those with serious problems. A teacher at the Child Study Center in Fort Worth, Texas and as a youth coordinator at the Maumee Valley Youth Camp, a correctional institute for juvenile delinquents, he found that many of the problems stemmed from an inability to form trusting relationships and solid friendships. Everybody needs a friend. Mr. Porter discusses some ideas on being a good friend.

What is a true friendship? Should you have set rules for it? Do you have set rules that you are aware of? Do you have principles concerning your friendship? Should you have some? Do you know what would happen if you were to tell a secret that one of your friends told you in confidence? Would you understand if one of your friends told one of your secrets?

You and I know there are not set answers for these questions, but I do hope you will think about them. I think you should begin to question some things about friendship now. Are you a good friend? What makes a good friend? What makes the difference between a friend and an acquaintance?

There are some common ideas of friendship that never change. They are honesty, faith, understanding, and communication—four priceless qualities that affect all relationships, especially friendships.

To be honest with your friend means more than just telling the truth. Don't be afraid to express your feelings and stand firm in your beliefs. Included here is also the quality of faith—faith in your personals ideas and

"Honesty, faith, understanding and communication are the four priceless qualities that make a friendship."

Many lasting friendships begin at the MISS TEENAGE AMERICA Pageant Finals each year. Among the girls pictured above are Debbie Patton, MISS TEENAGE AMERICA 1970 (top right) and Sandy Roberts, MISS TEENAGE AMERICA 1967 (identified by badge in lower right photo).

85

decisions and faith in your friend to accept you as you are and want to grow in your relationship.

Understanding is an important facet that has to be involved in any meaningful friendship. If your friend's opinions vary greatly from yours—can you accept them for what they are and build from there? Respect of an individual's decisions is necessary all through life.

The last and all-encompassing factor is that of communication. Communication needs to be brought into play when discussing problems and expressing feelings. Talking things out will serve to either strengthen your friendship or point out to you that you wish to conclude the relationship.

Remember that building meaningful relationships requires you to play an active role. You need to seriously consider just what it is that you hope to give to a friendship and what benefits you expect to receive.

Because a true and strong friendship is one of the highest forms of love, I wish for you an everlasting friendship.

Attitude—Your Approach to Life, Love and Beautiful Friendships

BY
ELIZABETH LACEY
Oklahoma Association for Mental Health

Elizabeth Lacey not only writes about people and talks about people—she also works with people who are seeking attitude opportunities. When she writes about attitudes, she does so from an extensive background of personal achievement. Your attitude is an important part of your relationships with others, whether it be your friends, your family, or that "special someone" in your life.

Let it be understood at the outset that I am neither a psychologist nor a psychiatrist, but am fortunate in that my work with the Mental Health Association has brought me into contact with many leading professionals in those fields. Similarly, it has provided access to the expanding number of publications dealing with behavior, both as diagnosis and as day-to-day advice for those troubled or curious about their relations with others.

Virtually all sources agree that "attitude" is a key ingredient in the success of any life endeavor, be it getting the chores done at home or realizing your heart's desire to be selected a cheerleader, yearbook editor, homecoming queen, MISS TEENAGE AMERICA or what-have-you.

Your attitude—your approach to life in all its aspects and, perhaps most importantly, particularly the difficult or disagreeable aspects—is visible to all around you even on "first impression" and is ever more so with the passage of time. Just as the features of your face have become more pronounced as you've grown from infancy, and will continue to do so as your age advances, so have the "features" of your personality, your attitude. Of course, if you dislike your nose or your chin, it is possible to have them changed, but that's a very involved procedure. Your attitude is far more malleable in many respects and you can change it by awareness and concentration. In fact, give a change in attitude, you may not need or want to change your nose.

Once upon a time, I knew a young man named Bill. Good-natured, ebullient, interested in everything going on around him, and warmly interested in the people he met, Bill was a "must invite" no matter what was going on. He was fun and a joy to be around, and one day another friend and myself were exclaiming over him when a third person made a passing reference to something about Bill's left leg. "His leg? What's wrong with his leg?" While still quite young, Bill had been crippled by polio, yet the adjustment he had made, the attitude about himself which he took forward in his life, was such a positive and healthy one that it practically obscured the impairment. Similar examples of the triumph of attitude over handicap are legion, and probably you know more than a couple yourself.

On the other side of the scale are the equally countless numbers of people whose attitude is completely the reverse. Everything that happens to these people is the end of the world, including hangnails. Their attitude conveys a pessimism which often verges on the bitter, and heaven help you should you need to call on them to give you a hand with something a little difficult! If you do so once, chances are you won't ask a second time, because to them everything is a chore and a nuisance and a bother and with their unwilling help the simplest operation soon becomes a distasteful boondoggle to everyone involved. And I'm sure you know your share of *them*! They can be—and many are—physically beautiful people, but somehow they are not remembered as beautiful and are recalled only as a whine or a frown.

Beauty, we're told, is in the eye of the beholder and our own eyes, our own experience, behold that attitude manifests itself as beauty, or the lack thereof. The important thing is that it is manifest. Consequently, while very, very few people in this world are endowed with the range of physical attributes which constitute popular definitions of "beauty," still the world is full of people who are beautiful by any definition.

Perhaps you've read Oscar Wilde's *The Picture of Dorian Gray*. The plot concerns a young man so vain of his good looks that he dreads to see them lost to age, and he is granted his wish that time and the ravages of his dissolute nature be manifested not on himself, but on his portrait. With each act of faithlessness and cruelty, he sees the portrait image grow more abhorrent. Among many points which the story makes is the uselessness—even destructiveness—of physical beauty unmatched by beauty of attitude or character, and it insists that the faults of the latter shall be visited on the face, one way or the other. In the end, of course, it all caught up with Dorian as it does with everyone.

Granted, then, that attitude is a significant feature of personal loveliness and an important factor in the achievement of whatever happiness you construe as success. How can you go about gauging your own attitude in order to make any adjustments which you decide upon? Probably the easiest and surest means is by a careful observation of two kinds of people: the ones you like, and the ones you don't like.

Begin by assessing the people you most enjoy being with, those whom you trust and respect, the people you are genuinely and instinctively drawn to. What is it about them that you most cherish? Maybe they possess a good sense of humor, they're not stuck up or stuck on themselves, they tend to be cheerful and honest—and probably you feel that they like you. Within those several traits are important attitudes such as the ability to maintain perspective and not let every little thing bring on doom and despair, the ability to see one's self as part of the world and not as the whole show, yet to enjoy it all. All of that implies a certain level of integrity, a clarity of vision. Given all that and more, still such a person probably won't appeal to you a bit—might even rankle you dreadfully—unless you sense in them some appreciation of *you*.

How about the people you just really can't tolerate? Doubtless you have many epithets for these: nosy, untrustworthy, arrogant, spoilsport, jealous, spiteful, selfish. They will include such people as those whom you know will lie to escape blame or the consequences of their own actions, those who will betray a confidence, those who are obviously only concerned for themselves. Something there is about these people that gives you no incentive to win their friendship or esteem, even though they may be making a great effort to win yours. You may even see them succeed in winning esteem, honors, position through what is to you sheer duplicity, but for all of it, they're not your kind of folks—for when it comes right down to it, they've shown you reason to feel they have no true consideration beyond that for the image in their own mirror.

The attitudes of both types of persons, those you prize and those you don't, most clearly emerge in the way you perceive their reactions to you. Do they give you a chance to express yourself, or do they dominate whatever expressing is going on? Do they take your faults and mistakes in stride or react with exaggeration, possibly ridicule? When you ask their help, either by direct request or by verbalizing a need, is their help prompt and cheerful or slow and begrudging? And, do they deliver what they promise in a timely manner, or is it like pulling teeth to get them to live up to their word, if indeed they do so at all?

Now, very quickly, spin that around: in a group, do you feel you have to be the one doing all the talking or are you interested in giving others an opportunity for expression? When someone makes a blunder, do you feel constrained to call their attention and everyone else's to it, or, knowing how it feels, do you help smooth things over? When called upon to help someone else in some activity that doesn't exactly qualify as your favorite sport—your mother asks you to dry the dishes while she runs to the store; a friend needs help changing a tire in the rain—what comes of it? Do you tell your mother, "I'll take care of it," but when she gets back, the job is still undone because you couldn't tear yourself away from your tape deck; and does your help with the tire come reluctantly, accompanied by grousing about buying the wrong kind of tires in the first place and pulling off in the muddiest spot on the road.

You perceive the attitudes of others, positive or negative, in the way they react to you. And others perceive your attitudes by precisely the same means. Ultimately, it is your own reaction, particularly to difficult people or under difficult circumstances, which reveal your motivation. The quality we are dealing with here as "attitude."

The inner you simply cannot be separated from the outer you. If you're down in the dumps and out of sorts, it's going to show. What equalizes the impact of events on your complexion is the attitude you bring to those events, the attitude you have about yourself and others.

Essential to that attitude is your realistic recognition of the fact that being a "beautiful person" does not guarantee by any means that promptly at 9:45 tomorrow morning, you will be transported to untold heights of fame, honor and appreciation. No, it reaches to something far better: that you'll be happy and productive without that trip, able to function both creatively and contentedly even in the face of disappointment.

With that sort of an attitude, it will probably come as a surprise one day to hear someone say to you, with obvious sincerity, "You're really beautiful."

The Common Sense

A Sense of Humor

BY
DICK HITT

It has been said that Dick Hitt's daily and Sunday column in the Dallas Times Herald *has accounted for more out-of-town subscriptions than any other feature in the evening paper. Read a single Hitt column and you are certain to be one of many who eagerly await the next one. More than a humorist, Dick Hitt finds that human side of life that is often warm, often helpless, often bold and dashing yet always just a little bit unmanageable for a mere mortal. When you read him, you find yourself laughing at that thing called the human race while remembering that you are, after all, a part of it.*

A sense of humor is serious business. For various reasons, everyone needs one. You can judge for yourself whether this is true, right now, by picturing those of your friends and acquaintances who have a sense of humor, and those who don't. Is one list longer than the other, and are the "haves" leaping into your mind a little more quickly than the "have-nots"? Do the people who can laugh seem to be fuller and more complete in their chemistry, and in the things they have to offer that make their friendship worthwhile?

A human being is born with a sense of humor, or at least with the propensity for one. Homo sapiens is the only creature that laughs, the anthropologists say. The same observers say that when we see monkeys in the zoo or the family dog on the floor, scratching themselves and baring their teeth, seeming to smile, they aren't laughing, they are expressing pleasure or relief. Which leads to the conclusion that laughing is pleasure, while pleasure isn't necessarily laughing.

Perhaps what I just said could be offered as a fairly good example of pomposity, which is the natural enemy of a sense of humor. Like cobras and mongooses, pomposity and humor lie in wait for each other in one of the continuing conflicts of humanity. Properly placed humor will puncture pomposity where it occurs. And unfortunately, properly placed pomposity, as in high officialdom, for instance, will stifle a lot of humor.

Politically, humor can be a tool, a weapon or a cushion. We remember Abraham Lincoln's wryness along with his greatness. Lincoln's dependency upon humor actually increased as the troubles and agony of the Union did.

There is a pressure-valve point in the human condition that requires the relief of laughter. One pretty fair humorist who recognized this was William Shakespeare, who invariably threw in some funny business after the tragedies in his plays.

When President John F. Kennedy caused a furor by appointing his brother Attorney General, he softened the news for a lot of people by cracking, "Bobby can use the experience before he starts his own law firm."

It was Kennedy's frequent use of humor, injected perfectly, that contributed so much to his image of elegance. On the other hand, there are Presidents remembered chiefly for their bleakness; Calvin Coolidge telling the nation, "When more and more people are thrown out of work, unemployment results." More recently, the only people in the country who didn't make light of Watergate in the early stages of the cover-up were the ones who probably should have, the officials of the Nixon Administration.

From earliest times, people have craved laughter. The kings had their court jesters, who had to view the humor business as serious stuff; if the monarch didn't like the act, the comic ended up at the chopping block. We are slightly more civilized now; they just cancel the comic's show instead of the comic.

But the purpose of this treatise is not to produce a generation of comediennes, but to convey to you the thought that it's a good idea to have a sense of humor.

In a literal meaning, a sense of humor is more than the ability to be a teller of jokes. It is the ability to be a "tellee."

Personally, I think I'd rather listen to a good joke than tell it. In the first place, as a listener, I don't have to remember a lot of jokes to tell at the right time. In the second place, I've heard all my jokes.

A successful joke teller knows when to stop telling and start listening. How else are you going to learn any new jokes? There is nothing less funny than a card who won't let anyone else tell a joke. One of the most uncomfortable evenings I ever spent was at an after-hours restaurant at a table with four or five professional comics who were trying to outdo each other. They were stepping on each other's lines with blood in their eyes and humiliation in their hearts, defeating the purpose of humor.

For something as universal as it is, humor is an elusive thing. It's amazing what'll get a laugh, or what won't. Professional students of humor have a theory that different nationalities laugh at different things. My only personal involvement with this is that once I asked a German to tell me what he considered a good German joke. He said there was a guy who went to a restaurant in Hamburg that claimed it could produce any kind of sandwich that anyone could possibly want, on a moment's notice. The guy went in and ordered an elephant-ear sandwich. "And make sure the elephant ears are done medium-well," he said. In a moment the waiter was back, apologizing that they couldn't make him the elephant-ear sandwich. 'An ha!" the customer said, "you don't have elephant ears!" "Not at all," said the waiter, "the problem is that we are temporarily out of the large buns."

The technicians of humor call that the double switch, or the inverted surprise. Not all humor is as complex. I once knew a dryland cotton farmer in West Texas who broke into laughter one afternoon, just because it was raining after thirty days of drought.

According to the dictionary, humor is such an elemental part of humanity that in medieval times, "humor" itself was thought to be "One of the four fluids entering into the constitution of the body, and determining by their relative proportion a person's health and temperament."

This is heavy stuff indeed, but I will hasten to use it because it means the ancients bear out my contention that a person without humor is somehow an incomplete person. In many ways, I wish the ancients had been physiologically right and "humor" had been an organic element. I know some people who would be the better for being plugged into a Humor-Augmenting Machine, the way kidney patients are connected to dialysis machines.

The dictionary offers some more standard definitions of humor: Humor is "Action revealing the oddity or quirk of a human temperament; whimsical or fantastic actions." It is "The faculty of discovering, experiencing or appreciating ludicrous or absurdly incongruous elements in ideas, situations or happenings."

Now, to creep up on the point of all this, and laugh at it, ask yourself if you're going to be able to go through life without encountering an oddity or quirk of a human temperament. Are you going to be able to avoid ludicrous or absurdly incongruous elements in ideas, situations or happenings?

"You're Beautiful When You Smile!"

Having a sense of humor, and showing it, is the best way I know, within reason, to reckon with situations beyond your control.

There are lots of ways the value of having a sense of humor can be expressed. You can sit around making profound observations like "Laughter is the shortest distance between two people," or "A sense of humor doesn't help explain life's hard edges, but it sure makes them tolerable."

Those happen to be two of the principles I have followed in my job as a daily newspaper columnist specializing in the humors and ironies of our times. Most people are anxious to find some lightness mixed in with the disasters and dross of our age.

Not everything is funny. That goes without saying. Forget I said it. We all have our foibles and our sacred cows, and if I may inject another personal opinion, I sincerely hope that no matter how finely you develop your own sense of humor in the future, you will never, never laugh at the term "Banana split." There's nothing funny about that.

I leave with fond wishes for a lot of laughs in life, and a reminder that a banana split is the shortest distance between two dips.

Why, you're beautiful when you smile!

Hey, Look Me Over

What Guys Look for in the Girls They Date

BY

The Gary Moore Singers
As related by Gary Moore

Snips and snails and puppy dog tails may be what little boys are made of, but when they've grown into young men like the Gary Moore Singers—well, they've come a long way, Baby!

A distinguished vocal chorus, the Singers have performed on the MISS TEENAGE AMERICA *National Telecast for the past five years. But they bring much more to the Pageant than a pretty sound. Along with the warm smiles they wear, the guys offer moral support, friendship, understanding and even humor. But, most important, they possess that unique quality that only a guy can offer a girl—that wonderful way of making her feel important and very special, even if she doesn't go home with the* MISS TEENAGE AMERICA *Medallion.*

How good is your imagination? Can you suddenly put yourself in the place of a seventeen-year-old boy who has just been told by his choir director that he is going to fly to another city, check into a hotel and with forty-nine of his buddies, be the escort, friend, brother, co-worker, comforter and companion of fifty of the sharpest most attractive, dynamic, intelligent, fun-loving, hard-working girls in America? If your imagination is that flexible, you might be able to experience a small portion of the excitement and anticipation that has been felt by the Gary Moore Singers for the past five years upon finding out they have been invited to participate in the MISS TEENAGE AMERICA Pageant for another year.

MISS TEENAGE AMERICA asked that we get the Singers together and let them express their views on teenage girls so that girls could have a fairly candid impression of "how the other half thinks!" Granted, all of the guys are members of the Chapel Choir of the First Baptist Church of Dallas, Texas, but don't let that "choir boy" image fool you. They are fifty red-blooded American boys who like football a lot more than

Gary Moore Singers, dressed in Bicentennial wardrobe for MISS TEENAGE AMERICA "New Spirit of '76" telecast production number in the 1976 Pageant.

Beethoven and who like girls a lot more than *football!* So, having assembled these experienced girl-watchers together for a roundtable discussion, we began to try and cover topics from which girls could benefit by knowing what the guys like and what "turns them off."

The first question they pondered concerned telephone calls. I asked them what they thought about girls calling boys. Like most teenagers, they started bombarding me with requests to be more specific. Did I mean on a regular basis? Did I mean the initial call? Did I mean for a date? Did I mean for advice? So I quickly and (brilliantly) answered "Yes!" That way, they answered "All of the above."

The first comment was, "It depends on the reason." It soon became obvious that most of the guys did not want girls calling on a regular basis. They feel that while it may be very flattering for a girl to call in the early stages of a developing relationship, that the first call should be theirs and that generally it should be the boy's initiative that starts the conversation. It seems from the general direction that their comments took that "chivalry is not dead" and that the telephone has replaced the sword and shield for a twentieth century knight to woo and win his fair lady. So girls, even in this day of Women's Lib, the fellows say, "Leave the sword alone and let 'Sir Lancelot' make the first move!"

The next topic of conversation which emerged was clothing. This really sparked some lively dialogue. Clothes seem to have a symbolic and aesthetic dimension which goes far beyond the basic needs of covering, warmth, comfort, etc. They seemed to be expressing the idea that clothes have a psychological effect that is a highly indicative barometer of a person's personality and even character. One of our more uninhibited members blurted out, "You can tell what a girl is like by how she dresses." On the surface this may seem to be a rather broad oversimplification of the situation, but after discussing the topic for a half hour, all of the statements seem to point back to the fact that this is a rather accurate appraisal.

The boys wanted girls to "dress sharp" and they wanted that for a number of reasons. First, they enjoyed looking at girls whose clothes were stylish ("classy," they said), and as you'll see later, appearance is a large part of what attracts and keeps a boy's attention. Beyond that, however, they were concerned about what other people thought about the girls they went with. Here is where clothes took on a dimension of status. The guys wanted people to admire their dates for their good-looking clothes because it was also a reflection on *them*! How about that! Isn't it amazing how interwoven our lives really are?

Naturally the subjects of modesty and propriety are connected to decisions about clothing and it was really interesting to hear the guys express themselves on this point. Being boys and being honest, they admitted that they liked to look at girls whose clothes were . . . well, how should I phrase it? . . . how about "highly indicative of their femininity"! (How's that?) In almost the next breath, however, one of them said, "Yeah, that's O.K., but would you want your *sister* to dress that way?" That really spoke volumes! What it said was that the girls they really cared about and had deep relationships with were special people and they didn't want them to be "on display." That really ties back to their comments about other people's reaction to their girlfriend's clothing and how that reflected on them.

Some of the words they tossed out in talking about clothes were, "stylish," "smart," and "sharp." To say that someone is a "smart" dresser has taken on the meaning of chic or fashionable, but it could be taken at face value and mean that a girl ought to dress "intelligently." Therefore, to dress in a way to make guys look at, like, and respect you is really "dressing *smart!*"

The topic that evoked the most "wisecracks" as well as information was the subject of make-up. Guys are not "emotionally involved" with make-up. I mean by that, they are not personally affected by make-up, since they don't use it. They are the "view*ers*" and not the "view*ees*." That naturally affects their point of view.

The word they used most often was "natural." They all agreed that make-up helped a girl and that it should be used, but they felt that the real secret was to use make-up in such a way as to make it difficult to tell that a girl was wearing it. One of the guys told about going to visit a friend one morning and when she came to the door he didn't recognize

"Appearance, personality, and an ability to get along with others are some of the qualities guys look for in the girls they like to date."

her. He was so accustomed to seeing her heavily made up that without make-up, she looked like an entirely different person. It was quite a letdown for him. If she had used only a minimum of make-up, the change would not have been so dramatic.

Another one of the singers related how he went swimming with one of his friends from school. "Wow," he said, "she dived in and when she came up, she left most of her face floating on top of the water!" Again, girls, remember if the amount of cosmetics you use is very slight, just enough to highlight your natural features, the guys won't ask if your sister is home when you come to the door "without your face."

We had been discussing these topics for about an hour when a subject occurred to me that we had not covered yet. "How important is a girl's sense of humor?" I asked. Immediately, the boys tackled this one with real enthusiasm. One could sense instantly that this was something they really wanted in girls they date. Most of them considered it an absolute necessity. Humor, of course, is a basic component of personality and this ultimately determines how lasting a relationship will be. The boys may be attracted by beauty, clothes, etc., but that was just the beginning. A sense of humor and how it is used has a lot to do with "compatibility," and that is exactly the word they used. They want girls who have a spirit of fun and good humor, but they also felt it should not be excessive. To be cutting up or joking all the time was not attractive to them. "She also has to be able to be serious," one of them said. Another remarked, "I'm about half crazy and don't want a girl who is a drag!" The lesson they seemed to be teaching here was a girl needs to have a sense of humor, but she also needs a "humor with sense."

I asked them to name the things they considered most in looking for girls they wanted to date. We even thought of arranging them in descending importance, but everybody placed different values on each one so we just decided to list them as we thought of them and say that each one was important in contributing to the image of the ideal girl. They are: appearance, attractiveness, personality, ability to get along with others, respectability, humility and poise, good habits, high morals, a good spiritual life, self-confidence, maturity, predictability, and compatibility.

I never tried to influence the train of thought of the boys, but rather, I tried to let the discussion take a normal pattern and course and be a very representative sampling of how they felt about each topic. However, one of the boys mentioned, "We haven't said anything about a girl's spiritual qualities." This was a topic I knew we should discuss because it is vital to a person's life and happiness, but I feel that I should wait until the boys brought it up so that I would not be putting words in their mouths. It really was startling, because I took off on that statement and asked them how important to them a girl's spiritual life and moral standard were, and in a veritable barrage of answers, they touched on every other thing we had talked about all afternoon. They felt that her relationship to God affected how she thinks, how she acts, what she says, and how she looks. Of course, you may expect this kind of response from our boys because they are all members of a religious choir and they have all been raised in homes that honor the Lord and their faith and trust in Him is strong. I have always felt that this made them different from other singing groups and that this was one of the reasons they have been selected for the MISS TEENAGE AMERICA Pageant, because the Pageant stands for the very best in American life, and life without a trust in God is void of true meaning and purpose.

One of the boys *really* summed it all up. He said he had been to a seminar where the leader had drawn this diagram:

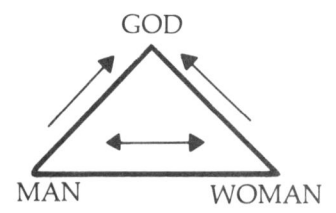

GOD
△
MAN   WOMAN

He then said that when two people get closer to the Lord, they get closer to each other.

So, there you have it . . . two hours of "brain picking" by the Gary Moore Singers. We hope this has helped you. We believe in MISS TEENAGE AMERICA; we love it because it brings out the best in us and because every year we see so many great girls realize that each and every one of them is "a winner."

Questions Teenagers Ask the Most

From the Files of Jean Adams

BY
JEAN ADAMS
Syndicated Columnist and Lecturer

Every day, thousands of young women and young men write Jean Adams for advice about problems of a very personal nature. Through her daily syndicated column, "Teen Forum," she gives them a "no holds barred" answer that provides constructive criticism as well as advice.

Here are a collection of frank and revealing questions and answers that have appeared in her widely read column.

Today's teenager can flip a switch on a television set and receive "instant" news from thousands of miles away; the same teenager may walk into the next room and be unable to communicate with his or her parents.

When I first began writing *Teen Forum* column ten years ago, I received questions concerning simple things like how to dress. Today, the popular topics are dating, parents, sex, jealousy, shyness, marriage, drugs, smoking, conversation, French kissing, stealing, interracial problems (in that order).

Scientific advances may reshape our world, but human problems remain, and they are *not* always the same as those of previous years.

It is easy in this complex environment for a young person to sometimes feel confused and in search of answers. It can be an exciting, fast moving, and beautiful world, but it can also be a harsh and difficult one. The teenager of today moves toward an honest, open, and reasonable discussion of problems.

The following recent letters that have appeared in *Teen Forum* column are typical examples of the topics I receive most.* My philosophy in answering these letters is not to preach or say "You must," but to tell young people the price they will pay for any of two or three choices.

DATING

Dating is a subject on which I get many letters. Parents and teenagers generally agree that going steady is permissible. But age is a consideration. Here are some examples of letters in this category.

"FRED, SOMEHOW I FEEL THAT OUR RELATIONSHIP IS A BIT TRANSPARENT!"

Q. I'm seventeen and out of high school. I really am beginning to like this sixteen-year-old dude. He's a junior and I know I should go for older men, but he seems like he could do a lot for me.

The good thing about him is that I can enjoy being with him—not sexually, just being in his company.

We're not hung up on sex. You don't have to have sex in order to love someone.

Can you help me? ——Wondering in Indiana

A. You're right about one thing—you don't have to have sex to love someone.

You're wrong, however, if you think this boy is too young for you.

Q. Tim and I are both eighteen and we both work at the same place. He doesn't have a girlfriend and I don't have a boyfriend.

We talk to each other and have a few things in common, like swimming, tennis, baseball, music, and history.

How can I tell him that I like him? Because I do! ——Very Much in Maine

*All of the letters and replies were originally published in my column, *Teen Forum*, by United Feature Syndicate.

A. Invite him to call you on the telephone.

Or invite him to visit you at home some Saturday or Sunday when you know your parents will be at home.

Q. I called Peggy up and asked her to go out with me. She said yes, but all of her friends tell me that she is going out with another boy, and doing other things with him too.

She tells me this is not so, but I just can't tell if she is telling me the truth. Will you help me, please? ——Unsure in Indiana

A. You asked Peggy for a date. She accepted. This does not give you the right to cross-examine her. It does not give you any control over her past, present, or future.

Apologize to her for what you have done. If she accepts your apology and you remain friends, be honest with her and respectful of her in the future, and hope that she will be the same with you.

Q. You see, I like Cindy quite a lot, and since we are good friends I would like to ask her for a date. I think I could find enough courage for that, but since she is so popular around school she is always at a meeting or other people are talking to her and I can't get her alone to ask her.

Please tell me what to do. ——Trying in Michigan

A. Don't let Cindy's popularity stop you. Sometimes the "busy" person, surrounded with people and activity, is really lonely and would like a genuinely close friend who cares.

Look Cindy's number up in the telephone directory, call her, and ask her for a date.

Q. I'm fourteen and would like to know if I'm too young to go to movies and parties with a boy. He is nice and wouldn't do anything to harm me. ——Waiting in Alabama

A. You may be a little young for regular dates, but you are not too young to meet boys at parties, movies and the like. These are good places to learn how to get along with boys.

Q. My two best friends are breaking up. I feel it's my fault and I want to get them back together again. What should I do? ——Concerned in Kentucky

A. I can't tell exactly what you did to break them up—maybe nothing.

In any event, patching other people's problems is seldom successful.

Let them work out their own solution.

And if you did contribute to the breakup, stay out of their hair in the future.

Q. Marj (sixteen) and I (fifteen) are good friends. She doesn't have a steady boyfriend. I would like to get to know her better, even though I have never dated and am not very good-looking or popular.

Should I try to win her love and risk turning her off and losing her as a friend, or should I just be content to keep her as a good friend? — — Interested in Alabama

A. Most cases of love and marriage grow out of a friendship such as you and Marj now share. Go ahead? Of course. Give yourself and Marj a chance. Call her on the phone. Ask her for a date.

PARENTS

Much discussion has centered around the communications, or generation, gap between teenagers and older generations, particularly parents. In a few cases, communication is so poor that the teenager considers running away, or even commiting suicide. Even in happy families, the teenager will frequently write about milder problems such as the length of hair. They simply cannot communicate with their parents on these issues. Much of my mail concerns parental hangups, where the teenager is caught in the middle of an unhappy family situation such as divorce or alcoholism.

Q. All the time my parents and brothers ask me what did I do on a date and where did I go. They say I should not kiss my boyfriend more than twice on a date.

I have never done anything wrong and I have never done anything behind my parents' backs. My boyfriend and I have been going together a year and a half. I am 18½. We go out about twice a week and are together for three or four hours.

Please help me. — —Quizzed in Connecticut

A. You do not really seem to need any help. As far as I can see you are doing quite well.

It is natural for your parents, and your brothers, too, to be interested in what you are doing. They should *not* count your kisses. But their comment on this seems to be in the form of an opinion rather than a command.

Q. Up until last year I lied a lot. But I saw it was costing me so I stopped. But now when I tell the truth my parents won't believe me.

For instance, my father had a coin collection. Somebody stole all the coins. My dad thinks I did. I didn't touch them, but my parents keep hassling me. How can I make them understand and care about me again instead of hating me? — —In Pain in Maine

A. It is unprofitable to lie, as you have learned.

"MY MOTHER HAS INVITED YOU FOR DINNER."

But what one has done in the past should not be charged up to him or her forever. Once a child has asked forgiveness and corrected a mistake, whatever it was, the parent should forgive and restore trust.

Have you told your parents you have changed? Have you asked them to forgive you for the lies you told in the past?

Q. I am fifteen and am stuck on a girl who is thirteen. We really like each other, but her mother won't let me take her out. Should I go to her mother and talk to her? ——No Luck in Louisiana

A. Talking with her mother is an excellent idea. She will probably say (and I would agree with her) that your friend is too young for dates. But she may allow you to visit the girl, which I surely think would be a good start.

Q. Last week I took an overdose of pills. I was mad at my parents for not letting me see my boyfriend every night. Lucky for me, my mom had that so-called "mother's feeling." I'm O.K. now.

That was a stupid stunt I pulled. I was trying to scare my parents, but what I really did was hurt them and myself. There are really no words I can say to them to make them realize how sorry I am.

Kids think their parents are the meanest people alive, but they are there to help you when you do dumb things like I did. Your parents really love you and want what's best for you. ——Sorry in California

A. Thank you for a letter that should help many *Teen Forum* readers.

Q. I am a straight girl. No drinking, smoking, drugs, parties. I don't have a bad reputation. I don't hang in crowds. I am seventeen and plan to finish school and go to college for four years.

My mother, however, is on my back all the time. She tells me what to do, whom to talk to, whom I can go out with. I feel I am old enough to make some of my own decisions. What can I do? ——Harrassed in Maine

A. You are already making decisions. You list several, and they seem to be good ones.

Do not, however, be self-righteous or arrogant about them. And try to be friendly with your mother. She is having a hard time letting you go, but she will eventually have to.

Please show her this, and keep assuring her that she can trust you.

Q. You know how boys are wearing their hair longer today. Well, my mom is against it. She let me have it long once and all the girls liked it. But now she makes me get it cut very short. I'm ashamed to go to the dances and things at school.

What can I do? ——Peeled in Pennslyvania

A. Your mother wears her hair the length she likes it. She no doubt feels it is her right to do that.

Ask her to recognize your right to do the same thing.

SEX

Young people of today do, in many instances, indulge in sex. And it is much more common to find young girls pregnant during their high school years. Frequently neither the boy nor the girl in this situation has had an open discussion about sex with their parents or in a sex education class at school. But many other teenagers are much more knowledgeable about sex than were their parents at the same age. This can be a plus factor in growing up if the teenager gets this knowledge from parents or school sex education courses.

Q. I am a freshman in college and I have been having serious problems with my boyfriend. He wants me to sleep with him and I'm not sure if I should do it or not. I would deeply appreciate your advice. I am eighteen. ——Pursued in Pennsylvania

A. Time after time our inner selves speak to us. We call this inner self our conscience. I am strongly in favor of listening to one's conscience.

If you have a question in your mind about the rightness of doing something, don't do it. In this specific case, you do have a question!

Q. Arnold tried to get me to do you-know-what the first time I went out with him. I went out with him two more times and he tried both times. That was just a week and a half in all that I had known him.

Then he broke up with me. Now he won't even talk to me. I think I really love him and could make love to him if I were going out with him. But I'm not. How can I get him to see that I love him but can't prove it if he won't give me a chance? ——Ignored in Massachusetts

A. Arnold does not love you and was never interested in you except for sex. Do not waste your time thinking about him, or any other boy like him.

Q. Jim tells me he loves me only when we are having sex. He doesn't come over much anymore, either. How can I tell if he really loves me? I really love him.

We are both fifteen. I have been going out with him for eight weeks. ——Unsure in Pennsylvania

A. It is definite that Jim warmed up fast. He seems to be cooling it just as fast. This often happens when a boy gets everything too easily and too quickly.

You have been too easy. Let Jim go, and don't be so easy with your next boyfriend.

Q. J.D. has asked me to have sex with him. I am scared at one time and want to at another time. I do not think it is bad for a girl of fifteen to have sex with her boyfriend.

I have told my mom about it and we have talked it over but my father doesn't know anything about it. I would like to have your opinion. ——Mixed-up in Maryland

A. Your letter is signed "Mixed-up." That means your emotions are mixed on this matter. As long as you are not sure about a step—especially a big one like this—you should not take it.

Congratulations on talking with your mother. Many girls who write me need to do just that. If they would, or could, they would have fewer problems.

JEALOUSY

I receive a lot of mail from jealous girlfriends or jealous boyfriends. I always counsel the teenager not to try and konsel someone else's life. Dating and going steady can be a lot of fun, but it doesn't have to be a lifetime proposition with any one person.

Q. Nina is the kind of girl who will not even hold your hand. She was taught not to. She will not date, either. But she gets angry when I dance with someone else and I get jealous just thinking about her dancing with another boy.

She likes to talk to me on the telephone. We argue about everything, but make up. She always insists that she is right, even when she is wrong.

How can we stop fighting? I love Nina very much. She is sixteen and I am fifteen. ——Jealous in New Jersey

A. Except for the non-dating and the non-hand-holding, you and Nina seem to be a typical boyfriend and girlfriend. You have good times and bad, you fall out and make up, you both are possessive.

Be thankful for your friendship. Enjoy the good times, live with the bad times. Talk openly and frankly with each other, and Nina, I predict, will eventually see that dates and hand-holding are right for her, just as they are for other girls in their mid and upper teens.

Q. Peter thinks I go out with other guys, which I don't. He doesn't trust me. I don't know how to get through to him that I wouldn't go out on him. I think we should have a mutual trust for each other. Please tell me how I can convince him that I love only him. ——Unbelieved in New York

A. It is correct that mutual trust is very important. But talking about it and insisting upon it do not necessarily make it come true.

Sometimes we complain of our own faults when we see them in others. Do you trust Peter? Do you really love him? If you do, stop debating with him, and maybe he will stop debating with you.

Q. I have been going with Mark five months. All that time his ex-girlfriend has been calling him and going over to see him.

He has given her hints to get lost, but will not come out and tell her to. He says he is not that type of person.

We have fights about it. What can I do? ——Seething in South Carolina

A. You can admit to yourself that if Mark really wanted to get rid of this girl he could. He apparently likes her.

This does not mean he does not like you. And it does not mean you cannot date him and enjoy your times with him.

If you cannot accept the situation, continue to date him and don't discuss her with him. But if you have to fight him all the time because you can't face facts as they are, you would be better off to let him go.

SHYNESS

Often, a young person writes about the great difficulties he or he has in meeting and talking to other people, particularly members of the opposite sex. The teen years can be a great experience in becoming "your own person." But it is not uncommon to feel left out and lonely. Being your own person means developing the things you do best. The confidence gained will help you to reach out to others.

Q. What is your advice for a person with a bad case of nerves from fear of starting her first year of high school? ——Upset in Alabama

A. Take comfort in the fact that all the other new high schoolers in your home room and in your classes are nervous too.

Try to make those around you comfortable and happy. This will help you to forget your own discomfort. Then before you know it you will feel at home in your new "home."

Q. I don't have any friends because I am ugly. It's not just in my mind. Kids tell me I am ugly. I've had kids I've never seen before come up to me and say, "You ugly dog. Did you ever look in the mirror?" Sometimes kids will walk up to me and bark in my face.

I am eighteen and a senior. My only friend is in the eighth grade. I like her very much, but I would like to have friends my own age also. ——Dog Face in Mississippi

A. It is possible to be very homely and still have a world of friends. This is true for both males and females.

Try to stop blaming your looks for your loneliness. Seek out friends, both boys and girls, of your own age.

I have one other suggestion. I am not a strong advocate of self-improvement courses, but I think a good one might help you. It would teach you how to improve both your appearance and your self-confidence.

Q. Two girls have dropped me like a hot rock. It really hurts me and I stay depressed for weeks. I really loved the second one and still do. She said I was too shy and boring. Should I just give up everything? I am fifteen. ——Loser in Louisiana

A. Lots of boys haven't even started at fifteen, so don't give up.

Instead, study the two clues your friend gave you—that you are shy and boring.

The more girls you go out with, the less shy you are likely to be. The more experience you have, the less boring you are likely to be.

For more experience, date several girls instead of just one. While you are dating, look for a girl like yourself—maybe a little shy and not an accomplished talker. Together, you may be able to work on your conversation and your self-confidence.

MARRIAGE

Many young people fall in love and think that the only solution to their situation is to get married. I encourage teenagers with these feelings to enjoy knowing one another and not to jump too hastily into such an important decision. People change a great deal as they emerge into adulthood, and what seems great today may pale tomorrow.

Q. My boyfriend wants to get married in September. I told him I would!

But my mother doesn't like him, because my aunt doesn't like him. She hasn't even seen him. How can I get her to like him? How can I tell her we are getting married. What should I do? I will be sixteen in October. He will be twenty-three in November. ——Engaged in New York

A. Put first things first. What your mother and aunt think about your boyfriend is less important than the fact that you are much too young to be married now.

Tell your boyfriend that, and don't let him re-talk you into promising to marry him next month.

If he remains friendly, introduce him to your mother.

Q. Johnny is twenty-two and I like him. Not long ago, however, I found out that he had been married and has a small daughter. I told my parents and they don't think I should go out with him. They are afraid I will want to marry him. I know I won't marry him soon, because I have a lot planned for the next few years.

By the time I am ready to marry him, his daughter may be six or seven years old. Do you think that she would resent me? ——Seventeen in Texas

A. How a stepdaughter feels toward a stepmother depends upon how the stepmother feels toward the stepdaughter. But you seem to be putting undue stress upon a problem that may never arise.

By the time you get all the things done that you are planning to do, Johnny may be married to someone else, and you may be ready to marry someone else. I think that would be a good outcome for all concerned.

DRUGS

Often a teenager sees a parent misusing pills or alcohol and cannot understand why that same parent is opposed to smoking marijuana. Once again, this is where two-way communication and respect are important. Parents and teenagers who can talk to one another about these problems and have a mutual respect for one another do not write me distraught letters about drug abuse. And many, many letters from hard drug users urge me to tell other teens to abstain.

Q. I am seventeen. She is sixteen. I love her and she loves me. But she smokes pot and drops downers and speed, which is why I ask for help.

I have tried drugs and know they are dangerous and a sick way to feel good. Please help me. I love her too much to see such a beautiful girl destroyed by drugs. ——Unhappy in Pennsylvania

A. As one who has been there, you can tell her about your experiences and what they have taught you.

Do this, and if the lesson works, be glad.

But if it fails, do not blame yourself for what is happening to her.

Q. Ron got in with the wrong crowd. He is taking LSD and stuff like that. Please tell me how I can help him. I want us to work it out together. ——Penny in Pennsylvania

A. Ron will have to want to help himself.

Try to get him to talk with a responsible adult whom he respects about what he is doing, and where it will inevitably lead him unless he stops.

SMOKING

What else can be said about smoking that has not already been said? It is injurious to health and unpleasant for those who don't smoke. But there are many teenagers who talk up the habit and think they are defying their parents rather than realizing the health hazard it is.

Q. I have been smoking for a long time. My mother has been trying to get me to quit. Every time she has caught me at it she has grounded me for three days.

But last week she caught me and beat me with a stick. I'm sixteen and too big for that.

How can I convince her I'm not doing anything bad? ——Bruised in Pennsylvania

A. You can't convince *me* that you aren't doing anything bad, so I can't tell you how to convince your mother that you aren't.

I think smoking is bad for you and that you should stop.

I agree that your mother shouldn't beat you. But you know how to stop that. Stop smoking.

Q. I smoke and am kind of afraid to tell my parents because I don't know what they will say. Should I sit down and tell them straight out, or should I just keep quiet and let them find out the hard way? Could you please give me some advice? ——Fifteen in Texas

A. I believe you would be more comfortable telling them. It may be that they will ask you not to smoke at home, or not to smoke anywhere. If they do, consider their request seriously. The less you smoke the better your health is likely to be. No smoking at all is best of all.

CONVERSATION

What if you have trouble talking to people in your class or some other group? This teenager states it like this:

Q. I can't hold a conversation. The things I talk about to my friends don't appeal to them. I have the same problem with girls. I lie to try to interest them.

It seems to me that what I say has no meaning. I have tried to talk and act like some of my friends who have no trouble talking, but it doesn't work.

Please tell me what to do. ——Poor Talker in Texas

A. Do *not* do either of the things you are doing now. Do not lie and do not try to copy someone else.

Instead, be yourself. Your effort to hide yourself from others is what is mixing you up. If you will be honest about yourself and what you are and think and like and dislike, you will stop being mixed up and you will stop turning off those you talk to.

FRENCH KISSING

I received the following letter from "Disgusted Father in Oklahoma."

Q. I was most horribly shocked at your obscene advice. You advocate French kissing! Gawd amighty! Don't you have any decency whatever? A boy and girl should have the *hell* beat out of them for even thinking about such a vulgar thing. ——Disgusted Father in Oklahoma

A. The sixteen-year-old boy asked how to kiss and how to French kiss. I told him this: "You can kiss lightly or lingeringly. Your lips can just touch the girl's or they can press. The mouth can be closed or open. Tongues can touch or not. It depends upon the girl, the time and the feeling."

That is not obscene.

I happen to know that older teenagers are much interested in French kissing and I try to be realistic about it. I am afraid you are not realistic—just bigoted. And your language is dirty.

STEALING

Sometimes a teenager loses a prize possession that might have taken a long time to acquire. But hasty judgments about a thief might be dangerous, as in this case.

Q. My baseball glove was stolen. It meant a lot to me. I miss having it. I think I know who has it. But it had my initials on it and they have been blackened out. How can I get it back? I am 80 per cent sure it is my glove, but not 100 per cent sure. ——Victim in Virginia

A. If you are not 100 per cent sure, do not try to get it back. To do so might be to accuse someone unjustly. That could cost you a lot more than the glove is worth.

But *do* learn from this experience, and be more careful to protect your property from now on.

INTERRACIAL RELATIONSHIPS

In a diverse society, we meet and get to know people of different backgrounds from our own. Most social scientists consider this one of the great strengths of American society. In high school, boy-girl relationships can become much more difficult for an interracial couple unless parents and others are very understanding. Here is one of the recent letters I have received on this subject.

Q. I am in love with this black boy and he loves me. We had a baby but it died. We are planning on getting married.

The problem is my mother. Someone told her that he and I were getting married and she said that if I had anything else to do with him she would kill herself. What should I do? ——Seventeen in South Carolina

A. If your boyfriend were the same color you are I would counsel you not to marry him now. This is because of your age, not because of what your mother says or thinks.

Concerning him, I give you this same advice, and for the same reason—you are very young.

When you are nineteen, or twenty, or twenty-one, you will be better able to decide whether he is the one for you for a lifetime. At that time you will also be an adult and on your own.

Teenagers often wonder what characteristics the opposite sex likes best. I have talked with many teenagers in many different towns and cities throughout the U.S.A., and here are the lists that appear most often.

CHARACTERISTICS BOYS LIKE BEST IN GIRLS

1. Appearance
2. Personality
3. Good fashion and grooming
4. Honesty
5. Sense of humor
6. Intelligence
7. Good manners
8. Not a showoff
9. Thoughtfulness
10. Knows what to say, when
11. Respect for the boy
12. Positive outlook on life

CHARACTERISTICS GIRLS LIKE BEST IN BOYS

1. Respect for the girl
2. Good appearance
3. Sense of humor
4. Good manners
5. Good fashion and grooming
6. Honesty
7. Pleasing personality
8. Thoughtfulness
9. Intelligence
10. Athletic ability
11. A positive outlook on life, plus ambition
12. Freedom from the urge to show off

I believe that these lists of qualities indicate how teenagers *can* make sensible decisions about their problems if they can communicate with forthright, open, and reasonable adults. But teenagers can make mistakes, just like adults. Giving them forgiveness and understanding may be the smartest thing a parent ever does.

Sometimes it is easy for a parent to say no to a teenager and refuse to discuss the matter further. Or to preach one thing and act exactly opposite. The hypocritical adult will never communicate with today's young people.

A young person will not respect an adult because he or she is an adult. The adult must act in such a way to merit that respect.

The contemporary teenager has more magnificent opportunity available than ever before—and faces a more complex world than ever before. A world of adults who care more (and can show it) and criticize less may make the difference in their future.

ADVENTURE III

Making Your Femininity a Beautiful Part of Your Life

Woman or Lib?

You can be a railroad engineer or the Governor of a state or the head of a corporation. You can be a horse race jockey or a professional golfer. You can wear pants and jeans. You are free to make your decisions and choices about your life and your future.

Not too many years ago, these statements related only to men. The women's movement has been instrumental in bringing many of these things about for women, but at the same time this flow of new ideas concerning women and what they should or shouldn't do or be allowed to do, has also brought about some confusion.

Some girls make the mistake of thinking in terms of "doing what a man can do." They sometimes confuse liberation and equality with masculinity. In other words they think only of the "lib" and forget the "woman."

The liberation part simply means that you can do anything you really want to do and you can be anything you want to be, provided you are willing to put forth the effort. You can even decide just how "liberated" you want to be.

Some girls think that a liberated woman cannot be a housewife and mother. But many liberated women choose this route. It's what they want. It's where they find happiness and satisfaction, just as other girls find their happiness and satisfaction in a career.

There are so many choices available about the many ideas and opportunities that will come your way. Sort them out carefully and decide what you really want to do, not what you think the trend is, or what other women may be doing.

You control your mind, your body and your future, by the choices you make.

As you make these choices remember that you are a *young* woman. Don't ever give up your femininity. Don't be afraid of being a lady and of being ladylike. It's natural and it's an asset. Be proud of it.

The next chapter deals with the blossoming of womanhood and the sharing of love between a woman and a man. These are unmistakably feminine experiences and a beautiful part of your life.

How to Survive Adolescence

BY
THE EDITORS
(Who Have Been There)

You say every single girl in your class except you has a reason to wear a bra—and when you secretly shaved your legs everybody knew because you gashed your shin and it's been two weeks and it still shows—and your father hit the roof because you used *his* razor—and this morning a huge pimple popped out right smack on the middle of your nose—and the elastic on your half slip gave way just as you stood up to recite in front of the entire class—and the guy you have a crush on likes your older sister—

Take heart, MISS TEENAGE AMERICA. You *can* survive adolescence! Millions have.

It's just a part of growing up. Sure, you have special problems, special thoughts, and special worries. But you're not as alone as you think. Every other girl your age shares those same feelings in some way.

A junior high teacher in a boy's school used to say he was in the pre-people business.

This is a wonderful time of your life when you are becoming your own grown-up person—no longer a child, but a unique, special, one of a kind, bonafide, genuine lady.

Everything is new. You have new emotions, a new body, and a whole set of new experiences to deal with. And with all of this newly acquired strangeness, would you believe that it is all completely normal, healthy and, yes, even beautiful.

Another thing you won't believe is ten years from now you will sit back and "die laughing" at all of those experiences that seem so dreadful now.

So forget ten years from now. We're talking about surviving the present. Let's tackle some of those special worries.

Most girls between the ages of eleven and nineteen, especially the younger ones in that age group, have a poor self-image, particularly as it concerns their figures and appearance. Everyone dreams of being a knockout in a bikini and when the image in the mirror doesn't measure up to that voluptuous mental image, a feeling of inferiority usually takes over.

When girlfriends the same age have curvier curves, shinier hair or clearer skin, that feeling of inferiority grows even worse.

So isn't it nice to know that girls who feel that way (and who doesn't?) almost always look much prettier than they think they do.

For the salvation of your ego, remember that you are unique—special. Don't compare yourself with your friends. For instance, if you have dark hair, you may need to shave your legs sooner than a girlfriend who is very blonde. Everything does not happen at the same time with every girl. Some girls will develop curves earlier than others, body hair appears earlier in some girls than in others, and the arrival of your first period may even be by several years before (or after) that of some of your friends. It's O.K. It's normal. Everything's cool.

That day you've been waiting for—the day you *need* to buy a bra will also differ from your friends timewise. And if your best friend or your worst enemy ends up with a "C" cup and you're stuck with an "A," don't fret.

You are fortunately living in a day where the size of a girl's bosom is of minor concern as it relates to beauty. As a matter of fact, many of today's beauty idols are literally flat. If you're still not convinced, please don't waste your money on creams or machines which claim to develop your bust. No preparation or gadget is going to work miracles. The best thing to remember is that *all* breasts are beautiful. They are one of the loveliest parts of your femininity. And no matter what size or what shape, they are equally capable of producing nice feelings and, later in your life, if motherhood is your choice, nursing your babies.

Even in the current times, bras are still recommended. If your breasts are large, it is really a must. Do yourself a favor and make sure you are properly fitted. Also, it's good to get in the habit of a monthly breast self-examination even though it's highly unlikely that you would find anything wrong in your teen years. The American Cancer Society has a free booklet.

Your first period marks your entrance into a woman's world. It may show up as early as eleven or twelve years of age or it may wait awhile and make an appearance on your sixteenth birthday. Somewhere between the ages of eleven and seventeen is in the normal range. The average menstrual cycle from the beginning of a period to the start of the next is twenty-eight days. But a shorter or longer cycle is perfectly normal. At first, your cycle may vary from period to period. Your body has to have a little time to "get in gear." The length of your period may be seven days, or it may be only two. Again, both are normal. Sometimes cramps accompany your period. Women used to take to their beds on those occasions but it has since been discovered that exercise is a key factor in lessening cramps. The more the better, all month long. Make sure you're not making a mountain out of a molehill. A little ache and pain is normal. On the other hand, if the pain is excruciating, you should check with your doctor.

And that's another thing. There's no reason to feel embarrassed about discussing your period—or any other feminine problem—with your doctor. Your period and every other female thing about you are normal. There's certainly nothing wrong with being normal. If you have questions about menstruation or womanhood in general, your doctor probably has or can recommend some good reading material for you. Also, the companies that manufacture feminine products usually have free booklets on those subjects.

And then there's skin. Talk about a Jekyll and Hyde! Yesterday, there was that smooth baby face—and today, the end of the world. Don't take it so hard. There is help.

You may think you're in the middle of an oil crisis, except you're oversupplied instead of running short. Proper care will bring results. Frequent cleansing, even several times a day, will get rid of the excess oil and the dirt it attracts.

A pimple or two is one thing, but acne, where the bumps are more in proportion to freckles, is another. That calls for medical help, and a dermatologist (a skin specialist) *can help*. Antibiotics and special treatment today have created many complexion miracles. Don't let a troubled skin delve you into deep depression. First of all, there are things you can be doing about it and secondly, remember that just about everyone your age has an understanding of your problem because it's one they share—even boys.

Adolescence is a time of almost constant self-appraisal. If you're like most teens, you're probably too rough on yourself. You hate your nose, you're too short or too tall, you haven't smiled in two months because of your braces, your hair won't do right.

Have you ever thought about the fact that Cybill Shepherd (a former MISS TEENAGE AMERICA Friendship Award Winner) and Catherine Deneuve probably felt the same way when they were your age? The beautiful television actress Karen Valentine (1964 Talent Winner) cried when she arrived at the Pageant "because she was so ugly." And while you're sitting around moping about the fact that all of your friends are prettier than you are, they are probably all worrying that they are not as pretty as you are.

Instead of dwelling on the things you don't like about yourself, think about your good features and qualities. There are so many.

Think about the nice things there are about being a young woman, about how wonderful your femininity is, about all of the special feelings and emotions that only a girl can know.

See, you *are* very special.

Human Sexuality: More Than Only Natural

BY
ERIC W. JOHNSON

Eric Johnson is a graduate of Harvard College and earned his M.A. at the Harvard Graduate School of Education. During World War II, he worked with the American Friends Service Committee (Quakers) on refugee and famine relief projects in Portugal, Morocco, Algeria, Egypt, and India, and from time to time since that war, he has served with the A.F.S.C. in other countries. Most of his life, however, he has spent as a teacher of English, history, and in the past decade, sex education. He was headmaster of Friends' Central School from 1948 to 1952 and later head of the junior high school at Germantown Friends for eight years. He now teaches sex education there, part time.

He also writes books; some are language arts texts, some are children's fiction, and some are to help parents and students deal with academic and social problems. The best known in the last category is How to Live Through Junior High. *In addition, he has written four books on aspects of sex education. Two of these are named in the booklist at the end of the article.*

Part of the nature of human beings is that they are sexual: they are male or female, they reproduce their kind by intercourse, and one of the great influences on their lives is the power of sex. There is a great difference between human sexuality and the sex behavior of other animals. Human beings decide when and how they are going to express their sexuality; most animals have the decision made for them by instincts which are unchangeably programmed within them. We make choices; they are limited by their seasons; we are responsible for our decisions and choices; they have no responsibility, no choice; we have much to learn; they do not learn at all, except, in some cases, by imitation. That is why I entitled this chapter "Human Sexuality: More Than Only Natural." If our sex lives and behavior were only natural, there would be no need to write about them.

What are some of the things we learn about sex? I shall mention just two categories of learning. If we come from an enlightened family or attend a forward-looking school, we learn what are commonly (and I think somewhat foolishly) called "the facts of life"—where babies come from. I shall not recite these facts here, for most teenagers already know them, but many, even some who are intelligent and otherwise well-educated, do not have it all straight, and I think it is their responsibility to get it straight. At the end of this chapter, I name a few books that will give you all the facts.

We also learn from American society; we learn two powerful and conflicting lessons: one, that sex is the most exciting, important, rewarding, status-giving turn-on there is, that it will sell anything and that we should all become as sexy as possible; and two, that sex is a no-no, that we should stay away from it or we'll be punished, lose our reputations, and mess up our lives. Given this double voice of society, no wonder many of us—teenagers and adults—are confused.

How can we straighten out our confusions? One easy way is to decide to abide by the rules of behavior and morality set down for us by our parents and our church. Most commonly this moral code says: no sex except for mild expressions of affection (hand-holding, a friendly hug, a gentle kiss) until marriage, and after marriage, sex limited to one's spouse. For millions of people, young and old, this code works well and provides a sound base for a happy, stable, rewarding life.

However, it would be denying the facts of life today to maintain that most teenagers are willing simply to accept these traditional rules of behavior. Teenagers, and many adults, too, are questioning, seeking, trying to establish their own values and to choose for themselves how to express their sexuality. They will do well not to ignore the wisdom of tradition, which has been evolved over centuries of trial and error and success, but they want to examine the tradition in the light of the circumstances of today and to make their own choices.

Such freedom of choice presents vast possibilities for rewards and for tragedies—but, then, so does the unexamined acceptance of tradition. To have to make choices can lay on us a heavy burden, but to make the right choices can bring enormous joy and satisfaction. To aid teenagers, and the rest of us, to make their choices, I want to suggest some values which we can supply to our sexual lives (and to much of the rest of life, too) and which I think will help us make satisfying, responsible, life-affirming choices throughout life.

INFORMATION

Correct information—the facts—is better than ignorance or rumor. People get into trouble sexually not because they know too much but because they know too little or their knowledge is spotty. Information, contrary to a widely-held notion, does not lead to irresponsible sexual experimentation; ignorance, and the frantic desire to find out does that. What you don't know may hurt you; what you do know will help enable you to act responsibly. Information does not "put ideas into people's heads." In the sense in which this expression is used, the "ideas" are already there. Information will help people deal intelligently with the ideas.

A part of this information, by the way, whether one is Catholic or not, should be the facts about contraception. Knowing the facts is not the same as advocating the practice. The book *A Catholic Parent's Guide to Sex Education*, approved by the Church, states that young people "should have some knowledge of the Church's teaching about contraception and of the different methods that some people who do not share Catholic beliefs use for this purpose." It is not true, I should add, that knowledge of contraception leads to a sudden increase in teenage intercourse. A sad fact is that most early teenage intercourse takes place "unprotected," which is one reason why so many unwanted babies are born to young girls today.

Other needed information, given elsewhere in *Miss Teenage America Tells How to Make the Good Things Happen* concerns venereal disease and abortion.

COMMUNICATION

It is good to be able to talk with others about sexual matters, with people of the same sex and of the opposite sex. Otherwise, how can we share feelings, know how others may behave, correct our own misconceptions and help modify those of others? Much of the pain and suffering involved in teenage sexual activity arises from a lack of knowing how the others (a partner, a parent, a classmate) feel. Much of the unhappiness in marriage is caused by the inability of husband and wife to tell each other how they feel, physically and emotionally. Sex education classes in schools are a good way to start and facilitate such consideration.

PLEASURE

Society is so afraid that teenagers will "go wild" if they find out that sexual activity gives intense pleasure that most books and courses in schools never mention it. And yet it is a fact—a wonderful fact and one that helps to bind man and woman together in loving relationship—that sex is pleasurable. The pleasure of sex is one of the values we should not deny as we consider our choices. It is not healthy to wish that sex and sexual pleasure would go away and stop bothering us or to believe that to enjoy sex is somehow to surrender to the "beast" within us. The beasts copulate because of instinctual needs to release tension; human beings have intercourse—the word means so much more than copulation—and, under the right circumstances and within the right relationships, it affords deep and wonderful pleasure, both of body and emotion.

CONTROL

Sex is a power and, like any power—language, intellect, muscle, cars, fire—can be used for good and bad. A mature person will have his or her powers under control rather than controlled by them. In respect to sex, it is well for people to decide *in advance* of the sexual situation what they think it right to do, and what wrong, so that in the heat of emotion and feeling they will not lose perspective and control.

It is important for boys and girls, and men and women, to know that in normal human beings there is no overpowering, uncontrollable animal urge to copulate. The *desire* to do so can be very strong, and the *feelings* one has are not readily subject to control, but the *action* of having sex can be controlled if a person wants to control it. It is a cop-out to say, in effect, "my urges took over; it wasn't my fault."

SPONTANEITY

After emphasizing the importance of control, how can I place a value on spontaneity—acting on the basis of unrestrained, unpremeditated impulse? I certainly cannot advocate that for young teenagers, but it is one of the joys of living as a firm, lovingly bonded married couple that the sex life of husband and wife can take on a freedom and spontaneity that is joyous and exciting and improves as the communication and sexual learning of the couple deepen. Then sex can be freed of the burdens of heavy thinking and guilt.

CONSIDERATION

The sexual activity of all of us should be governed by a considerate caring for the other involved—not only the sexual partner but others less directly involved: friends, parents, the community, society. Consideration—respect, caring, unselfishness, love, call it what you will— involves an exercise of imagination, a unique human quality. We must be able to imagine ourselves into the minds and bodies and emotions of others and to feel with them. Only thus can we care for and consider them. It is a mistake to act on the assumption that your partner or your spouse feels and wants just what you yourself are feeling and wanting. Without communication, and much of it is nonverbal, consideration is impossible.

MARRIAGE AND THE FAMILY

These days there are many strains on marriage and the nuclear family, and yet I believe that the loving family, in most cases, provides the best way for a man and a woman to relate to each other and to bring up happy, confident, eventually mature children. This is not to say that everyone should get married. Many single people are single by choice, are very happy and contribute greatly to the health, richness and joys of our society, and I think it is an immoral form of coercion to press young people into marriage. It is to say, though, that we should conduct our sexual lives in such a way that the strength of families is increased and the rewards of marriage enriched.

RESPONSIBILITY

Responsibility means knowing and keeping in mind as well as we can the consequences, good and bad, present and future, of any actions we might perform, and then deciding to take or not to take the actions in the light of our knowledge of these consequences. For example, it would be irresponsible for a young unmarried couple to engage lightly in sexual intercourse without using contraception. One consequence might be a moment of intense pleasure and even joy, but the other consequences might be guilt, loss of reputation or self-respect, venereal disease, pain on the part of parents, a feeling on the part of one or both of having been used, and pregnancy—the starting of a new human life that was not consulted about the matter and for whom loving, long-time care was not assured.

THE ULTIMATE WORTH AND DIGNITY OF EACH INDIVIDUAL

A fundamental concept of our society is that each individual, and his or her conscience, rights, and welfare are of supreme importance. This is inherent in the Judeo-Christian part of our heritage and perhaps the essential value, also, of humanists, who are not religious in the conventional sense. We should conduct our sexual lives and make our choices of sexual behavior in ways that respect and in no way reduce the worth and dignity of the individual. There are two ways in which we have traditionally failed to do this. One way is by applying a double standard to sexual morality, one for men (it's O.K. to play around, get experience, sow your wild oats) and another for women (you must maintain your virginity, not show an active interest in sex, and save yourself for marriage). The second way is by allowing our society to press men and women into stereotyped sex roles and personality traits. Women, according to the stereotype, should stay at home, bear and bring up the children, do the housework, support and encourage their husbands; they should be gentle, understanding, intuitive, lovely and sweet. Men, on the other hand, should go out and earn the living, provide a vigorous model for their sons, respect and protect their wives and children, make the important decisions, be head of the household, lift heavy loads, open stuck jars, and be logical, ambitious, decisive, somewhat aggressive, and not too emotional, except for righteous anger.

For some people in some societies—and it is deeply engrained and cherished in parts of American society—the double standard works. If it does, and both the man and the woman find it equally satisfying, no one should be forced to give it up. But too often the double standard means freedom for the man and submission for the woman. And the man may not feel really comfortable with his freedom, especially when he should know that the woman probably resents and feels humiliated by her need to submit, though until recently she has rarely felt free to say so.

As for sexual stereotypes of personality and social functions, they tend to deny the worth and dignity of both men and women. To be forced into a social mold rather than to be allowed to fulfill one's individual nature is to be reduced and to have one's potential denied. If some women and some men find the stereotype to be the best way to fulfillment and to harmonious complementarity, these people should be free to choose that style of life. For millions, it does bring happiness and success. For other millions, however,—both men and women—it is reducing and denigrating. As we make our choice of sex-related behavior, we should keep in mind the effects of the double standard and of stereotyped roles and try our best to act so as to enhance the individual and help him or her realize full worth and dignity. Today our society is an extremely flexible condition. Young people have more choices to make than they ever did. The family is having to find new bases for stability, bases other than those of economic and reproductive necessity. Religious and social codes, for better or worse, are subject to critical examination and rejection. Further, it seems likely that we shall soon have foolproof, harmless methods of contraception, involving no bother and no expertise; and some public health officials predict that the day is not far distant when V.D. will be eradicated. Thus, the traditional restraints on sexual intercourse, that is, the fear of pregnancy and disease, may soon be removed.

And so the choice of what people will do with their sexuality will fall increasingly upon us as individuals, to be made in terms of our beliefs, priorities and values. It is my hope that our sexual learning will be soundly guided and that we may come to express our sexuality in ways that exploit no one and fulfill life for all, physically and spiritually—in ways as varied and meaningful as human beings are varied and meaningful. There could be no greater challenge for teenage Americans than to achieve this goal.

RECOMMENDED READING ON SEX EDUCATION

Love and Sex and Growing Up, by Eric W. Johnson and Corinne B. Johnson.
(The facts and their consequences, presented with a broad social context; written for boys and girls aged 8-12; published by J.B. Lippincott Co., East Washington Square, Philadelphia, Pa. 19105.)

Love and Sex in Plain Language, by Eric W. Johnson
(A plain statement of all the information needed by teenagers and a discussion of the issues arising from the information; written for ages 11-15 but

informative for any age; published by J.B. Lippincott (see above) and in paperback by Bantam Books, 666 Fifth Avenue, New York, N.Y. 10019.)

Growing Up with Sex, by Richard F. Hettlinger.

(A thorough discussion of sexual behavior and the moral questions involved, but without moralizing; gives "the facts" in the appendices; written for ages 15-18; published by the Seabury Press, 815 Second Avenue, New York, N.Y. 10017.)

Sex Isn't That Simple, by Richard F. Hettlinger.

(An excellent book to prepare young people to deal with the increased freedom of sexual choice that will be experienced in college—or on the job; published by the Seabury Press –see above].)

ADVENTURE IV

Making Your Own Success Story Happen

THAT IMPORTANT ONE THIRD OF YOUR ADULT LIFE—
YOUR CAREER

By the time you are reading this, at least a dozen well meaning but misguided interested people have insisted on knowing what you plan to do as an adult.

Probably, you have developed a pat answer that closes that avenue of conversation. But the fact remains that you have now come to the day where the question deserves some consideration.

This does not mean that you must put gold paint on a shining goal and bravely press forward to the end. The chances are excellent that you may change your mind many, many times as new horizons develop from expanded opportunities to observe others in a career capacity.

At least a general idea of how you may wish to display your talents will be helpful in plotting a course for additional education or on-the-job training and will provide even a tentative road map with your career as a destination.

The chapter that follows this one talks about education and special training. Once you have in mind even an inkling of what you think you might like to do after high school or college, you will be better prepared to make decisions about your future education—choices like college vs. vocational school, college major and which school has the best training to offer you.

Unlike the day of your grandmother, and in many cases your mother, today there are virtually no career doors that remain unopened to women. If you can compete competently and fairly, without expecting special consideration for your sex, and deliver results and high performance achievement then the world of your chosen career is wide open and available to you. Have no fears.

The editors have collected, from women who are already employed in a given field, or from people knowledgeable about a special career opportunity, a brief survey of some of the fields of endeavor worthy of your time and talent.

We make no claim for complete coverage. If there is one particular field not even mentioned, that interests you greatly, just seek out a person employed gainfully in that area, and request a time when you can meet with them and discuss the possibilities and probabilities of employment in their bailiwick.

It's Your Choice

BY
MARGARET EPPS

From the *Encyclopedia of Careers
and Vocational Guidance*, Third Edition,
vol. I, Copyright © 1975, 1972, 1967
by the J. G. Ferguson Publishing Company

... *Jane Thompson, a ninth grade student in a small, midwestern junior high school, finds making friends easy but school work hard. She earns a "C" in most of her subjects and is very concerned about what courses to take in high school that will prepare her for a satisfying job in the future.*

... *Jim Trendel, a tenth grade debater, easily does superior work in all school subjects. His family has always planned on many years of schooling for Jim, and eventually, a professional career. He wonders which college will have the best atmosphere for him, and what kind of high school record of activities, clubs, and courses will make him attractive to that school.*

... *Tony Cuevas, an eighth grader, who is an American of Mexican descent, has parents who insist that he stay in school and get an education so he can earn a good living. He struggles along, earning a "D" in English and history, and a "C" in math and shop, while he would rather be outdoors, actively working with animals. Are there any high school courses which might prepare Tony for a career that he will enjoy?*

These are typical problems faced by many teenagers each school year. To solve these problems and thereby pursue studies which will lead to a satisfying career, each student must study himself—his interests, abilities, and values—and then study the work roles in society to see where he will contribute the most and be the happiest.

When entering high school, students have their first opportunity to choose their own courses. Selecting the subjects one wishes to study is fun and challenging but also difficult.

The school counselor will try to help students with this choice but each student must, of course, make his own decision. He or she must decide first and foremost the basic curriculum he wishes to study—the college preparatory, business (commercial), or vocational curriculum.

In each of these curricula, teachers emphasize different goals. For example, in the college preparatory curriculum, instruction is aimed at preparation for more formal education and teachers give information and encouragement about college admission and college life.

In the business or commercial curriculum, teachers stress more specific on-the-job skills such as shorthand and bookkeeping. They also concentrate on how to find a job and how to succeed in relations with fellow workers. Teachers in the vocational curriculum, which consists of courses such as sewing, automobile mechanics, and carpentry, emphasize employment requirements and industrial levels of performance.

It is very important to remember that it is difficult to transfer from the vocational and business curriculum into the college preparatory courses but it is easy to adjust in the reverse direction. Therefore, if students have doubts in their mind and feel confused, this fact might be very helpful.

30,000 DIFFERENT JOBS

There are 30,000 different jobs you have to choose from in the world of work. A specific choice is years away and by that time the succession of "choice points" along the way will have sorted more and more meaning out of the confusion of where you fit into the world of work. Our educational system requires students at definite points to make certain decisions such as course of study or kind of education after high school. Each decision narrows the broad range of possibilities; at the same time, each decision increases the understanding of one's self—one's interests, aptitudes, and abilities—and clarifies an individual's view of where he can best fit into the occupational scheme.

As mentioned earlier, the curriculum a student selects early in high school leads to more formal education after high school. At grades eleven and twelve, students decide either what college, business school, or vocational school to attend and learn how to be admitted to it; or what kind of job to seek after high school and how to obtain it.

In college, students pick a major field of interest. At work, a first job will probably involve a particular line of service. Each of these "points" is one more step in an individual's vocational development, one more step in the general direction toward one's major life's work.

The best decision can be made at each of these choice points if an individual has analyzed himself. What do you know of your interests, values, needs, aptitudes, and abilities? How do you model yourself in relation to your parents? What community resources are available to you? What is the level and quality of your educational background, and the occupational trends and attitudes of your community? If all of this sounds complicated, just remember it is to teach you a method of analyzing yourself so that you can apply it each time you are required to make a decision.

In order to learn more about yourself, look over the following list of general goals and pick one or more that interests you.

Do you want to:	*Then consider:*
Help people who are ill, old, or handicapped?	Health careers, hospital jobs
Organize activities and deal with people?	Business or sales careers, public relations positions
Provide better housing, eliminate slums?	Engineering careers, city planning or construction positions
Help people understand each other better?	Public service careers, social work or labor relations positions
Help people live better?	Marketing careers, food service positions
Work with your hands	Engineering or mechanical careers, artistic positions
Raise food and improve living standards	Agricultural careers, health or social work positions
Help people receive a better education	Educational careers, acting, writing, or library positions

If one or more of these general goals appeal to you, why not learn more about them through volunteer and club activities in your home, school, church, and community? Just a few activities which might interest you are listed below. Make out a chart like the example that follows for yourself and obtain suggestions for other activities from your parents and friends.

General Goal	Home	School	Church and Community
To provide better housing, eliminate slums	Clean up yard. Learn to do small home repairs. Encourage family discussion of local housing needs	Learn drafting. Learn about effect of slums on people. Learn woodworking. Actively welcome students who come from poor communities	Clean up trash accumulated on empty lots. Join work crews who repair houses of elderly people.
Work with your hands	Learn to cook. Learn to sew, paint, and clean. Maintain a garden	Make club emblems for sale or gifts. Make posters. Help pick up a yard.	Create new hair styles. Make games for Christmas baskets. Start your own business of stringing beads or trimming poodles.

YOUR PERSONALITY AND INTERESTS

Write your answers to the following questions so you will have an even more complete file on yourself to help you make future course decisions.

1. Mental characteristics—describe your grades, hobbies, and leisure activities.
2. Social traits—do you prefer being in a group or being alone, do you like to see new places and new people or stay near home and family, do you like to talk people into your opinions or care little what they think?
3. Physical traits—is your health generally good, do you have good physical endurance?

4. Character traits—are you ambitious, do you work well under pressure, are you patient and sympathetic in helping others, do you like to discover new ideas or prefer to have your work laid out for you?

Interests are a good indicator of the things which make your vocational goal appeal to you. They change throughout your life as you are exposed to new things. You will learn the difference between a temporary excitement and a lasting interest which will carry you through the dull routine, disappointments, and even setbacks which are somewhat involved in every job.

Remember, too, that interests are inclined to change as your life broadens.

The following factors can often produce superficial interests and you must beware of them when you judge your own interests.

1. Money and the things it can buy tempt lots of people into taking the first job that comes along, regardless of whether it uses their aptitudes or will take them where they want to go. You will get off on the wrong foot in developing career experience if you let money lure you into a job you don't like or keep you from getting as much education as you should have.

2. Change and newness in a job wear off unless the job develops your aptitudes.

3. "Everyobdy's doing it," the old social-approval or conformity drive, is one of the strongest lures to the young adult. Try to distinguish between the things you do because you like to do them and those you do to stay "in" with your crowd.

4. What someone else has done, what your hero, favorite player, or father has done will work for you only if you have the necessary aptitudes to do what they do.

5. What your parents want you to do is one of the strongest inducements to many young people; a strong prohibitor to others. Such interest must be closely related to aptitudes and ability to be real.

YOUR APTITUDES AND ABILITIES

The difference between aptitude and ability is that aptitude is potential and ability is developed; in other words, an aptitude must be developed by practice and training to become an ability. An aptitude is not easy to discover, and abilities rarely appear fully developed. Some aptitudes can be discovered by tests, but for others no accurate tests have been developed. Discovering and developing them is a process of daring to try new things. High or low aptitude in a given area does not mean good or bad. It just means that you fit into the requirements of one job better than into another.

TIE TOGETHER WHAT YOU ARE AND WHAT YOU CAN DO

Now consider the general goal or vocational purpose you listed at the start and review the above picture of your interests, aptitudes, and abilities. Our next step will be to fit these into a career that stresses your goals and needs a person with your abilities.

Use one or all of the methods listed below to find out specific details about occupations. Pay particular attention to what people do on their jobs each day, the advantages and disadvantages, the educational and personal requirements, the advancement opportunities, and the employment outlook.

1. Read good books like the *Encyclopedia of Careers* and career articles in magazines.
2. Talk to people currently working in various fields.
3. Write associations for pamphlets on occupations.
4. See occupational movies, or attend a career conference in your school.
5. Try working at some of your possible choices, if you can. After-school jobs, vacation jobs, high school activities, and volunteer work can all provide experience. In whatever work you do, keep your eyes open; try to see other jobs which are like the one you are doing; try to imagine what it would be like to work at the jobs you see around you; and notice how differently people in the same job do their work.

Before you have gone very far in gathering information about careers, you will find that the recurring theme is "how much education you need to succeed." No longer can a person count on working his way to the top by being alert and ambitious. Many more people are going to universities, two-year colleges, or technical institutes to gain technical or professional knowledge. Employers looking for people to promote from within the company select college graduates first. You can still work your way up to a managerial position in a bank, grocery store, drugstore, or supermarket, but it is easier and quicker with a college degree.

If the cost of college scares you, consider living at home and going to a local college or institution, thus saving the cost of room and board. Consider getting a job during the day and going to college at night, or working one year and going to college the next. Get information about scholarship and loan programs. See if you qualify for one of the military academies which would mean the government will pay you while providing your advanced education. Or enlist in one of the military services and take the college credit courses the government provides.

DON'T RUSH INTO A LIFELONG CAREER DECISION

All you need to decide right now is your course of study for next year. There will be later decision points when you will make further vocational choices. Every time you come to one of these career-oriented decision points, you should review your knowledge of yourself and then ask two questions:

1. What is my real and immediate career problem right now?
2. What are the alternatives available to me?

Then try to make the decision which will keep the most career possibilities open to you.

Decision making and particularly career-oriented decision making is a very difficult task. However, it is also extremely exciting since this process can change your entire life. It contains all the adventure of the unknown—the new and different and unexplored. And it is particularly exciting because you are the master—it's your choice!

A Sampling of Opportunities in Communications

JOURNALISM

BY
NIKKI NIXON
(Miss Teenage Hammond,
Indiana, 1966)
Women's Page Editor
Michigan City, Indiana,
News Dispatch

Nikki Nixon finds journalism exciting.

Combine glamor with hard work, curiosity with skepticism, and public service with dedication—and you have journalism. In all its forms—press, radio, television and magazines—journalism draws and challenges bright minds, eager to examine the contemporary scene and inform others.

Is it for you? Do you have a nose for news? Do you like people? Do you like to talk to them? Can you work under deadline pressure? Can you overcome shyness and ask probing questions? Do you like to write?

If you've been answering yes, consider journalism. It probably won't make you rich in money, but you'll be rich in experiences. You'll have a front seat at community and national events. Your press card is a passport to all kinds of interesting places with interesting people.

Contrary to what you see on the *Late Show*, journalists do not imitate detectives tracking murderers, nor do they yell, "Stop the presses!" or go around with press cards stuck in their hatbands. Rather they work eight-hour days (most of the time) in normal-looking offices where they sit in chairs, not on desk tops.

As editor of women's interest news for a small daily newspaper (18,000 circulation), I spend my mornings preparing news submitted by club women, local organizations, brides, new parents, and others. I edit the copy, write headlines and determine its placement on the page, which is like putting a puzzle together.

Every day is different. My morning work is done quickly under deadline pressure. After the day's paper is published at 1 P.M., my afternoons are free to interview and photograph good cooks, clever hobbyists, remarkable personalities, community projects and other things of interest. Smaller papers often assign you more varied tasks, such as writing, photography, editing and layout. Larger metropolitan papers often call for more specialization.

High school provides some opportunity to prepare for a journalism career. It's the time to get a sound command of the English language and all its grammar peculiarities. A typing course will stand you in good stead. Working on the school paper and journalism classes are helpful but not necessary if you plan to pursue a college degree in journalism.

The trend today is toward hiring college-trained journalists. The important thing to remember in college is to get a broad liberal arts education along with the journalism skills. Too many journalism students work on the college newspaper all four years and let it monopolize their time. It's stimulating and it's good experience, but a couple of semesters is enough. It's more important to learn about government, sociology, history, psychology, economics and the arts. Everything you study is of potential value to you in your quest for news.

Sound exciting? It is. And journalism can be a springboard into other exciting pursuits. Jacqueline Onassis, then Jacqueline Bouvier, was a reporter on assignment when she interviewed John F. Kennedy, then a senator. A year later they were married.

No telling what could happen to you!

TELEVISION— ON CAMERA

BY
TINA COLEMAN LOY
(Miss Teenage Jacksonville, Florida, 1970)
KCST-TV, San Diego, California

Tina Coleman Loy at the time she was a MISS TEENAGE AMERICA Candidate. She was Second Alternate in the 1970 Pageant.

So you want to work in television. Be prepared to search high and low since the broadcasting industry has always been traditionally tight in terms of employment. Luckily, pressure from women's organizations and other minority groups on national and local levels has done a great deal to institute fair and equal employment practices, and women are now employed in every area of the broadcasting field—from camera operators and video engineers to management—at both local affiliate and network levels.

But how did the women who have jobs get them? A degree in communications is a good idea for starters, and there are several excellent programs and curriculums offered. Some schools have their own radio and/or TV stations right on campus, or sponsor on-the-job intern programs with local stations enabling students to work and observe actual station operations. Several major broadcasting corporations (such as Storer) offer scholarships for on-the-job training at their stations for tuition or other compensation. Both these and any other possibilities that could provide you with actual job training will prove invaluable when trying to find work after graduation. When choosing a school, it would be wise to investigate what opportunities exist for either commercial or simulated commercial television operations experience. You'll be that much farther ahead in the race for broadcasting jobs. Experience (no matter how little) naturally means more to an employer than just a degree. School can give you the basics, the theory, but it can't give you the details—and that's what counts in the long run. If you're able to combine the two, your chances are increased.

Also something to consider is the fact that the television industry encompasses many professional fields: engineering, electronics, art, theatre, literature, journalism, research, public and social services, advertising and public relations, sales, business administration and more. Get any experience and/or education you can in any related field.

Broadcasting, like most, if not all, professions is one in which you can expect to work from the bottom up. When applying with little or no experience, choose stations in small market areas. The freedom and experience you'll gain more than makes up for the usually low salaries. Smaller stations are usually more receptive in terms of employing less experienced personnel, and you'll be able to learn more without the restrictions imposed by the unions at larger stations and markets. Also, because of the smaller staffs you'll be able to investigate the mechanics of various departments and get a better idea of what area you might like to pursue later.

What kind of job can you expect to find? Realistically speaking, the best rule of thumb is to take what you can get. Many former production secretaries are now directors and producers! Don't turn down a clerical job if it's in a department related to your professional goal. Almost all stations promote from within, and you'll be in an excellent position for advancement when an opening does come along. Also, you might consider taking a job that is not directly in your field just to get a foot in the door, but be careful. Check out the individual station's policy in regard to interior mobility. A "foot in the door" can sometimes just get you caught in the door jamb!

Other beginning job areas and possibilities can include production assistant, promotion, programming, film librarian, sales assistant, traffic, public affairs, news production assistant, and more. Again, your best chances for landing one of these jobs fresh out of school is in a small market. And be sure not to overlook public and cable TV systems.

My first experience in broadcasting was in the area of public affairs at WJXT-TV in Jacksonville, Florida. I was hired as a talk show hostess and the job developed into Associate Producer of Public Affairs Programming, which included producing three public service oriented talk shows. My individual duties consisted of originating and developing program topics and ideas, finding the guests to execute these program ideas, writing and producing all promotion for the shows, formatting each individual show and acting as hostess/moderator. I also shot film and slides to supplement interviews and provide additional visual interest, and produced a series of mini-documentaries on consumerism. Since it was a relatively small market and station, I was able to "float" into many other areas outside public affairs since my duties also encompassed promotion, public relations and film. That's the kind of flexibility small stations allow.

Following marriage, moving, and a tour of the advertising business with two agencies, I became Assistant Promotion Director at KCST-TV in San Diego, California. My main duties are writing and producing all station promotion—print, radio and promos that run on our air (of which four are produced daily), scheduling and trafficking these announcements and ads, writing all on-air copy (except commercials), producing visual aids for the Sales Department, station public relations and special projects. Our most recent special project was the coordination of the Mike Douglas Show's visit to San Diego. They taped two weeks of shows here, and we handled all advance publicity and promotion—everything from arranging interviews for local entertainment editors with Mike and his guests to planning entertainment for cast and crew—even a shopping trip for Mrs. Douglas! Promotion is a job that requires a good background in advertising and public relations as well as television in that it is the department that literally advertises the station and its product (programming). My years in advertising were a major factor in qualifying me for this job, which points out the importance of working in a related field if you can't find a job in broadcasting right away. Any related experience you can get will help.

A career in broadcasting is naturally exciting and challenging. There is a great deal of pressure and responsibility involved and tremendous attention paid to detail. If you're planning to pursue a career in this field, be prepared to work:

Hard and long—including holidays.
(Have you ever heard of cancelling all TV programs because it's Christmas?)

Weird hours
(Yes, someone *is* up at 5 A.M. on Sunday mornings!)

Under varying amounts of pressure.
From producing and taping a thirty-second commercial in three hours' time (sometimes it takes that long and longer!) to preparing a news show that airs live at 5 P.M. when reporters are still writing copy and editing film at 4:56!

But the joy and satisfaction comes in beating the pressure and frustration, praying for miracles and making them come true. If you can handle it, the rewards and recognition are far-reaching. Nowhere else do you have the ability to communicate your message to millions of people instantly from almost any corner of the world. The possibilities and opportunities are limitless—there's a constant need for new ideas, new methods, new faces.

One of them could be yours!

Until recently, most opportunities in television were open only to men. Now women can work in virtually every area of that profession.

TELEVISION — BEHIND THE SCENES

BY
DORIS WILLIAMS
Manager, Practices
NBC Television Network

For many years predating the push for Women's Rights, the National Broadcasting Company had a woman Vice President for Radio, several women producers, women lawyers and women, of whom the writer is one, in management positions in various departments. However, up until the quite recent past, most business and industry was not the greenest pasture for women on the management level. When an opening occurred for a management position, women were not considered as a general rule.

With the advent of Women's Liberation and the enactment of anti-discrimination laws, all this has changed radically, so that now it is no longer true that a woman in a position ordinarily held by a man has to work twice as hard. Today there is no position within the broadcasting industry that a qualified women may not hold, and the networks have made every effort to place women in executive and technical positions. There are now women technicians and engineers; sales executives and salespersons; station relations district managers; programming executives; researchers; personnel executives; producers; directors; writers; business affairs executives; public service executives; sports executives; and news executives, as well as newswomen on the other side of the camera.

Today when a woman is employed by a network she is asked to list the department she ultimately hopes to work in and her qualifications. Thus, when an opportunity arises, in the area of her choice, she will be considered. The majority of new employees indicate production as their first preference, and obviously they all cannot be accommodated there. However, it often happens that a person who thought she preferred a particular area becomes so engrossed in the department in which she is, that she opts to remain and make her way there.

Television requires specialists in many different areas of endeavor. Those interested in seeking a career in this medium should be aware that, although television is one of the so-called "glamor industries," the glamor is reserved for the end result seen on the television screen. To get to that point requires an enormous amount of hard work and attention to detail by hundreds of unseen and unsung individuals, each of whom makes his or her personal contribution in his or her own field.

At present, it is comparatively easy for a woman to advance to the management level. However, as the number of women on the executive level increases, so does the competition for such jobs. So I urge you, whatever your chosen field, to recognize that all business, and certainly television, as a billion dollar industry, is a serious affair, which requires that you bring your very best to it each day.

Therefore, one should acquire the finest training obtainable in her chosen field, whether it be in the business or creative area of television. This is vitally important for several reasons, the obvious one being that the more knowledge and expertise one possesses, the more competitive and efficient one will be.

There is another consideration, however, about which I personally feel strongly, and that is, because women are just coming into their own in previously male dominated fields, they are under intense scrutiny until they prove themselves. When a man performs poorly, it is considered an individual failure. When a woman performs poorly, it is considered a failure of all women. Never strive to be good at your job; strive to be the best at your job. You owe this to your employer, to all those who have worked for equal opportunity for women, to all those who will follow you, and most of all to yourself.

A Sampling of Opportunities in Education

CLASSROOM TEACHING

BY

SUZANNE MEADOWS TAYLOR
(Miss Teenage Wichita, Kansas 1969)
Teacher, Pat Neff Middle School
San Antonio, Texas

Suzanne Meadows Taylor at the time she was a candidate in 1969.

Do you enjoy working with people? Do you want a job that is a challenge? Do you have the patience to work towards making society a better place to live?

If you answered yes to these questions, then maybe teaching is the career for you. If you have found that you are excited by helping people and by working closely with others, then teaching could be a job that you would enjoy.

A teacher's life is a busy one. Sometimes it is frustrating and disappointing, but most of the time it is exciting and rewarding. It really gives you a great feeling when you know that you have helped another person be a happier adult.

Some people have the misconception that teaching is just babysitting. They couldn't be more wrong! There are only a few teachers around who function as a babysitter. Most teachers really want to help their students in whatever ways they can. These teachers strive every day to make school interesting and relevant to the students.

Many of the problems that we face as a society can be solved or at least minimized through the schools. Think about how much of your time is spent in the school.

Where do you form your ideas? Where do you learn the things that you need to know to get a job? Where do you find out what is happening in your world?

In the school. It's obvious therefore that the teacher is a pretty important person. He or she is the one that can make school fun and interesting, or dull and boring.

That is why I say that teaching is a challenge. It's not easy to stay on top of things and keep your class exciting every day from eight until three. However, it's really worth it in the end. When you see your students starting to care about themselves and about their fellow man; or when you know that you've reached that one student that's been troubled all year, then you're glad that you are a teacher.

Don't ever let anyone put down teaching as a career. It is very definitely a professional job. You must be willing to give of yourself in order to be a good teacher.

If you think that you are interested in teaching, you can do volunteer work while you are still in high school at your local YWCA or Sunday school. This will give you an opportunity to see if you like it. Also, your school might have a Future Teachers Club which allows the students to take over classes for a day.

In college, you need to see an advisor to help arrange your classes. All states will expect you to fulfill specific certification requirements.

This can usually be done in four years. Then you are ready to teach. The first few months of teaching can be pretty scary, but once you get into it, there is never a dull moment!

Teaching is valuable and exciting. Every year is different. Every student is different. There are great opportunities open for the teenager who becomes a teacher. The challenge, the headaches, the papers to grade, the tears at the end of school, the many beautiful memories of special students who make it all worthwhile . . . teaching is fulfillment!

COUNSELING

BY
DIANE MORISATO
Assistant Director of Student Activities
University of Hawaii

Of course I'm biased. Having chosen counseling as my career, I'm inclined to think of my vocation as being special as well as one of the most interesting, challenging and gratifying professions one could choose. Being with people, talking with people, and helping people to help themselves is a source of tremendous satisfaction for me personally.

The rewards that I receive, intangible though they may be, make me feel that I may have contributed something towards the development of an individual with whom I've come into contact—and that's all I could want. A smile which says "thank you," a sigh of relief, or the laughter which comes from mutual trust and enjoyment is enough to truly make my day.

Counseling as career can be a hundred different things. The profession is so varied that it can touch almost all aspects of our lives. We often think of counseling at the same time that we think of mental illness. Nothing could be farther from reality than that statement. Counseling is *helping*. Whether it is a person with an academic problem, a career choice decision or a social dilemma, the task is to help.

What can one expect in a career in counseling? The answers are as varied as the field of counseling itself. There are, however, some givens.

This career will always mean working together with people. If you feel a genuine love of people, a desire to want to help in their development, then perhaps you have set your feet in right direction.

Counseling will mean caring, an objectivity about a situation, to be sure, but an appreciation of the uniqueness and worth of each individual with whom you come into contact. This will mean an acknowledgment that each individual has the right to make and accept responsibility for his decisions. Counselors don't make decisions for their clients; rather, they are there to help them to make their own decision or decisions.

If this is essentially what counseling is all about, then it is probably natural that its antithesis be discussed.

Counseling is not synonymous with rigidity. The clients you will meet will differ greatly. There are no set formulas in the counseling setting. Time, place and space will change and the counselor will have to adapt to different situations and/or problems as they occur.

Counseling is not the offering of sympathy. Feeling sorry for a person is not a position a counselor can afford to assume. Sympathy or feeling sorry for a person connotes a one-up-manship in the counselor-client relationship; a relationship where the counselor is supposedly superior to the client. Authoritarianism or the insistence on your own way is not counseling.

Counseling cannot mean that the counselor has too great a need for other people. Too great a need for others will often lead to a reverse dependence upon their clients and will ultimately lead to too much mutual dependence by the client upon the counselor and perhaps, in extreme cases, the roles may be reversed entirely.

Counseling is not an over-identification with the person or problem the professional is dealing with. Empathy is one thing, but reflecting on a problem by saying that you had exactly the same problem, ". . . and this is how I solved it. . . ." is not helping the client to evaluate his position objectively. Above all, the counselor is objective.

Counseling is not a shoulder to cry on. It is a discipline with an ethics code; it is not a gossip session but a discussion of the problems of people who avail themselves of the services the counselor can provide.

If you decide that counseling seems to be what you're looking for in a vocation, you may want to explore the different possibilities within the field.

We know that counselors work in school and colleges but they are also an integral part of the world of business and day-to-day living. The field is generally divided into three general areas: school counselors, employment counselors and rehabilitation counselors.

School counselors make up the largest single grouping within the profession. They may be divided into two subdivisions, elementary/secondary school counselors and college/university level personnel.

Elementary and secondary school counselors are concerned about the educational, career, and social developments of students. Using the results of educational testing, they help to develop an educational plan that fits the student's abilities, interests and career aspirations. Secondary school counselors often maintain libraries which contain occupational and higher education literature for students to use as reference material in planning their respective futures. Elementary school counselors help children make the best use of their abilities by identifying these at an early age. They observe children in classroom as well as in play activity to furnish information and clues about their clients.

In order to become a school counselor, most states require that such personnel have counseling and teaching certificates. Students interested in becoming school counselors usually take a regular program of teacher education with additional courses in psychology and sociology. In all cases, however, a person who plans to become a counselor should check the requirements of the state in which he or she plans to work.

College and university level personnel are most often referred to as college student personnel workers. These people are assigned the responsibility of providing for the housing, social, cultural and recreational needs of students attending their particular college or university. Admissions officers, registrars, deans of students, placement officers, student activities and college union personnel, student housing officers, financial aids counselors, foreign student advisers, and counselors in the counseling center of the college are typical areas of employment in colleges and universities.

Since there is such a diversity in duties and job descriptions of college student personnel workers, the educational requirements vary greatly. A bachelor's degree is the minimum requirement in most instances and more and more master's degrees are being required by many institutions.

College student personnel workers, as a rule, must have the patience to cope with persons of all backgrounds and ages, with conflicting viewpoints of students, faculty, parents and the community, and with the rapid changes of thinking and types of activism that occur on college campuses.

Employment counselors deal with all age groups, the young and old. They are, by description, concerned with career planning and adjustment. Their clients may be the able-bodied as well as the handicapped. The extent of counseling services given by employment counselors varies, depending upon the jobseeker and the type of agency the counselor works for. They help the jobseeker evaluate their abilities and interest so that they can choose, prepare for, and adjust to a satisfactory field of work.

Students who are interested in becoming employment counselors are usually advised to enroll in courses in psychology and basic sociology. At the graduate level, requirements become more specific, usually dealing with courses in counseling techniques, psychology and testing assessment.

Rehabilitation counselors work with persons who are physically, socially or mentally handicapped. While their emphasis is most often job-oriented, personal counseling is also often involved. The counselor helps the disabled person to evaluate himself—his physical and mental capacity and interest—in relation to finding suitable work for himself. Together, they then embark on a plan of rehabilitation with the aid of other specialists. Rehabilitation counselors must maintain close contact with the families of their clients.

A bachelor's degree with courses in counseling psychology and related fields is the minimum educational requirement. More and more, employers are placing increasing emphasis on the master's degree in vocational counseling. Since rehabilitation counselors deal with the welfare of individuals who may otherwise be unemployed, the ability to work independently and to motivate others is essential.

The *Occupational Outlook Handbook 1974-1975* which is published by the U.S. Department of Labor is an excellent source of more detailed information. You may want to consult it if you think that counseling has career possibilities for you.

I truly enjoy my work. There is nothing routine about the job. Counseling is not a glamorous occupation, its salary ranges will never make you rich, but its rewards are tremendous.

EDUCATIONAL TELEVISION

BY
JAN PAULICH JONES
(Miss Teenage Cleveland, Ohio, 1963)
Teacher/Performer
"Telewave Reports"
Cleveland, Ohio

Almost exclusively the television teacher must have a teaching degree and be an experienced classroom teacher. The close student contact and on-the-spot performance in class give the TV teacher an added dimension to draw upon in front of the camera.

In general, a teacher does her own development for a TV course. Consequently, not only should she be aware of the facts she's presenting but, most importantly, she must be aware of the *best ways to present* the facts.

Jan Jones—chose a combination of teaching and performing.

You want to keep your audience actively interested in what you're presenting. There's no better background for this than one's own teacher-student relationships. The feedback you receive daily in your own classroom can help you make the right decisions when developing your television program.

Aside from college education courses, definitely enroll in theater arts classes. Sometimes they are even more valuable than TV courses. Television teaching encompasses a good deal of performing. In fact, if you try amateur theater and are successful, it may be a strong cue that you could be successful in a television endeavor.

Of course, the two realms are different from one another; however, any theater experience will help you gain poise and confidence in your ability to perform. Should you want to be a television teacher, knowledge of your subject will be assumed . . . the performing angle will have to be proven.

If you become involved in theater performance, it will give you a good guideline toward your performance as a television teacher. You may want to take one or two television classes in order to understand the television media. You'll then learn what will work on TV and how to put your ideas together in an appealing way.

The number of opportunities to get into educational TV are not great, but don't hesitate to call your educational TV station and ask the program director how he handles auditions. Courses available range from primary work to adult education, physics to yoga. There is some luck involved and, of course, the experience of the candidate has to fit the needs of the position. But, the right combination of experience, training, interviews and auditions could see you to a TV job.

In my personal case, I was a junior high English teacher with a strong background in theater arts. My series, "Telewave Reports" was basically a "how to study" program aimed at the junior high audience. There is nothing more boring than trying to teach, or learn, "how to study." Consequently, I decided the best way to attack the problem of boredom was by entertaining the audience.

Pulling from my background in performing arts, I developed the series around a reporter, me, who brought her assignments to the television audience in an appealing, exciting way. The teaching process may have been camouflaged, but it worked!

Because you develop your own programs, the job is unique and is certainly not a time-clock punching career. The time you spend working largely depends on the number of programs you have and your time schedule.

If you have many shows to complete in a short amount of time, you could be working seven days a week, and the job could be all-consuming. On the other hand, you may be in a situation where you come to the studio twice a week and do the majority of your writing and researching at home. The actual everyday work schedule is quite varied. Although there is reading involved and you must write scripts and put your ideas together, this is not really a desk job.

You have to come up with things to do that will fit the needs of your program, the needs of your audience and the needs of you, the teacher/performer. You will spend time chasing down props, interviewing people, shooting film.

The pace can be hectic and the work is demanding in every respect. Not only must you know your subject well, you must know how to present it, to an unseen audience, through television, in an appealing, interesting manner. A profession in educational television is unique and exciting. Once you've thrown so much of yourself into it, you certainly realize personal reward and fulfillment.

Melissa Galbraith, MISS TEENAGE AMERICA 1973, like almost every other girl alive, loves clothes and fashions.

A Sampling of Opportunities in Fashion

MODELING

BY

JAYNE MODEAN
(Miss Teenage Clifton, New Jersey 1975)
Professional Photography Model

Modeling is an exciting and "glamorous" career and it offers tremendous opportunities if you are willing to work hard, have what it takes, and get a little bit of luck.

It takes a lot of dedication, determination and discipline as one must spend endless hours seeing potential clients and making test pictures. These pictures are necessary for someone just starting as a model as it is very important to have an up-to-date portfolio. This gives the client and photographer an idea how you photograph, which is the first step in getting the job. Personality and enthusiasm also count as the client and photographer want a model they can work with, one with expression, and one they know will sell their product.

It is not necessary to go to modeling school to become a model. One must arrange for an interview with a reputable modeling agency and they will tell you in a few minutes whether you have potential or not. Once an agency agrees to handle you as a model you are ready to begin your career. The agency can only open doors for a model; the rest is up to you.

It is good to be 5'7" or taller because clothes are not made for short girls. A girl should also have a good height and weight ratio, good body proportion, good legs, and a good face.

One must always look well groomed and have plenty of rest. It is important to get plenty of exercise and watch what you eat.

Most models fix their own hair but occasionally a professional hair stylist is hired. Most models wear shoulder length hair or shorter because it doesn't cover the neckline of the garment being modeled and it is easier to handle at that length.

Special talent also helps a girl get jobs because one never knows when they'll need an acrobat or a swimmer for a special job.

A model gives the client a composite on every interview. A composite is a few recent pictures showing the client how you photograph and also listing your vital statistics and agency name. The agency also sends out a head sheet every month to clients and photographers showing which girls are available and listing where recent photos can be found in current magazines.

Once the client or photographer decide on the model they want to use, from those interviewed, they call the modeling agency that handles you. The agency notifies you and tells you the time, place, number of hours, and day the job will be done. The agency gets ten to fifteen percent commission for handling you.

It takes a lot of go-sees or interviews before you get that first job. The competition is always great; therefore, many girls get discouraged after a few months and "drop out." It is a way of life that is exciting! It is like entering a contest every day and waiting to hear if you have won.

You never know when your lucky day will come, so have confidence in yourself and one day your agency will call and tell you the client wants you for the ad.

Jayne Modean, a successful teen model. These are the photographs she chose for her composite.

I started modeling through a children's modeling agency at age six. It has been easier for me to make it as a teenage model because I had many years' experience and knew many of the clients and photographers. The opportunities are unbelievable, with chances for national television commercials, location jobs in Europe, Bermuda or even Florida or just the fact that your beginning pay as a teenage model is $60.00 an hour.

I don't consider myself any different for having modeled for eleven years, but sometimes classmates consider you different, so you have to work hard at being friendly to everyone so you're not considered a snob. My biggest problem this year has been to find time for school activities as well as time to go to New York City almost every afternoon after class.

161

You sometimes wonder if it is worth all the rushing from one interview to another only to find out the garment is too large or too small or the client has already booked a girl. But when you get the job and you see a full page ad of yourself in a national magazine you know it was worth your time and you feel a certain pride to think they chose you over all the beautiful models because they thought you were right for the job, that you would sell their product, and people all over America would identify with you.

FASHION RETAILING AND PROMOTION

BY
JEANINE ZAVREL FEARNS
(MISS TEENAGE AMERICA 1964)
Fashion Coordinator

Jeanine Zavrel Fearns, at the time she won the MISS TEENAGE AMERICA 1964 title. Her career choice was in fashion coordination and retailing.

Fashion and retailing are areas which I have always found fascinating.

How did I ever enter that world in the first place? It's not a long story nor a very typical one. My experience as MISS TEENAGE AMERICA certainly had a great deal to do with it.

I have always been interested in clothes and hair styles, a trait inherited from my mother. This was fostered, of course, by my participation in the pageant.

My training for a career in the fashion field was received more through practical experience than through formal schooling.

My first exposure to the professional side of fashion came at age sixteen when I became a teen board model at a suburban department store. The interest engendered there developed steadily through my college years, and I spent each summer working and modeling at the same store near my home.

I was exposed to the business end of retailing through their executive trainee program—a marvelous introduction to a fascinating, vital profession.

About halfway through college, I decided that this was the future I wanted, and became concerned that my academic training was not suitable for the career I had chosen.

I was repeatedly assured by both guidance counselors and store management that a retailing or fashion degree was not necessary for success.

I continued work on my English major and filled my academic year studying literature and related liberal arts. My summers were spent modeling for a department store.

I was learning not only how to merchandise clothing, but how to sell myself as an acceptable adult in the business world. This exposure to the consumer public helped me to develop my self-confidence as well as my business sense.

Upon graduation I received several offers from major department stores for management training positions. I decided upon one and started from the bottom—floor walker, service manager, all-around assistant to everybody—that was me for about six months.

Having completed this broad basic training, I took a position in a women's ready-to-wear area as assistant buyer. From there I moved into a department manager slot in one of the suburban branches, learning more each day.

Though this was fascinating, demanding work, I still nurtured the hope of getting into the "glamor" side of the business—fashion promotion. I felt I had the basic talents required, all I needed was the "big break."

After eighteen months, it came, like a bolt from the blue. Obviously, the powers in management saw the feeling I had for fashion and display, as I was offered the job as fashion coordination head for the branch store.

I spent the new months of my career on top of the world—I had truly achieved my ultimate goal!

Working side by side with the display staff, I selected all the fashions for the store windows and displays, contracted fashion shows for the public and for the employees, directed the teen board activities, taught classes in wardrobe selection for the charm school run by the store, and functioned as the liaison between the corporate fashion office and my branch store. It was my job to get all the latest fashion news from the fashion director (and many other available sources) and to relate the trends to our customers and our employees—to convey the proper fashion image for my store as put forth by the corporation.

And where did I learn all this? From many sources—keeping abreast of the latest in fashions through publications, attending seminars, having my ears and eyes open at all times, and of course, tempering it all with taste and common sense! These are qualities no one can teach you. You learn by doing, by watching, listening—and of course, through your own mistakes! That "school of hard knocks" is worth more than a thousand retailing degrees. I'm not discounting the value of such a degree, but I do feel that it is not a necessary prerequisite. In my case, it was not available to me on the college level, so I made use of practical experience combined with my own talents to teach myself what was needed.

And how do you know if you're suited for it? Well, that's a bit harder to explain than how to go about it. For me it was an interest nurtured through many years of varied experiences—a rounded education in general fields which led to an isolated opportunity. I always knew I loved fashion and had the feeling for it! I merely relied on this self-knowledge and took an opportunity which was presented to me.

You think you can be successful in a field you would love to enter, but you never really know until you try. My admittance was gained through department store retailing, but there are other avenues—vocational schools, modeling, commercial art, fashion display, to mention a few.

Success in a chosen field is a marvelous achievement, but knowing what you really want is the first big step. When you've made that step you're on your way! Good luck!

You've heard from a former MISS TEENAGE AMERICA *who made it in the world of fashion retailing and promotion; now here is some advice from the potential employer.*

MORE ABOUT FASHION

BY
MARY KERNAN
Director of Training
and
ESTER BOGART
Employment Director
Lord & Taylor

There are a variety of approaches for a high school graduate interested in a career in fashion. During peak seasons, part-time or temporary jobs are often available to high school students, which might give you a slight advantage in being considered for a permanent, full-time position. You can begin in a sales, stock, or clerical position right out of high school.

If you do go to college—a two- or four-year school—you will be eligible for the training program offered by most major-sized retail firms. Your college major can influence the decision on your application. Helpful courses of study include clothing and textiles, fashion merchandising, business administration and marketing. However, your projection of your interest and enthusiasm for the business is your best selling point in obtaining a job offer. An employer will definitely look at your extracurricular activities with an eye to finding out whether or not you like to participate in campus affairs and will be especially interested in such personality traits as poise, maturity, a sense of humor, and the ability to articulate your ideas.

If you do join a retail store such as Lord & Taylor as an executive trainee, you will be given formal training initially to help you develop the necessary basic skills. Most of your training, however, will be on the job, usually in a buying office or in a management position. As you are promoted you will again be given formal training in the various aspects of that position. Training programs vary according to the store; some are more formal than others. For those who are interested in becoming a buyer, the time required to reach that goal can vary from three to six years, depending on the store, but that is only one of the many opportunities in retailing.

Get your toe in the door and get started. With drive, determination, and dedication you're bound to go straight to the top of the retailing world.

A Sampling of Opportunities in Government

WOMEN IN GOVERNMENT

BY
U.S. Representative DALE MILFORD
and Mrs. DALE (MARY)MILFORD

One of the largest and fastest growing sources today of employment for women in the United States is government: federal and state.

Of the 30.1 million women employed in non-agricultural and non-postal full-time positions in the United States, the federal government employs 3 percent and state and local governments together employ 18 percent.

Women enter government service by means of Civil Service merit systems, executive and congressional appointments, and, increasingly, by election to public office. In the federal service women constitute 48.2 percent of the clerical workers, 28.9 percent of the technical workers, 16.1 percent of the administrative workers and 18.7 percent of the professionals.

At the managerial levels they make up 3.9 percent of the mid-level ranks (GS 13-15) and 1.5 percent of the super-grades (GS 16-18). On the sub-professional and professional levels, women hold many and varied positions in such areas as medical technology, air traffic control, urban planning, architecture, personnel, actuarial science, law, engineering and marine technology.

In the area of presidential appointments, in the Ford Administration there are forty-six full-time women appointees, including twelve judges, four ambassadors and the third woman Cabinet member in the entire history of the United States, Carla Hills—the Secretary of Housing and Urban Development. Especially since the Nixon years there has been an overt effort to recruit and hire more qualified women to high level positions within the Executive branch and agencies. In addition to these forty-six women, there are twenty women who were appointed to non-career high-level positions (meaning GS 16 and above and outside the Civil Service system) within the administration bringing the number of high-level, full-time women appointees to sixty-six.

As a result of Circulars 5901 of November 23, 1970 and 3745 issued in August 1971, the area of the Foreign Service has been opening up to women—both married and single—in secretarial positions as well as policy-making positions in *every* geographic area. In fiscal year 1972 alone there was an increase of women officers from 7 percent in 1971 to 21 percent. According to Gladys Rogers, Special Assistant to the Deputy Under Secretary of State, "The Department of State has made a commitment to its women employees to: redefine their status, provide essential resources to achieve that status, establish radically new policies, and make the concerns of women a key element in management reform. An honest beginning has been made to deliver on the commitment."

Women seem to be making the most overt strides, however, in the political arena, especially in the last two general elections. Currently there are seventy-two women in Congress, one woman Governor (Connecticut) and one woman Lieutenant Governor (New York).

In 1974 the first woman was popularly elected to the office of Chief Justice of a State Supreme Court (North Carolina) and in Alabama Janie Shores became the first woman Associate Justice of the State Supreme Court.

Also in 1974 two women were appointed to the prestigious House Judiciary Committee: Congresswomen Barbara Jordan of Texas and Elizabeth Holtzman of New York.

Party politics also have undergone some changes where women are concerned. In 1972 (now U.S. Representative) Yvonne Braithwaite Burke was selected Vice-Chairman of the Democratic National Convention; former Ambassador to Luxembourg Patricia Harris chaired the Credentials Committee at the same convention and Jean Westwood was elected chairperson of the Democratic National Committee. Mary Louise Smith was appointed in 1974 as the new chairperson of the Republican National Committee.

It is clear then that opportunities are opening and expanding for women at all levels of government and women are taking advantage and are using their talents, perspectives and expertise to the benefit of the American people.

This should not be read to suggest, however, that the government is free from injustice and discrimination against women applicants and employees. Private industry and academia are not immune. Neither is the United States government. Women still are largely clustered at the lower rungs of Civil Service grades. Women still only constitute 3 percent of Congressional membership and 9 percent of state legislatures in spite of the fact that there are seventy million women of voting age, seven million more than the number of men of voting age. However during the past several years the government has committed itself to re-evaluating the role women could and should play in the domestic and foreign operations of our nation. "An honest beginning *is* being made to deliver on that commitment."

WOMEN IN THE ARMED FORCES

BY
ANNE TAUBENECK
Editor,
Lady Com Magazine
In Cooperation with the
Department of Defense

One career opportunity that should not be overlooked is service in the armed forces. All branches of the military have opened up almost all occupational specialties to women. The only fields that remain closed to women are combat-related. Women in today's armed forces serve as pilots, mechanics, policewomen, and air traffic controllers as well as in the more traditionally feminine occupations like nursing or administration.

More and more women are serving in command positions. They are, increasingly, in the mainstream of the armed forces, leading and working with men, in jobs formerly closed to women.

Of special interest to the high school girl looking toward graduation is the chance to compete for admission to one of the service academies, which have just opened their doors to women. The United States Military Academy at West Point, the Naval Academy at Annapolis and the Air Force Academy in Colorado all offer exciting educational programs.

A career in the armed forces offers a chance to travel, an opportunity to pursue an occupation in a challenging field. Pay and benefits are excellent.

Basic enlistment requirements for servicewomen are essentially the same in all the armed services. Concerning high school education or its equivalent, these guidelines apply: The Coast Guard does not require a diploma, the Air Force finds a diploma desirable, the Army and Navy require diplomas or GED equivalents and the Marine Corps requires a diploma but may grant waivers in some cases by accepting GED equivalency.

Applicants cannot be less than seventeen years of age (the Navy, Marine Corps and Coast Guard accept enlistees from seventeen to eighteen with parental consent; the Army accepts women seventeen and one-quarter into the Delayed Entry Program to begin active duty after age eighteen is reached; and the Air Force requires parental consent if the woman is under her home state age of majority). Other requirements for enlistment include good health and high moral standards. An applicant may be married but must have a waiver for dependents other than her spouse (the Coast Guard and Marine Corps do not allow for enlistees with children).

Minimum enlistment periods are: three years for Women Marines, women in the Army and Coast Guard and four years for women in the Air Force and Navy. Longer enlistment options are available in all services. Women enlistees can, in many cases, be guaranteed a choice of a specific type of training. For example, most of the Army's enlistment option guarantees are open to women and the Air Force allows them to enlist in a specialty of their choice under the Guaranteed Training Enlistment Program.

RECRUIT TRAINING

Recruit, or basic, training is of six to ten weeks' duration depending upon the individual service. This training provides each recruit with essential knowledge and skills early in her enlistment. It also emphasizes teamwork, discipline and responsibility toward the service concerned as well as the high individual standards expected of all women in the service. Recruit training for women in the Coast Guard is, as far as practical, coeducational with the men. They attend the same classes, the same drills and are given the same responsibilities. Housing facilities are separate.

GENERAL INFORMATION

Living Arrangements. Most young women on their first enlistment are assigned to posts and stations with a women's strength of fifty or more. Facilities in barracks or dormitories usually include sewing machines, hair dryers, kitchenettes, lounges, TV rooms and laundry rooms with automatic washers and dryers.

Career Fields. Jobs open to women are not exactly alike in kind or numbers in each of the services. Women in the Army and Marine Corps may serve in any career field with the exception of those directly related to combat. Before enlisting, a young woman should find out whether the service of her choice offers the career fields in which she is interested.

Pay and Benefits. Servicewomen receive exactly the same pay and benefits, including retirement rights and annual leave, as servicemen in the same pay grade and the same time in service.

Military Duties. Aside from regular job assignments, these duties include standing inspections, charge of quarters and other military duties concerned with maintaining security.

Working Hours. Most servicewomen work an eight-hour day and a five or five-and-a-half-day week, although in some cases, as in civilian industry, working hours may be on a "shift" basis.

Wearing of the Uniform. In peacetime, civilian clothes are usually worn during off-duty hours.

Service Schools and Off-Duty Education. Servicewomen are eligible for service school training in most of the career fields to which they are assigned. Opportunities for off-duty education are identical to those of servicemen.

Overseas Duty. Women in all the services are eligible for overseas assignments. Servicewomen are presently assigned to a number of overseas bases—Europe, Hawaii, Panama, Far East and Middle East.

Marriage While in the Service. A servicewoman may marry, but she may not leave the service solely for this reason. The separation policy for marriage varies among the individual services.

COMMISSIONING OPPORTUNITIES

College graduates may apply directly from civilian life for a commission as an officer or to attend an officer candidate school or course. Enlisted women can qualify for certain officer candidate programs. Generally some college education is a prerequisite.

ACTION PROGRAMS—
THE PEACE CORPS AND *VISTA*

(A VOLUNTEER Program)

BY

BETTY MURPHY
Office of Public Affairs

Have you thought about someday becoming a volunteer in the Peace Corps or VISTA (Volunteers in Service to America)? Do you know what these ACTION programs are—what they entail; what they could do for you; and, more important, what you could do by joining one of them?

Being a Peace Corps or VISTA volunteer is not a career. It is a term of service that should be viewed as a supplement to a career, not as an alternative; an integral part of your education, not a step sideways. Your ACTION experience could help qualify you for a good position in your chosen field.

Both the Peace Corps and VISTA are part of ACTION, our country's federal volunteer service agency. The Peace Corps, founded in 1961, and VISTA, authorized by Congress in 1964, both joined ACTION in 1971, when the agency was established to coordinate all federal volunteer programs.

The Peace Corps is the international arm of ACTION. About 7,000 Americans serve as Peace Corps volunteers and trainees in sixty-eight developing countries in Latin America, Africa, the Near East, Asia and the Pacific. Its goals, as originally set by Congress, remain unchanged: to help developing countries meet their needs for trained manpower, and to help promote mutual understanding between the people of the United States and the developing nations.

VISTA is a national corps of volunteer men and women of all ages who work to alleviate poverty in the United States, Puerto Rico, the Virgin Islands and American Samoa. More than 4,000 VISTA volunteers and trainees live and work among the poor under the sponsorship of local organizations.

The overall goal of both volunteer programs is to *help people help themselves.* This is far more demanding than handouts or armchair advice. These are not turkey basket, or token service programs.

You may have heard that Peace Corps volunteers travel to exotic, faraway lands—live in quaint, picturesque South American villages; find adventure in African wildlife preserves; glory in the rich heritage of the Near East; or bask in the tropical sun on romantic Pacific isles.

These are postcard pictures, not the real message. Wherever you go with the Peace Corps or VISTA, giving, not receiving, is the name of the game. And being a volunteer in either ACTION program is not a game.

You have to be prepared to do without many things that you take for granted now. You may not have such luxuries as electricity, indoor plumbing, hot or even running water. You may have to sleep on a straw mat in a mud hut, eat strange foods that would seem indigestible to you now and learn to speak in a new language.

There are many hardships to endure wherever you serve as a Peace Corps or a VISTA volunteer. But there are also many rich rewards—particularly if you don't expect to perform miracles. You are not going to wipe out poverty, illiteracy or disease on a community-wide basis, no matter how hard you try.

You may help a handful of disadvantaged children to read and write, show a few farmers how to improve their crop production, or improve the health of a few malnourished families. Then again, the effects of your efforts could be far-reaching and long-lasting. You might build a well for a town that never had its own water supply or plan a curriculum for a developing school system.

It takes a lot of patience to be a Peace Corps or VISTA volunteer. You have to give deeply of yourself, but you have to have something more than yourself to give. You must have a skill that is needed in a developing country abroad or a disadvantaged community at home.

First, you must be a United States citizen in good health and at least eighteen years of age. Both the Peace Corps and VISTA prefer to recruit college graduates with some professional or technical work experience. However, if you lack a degree but have needed skills and experience, you also might be highly qualified.

The needs change from time to time—from project to project with VISTA, and from country to country with the Peace Corps. But virtually all technical skills are needed at one time or another.

Teaching positions in ACTION programs both overseas and at home offer unique and challenging opportunities to education graduates and experienced teachers. From remote villages in Africa to migrant farm camps, Indian reservations and urban ghettoes in the United States, teachers are needed in almost every field.

There is a growing demand for agriculturalists, particularly in the Peace Corps, but also in VISTA. If you have training or farm experience in horticulture, animal husbandry, forestry, fisheries or any other agricultural specialty, your skills could be a vital asset to a rural community in a developing country abroad or disadvantaged community at home.

Health professionals and technicians are in great demand by the Peace Corps and VISTA. Doctors, nurses, dentists, pharmacists, medical technologists and physical therapists are needed, not only to care for the sick but to train nurses, technicians, paraprofessionals and other hospital and health workers. Health volunteers also are needed to teach nutrition, sanitation, disease control and preventive medicine.

Trades people who are most often in demand in both ACTION programs are carpenters, mechanics, electricians, plumbers, masons, tool makers and welders.

The Peace Corps and VISTA also need architects, engineers, city planners and businessmen and women to volunteer their services at home and abroad. The more skills you have to offer in these and many other professions, the more you will be able to contribute to developing communities throughout this country and in Africa, Latin America, the Near East and the Pacific.

For some volunteers, service in these ACTION programs has changed the course of their lives in very positive directions. By facing challenges, solving problems, learning new ways of life and utilizing their skills to the utmost, many have carved new dimensions in their chosen fields or have found more satisfying careers to pursue.

If you are interested in becoming a Peace Corps or VISTA volunteer, you should submit an ACTION application no more than twelve months before you are available for service. You may state where you would like to serve on the application. If you qualify for service and if your skills are needed in your chosen area, ACTION will try to place you there, but there is no guarantee.

For applications and further information on the Peace Corps, VISTA or other ACTION volunteer programs, you may call 800-424-8580 toll free.

"NOW CLOSE YOUR EYES."

A Sampling of Opportunities in Medicine

HEALTH INDUSTRY CAREERS

Courtesy of
Texas Health Careers Program
Texas Hospital Association

The health industry is one of the most fascinating industries in the world today! The search for good health is as old as human living. Today, however, health is synonymous with continually expanding horizons and undreamed-of frontiers. Did you know, for example, that within the span of your own lifetime that health sciences have developed more "firsts" than in any other period in history? Transistorized pacemakers, wonder drugs and vaccines, nuclear medicine, organ transplants, dialysis machines and literally hundreds of other health discoveries have affected the health of us all.

Modern health care is in a constantly changing state. New techniques, new equipment and new ideas are being put to work to save lives and prevent diseases. Peoples' attitudes toward health care in our country are also rapidly changing. More and more people now feel that health care is something that should be accessible to everyone. Consequently, the government has become a major health provider in our times. Moreover, many people now are just becoming aware of the importance of preventive medicine and proper health planning.

This constant change has also created a great and immediate need for tens of thousands of health workers. The present shortage of health manpower affects the quality, quantity and cost of health care for almost all Americans, especially those who live in rural and medically under-served areas. Young people now entering the health field have almost unlimited opportunities for employment and personal fulfillment because of this need for health manpower.

The health care field is really many different kinds of careers. People are needed to be doctors and nurses, of course, but the health care team is made up of more than three hundred different careers. There is a good chance that there is a place on the team for you.

Health careers are open to anyone who is qualified. The health field needs people with different educational backgrounds, different skills, different social and ethnic backgrounds, and different personalities. Would you like to work directly with patients? Or would you rather have a career oriented toward research or education? Do you have an interest in administration or clerical work, building operation and maintenance—they, too, are health careers. It takes all kinds of people with all kinds of skills and capacities to make up the health team. Whoever you are and whatever you are good at, health employment is a field where you could use your best talents and do the kind of work you like best.

Some health careers are devoted especially to maintaining physical health; others specialize in helping people toward better mental and emotional health. In some health careers you can help individuals with their specific health problems; or you may want a career aimed at improving the general health of the community.

There are a variety of approaches to health problems, too. Healing diseases and injuries is the goal of some types of health careers while other work to prevent disease and injury. There are even health careers which help people by providing health care for animals.

The best way of determining what health career might be right for you is to look at your own interests and abilities and identify them with related health careers. If you like home economics, you may wish to consider a career in dietetics or food service, executive housekeeping, nutrition or homemaking rehabilitation consulting. Careers in biomedical research, computer programming or health statistics require a keen interest and ability in mathematics. English and journalism majors would have a good background for careers as health educators, medical librarians, public information specialists, in public relations, as well as scientific and technical writing. Budding musicians can become musical therapists. For those who are interested in business and finance, there are health careers in administration and accounting. If you are interested in art, electronics, business skills, languages, industrial arts, model making, photography, education, social studies or science, all of these school interests have related health careers.

Preparation for a career in the health services begins in high school. High school courses in mathematics, communicative skills and physical sciences are an excellent groundwork for any health career. Some high schools have special training in health occupations education available.

The only requirement basic to all health careers is a sincere desire to help people. Among the more important personal requirements for those considering health employment are a strong sense of responsibility, an ability to communicate and get along well with others, manual and mental dexterity and dedication.

Education opportunities for health careers range from a few weeks of on-the-job training to eight or nine years of formal training and education at a university. After high school, there are a variety of educational programs to choose from. The most important variable in recognizing any career goal is the right education for the right job. This is especially true of health careers.

On-the-job training offers jobs for high school graduates who want to go to work immediately and learn a skill at the same time. On-the-job training is available for technical and clinical areas as well as the areas of administration, hospital maintenance and housekeeping, dietetics, and doctors' assistants. Other careers such as medical secretary, operating room technicians, physical therapy assistants and others require only months of preparation. Four years of college and a bachelor's degree represent the basic education for social workers, therapists, radiologic technicians, medical technologists and many other health professions. Some of these occupations require a year's internship after graduation. Still more extensive professional training is required in medicine, dentistry, and a few other health careers. After formal training many health careers require certification or licensure by professional organizations and state licensing agencies.

All health careers, no matter what educational preparation is involved, work together in a partnership to provide total health care for individuals and the community in which they live. Although each health career may specialize in the type of services provided, all health careers are interrelated and each contains some aspects of the others.

A physician who works with patients, for example, is involved both in healing disease and in preventing disease and helps patients toward better physical and mental health.

Most communities offer a number of employment settings. Over one-half of those employed in health careers are found in hospitals. Voluntary health agencies, health departments, industry, educational facilities, mental health centers, research organizations and private practice offer a variety of employment opportunities for those interested in health careers.

Salaries for the many hundreds of different careers in health vary greatly, depending on your responsibilities and education. On-the-job training usually pays the minimum wage to start, with salary increases after the training period. For other types of health careers, beginning salaries can range from $5,000 to $30,000 annually. As with most careers, experience and additional education command higher earnings.

The rewards that come from employment in a health career, however, cannot be measured in dollars and cents alone. Your work in a health career will be rewarding by making a contribution to saving lives, easing pain and preventing disease. The knowledge that you are really needed to help people means job satisfaction that few career fields can offer.

There are a number of indications that the need for health workers will continue to grow in the years ahead. Advances in medical know-how which enable treatment of more health problems create new skill and employment demands. More and more Americans are participating in private and governmental insurance programs which enable them to get medical care when they need it. The growing emphasis on health planning and preventive medicine will require more manpower. As more people seek adequate health care, a corresponding increase in demand for workers is created. Americans will continue to demand high quality health care which in turn will maintain a strong need for future health care workers.

Health care is, and will continue to be, a big business. Nearly $115 billion was spent in 1974 by Americans on their health. This sum made health care the largest money generating industry and the second largest employer in the nation. It is a big business, and yet, it is much, much more than a business. It is an experience in human endeavor where one person can reach out and improve the life of someone who is or may be sick. Health careers are more than building, knowledge, money and machinery—they are the highest manifestation of love. Health is people who care.

If you care—there is a place for you in health careers. You can put your talent to work in the health field. Do not make the mistake of minimizing your own abilities and individual worth. You as a person can make a contribution to provide better health for people. You can do it!

MEDICINE

BY

JUDY HARVEY

(Miss Teenage Springfield, Missouri 1972)
Medical Student
University of Missouri

Judy Harvey—looks forward to "hanging up her shingle."

I remember when, as a fifth grader in our class of about thirty students, a teacher asked everyone what we wanted to be when we grew up. I don't remember another thing that was said. I was sitting there at my little desk thinking "I want to be a doctor, but women aren't doctors." What a predicament! To this day I don't know why I didn't accept that "fact," but I assure you, I'm very happy that I didn't. Being somewhat of an individualist, I wanted to make a worthwhile contribution of my own to society. So, it was left up to me to decide what type of contribution to make to society and how to do it.

In school, the subject I liked most was biology, which helps form a solid basis for a science career. I'd been well-exposed to the hospital through my father, observing treatment of emergencies, operations, working in his medical office and talking to the patients there.

178

A major factor influencing a girl's decision to go into medicine is how well can she perform in that field and enjoy a satisfying family life at home, having and rearing children. We must keep in mind that medicine has changed drastically during this century, especially during the last forty years.

Doctors see most of their patients in the office or in the hospital. People have means of fast transportation now, so it isn't mandatory that the physician rush out to the home because a child has a fever, or someone has been injured severly. We have trained emergency personnel with ambulance service for most of the population, so ill patients can be delivered safely to a center where the physician can devote his or her time to the actual performance of care rather than spending time on the road. Also, the necessary diagnostic aids are available to the physician if the patient is delivered to the physician's care location. The so-called miracle drugs have contributed greatly to the "revolution" in medicine, so the physician can actually provide a specific remedy for a given disease where years ago they, many times, could only provide physical support and encouragement while waiting for the disease process to run its natural course.

Not being exceptionally wild about school rules, deadlines, etc., for any longer than necessary, when I heard about the Six-Year Program at the University of Missouri—Kansas City, I was excited. I loved it!

UMKC has developed a new, unusual program for improving education to prepare young people straight out of high school for a lifetime of skilled production work as physicians. Instead of the traditional four years of pre-med followed by four years of medical education, the freshly graduated high school student entering this program attains baccalaureate and M.D. degrees through six years of concentrated educational effort.

Our Six-Year Medical Program reveals early that doctoring is much more than just science. Technical knowledge is a must, but a genuine concern for people and the desire to work with and help them is an extremely important qualification for a beginning physician as well as for those physicians who have been practicing over the years.

Our curriculum is scheduled for forty-eight weeks each year and its nature provides a realistic working knowledge of community health problems and resources. This program isn't just eight years' work condensed into six by any means. We have early and continuing contact with patients, clinical experiences starting at the beginning of Year One in our program. Traditional students usually are exposed to similar experiences no earlier than their second year of their four-year program, whereas we are exposed to these experiences throughout our entire six years in the program. For those who worry about the shortened period of educational requirements for acquiring the M.D. degree, we say, don't worry, we are actually in school longer than those medical students in the traditional schools according to the statistics. We do not receive the long summer vacations that are enjoyed by many medical students in the traditional schools.

Some basic objectives of the UMKC Six-Year Medical Program are: 1) help overcome the shortage of physicians, 2) improve the health-care delivery system, and 3) reduce the cost of medical training. UMKC is trying to help provide the needed physicians in rural areas. The school demonstrates through the student selection system that there is equality, and availability of educational opportunities regardless of race, creed, color, sex, or socioeconomic status.

During the first year we are introduced to general medicine. The basics of medicine are acquired, such as the language and vocabulary. We also learn about the factors influencing illness, including social, psychological, and economical aspects. We spend a month working in "orderly-like" jobs.

Frequently we are allowed to dress in a cap, mask, and gown to watch surgery. I was hoping to avoid fainting under those circumstances but on the contrary, I was fascinated with everything I saw and had a chance to do. We also attend the summer session at UMKC and have a one-month vacation during the first summer. During year two we are introduced to the infant, child, and adolescent in pediatrics. We acquire a broad aspect of the woman during "OB-GYN," obstetrics and gynecology. During the summer, after completion of the second semester of the second year, we are assigned to a preceptor who is a physician in general or family practice, whom we follow and observe for one month. Many times the student will live with the doctor's family during that period and really experiences the night calls, emergencies, and every aspect of the private practice of medicine. Another month of this summer is spent learning about emotional factors in illness. We spend all day of every day of that month at a mental health hospital. Another highlight of the summer is the independent study of pharmacology.

I no longer feel that I must give up all of my non-medical activities and interests to become a physician. On the contrary, I need to remain exposed to everyday life outside my medical studies to be able to relate to all individuals regardless of their background. Students in this program should therefore be well-rounded and thus better able to relate to and understand our patients. We have less pressure because we know we are already in medical school, so that we can find time to engage in non-medical activities and interests just like every other college or university student.

My class, being almost 40 percent women, is only one of the many evidences that UMKC actually reaches out to help all qualified interested individuals regardless of their location or status in life.

I have seen everything ranging all of the way from the excitation of seeing a new baby brought into the world to the other end of the scale, where relatively grim periods have been spent with the bodies of our patients being autopsied in the morgue.

If you think medicine may be for you, this information may interest you. I know of at least thirteen medical schools offering medical education programs, very similar if not identical to the program in which I am working. They are as follows: University of Missouri—Kansas City School of Medicine; Louisiana State University School of Medicine in Shreveport; Boston University School of Medicine; Northwestern University Medical School, Evanston, Illinois; Albany (N.Y.) Medical College; Jefferson Medical College and Hahnemann Medical College, both in Philadelphia; South Carolina College of Medicine in Charleston; State University of New York at Stony Brook Health Science Center; University of South Florida College of Medicine at Tampa, Florida; Rush Medical College, Chicago, Illinois; University of Nevada School of Medical Science at Reno, Nevada, and University of Michigan's Interflex, Ann Arbor, Michigan.

Other materials that may be of interest to you include: *Medicine, A Woman's Career*, a little booklet of encouraging words on what it takes to be a woman doctor, is available for fifty cents from the American Medical Women's Association, Inc., 1740 Broadway, New York, New York, 10019.

Detailed information on schools, requirements, costs and scholarships has been compiled in a directory, *Medical School Admission Requirements*. The annual handbook which costs about four dollars, is ordered from the Association of American Medical Colleges, Attention: Membership and Subscriptions, One Dupont Circle, N.W. Washington, D.C. 20036.

Two Hundred Ways to Put Your Talent to Work in the Health Field describes careers related to medicine. Single copies of the brochure are free from the National Health Council, Inc., Box 40, Radio City Station, New York, New York 10019.

NURSING

BY
NANCY MEEK TAYLOR
(Miss Teenage Indianapolis,
Indiana 1970)
Surgical Nurse
Methodist Hospital
Indianapolis, Indiana

Nancy Meek Taylor—First Alternate in the 1970 Pageant, Nancy is now a practicing nurse.

Nursing is a challenging and rewarding profession, and I am happy to say it was my choice as a career. It has many advantages over other professions. Job opportunities are unlimited and the salary is above the average.

There will always be people that need physical and emotional care. One of the nicest benefits I've witnessed is that your education is relative to your everyday life. You use what you learn to obtain the most optimal health. In a society that provides little preparation from womanhood to motherhood, your professional knowledge should be invaluable in the future years. Whatever field of nursing you choose you can become an expert and specialize in that particular type of nursing.

I strongly advise any high school girl who has an interest in nursing to contact the nursing school of her choice early in her high school years. There are waiting lists to enter some schools. They will be most helpful in explaining their programs and advise you what is required for entrance. I feel it is important to have a good background in English, biology, chemistry, and mathematics. Many schools require the student to be in the upper one-third of their high school class and SAT tests are also necessary.

It is also important for a girl to have a lot of physical stamina. Not only do you take a full college course, but you will work in the hospital learning the practical side of nursing care and applying the theory you learn in the classroom. It takes a lot of patience, tolerance, and discipline to become a good nurse.

Since graduation, I have been working as a surgical nurse at Methodist Hospital in Indianapolis. I "scrub" or, rather, I am the doctor's assistant during the operations. I begin at 7 A.M. and many days assist with seven or eight operations by 3 P.M. Each day is different. It is very satisfying to know you are a small part in helping someone back to good health.

As the saying goes, "Not everyone is cut out to be a nurse," but for those who are, there isn't anything like it!

DENTAL HYGIENE

BY
KAREN P. HUGHES, B.S.,
Registered Dental Hygienist

A dental hygienist is the member of the dental health team that is primarily responsible for educating the patient in prevention of dental diseases. The hygienist may be employed by a private office, schools or other institutions, under the supervision of a licensed dentist. Additional employment opportunities include hospitals, clinics, federal agencies, as well as local and state health departments.

The dental hygienist's main functions in a dental office include performing oral prophylaxis (scaling calculus from teeth and polishing them) and educating patients in proper care of the mouth. She also may make preliminary examinations, and give fluoride treatments to help strengthen the teeth. Her duties include taking and developing X-rays. Usually a hygienist has her own operatory where she performs her duties. After she finishes a routine prophylaxis, the doctor checks the patient, and it is the responsibility of the hygienist to chart any decay he finds.

To prepare for a career in dental hygiene a background in biology and chemistry would be helpful from high school. High grades are important because the selection of a class of dental hygiene students is done on a very competitive basis. There is a large demand for hygienists nationally; consequently, the schools are besieged by applicants. Only a small minority are accepted.

There are two avenues to consider in becoming a hygienist. The first is to attend an accredited college for two years, and then enter a college of dental hygiene that offers a degree program for two more years. The second is to enter a two-year vocational program.

The degree program gives you a Bachelor of Science degree in dental hygiene with a minor in biology. With this the employment opportunities are a little broader, and there have been several cases of a hygienist with a Bachelor of Science degree going on to dental school for four more years and becoming a licensed dentist.

With the two-year vocational schools, she receives the same Certificate of Dental Hygiene as the hygienist with a degree. She is able to practice in private offices and her earning potential is about the same as the degreed hygienist. Where money is a factor, the degree program could be considerably more costly because the vocational schools are usually state funded. Both roads lead to an R.D.H. (Registered Dental Hygienist). The choice lies only in what she wants to do after graduation.

Prospective hygienists must know that the practice of dental hygiene is very demanding mentally. A future hygienist must be serious in her studies for she will be required to take courses in such things as anatomy, embryology and histology, physiology, biological chemistry, pathology, microbiology, and pharmacology. Late in her first year of dental hygiene school, she will actually work on patients under the supervision of an R.D.H. Upon graduation she then must pass the state and national examinations to be a licensed hygienist. The examination consists of a written portion and a clinical portion in which dental examiners check her work on patients.

The benefits of this career are numerous. Employment opportunities are available on a full-time and part-time basis, and the profession offers a high degree of prestige and security. It is the ideal profession for a woman who wants a career and a family too. Some doctors need a hygientist for only one or two days a week. Sometimes uniforms are required; but, if so, they and their maintenance are tax deductible. Dental hygiene is financially very rewarding. A hygientist may make from $800 to $1400 a month, depending if she is salaried or on commission. By law, a dentist can employ only one hygienist at a time. Consequently, in some parts of the country they are in tremendous demand and salaries and benefits are adjusted accordingly.

On the other hand, in recent years many vocational schools have opened in concentrated areas forcing lower salaries and job hunting in these places. There are not many drawbacks to dental hygiene, but the practice is physically demanding and, therefore, a prospective dental hygienist must be in excellent health, and free of physical impairment.

A hygienist is a student all her life. She has the opportunity to attend conventions with her peers to learn new techniques. Continuing education courses are offered throughout the year. There are professional groups who meet once a month for fellowship and learning.

Hygienists are the only members of the auxiliary group in the dental profession permitted by law to perform direct preventive services to a patient. Therefore, it is possible for a dental hygienist to volunteer her time to the community in various programs.

I find it a very gratifying and fulfilling profession and am proud to be a part of it.

A Sampling of Opportunities in Theatrical and Performing Arts

THE THEATER— A PRODUCER'S VIEW

A Practical Look at the Theater

BY

CHARLES R. MEEKER, Jr.

The only person who has been with MISS TEENAGE AMERICA *since its inception, President and Executive Producer of the National Telecast, Charles R. Meeker, Jr., has been in the business of the theater and entertainment for some forty years. He has experienced just about every facet of that profession—from press agent to producer. He has distinguished himself in his work with top-flight stars as well as guiding the careers of young people who are interested in the various aspects of the theater and performing arts.*

Ask any former MISS TEENAGE AMERICA *Candidate about Mr. Meeker and she will tell you that he is one of the most inspiring people she has ever met and a very special person in her life. Once he has touched your life, you'll never be quite the same.*

Breathes there a girl with soul so dead that to herself hath never said, "I was born to be the theater's biggest and brightest star."

A favored few have made the dream come true. Many have had the chance but faltered.

Most, having made a practical and honest evaluation of their talents, have wisely chosen a career in a different field.

Although the press agent's stories continue to regale the readers with "instant successes," they are rarely true. It is also worth remembering that very little is written about the "instant failures."

One of the more accurate statements came from the actor who said that it took him only twenty years to become an "overnight star."

If, however, you are determined that the world of entertainment must make a place for you, then read on.

The best way to start is to erase the sugarplums of "glamor," "fame," "fortune" and perhaps "total adoration" which may be dancing in your head.

Speaking to and with young people is Mr. Meeker's favorite form of recreation. "It's my golf game," he claims, "and I'll promise you it's more stimulating and exciting than any sport you can name."

Much of Mr. Meeker's theatrical career has been spent in guiding the careers of young people. "One of the basics," he says, "is the ability to communicate an idea and in return receive an emotional response at the closing curtain."

If you can approach your objective with the same careful consideration you would give to becoming a doctor, lawyer or Indian chief you will not only improve your chances but you will surely avoid many disappointments along the way.

Formulas or sets of rules for success in career matters are rarely valid. Too much depends on individual ability and individual application to the immediate task. The theater world does not have a corporate structure or a table of organization.

In almost every case a performer stands alone once the curtain goes up and the margin for failure or success depends not only on what you are capable of doing but also on how your audience will accept your offering.

There are, however, some valid and workable ideas. They will not guarantee success in the theater world but they will enhance your personal chance if an opportunity to perform comes your way.

Of primary consideration, remember that the values of a sound and thorough education are innumerable and many of these values are rooted in practicality.

To be employed, while seeking an opportunity to perform, substantially increases your chances. Your choice of studies should include this very important consideration.

The basic premise of the world of the theater is simply communication. The more you know, the more you will be able to communicate. The more you understand, the more you can embrace another's ability to understand.

You simply cannot communicate that which you neither know or understand.

Those whose purpose is so single-minded that it fails to include the other facets of living end up in a very narrow world indeed.

Maturity has little to do with age but a lot to do with being able to apply knowledge. The day of "beautiful but dumb" is gone forever, simply because lack of instant comprehension usually causes delay which increases the cost of the project.

Fortunately the theater occupies a higher position in society than it did a generation ago when theater and carnival were held in about the same esteem.

This has come about because more people from the entertainment world have accepted the responsibilities of good citizenship rather than those who have exhibited both their ignorance as well as their sense of values in search of a headline.

The extra years you spend in completing your education and in discovery of today's world will return dividends galore when you have come to that time of opportunity, and someone will be interested to determine if you really know "what it's all about."

In conjunction with your formal education, practical experience ranks significantly as one of the best teachers.

Historically it was about 400 B.C. when the Greeks added speech to pantomime and the verbal theater was born. Since the time when the simple but classic Greek dramas established the foundation for today's world of entertainment we've added a lot of tinsel.

Scenery, lights, microphones, cameras, costumes, properties, assistant producers and directors, script girls, make-up artists and a myriad cast of people and an endless list of items comprised of animal, mineral and vegetable have been added along the way.

The basics, however, have not changed one iota. The ability to communicate an idea and, in return, receive an emotional response which at the closing curtain will bring either approval or disapproval is still doing business at the same old stand.

The fact remains that the people and items listed above are going to remain for the foreseeable future and be a part of any serious consideration of a performing career.

So you need to know something about the "mechanics" of your chosen field in addition to the skill you may acquire as a performer. The most skilled actress who is so unknowing that she turns her back to the camera will be flirting with oblivion.

All this means that you need to have a working knowledge of all the pieces that, when properly assembled, complete the puzzle.

How is this accomplished? By doing. Seize every opportunity to inspect and study every aspect of your chosen field of performance until you know what it does, where it goes, and how it can best serve you.

This does not mean that you must learn how to take a spotlight apart, reassemble a microphone, or handle the fly loft. It does mean that you should know where things are, what they do and who is responsible for their function and operation.

Finally, if you aspire to be an actress, then act. Learn about an audience.

In this highly competitive field, formal training is vital. There may be "natural born actors and actresses" but most of them are unemployed.

The basic fundamentals of all of the arts are applicable facts, not theory, and have been tested to the extent that they are universally accepted. They are necessary for survival.

A competent producer or director will have little interest in furthering your education. The cost in time (which is expense) simply will not permit it.

After you have completed your training there will still be one missing ingredient. An audience.

Every opportunity you have to appear before two or more people will be a learning experience. Treasure every one.

You may never come to the point where you will "understand the audience" but without that ingredient, the theater in every form is indeed a very lonely place.

To get to that point at which you begin to worry about the audience reaction and your effectiveness as an actor you will first need to experience the audition.

"By your audition shall ye be known" is a meaningful phrase to remember. More budding careers have been left on the audition room floor than can be imagined. It could happen to you.

On the other hand, the application of a small amount of common sense can secure an advantage. It will not improve your basic talent but it will give you a better chance to exhibit what you possess.

The following are basic to nearly all auditions. Study them. Think about them. Give yourself the best chance.

- *Do dress up*—look your very best. Arrive for the audition in disarray and the person conducting the audition will only assume that your interest was so small that you cared very little about what he might think of your appearance.

- *Discover the purpose of the audition*—know what the person conducting the audition is hoping to employ. This can usually be done in advance by a phone call or by asking if any descriptive material is available. If the auditions have been advertised or publicized and you arrive without the knowledge of what is happening, you will probably be marked "stupid."

  If the audition is for dancers and you are a singer then stay away. The next one may be for singers and if you showed up the first time, your first impression will be a hindrance.

- *Try for originality*—abandon the hope of knocking Barbra Streisand or Gwen Verdon "out of the box." The very minute that you offer an imitation of a successful performer, you have locked yourself in a comparison of the very best. The cards are against you. Strangely enough, no one is looking for another Streisand because there already is one. There are literally hundreds of "standards" in the field of music as well as dance. They can serve you well and you can avoid a disparaging comparison.

- *Be brief*—take your best shot at the very beginning. Avoid being stopped.

  An experienced auditioner will be looking for quality not longevity. Should he have interest in seeing or hearing additional material he will ask for it. Then be prepared with a second number and even a third.

  One veteran auditioner says at the beginning of each audition, "Avoid the verse—start with the chorus."

  Consequently when someone pays no attention and starts with the verse he automatically eliminates them. He assumes that their ability to take instruction or direction in a simple matter would make them difficult to work with.

- *Make your audition in keeping with your abilities*—if you are a singer, select a number that is comfortably in your range. Stay away from the note that you must "reach" for. The person holding the audition will most likely be interested in the quality of your voice, not its range.

  If you are a dancer select a routine that best illustrates your coordination and your ability to move. Don't try to "dazzle" the auditioner.

  Selecting the most difficult steps (unless you are especially skilled) increases your chance to prove yourself ineffective.

  Here again, the person conducting the audition will not be very interested in your "routine." Rather he will be thinking as to whether or not you can fit in his choreography.

- *Radiate*—nothing catches the interest more than a smile and an exhibition of enthusiasm for what you are doing.

Along with these suggestions to remember are several practices not to indulge in.

Don't explain in advance what you are going to do—just do it.

Refrain from making an excuse in advance as to health or inability to perform at peak ability. No one will care.

Forget about announcing that your material is "original"—if the auditioner is interested in the material he will ask where it came from.

Don't ask to be "moved up" or "moved back" in the order of audition because of other engagements. It is always assumed that if the audition is of sufficient interest you will make arrangements to be available at the convenience of the audition.

Don't fail to bring proper accompaniment or proper, clearly marked music for the accompanist. Music that must be transposed at sight by the accompanist is an unnecessary burden which you should make all efforts to avoid.

Don't ask time to "warm up" before you audition. You should have "warmed-up" before you came, or backstage prior to your audition.

Extend the same courtesy you would like to receive. Noisy or inattentive behavior while others are auditioning is inexcusable.

Refrain from asking the auditioner his or her opinion of your performance.

All in all, treat your audition in the same manner you would treat any job application. Look your best. Do your best. Realize there is a viewpoint other than your own.

Don't be afraid to fail. It is part of the learning process.

As a final reminder —

STAY WITH IT.

The theater is no place for the faint of heart.

Determination and the ability to pursue your goal are the two most important qualities next to ability to perform.

In most successful careers, rejection is par for the course at the beginning. Learn from each experience.

When the day of opportunity does arrive, as it will if you will not give up, be equal to it.

THE THEATER— A VIEW FROM THE STAGE

BY

BARBARA SIGEL

(Miss Teenage Philadelphia, Pennsylvania 1968)

Film and Television Actress

To make it as an actress it takes 90 percent perseverance and 10 percent talent. It is the hard worker who makes it, not the ones who are born with exceptional talents.

On the other hand, it is not all glamor and fun. If you are willing to work hard, to deal with rejection and still enjoy the profession, then go ahead and give it a try.

Barbara Sigel—Her first major film was *Time to Run*, the Billy Graham film.

You can start your career right where you are by getting involved. There are many opportunities available which help to develop poise and confidence in yourself and as a performer in front of an audience.

School plays, community theater, college and professional theater, as well as summer stock offer exciting openings for you. If you don't get a lead, try for a smaller part, or work behind the scenes in a capacity other than acting.

Public speaking, debating, or working in radio as an announcer or disc jockey also help to gain an awareness of your voice and its qualities as well as an overall heightened sense of your self.

Modeling is a beneficial way in which to acquire an impression of the way others see you and just how you appear in a photograph.

Another thing to remember is that physical exercise is essential, whether it is in sports or dancing. Besides helping to stay healthy, it will develop grace.

While watching television, films, and plays, try to analyze the actors' performances. Read as many plays as possible and familiarize yourself with books written on acting by Stanislavsky, Strasberg, and Uta Hagen.

Be inquisitive. When you meet celebrities and actors, ask questions about their profession and how they got started. Any information they offer may aid you in getting started on your own career.

Keep in mind that there is no such thing as an overnight star. Even Lana Turner wasn't discovered in a drugstore. A lot of young people feel that they will make it overnight. It takes many years, at least two years of studying before good parts roll your way. Mary Tyler Moore and Lucille Ball were both in the business about ten years before they really made it.

Don't think that good looks alone will get you a part. Pretty faces are a dime a dozen. A particular look or style may be beneficial at times, but acting ability is what will get you the part.

Education is a necessary key to opening doors that will further your career. Several large universities have gained favorable reputations for their theater departments. Some of these are N.Y.U., Yale, Carnegie Tech, Northwestern, Catholic University, and U.C.L.A.

If you prefer an acting school, some of the finest are located in New York City. The Herbert Berghof Studio, the American Musical Dramatic Academy (A.M.D.A.), Neighborhood Playhouse, American Academy, Warren Robertson Studio, and the Actors Studio are a few of the best known.

If you are more inclined toward California and Hollywood, several acting coaches who have earned a name for themselves are Milton Katselas, Sherman Marks, Ned Mandarino, Jeff Corey, Charles Conrad and Peggy Fury.

Whatever path you choose, the more experiences that you can gain through your educational pursuits will serve you advantageously later.

When the time comes for you to seek an acting job your means of making yourself known and meeting prospective employers will be through interviews.

It is helpful to be friendly, say what you have to say, be honest and, most importantly, be yourself. In the beginning you will be nervous, but the more interviews you encounter the easier it gets.

Make a sincere attempt to remember names and faces. We all feel good when we are remembered by someone we have met only briefly.

When you go on an interview, you will be asked for a composite, which is a set of pictures showing different looks you can achieve and a physical description of yourself, and a resume which is a listing of all your credits and any talents or special abilities that you have.

It is challenging and fun to go up for all the different kinds of roles available in acting. It is very important to know what *type* you are. Ask people what kind of roles they see you in. Know what you are first and learn to play those kind of roles. The character roles can come later.

In order to best prepare yourself, it is in your own interest to be aware of a few prerequisites for all actresses.

Importantly, you need a respected agent who can be found by choosing one from a list put out by the Screen Actors Guild (S.A.G.) or it can be one recommended to you by a friend. There is a S.A.G. branch in most large cities which can save you a lot of useless knocking on doors.

If you have worked in a film or on TV, or in a commercial, you can probably join S.A.G. or the American Federation of Television and Radio Artists (A.F.T.R.A.). After one year in one of these unions or in Equity or American Guild of Variety Artists (A.G.V.A.), you can join one of the other unions.

An actress also needs film footage on herself. You can get this by asking for a copy of any work done in a commercial or industrial film, and a studio will lend out any film you have done.

If you have none of these, there are other ways to secure film. Many of the larger universities have excellent film students who are always looking for talent.

Another good thing to do is to send a photograph of yourself to the Academy Players Directory which contains pictures of the various types of actors and actresses—ingenue, character, leading types, etc.

It is helpful to buy the trade papers such as *Hollywood Reporter*, or *Variety* which relays information about auditions for film, TV, and stage. This is especially useful in your pre-agent days.

One last necessity is your phone service. It costs only a small amount a month to have a separate number so that agents and other people can get in touch with you when you're not at home.

Initially, you will want to decide whether you want to concentrate your efforts in film and TV or in performing on the stage. As you gain experience and begin to perform more your direction and preference may change.

Acting on stage is different from acting in film in many respects. A single eye movement can mean a great deal when blown up on the screen. This same eye movement would be lost on stage. In film, much of the emotions and reactions are seen in the face and eyes.

On stage, however, the whole body is used and the movements are much larger.

One of the challenges of a play is the excitement of doing that story in one evening, and feeling the reaction of the audience. If you give a bad performance or make a mistake, that is something you can't erase.

In film, there is no audience to work in front of, but if you are not happy with the scene, you can do it again. Also, your work is on film and can be seen again and again.

When working on screen, you must have total concentration. There are hundreds of crew members walking around setting up camera angles, changing the lights etc.

You must be involved with whatever is going to happen in the next scene. You must also remember what you have done so that it matches in the other angles shot for that same scene.

Sometimes, when you are working with a star, the scene will be read with the script girl because the star is busy, and this is very difficult. This doesn't happen very often. Most stars will go out of their way to be there. This is another reason why you must have your craft down pat.

When you finally get the opportunity to work on a film project, be friendly and warm to the crew members. They really want to be your friend. The technical members of the crew can definitely propel your career.

Be professional. When you get a job, know your lines, have your wardrobe prepared, be familiar with the location or the studio, be on time, and at the end of the day thank the director, producer, camera operator and technicians.

And most of all—don't give up.

A CAREER IN MUSIC

BY
LEHMAN ENGEL

It is rare indeed for a teenager to have the opportunity to hear the advice of such a prestigious, accomplished and respected expert as Lehman Engel.

A legend in the world of music, Mr. Engel has conducted over forty Broadway shows, composed music for over thirty more shows and has conducted and composed some thirty odd more. Mr. Engel has also demonstrated his vast talents in recording, television, radio, films and as guest conductor for great symphony orchestras.

As author and lecturer, he has provided the serious theater student with honest, direct and experienced knowledge through his excellent books on music and theater.

Pursuing a career in music, like everything else, changes with age. A century ago in America conditions were so different from the way they are today that there is little comparison. Travel was time-consuming but relatively inexpensive. More important to a career in music was the fact that there were few phonographs and still fewer recordings; no radio and no television. Popular music had its place—live only—in saloons, "music halls" (as the better ones were known), for dances and in some theaters. But live "serious" music was a model of its own kind—difficult to come by and, therefore, in demand.

Music study had two principal purposes: for those who hoped to follow concert or other professional careers, and young ladies who enjoyed performing for themselves and their friends and might, at some point, *need* to become teachers of voice or one of the more usual instruments: piano, violin or violoncello.

With the passing of time everything changed. Travel became easier, phonograph recording techniques were improved and became more plentiful and, finally, both radio and television became generally popular media—necessities in the home and offering music of all types—plentiful and within the reach of all. A personal appearance of Jenny Lind, "The Swedish Nightingale," or Paderewski, the great Polish pianist, or Fritz Kreisler, the eminent violinist, were unforgettable events when they could be booked for concerts in an American tour. In the fifty years between 1875 and 1925, however, the advent of recordings, TV and radio polarized such activities to such an extent that, far from being celebrated events, they were too often too expensive for the public and the opportunities for appearances grew less and less frequent for the artist.

Today, and certainly for an indefinite time in the foreseeable future, the role of the serious musical performer has become curtailed because of centralization and it is foolish for ambitious students to behave like ostriches, with their heads in the sand, not knowing the realities of their situations.

Concert managers can only book and will, therefore, not make contracts with performers who are less than already acclaimed popular stars. The concert *business* has shrunk to the point where Horowitz, Rubinstein, Van Cliburn, Birgit Nilsson and a few others in their very special class can be easily booked for appearances in whatever times they find themselves available and for rather enormous fees. Lesser-known artists obtain bookings with considerable difficulty and are infrequently sold at any price.

It is my considered opinion that accomplished instrumentalists (exclusive of pianists) are well-advised to become members of one of the major symphony orchestras which gives them invaluable experience, opportunities for first-rate music-making, predictable annual incomes and

Lehman Engel—a respected authority in music and theater.

more than sufficient time for whatever concertizing they may be able to acquire on a personal basis.

These and pianists should also be knowledgeable in musico-academic fields to qualify themselves for positions in conservatories and in college music departments. Such positions also embody the benefits listed above and, usually, provide a lifetime of economic security which is a necessity for every living being.

Singers—let us be honest—have small opportunities in the opera houses. Opera seasons are relatively short and few. Impresarios require the services of singers not only possessed of outstanding voices but of wide experience in a variety of roles. Such experience is nearly impossible to come by in America where there are few companies and the personnel engaged must have studied and performed—usually in small houses in Europe for little, if any, compensation—in many roles so that rehearsal time in America which is expensive, is cut to a minimum.

In the decades between 1945 and 1965, many potential opera singers were able to support themselves in the musical theater of Broadway but that, like everything else, is in a process of transition and the job opportunities have become fewer and fewer.

I can, therefore, only suggest that singers, like instrumentalists, equip themselves for careers in educational institutions. Many will teach and will often have opportunities to perform locally and, depending on their personal talents and accomplishments, in other places as well.

Everyone must come to grips with changes in the times. Nowadays, interested listeners are offered top-notch fare on radio, occasionally on TV and the best of everything on records. For an ambitious beginner to ignore these facts is to fly in the face of disaster. To come to grips with them is to plan and be able to carry out a life of security—a matter of prime importance—with the opportunity to work in one's chosen field and to find satisfaction in a continuing, rather than a sporadic, career. The time of instant fame and fortune in a musical career has been long gone, even if it ever did in reality exist.

Anyone with a musical talent and an unquenchable desire to pursue a career is well-advised to seek it out, methodically, by trying to become a part of existing organizations. There are enough rewards in such a career to make a lifetime undertaking of this kind invaluable. The choice of any other route is foolhardy and must lead to disaster.

BOOKS BY LEHMAN ENGEL
RECOMMENDED FOR STUDENTS OF THE THEATER

Planning and Producing the Musical Show (Crown)
Music for the Classical Tragedy (Harold Flammer)
The American Musical Theatre, A Consideration (CBS/Macmillan)
Words with Music (Macmillan)
Getting Started in the Theatre (Macmillan)
This Bright Day, an Autobiography (Macmillan)
Their Words Were Music (Macmillan)
The Critics (Macmillan)

A Sampling of Opportunities in Transportation

AIRLINE OPPORTUNITIES

BY
JOHN E. RAYMOND
Director of Public Relations
Southern Division
American Airlines

Over the past decade, the airlines industry has become a major provider of interesting occupations. Now, virtually all positions with the airlines are open to women, including that of pilots.

FLIGHT CREW

AGE: Minimum—21
HEIGHT: 5'6"–6'4"
WEIGHT: In proportion to height according to the airline's standards.
VISION: 20/20 without glasses in each eye separately
EDUCATION: Minimum 4-year college degree. It is realistic to counsel young people to consider Navy or Air Force pilot training, as 85 percent of recent hires were military.
EXPERIENCE:
1. Valid U.S. FAA Commercial Pilot Certificate with instrument rating.
2. Valid 1st Class FAA Medical Certificate without waivers.
3. Valid FCC restricted radio-telephone operator permit.
4. Minimum of 1000 hours of combined 1st pilot and co-pilot experience in jet or multi-engine equipment.

Recent hires have averaged 2300 hours of flight time with the great majority being in jet or multi-engine aircraft.

TRAINING: Initial training of three months conducted at AA Flight Academy, Fort Worth, Texas

What's it like to be an airline pilot? Colleen Fitzpatrick, MISS TEENAGE AMERICA 1972, tries out the flight deck.

FLIGHT ATTENDANT

AGE: At least 20

HEIGHT: 5'3"–6' (male and female)

WEIGHT: In proportion to height according to the airline's standards.

EDUCATION: High school graduate with some business experience. College and/or work experience preferred. Suggested prep course: English, psychology, public speaking, first aid, languages, home economics.

TRAINING: Six-and-a-half-week course at AA Flight Service College, Fort Worth, Texas

PROMOTIONAL POTENTIAL: To Flight Attendant Supervisor, Instructor at Flight Service College, and other management/specialist positions.

MECHANIC

Inspecting, trouble-shooting, checking, servicing and repair of aircraft, powerplant and component systems.

Must be willing to work rotating shifts.

REQUIREMENTS:

High school graduate or equivalency diploma; valid driver's license; FAA Airframe and Powerplant license (for line maintenance only) secured through military or FAA approved schools; minimum set of tools.

EXPERIENCE: Two years of experience closely related to job assigned

PROMOTION POTENTIAL: Crew Chief, Inspector, Technical Foreman and other maintenance management positions.

CLERICAL

Secretaries, records clerks, accounting clerks, statisticians, clerk typists, and stenographers. Duties vary according to area and assignment level.

PROMOTION POTENTIAL: Non-management salaried positions, Administrative Understudy, Executive Secretary, Statistical Analyst.

REQUIREMENTS: High school graduate or equivalent; some college preferred. Typing 50 WPM; shorthand 80–100 WPM.

TICKET SALES AGENT

Promote and sell air travel, give air travel and tour information, make flight and tour reservations, compute air fares, prepare and issue tickets, route baggage and prepare cash reports.
Must be willing to work with rotating shifts.

AIRPORT OPERATIONS AGENT

Duties similar to ticket sales agent, but at departure lounge. Also meet and dispatch flights, lift tickets, administer seat selection and boarding procedures, and maintain high level customer service with passengers.
Must be willing to work with rotating shifts.

TICKET SALES AGENT AND AIRPORT OPERATIONS AGENT

AGE: Minimum—20
EDUCATION: High school graduate plus two years' college or business experience
EXPERIENCE: Previous public contact experience
PROMOTIONAL POTENTIAL: Passenger Service Manager, Crew Scheduler, Management Understudy, other management/specialist positions.

PASSENGER SERVICE REPRESENTATIVE

Personalized service to passengers primarily at ticket counter, passenger boarding, or baggage claim areas. Assist the passengers by providing information, arranging for ground transportation and giving directions to inbound and outbound passengers.
AGE: Minimum—20
EDUCATION: High school graduate
EXPERIENCE: Some public contact experience and additional education preferred.
PROMOTIONAL POTENTIAL: Ticket Sales Agent, Airport Operations Agent

RESERVATIONS SALES, SERVICE, CONTROL

SALES AGENT:

Sell reservations and tours on AA, quote fares, give flight arrival and departure information (via telephone) and assist passengers in reaching satisfactory solutions to their travel needs.

SERVICE AGENT:

Complete and maintain passenger records, monitor seat utilization, call passengers to confirm reservations, compute complete fares and rates for complex itineraries.

CONTROL AGENT:

Monitor and augment SABRE (computerized reservations system) in regard to passenger space utilization and equipment substitutions.

AGE: Minimum—20

EDUCATION: High school graduate plus two years' college or business experience. Aptitude for telephone sales, as well as excellent telephone technique and a pleasant voice.

PROMOTION POTENTIAL: Management Understudy, other supervisory positions in Reservations.

AIR FREIGHT OPERATIONS, TELEPHONE SALES

FREIGHT AIRPORT OPERATIONS AGENT:

Process routing and rating of shipments; contact customer on arrival of shipments, and arrange delivery.

FREIGHT TELEPHONE SALES:

Quote rates, patterns of service and complete necessary shipping documents.

AGE: Minimum—20

EDUCATION: High School graduate plus two years' college or business experience

PROMOTION POTENTIALS: Management Understudy, other management/specialist positions

LADY AT THE THROTTLE
(Santa Fe's First Female Railroad Engineer)

BY

GEORGE T. GRADER
Sante Fe Regional Manager
of Public Relations

It was March 4, 1974. About two dozen newsmen representing newspapers, wire services and the television networks milled about. Camera lights flashed and glared and newsmen jostled to get closer. The object of their attention was a pretty twenty-one-year-old girl. Shiny brown hair reaching below her waist. Large, dark eyes with luxurious lashes. Five feet six inches, one hundred twenty pounds. A lush figure and a brilliant smile. Carefully groomed nails with pink polish. It happens to movie and TV stars in New York and Hollywood.

However, this was the Sante Fe Railway depot in Socorro, New Mexico, about seventy-five miles south of Albuquerque. The news media were there in the chilly, pre-dawn darkness to record for posterity Christene Gonzales—who would later appear in "Ripley's Believe It or Not"—becoming Santa Fe's first woman locomotive engineer.

When Christine (Chris to her fellow workers) took over the controls of that diesel hauling a rather unglamorous Sante Fe work train, she helped break a male-dominated tradition that has existed since the beginning of American railroads in the 1800s. She also became an instant celebrity and the question she faced most often was "Why railroading?" Well, when Chris broke the one tradition she also was upholding another that now spans four generations. You see, she's "railroad."

It began in Decatur, Alabama, where her great-grandfather worked for the Louisville and Nashville Railroad. Today Chris carries the gold railroad watch he used. Her maternal grandfather, Ernest Halbrook, now of Ruidoso, New Mexico, also worked for the L&N but later moved his family west to hire out on the Southern Pacific. He retired as a conductor on the SP's Sunset Limited in 1971.

Chris' father, Frank Gonzales of El Paso, is an SP conductor. Chris' mother, Betty Jo, went to work as a telegrapher at the age of fifteen for

Reprinted with permission from *Texas Railways*, Fall 1975

Christine Gonzales, America's first lady railroad engineer.

the SP in El Paso. Presently she is office manager for the Santa Fe trainmaster in El Paso.

It was from a chance remark by her mother that Chris first learned of new regulations granting equal employment rights, and that Santa Fe then was accepting applications for engineer trainees. She had been wrestling with the problem of what she wanted to do. She had graduated from Loretto Academy in her native El Paso, then worked in an oil company office in Houston. Courses at Houston Community College frankly bored her. "I didn't like the daily routine. It was always the same."

Returning home she enrolled at the University of Texas at El Paso but she still was restless. Finally, after much thought, she decided to fill out an application. Her reasons were quite clear. It presented an unusual challenge and, if successful, she would continue the family tradition. There was also another reason. "It's an exciting job and I could make more money in a week than I did in a month in an office."

After personal interviews and screening she began orientation at Albuquerque in May, 1973. As an engineer hostler she moved locomotives to and from the roundhouse. Later she rode with veteran engineers as an observer in road freight operations. In November, she was assigned to student training on freight trains operating between El Paso and Belen, New Mexico. She showed exceptional ability to absorb instruction and was recommended for final training at Santa Fe's Simulator School in Topeka, Kansas.

The simulator is similar to the famous Link Trainer which was used to turn out thousands of pilots during World War II. It simulates actual locomotive operations, complete with authentic sights, sounds, motion, backgrounds and crisis situations. During the 200 hours of accelerated instruction students learn operating rules, mechanical and air-brake operations, as well as many other fundamentals.

Chris freely admits that after the first day she was scared to death that she might not make it.

"Classes went from 8 A.M. to 5 P.M., and I realized how much more I had to learn," she said. "Besides, I don't think I had ever even held a screwdriver in my hand."

She needn't have worried. She sailed through her final examinations, scoring as high as a perfect 100 on her mechanical orals. Then came March 4.

Chris is a member of the United Transportation Union and as with all new employees she's low on the seniority roster. She's held varied assignments, including the work train, local freights and switch engines in the El Paso yards on the midnight to 8 A.M. shift. As this is written she is running a freight train between El Paso and various points in southern New Mexico.

She says she finds each day a new challenge and now understands what her father meant when he said, "Railroading gets into your blood." Chris works in blue jeans and gaily colored blouses or shirts—and her favorite pink nail polish. Her long, silky brown hair is braided and pinned up. In cold weather she wears a ski jacket.

Because of Chris, a new safety rule had to be written. It prohibits engineers from wearing loop or dangle earrings on the job.

A Sampling of Other Professional and Technical Opportunities

TAX AUDITOR

BY
JOHNNIE NELL YOUNG
Miss Teenage Forrest City,
Arkansas 1967
Tax Auditor
Internal Revenue Service

Johnnie Nell Young pictured in 1967 when she was a National Candidate.

Do you enjoy dealing with people?
Do you like to complete assignments on your own responsibilities?
Do you enjoy a challenge?

If you answer "yes" to these questions, you may enjoy working as an auditor. I did answer yes to these questions, and I am enjoying a rewarding career as a tax auditor with the Internal Revenue Service.

The I.R.S. makes investigations to ascertain that taxpayers' obligations are properly determined. The tax auditor has an important part in the enforcement of federal tax laws. He or she corresponds with the taxpayer to identify and explain tax issues and to determine correct tax liability. One becomes a specialist in resolving federal income tax questions and consults with taxpayers from all walks of life.

A bachelor's degree in general business and a master's degree in business administration provided me with an excellent background for this position. However, a four-year college degree in any field qualifies one for this position.

Upon appointment as a tax auditor, you are given several weeks of formal classroom training which includes an intensive study of income tax laws, auditing techniques, report writing, and tax research. On-the-job training is an integral part of career development where you apply the knowledge attained in the classroom. The training, with assignment to progressively more responsible duties, is carefully planned to develop your skills and abilities as rapidly as possible.

You can look forward to career advancement and recognition of your executive talents. Supervisory and mid-management training is offered to those who demonstrate potential for supervisory and high-level positions. With completion of twenty-four semester hours in college level accounting, you have an opportunity for professional accounting positions with the Service.

Most tax auditors work in Revenue Service District Offices located in fifty-eight major cities throughout the United States. Others work at local offices in the larger cities and towns in the United States. My first assignment was to the Little Rock, Arkansas, District Office, and later I transferred to the Forrest City, Arkansas, local office. So, no matter where you want to live within the United States, the Internal Revenue Service has an office nearby.

The Internal Revenue Service needs qualified women to fill professional positions. The Service recognizes that women represent an important resource of ability and talent and is working toward equality of opportunity for women.

Career-oriented women who hold positions which gratify them are extremely fortunate. If you would like to be such a woman, you should consider a position in the field of auditing.

A CAREER IN ELECTRONIC DATA PROCESSING

BY
JIM BATTISTONI
Corporate Recruiter
Electronic Data Systems, Inc.

The information provided in this article is designed to develop your investigative approach to any career, but in particular, data processing. The information is general, and requires your effort to reach the completeness you feel necessary, if you think you might be interested in a data processing career.

THE ELECTRONIC DATA PROCESSING INDUSTRY IN GENERAL

Many industries today are attempting to reshape thinking concerning women's place in their industry. The data processing industry is fortunate in that it is a modern industry. It has not experienced years of preconceptions and structures concerning aptitudes and responsibilities. Electronic data processing provides an opportunity to achieve technical skills, a marketable quality in today's business world. The accountant possesses technical skills, as does the lawyer, doctor and the data processing professional. These skills are tangible; a special coding language, a particular industry involvement and familiarity with a certain manufacturer's equipment.

In addition to the technical skills, a person has the opportunity to practice any management skills he or she may develop. A general overall statement of industry characteristics includes growing industry, rapid change, new career emergence and professional challenge.

WHAT IS EDP?

Electronic data processing, or EDP as it is commonly referred to, is an industry with far reaching effects, touching slightly or involved heavily in both the scientific and non-scientific communities. EDP can be divided into three basic divisions: *hardware*, which pertains to the mechanical and electronic features of EDP (this term is used as a synonym for the equipment); *software* refers to the procedures written, using specific rules recognized by the computer to perform desired tasks; *service* provides for a customer's EDP requirements utilizing hardware, software and the key ingredient, people. If one were to compare EDP to the music industry, these would be the parallel functions: Hardware is the stereophonic equipment, the sheet music would be the software, and your local radio station would provide the service. This article does not address the hardware industry, but is software and service-oriented.

BACKGROUND FOR ENTRY

There appear to be three probable avenues of entry to EDP; college or university graduation, technical school skill training and industry internal training programs. A person's choice of background development should be compatible with his or her personal resources and long-term goals.

POSITIONS AVAILABLE

There are numerous subcategories of EDP software and services positions, but they generally can be described by functions and grouped into three main titles: *Data processing support*, including the careers of data entry, coordination, and delivery; *computer operations*, entailing the physical control of the EDP effort; the *systems analyst/programmer's* function, entailing responsibility for the design and writing of programs to develop or maintain a system. Additional job titles and responsibilities are unique to particular companies.

ADVANTAGES AND DISADVANTAGES OF A CAREER IN EDP

Advantages offered by a career in EDP include: at present, relative ease in entry, withdrawal, and reentry into the labor market (there is a need for qualified technicians), the needs at present seem to be nationwide, providing availability of positions if family relocation is necessary, the industry is conducive to part-time and contract work (some companies allowing completion of work in the home), there are no unique physical requirements and a logical, orderly thought process tends to be the mental qualifier. Salaries continue to be an indicator of the need for qualified persons. Entry level salaries average $600 per month and tend to be governed chiefly by two factors—the size and the location of the installation. A decision to choose or eliminate an industry on the basis of salary information could turn out to be a costly one in future job satisfaction. The salary should be a factor weighted no more or less than other contributing decision factors. To some, disadvantages surrounding a decision to enter EDP include: odd working hours, commonly the first one listed on any list, EDP installations typically operate twenty-four hours a day and in many cases seven days a week; travel may or may not present a problem and is a function of some companies and not others; constant retraining and maintenance of technical skills may require attendance at manufacturer's schools, seminars, and conferences.

FINALIZING YOUR DECISION

Included in your research should be a visit to an EDP installation and a talk with practicing professionals. Listen to their reasons for choosing EDP. Are they compatible with things you are seeking? Research your library for additional information; then utilize this research if your decision is to pursue a career in EDP. Draw on this knowledge, preparation, and self-assurance in your employment interview; remember, you must make the good things happen. Good luck in *your* choice of a career.

Anita Columbo Morgan—a new field for women.

ENGINEERING

BY
ANITA COLUMBO MORGAN
Miss Teenage St. Louis, Missouri 1967
Electrical Engineer
C&P Telephone Company of Maryland

An engineering degree in any of the disciplines, whether it's chemical, civil, mechanical or electrical, will result in many opportunities presenting themselves.

With an electrical engineering degree I am working for the Chesapeake and Potomac Telephone Company of Maryland in the engineering department as a customer equipment engineer for large Private Branch Exchange systems—that is the switchboard and room of switching equipment in many businesses.

My primary responsibility is the design of the system, putting all the component parts together to create the working systems.

Along with this comes a lot of managerial responsibilities—coordination with other departments, budgeting and estimating the system costs.

As an added attraction we don't sit behind a desk all day as is the usual impression of an engineer. There is direct contact with the customers when determining their needs in the system.

The minimum amount of education is a bachelor's degree in engineering, but in thinking ahead to this sort of degree and career it is extremely helpful to study as much math and science as possible while in high school. Not only will this help in college, it will also help you decide on engineering as your chosen profession or that you never want to see an engineering text. In any event you are doing yourself a great favor.

If you have an analytical mind and enjoy your math and science classes, try to get a job in an engineering firm for a summer. You'll see an engineer in action, even if you aren't actually participating in engineering work.

And remember, there are a number of options with your engineering degree—research, management, patent law and design.

THE FLORAL INDUSTRY

BY

J. M. SCHMIDT
President,
Florafax International, Inc.

Career paths in the floral industry are quite varied and present many options. They can be exceptionally rewarding, not only from a monetary point of view but, more importantly, for a sense of personal achievement. In the terminology of behavioral scientists, an individual can achieve "self-satisfaction," "self-enrichment," and "self-actualization" from a career in the floral industry.

The careers range from pure artistic endeavor to the highly technical field of growing and reproduction. The educational needs and requirements are equally as varied and range from four-week floral design schools to doctoral degrees.

The utilization of artistic talent is best exemplified by the field of floral design. A floral designer takes raw materials—flowers, foam, ribbon and other accessories—and develops a finished flower arrangement. Many floral designers progress through the various supervisory and management categories within a retail flower shop and purchase or open their own business.

Cathy Durden, MISS TEENAGE AMERICA *1976*

Interior design is closely allied to floral design, and an increasing number of flower shops are offering interior designing to their customers and the public. Furthermore, diversifying with smart gift lines and antiques is prevalent in the retail segment of the floral industry, all of which creates the need for in-depth purchasing and marketing expertise.

Junior colleges are offering associate degrees in flower shop management. Curriculum consists of floral design courses, small business management, marketing and sales. A bachelor degree in ornamental horticulture would prepare an individual for retail flower shop management, as well as open doors into the nursery business.

The floral industry is also composed of flower growing operations. The flowers are grown either in open fields or in greenhouses. The best avenue into growing is by way of a university horticulture degree. The more advanced areas of growing and experimentation would require advanced education, such as a masters or a doctorate degree.

From growing, the next step is floral wholesaling. Floral wholesalers distribute directly to the retailing segment of the industry, which has been covered. The larger wholesale distribution centers employ floral designers, sales specialists, marketing specialists, credit specialists, and buyers. Degrees in business management or horticulture pave the way for entrance into wholesaling.

Floral wire services, such as Florafax International, Inc., are a major factor in the retail area of the floral industry. Positions for individual growth and development can be found in all levels of management, as well as the creative area. Necessary creative departments are editorial and promotional. Each major floral wire service publishes a monthly magazine. The content includes business articles; special articles, and requires considerable research that deal with how to use flowers in home or business. The promotional aspects of a wire service deal with developing floral promotions for the various holidays, including floral design and display. Here we can add as educational requirements degrees in journalism, advertising, art—and, again, ornamental horticulture.

If an individual has an artistic flair, enjoys working with flowers and plants, and prefers being in a people-oriented environment, the flower industry certainly fulfills needs, desires, and expectations.

From the standpoint of a young lady, the floral industry has many entertaining and fulfilling occupations available. The industry provides the opportunity for outside or inside work, displaying artistic talent, as well as using creative management techniques.

HOTEL SALES AND PROMOTION

BY
ANASTASIA RENE KOSTOFF
Director of Sales
Beverly Wilshire Hotel
Los Angeles, California

Anastasia Rene Kostoff—a lady hotel executive.

For the clever girl who can open her own doors to success and knows how to make the best of a situation, hotel sales promotion provides a panorama of the business world. It's a chance to get "behind the scenes" of a great variety of businesses with your own calling card as an introduction.

If the word "sales" scares you, keep reading; it scared me too. Just out of college I felt fresh and creative with none of the aggressiveness "sales" seemed to require. I've since learned that in the hotel business the word sales and all it implies is almost a misnomer.

The hotel business *is* fresh, creative and fun. Most of its interesting jobs must be filled by people who are persuasive, patient and personable. Hotel sales, in my opinion, is perfect for the outgoing girl whose enthusiasm has a conscience! You *are* selling. You must know your product, represent it honestly, then when you've made a sale you have a responsibility to see that your client receives the accommodations and services you've promised him. Once you've earned a client's trust and confidence your future dealings with him are practically guaranteed.

If you're wondering who your prospective clients are, think of your product. A hotel has something for everybody: sleeping rooms, of course, for the traveling executive or the family on vacation; restaurants and bars for hotel guests as well as businessmen and women; meeting and banquet rooms for private parties, corporate board meetings, sales meetings and seminars, conventions, etc. Your potential list of contacts is endless from professional trade associations and major corporations, to small local businesses—every industry from advertising to sports, from soft drinks to travel agencies. Most hotels have files already established in these categories for you to work from, but you may still create new leads of your own. You become the marketing specialist for your hotel.

Let your personality and charm do the work, live up to your promises and the road from there is endless. Stay in sales and you will travel to cities all over the globe attending conferences and calling on prospects. Broaden your knowledge and you may move up into management. By then you will have experienced enough of the workings of other industries through your countless contacts that you will have your choice of opportunities, and in many cases, cities. Hotels, even in the furthest corners of the world, have sales departments!

If this career sounds enticing, I recommend that you get a broad educational background in the humanities with some specialized courses in English, journalism and public relations.

Writing good persuasive letters is a key to good sales. PR teaches you to second-guess situations and how to solve problems. Good PR in a hotel is essential.

If the college of your choice offers hotel sales management courses, of course they would be great training. But don't depend on them; the final test is selling yourself to the Hotel Manager and Director of Sales.

Be vivacious, sincere, anxious and well-groomed and you'll get your chance to prove yourself. Don't stop at merely leaving an application and a resume. Get in to see the working sales staff; ask for referrals. Find out about the local chapter of Hotel Sales Management Association and attend a monthly meeting to introduce yourself. You'll be entering a field ever-changing, meeting new faces every day and reaping the rewards of invaluable experience.

Felicia Kaplan—a lady with designs

INTERIOR DECORATION

BY
FELICIA HEBERT KAPLAN
Miss Teenage Alexandria, Louisiana 1963
Interior Decorator

Interior decoration is one of the very few professions you may pursue with or without the help of a college degree.

If you are uncertain about your ability to succeed in "decorating" as a career, you might evaluate your personal tastes in several ways. Do you co-ordinate clothes you purchase with those you already have in the closet? Then, do you take the time to mix and match to find the best outfit to fit the occasion?

Do your friends compliment your "knack" for looking great? Can you take constructive criticism and evaluate the reasons behind that criticism? If you can, you could be a serious candidate for the decorating profession. These qualities express an innate sense of good taste.

You may be lucky enough to attend college. Your high school and college counselor can advise you whether or not to take a design curriculum or a well-rounded liberal arts curriculum.

Either way your degree will "open many doors." You will do sample projects from start to finish and probably see several design operations and how they work. Your degree will be a big factor should you want to become a member of ASID (American Society of Interior Design). You would be known as an interior "designer."

But if circumstances are such that you are unable to do so, there are other ways to work your way into this challenging, exciting, lucrative field.

Your next step is practical experience. You might apply for a "desk" job, i.e. receptionist, in a smaller furniture store where you can help out in floor sales or possibly look towards a manufacturer for contacts. In either case, I feel actual floor sales experience will be one of the main factors in your success. Practical experience, without a degree, means that you will be known as an interior "decorator."

Even if you've got that "knack," it might take you a little longer to get started. Some people, you may think, have very strange ideas about design. But it's up to you to gain their confidence, then tactfully lead them to a good design.

Sometimes this takes a while and you must work with your client to assure a "design" which is totally acceptable. But when it does—when you're happy and they're happy—you're on your way.

PUBLIC RELATIONS— MEDIA BUYING

BY

BEVERLY A. MARTIN
Media Director
Hal Lawrence Agency
Palo Alto, California

To most any girl, a career as media director in an advertising agency sounds exciting and glamorous. And, it's true, it is. But there's a great deal of hard work along the way to success and recognition.

From the standpoint of figuring out complex media schedules that tell a client how to get the most for his advertising dollar, you must have a real affinity for numbers. The job is part research, part calculation, part juggling, and part gut feel. First, you must develop a fairly thorough understanding of what your client is selling and to whom. If you're lucky, it's luxury cruises, cute gadgets, or wigs (you get some free). If you're not so lucky, it's electronic digital display systems, flanges, and resistors (you wouldn't take any free).

Then you delve into what media (newspapers, magazines, TV, radio, billboards) best convey the client's selling message to the segment of the public he's trying to reach. If you're lucky, there are plenty of brains around to pick. If you're not, you lose your eyesight reading the fine print about who reads or sees or hears what where, at what age, and when.

Meanwhile, every salesman in the world (it seems) calls to tell you why his magazine is superior to all the rest and, if you're lucky, you get a lot of free lunches. If you're not, you just get a lot of free advice.

Eventually, you list the media you've selected, along with circulation information, issue dates, deadlines, frequency discounts, and costs. You add everything up, and you're finished.

Except, at this point you discover you've spent $100,000 more than what the client had in mind, and begin juggling, adding, and re-adding.

You finally finish and proudly show your work to the account executive who handles this particular client. And, after several more revisions, the final schedule is typed and ready for approval by the client. You may or may not participate in presenting the schedule to the client. If you're lucky, your presentations are made to clients who think you're highly intelligent and silver-tongued. If you're not, your statements are met with inscrutable looks and silence.

Somehow, though, schedules do get approved, and you finally order the ads you've recommended . . . and find all the mistakes in your schedule. You refigure, fight with newspapers over rates, wonder why your ad appeared upside-down, on the wrong Sunday, in the wrong section, and cry on the salesman's shoulder, your co-workers' shoulders, and various other shoulders, as available.

But, in the end, when it all goes right, and the client thinks you're great, it's all worth the effort.

SALESMANSHIP

BY
EBBY HALLIDAY
President
Ebby Halliday Realtors
Dallas, Texas

It has been said that nothing happens until someone *sells* something—and this is true.

It's also been said that selling is the purest example of the free enterprise system—and that a good salesperson is never without a job—and this is true.

It is the selling of products and services that maintain our country's standard of living, the highest in the world.

It is the mastered art of selling, combined with the conviction that what you are selling has value, that you are in fact adding to another person's comfort and desires, that brings self-satisfaction and unlimited monetary returns.

The fact that most selling is based upon a fee or commission on how much one sells gives the salesperson unlimited opportunity.

Whatever the product—real estate, insurance, fashions, gifts, cosmetics, heavy machinery, typewriters, computers, or airplanes—the basics of salesmanship are the same: product knowledge, self-discipline, integrity, enthusiasm, selling techniques, the right blend of ego and empathy, and good grooming and good health habits.

There has been much discussion as to whether a good salesman is "born" or whether the art of salesmanship can be acquired. My observations are that while it helps to be born with an outgoing personality and a good mixture of ego and empathy, *salesmanship can be acquired.*

Authorities on the "ingredients" of salesmanship agree that most good salespersons are made up of the right blend of empathy and ego drive.

Empathy is described as "the ability to sense the reactions of another human being, and the ability to relate to that individual."

Ego drive is the hunger to succeed, a need to close the sale, a strong sense of self, self-enhancement, and self-gratification.

These two important ingredients of successful salesmanship must be well balanced.

Add to these elements good education, articulate speech, product knowledge, self-discipline, absolute truth and integrity, enthusiasm, good grooming and constant updating of marketing techniques and it spells success for the young woman preparing herself for the wonderful world of salesmanship.

A college degree today is, with few exceptions, the passport to career opportunity. For a selling career or management of salespeople, a BBA degree (Bachelor of Business Administration) is needed, and an MBA (Master of Business Administration) highly desirable. In today's world, unless one has the education ticket, opportunities to show what one can do become more scarce.

Such subjects as marketing, finance, accounting, real estate, organizational behavior provided in college courses give a good solid background for going into a chosen field of marketing, of selling.

But, even before a young woman reaches college, preparation for selling, for exploring our country's private enterprise system can begin.

The Junior Achievement Program is available in many high schools, offering practical role-playing experience in business. This program has the support of local businessmen and women, of the Sales and Marketing Executives International—the business community that feels the importance of exposing young people to the free enterprise profit system that distinguishes the United States of America from all other countries in the world.

Contrary to what many teach, profit is not a dirty word. On the contrary, profit assures consumers of the availability of goods and services, both now and in the future. Profit is the ingredient that makes our economy work. To meet its responsibility to society, business *must* earn a profit. A salesperson who sells at a loss, wouldn't stay in business long. It's that simple.

Selling for profit is a challenging career for women, a career in which equality with the opposite sex is assured. There's never a question of "equal pay for equal work." A salesperson, regardless of sex, has the opportunity to sell as much as he or she can—to make as much money as he or she desires.

The only limitation on salesmanship, on the rich rewards of selling—is the limitation the salesperson puts on his or her own efforts.

Selling, as a career, and particularly as a career for women, offers new vistas, new freedoms, new challenges and earning plateaus for the young woman willing to prepare herself for a sales career—the young woman who is willing to trade the security of a nine-to-five salaried job for the unlimited and unlimiting career of commission selling.

URBAN AND REGIONAL PLANNING

BY
JEANNIE GRUBER
(Miss Teenage Miami, Florida 1966)
Senior Planner
East Central Regional Planning Council
Miami, Florida and
Member, State of Florida
Recreation Technical Advisory Committee

The word that best describes urban and regional planning is challenging. More than any other profession, planning has the responsibility for shaping the future growth and development of our country. The planner has a broad perspective of the world; he is concerned with people and the interrelationships of the physical, social and economic elements that make up their environment and the total ecosystem. He is charged with managing change, with setting goals for physical and social improvements, and with finding the best ways to achieve them. In today's complex, fast-paced world, that is a challenge indeed.

There is a wide range of planning specialties; most of them are applied at the city, county, regional, state and federal levels of government, and many of them are applied in the private planning consultant industry.

A partial list includes planning for: land use, development, transportation systems, public services and facilities, housing and urban design. There is also social planning, environmental planning, criminal justice planning, planning for the aged, health care planning and policy planning.

The daily activities of a planner are just as varied as the planning specialties. Planners are generally expected to conduct research, gather and analyze data, project and evaluate future conditions, determine objectives and draft plans with feasible recommendations and proposals.

Such plans vary according to specialty from a twenty-year highway plan, perhaps, to a plan for a whole new community, or to a neighborhood action plan for economic development. Planners often involve private citizens, government officials, businessmen, industrial interests and technical experts from many fields in the planning process.

Once a plan is completed, planners are often required to devise a pro-

Jeannie Gruber—makes decisions that affect thousands of people

gram for putting the plan into effect. An implementation program may involve meeting with and advising political decision makers such as mayors, city managers or county commissioners. It may mean attending legislative committee meetings and hearings to answer official questions or defend planning recommendations. It could include meeting with citizen groups or the media to provide public information about the plan.

It may also involve working with various governmental agencies to obtain approval or funding assistance for a project. It is not unusual for the planner to participate in the legislative process itself. He may be a member of a committee or an assistant in the formulation of planning-related bills or regulations such as zoning ordinances or land use control laws. The planner's workday is definitely demanding, but usually just as interesting and rewarding.

Educational requirements for a planning career vary, but a master's degree in planning or a related field (such as political science or geography, depending on the specialty) or a bachelor's degree plus experience in planning are generally preferred for most professional positions.

There are over seventy-five American colleges and universities offering planning programs, most at the master's degree level. About a dozen schools offer bachelor and doctorate degrees in planning fields. An undergraduate background in the social sciences, liberal arts or even business administration is usually adequate preparation to begin master's level study in planning.

How can you tell if you're suited to planning?

Besides the educational requirements, you need to have an active interest in people and in your environment. You need to be able to research, analyze and evaluate problems and know how to apply your knowledge and skills in practical situations.

You need to be able to communicate effectively and tactfully with people, both verbally and in writing. And of course, you need to know how to exercise sound judgment and common sense. Most important, to be successful as a planner, you need a desire and a sense of personal commitment to contribute toward a better tomorrow.

To get started on a career in planning, contact your high school or college counselor for a list of colleges and universities offering planning or planning-related programs, or write for information to:

>The American Society of Planning Officials
>Advisory Services
>1313 East 60th Street
>Chicago, Illinois 60637
>or
>The American Institute of Planners
>1776 Massachusetts Avenue, N.W.
>Washington, D.C. 20036

Young Women and Private Enterprise

One Part of Self-discovery

BY
JOHN BENJAMIN
President
Youth Enterprise Foundation

Not only does our nation have millions of people who are successful and independent entrepreneurs; even more, throughout our work force we have tens of millions more whose success lies in the degree to which they think and behave like entrepreneurs, taking initiative on their own to hone their skills, to own or gain access to capital and equipment, to take calculated risks, and—perhaps most important of all—to so live as to establish a firm foundation and reputation of positive values: credibility and respect drawing the support of others in the form of loans, investments, and other reinforcement. For no one succeeds alone.

Males do not have a corner on the market of discovering the exciting and rewarding aspects of private enterprise. There are virtually thousands of young women today between the ages of sixteen and thirty who have found access to our economic system and all its tools and resources. What makes this important is the fact that in our economy, to a degree unique in the world, self-control and self-mastery of one's economic success not only is possible but expected. A stimulating expectation that embraces both sexes more so now than before.

The areas of private enterprise for young women are as diversified as the interests, talents and vision of the person involved. Everyday, faith and trust is transformed into credit-worthiness by financial institutions and individuals to support sound, potential profit-making ideas. In most cases, these votes of confidence are alive and working well:

>**••Bea Harris, 24, owns an Arlington Heights, Illinois, franchise of a professional employment agency whose profits she tripled in eighteen months.

••Susan Wohlfarth, a former Maryland MISS TEENAGE AMERICA candidate, operates her own ballet school at the age of 21.

••Judith Miller, 25, a graduate of the University of Florida Law School, started a firm that does legal reserach by mail for lawyers anywhere.

••Renee Weiss, 22, a Philadelphian with creative design talents, founded a successful business which manufactures girl's tops for sale to boutiques and specialty shops.

Though there are many stories that can be related, involvement by young women in private enterprise does not guarantee instant career success. Education (in some cases this means on-the-job training), hard work and dedication to a business operation are necessary ingredients.

America's future well-being requires that many young people undertake to explore the frontiers of business initiative, just as others will be needed to pursue corporate careers or devote themselves to public service.

It is real-life examples similar to the ones cited here that will act as the most effective stimulus in inspiring young women to discover private enterprise. Their influence on the attitudes of others will have a sizable effect on the survival of private enterprise and the preservation of private initiative in our country. For this is the heart of a free society.

Self-discovery by young women through involvement in private enterprise has always been one key to individual development. I believe Robert Frost described this point best when he said,

> "Two roads diverged in a wood, and I—
> I took the one less traveled by,
> And that has made all the difference."

How to Apply for a Job

Excerpts from *CASH FOR COLLEGE*

BY
S. ROBERT FREEDE

S. Robert Freede's book, Cash for College, *includes a chapter on part-time work and summer jobs, as a means of contributing to the costs of education. Whether you're looking for a full-time opportunity or an after-school job, Mr. Freede offers some sound advice.*

He discusses where to begin your search—your school employment office (if there is one), state and private employment agencies, classified ads in your newspaper and employment offices in private companies.

He especially recommends personal contacts as one of the best ways of looking for employment, saying "Tell everybody. If they don't have something for you, they might know somebody who does."

Here is a reprint from the "Stalking the Honest Buck" chapter in Cash for College, *Prentice-Hall, Inc., Englewood Cliffs, N.J.*

Let's get down to basics. To get a job, you have to know where to look, you need a social security card, maybe working papers, maybe resumes. You have to know how to fill out an employment application to your own best advantage and how to win an interview. These are the refinements of the job search that your competitors won't have.

Before we begin, a very important bit of free advice. There are some people whom everybody points to as having made it in life—whatever the criteria for "making it" are. They are the men and women who seem to have been touched by the golden hand of fate. This is nonsense. Success never drops out of the sky. Successful people learned (or were taught) to get off their duffs early. They know what they want and they go after it. Nobody is going to rush up to you begging to give you a job. If you want a full-time, part-time or summer job, start your search early, do some pre-planning, then expend some energy to get it. That's the only sure way.

Once you've made the initial contact, your chances of getting a job will be greatly improved if you have a resume (reh-zoo-may)—a written account of your background and qualifications.

Nobody likes resumes. They're a pain to write, people hate to mail them to strangers and be judged by them. They're also a pain to read and handle. Surveys show that interviews are greatly preferred as indicators of prospective job applicants.

So why bother? Like it or not, resumes are a necessity today—an entrenched fact of employment life. The press of time and numbers of applicants makes it mandatory for some employers to use them to help weed out the grossly unsuitable. A resume is your calling card and advertisement. You'll need one when you answer help wanted ads, when you make the rounds of employment offices, when you go on an interview and to pass around among friends.

Your resume will be selling you when you're not there. An employer gets applicants like a dog gets fleas. The flea that gets noticed is the flea that bites hardest. Your problem is to bite hardest. Master the skill of composing a good resume, and it is a skill, and you have it one over the rest of swarm.

Don't ever turn out a resume that's going to get lost. Take some time with it. A resume should be more than a dry rehash of your jobs pumping gas at the station down the road, or clerking for old Mr. Brockenschlager. It should look better, brighter and "bitier" than the competition's. So here is what you do.

Take some time with your resume. Two or three days wouldn't be wasted thinking about it, thinking about yourself. Why should the boss hire you and not one of the other sad-faced multitude milling around the waiting room? That's your assignment. To compose a resume with some character in it. Now I know it's going to be difficult turning your membership in the French Club and two summers at Camp Go-Ba-Na-Nas into a sparkling piece of sales literature, but you can.

Don't approach your resume as just a collection of facts. Look at it as an advertisement for you. Say something (or present it in such a way) that shows how you are unique, a giant among fleas. The idea is to create a desire to hire you. You do this by telling the boss (or whoever does the hiring), not that "I am good." Everybody's good. But "Why I will benefit you and your company."

How? By being very smart and a little sneaky. Your resume will include outside activities, your interests, achievements (in and out of school) and your working experience. Just make sure that everything has a purpose. Search your background for valuable experiences, things that will make you appear to be a better person and a better employee.

You'll see how this works when we finish discussing the mechanics of the resume. Remember, there isn't one standard format. Use one that looks best for you.

Name and Address—sometimes called "self-identification" in books that cost more than this one. It goes on top of the page. If you need any more help on this one: a) quietly close this book, b) lay it down, c) walk away, d) enter politics.

Occupational or Job Objective (extremely optional for you at this point). If you are looking for a career job, include a short effective description of what you're after. To repeat—should be left out at this point for most of the people reading this book. Go directly to *Education.*

Education. Interchangeable with *Work Experience,* below, depending on which you feel is more important. For most people, work experience at this stage isn't much to turn on to, so education is listed first. Doesn't matter. What goes here is schools you've attended and are attending. You should also include special training, technical schools, correspondence courses and so forth. *Optional equipment.* Some people prefer to list specialized courses, school activities and achievements here instead of under a *Miscellaneous* heading at the end. It does beef up the resume and give it a logical flow. Includes dates and graduation information if any.

Work Experience. Use your judgment. Exhaustive completeness isn't necessary. But be honest. Employers sometimes check (this goes for everything on your resume). If there's an episode in your past you'd rather forget, forget it. But don't add something out of your dream world. Don't be ashamed of your first job experiences either. Everybody had to start someplace. Early work shows that you got off your duff and earned a buck when some kids were blowing up beachballs. Employers like the idea of work more than the work itself. The fact that you're going to be an architect may not mean much to the office manager who wants to hire you part-time, but the fact that you ran a mimeograph to help pay your way might impress him.

So you list your jobs, in reverse chronological order, dates, job title if you had one. You might want to explain your responsibilities and achievements, but at this stage in your life it's optional. Give the company name and city address. Forget the street, zip code and phone number. I also wouldn't put the reason for leaving. If anybody asks, you can tell them something.

Personal. All kinds of things can go here, at your discretion. You will usually give your birth date or age and your marital status. Other physical attributes are optional and, I find, embarrassing. Height, weight, condition of health, color of hair and eyes may be called for depending on what kind of job you're applying for. You can include the first three if you're going to be a wrestler or watchman or unloader. A model or receptionist would want to add the last two.

Miscellaneous. Sometimes included under *Personal,* but I put it here to pad out your resume. This is the section that will sell you, make you desirable, wanted. Awards and achievements show you to be the outstanding person you are. Team membership tells the employer that you are well-rounded and alert. Community activities, your commitment, hobbies, sometimes; if they show your wide range of intellect or interests. (Forget the stamp collection unless you want a job in a stamp store. Forget your darkroom unless you want a job in the field. Get the point?)

References. If you did all of the above and your resume still looks like you just came off the boat, you may want to include these. But nobody takes references seriously. After all, who's going to list a bad reference? You can say "references available on request" or something equally as sparkling.

A sample resume has been shown. It looks dumb, but it shows a lot—it tells the reader that you're smart but active and good with your hands. It shows a wide variety of interests (sports, electronics, language) and that you can work with people (clerk, counselor) and ideas (magazine, dean's list).

You sound pretty good, don't you?

Monty Kristo
162 East 88 Street
New York, New York 10028
748-0225

EDUCATION
New York University, New York, Majoring in Electrical Engineering with a minor in Physics.
Graduated Erasmus Hall H.S., Brooklyn, New York 1973.
Academic course

WORK EXPERIENCE

1972 to present Junior Analyst and crew chief with the Port Authority
Summer, 1972   Stock clerk, Peterson's Variety Store, New York City
Summer, 1971   Counselor, Camp Wee-Wee-No-No, Laxawaxen, Pennsylvania

PERSONAL

Born: 10/7/55   Height: 5'9"
Marital Status: Single Weight: 155 lbs.

MISCELLANEOUS

Member, NYU German Club
Member, NYU Soccer Team
High School Dean's List—two years
Writer, High School Paper
Member, High School Track Team
Reading Knowledge of German
Ham License

References can be furnished on request.

THE MECHANICS

After you've composed this epic tome about wonderful you, don't shoot it down with its appearance. Use a good quality paper—an off-color or tint will help make it stand out. Use standard 8 1/2" x 11", nothing larger unless you want to make a little fold-over booklet. Don't use erasable bond.

Type neatly, no mistakes, no erasing. If you plan on saturating the market, have it offset at the cheapest place you can find. They all do a good job. Always carry a couple around with you to pass among your contacts, old ladies in the street, friends and to give to interviewers.

NO-NOS

NEVER, NEVER:

- Send a carbon copy of your resume
- List everything that has ever happened to you in your lifetime

- Get too personal ("My right hand hurts when it's going to rain, my sister, Barbara, age 10 1/2, goes to Jefferson J.H.S., my father died in 1969, my aunt sees visions." Don't laugh, it happens)
- Run down a former boss
- Make false or rash statements
- Use abbreviations, slang, slogans, poor English, the word "etc."
- Get political, ideological, philosophical ("I want this job because the world needs new blood, a person of my vision" See *Cover Letter*.)
- Oversell

BUT, do try to slant the resume to the job you're looking for. Play up those elements in your background that would make you, indeed, ideally suited for the job.

THE COVER LETTER OR LETTER OF APPLICATION

There may come a time when you'll have to write a very important letter, one that sells you as a product. It will either be a letter of application for a job, or a letter covering your resume. There are two schools of thought about which to use. One that says the resume should do your talking, and the cover letter merely something to introduce it, maybe highlighting a few important points. Some experts think that a good letter of application can be a better salesman than a resume. I go for the former.

In the simple cover letter, all you do is mention the job applied for, where you heard about it and mention a few background notes related to the job at hand. That's it.

The more ambitious letter follows the same rules as a resume, but in narrative form. Start off by mentioning the job and how you heard about the opening. Give a little background—school, activities and achievements. Then jobs. Tell why you think you'll be right for the position. End by requesting an interview.

Do I have to tell you to make it good? Or to use good paper, type neatly, be precise in spelling and grammar?

Use straightforward language, be brief and personal.

A rule of thumb. If you need more than one page, use a resume, if your resume is short, use a letter.

THE EMPLOYMENT APPLICATION

Okay, you wowed 'em downtown with your neatly typed and excitingly executed resume and you get a call/letter asking you to come for an interview. You're getting there!

First thing that happens when you walk in the office (a cluttered one room job off the workshop, or a sumptuous corporate affair in the Employee Relations Department) is you identify yourself and tell the receptionist you have an appointment with Mr. Bigtime. She will probably hand you an employment application.

"But, I have a resume," you say.

She'll give you a funny look. "That's okay, fill it out anyway." You fill it out anyway and curse me for making you write a resume. Wrong. Resumes are for interviewers, forms are for files and IBM machines, and for personnel records and information like social security and health insurance and like that.

You will be given an application form. Filling it out is more important to you than you might imagine. Believe it or not, a sloppy employment application is one of the major reasons for interviewers to reject job applicants. So, ask if you can take it home. Whether you do or not, be neat and accurate. Don't erase if you can avoid it.

Most of the questions will have been answered by your resume. A few things worth mentioning. Read over the questionnaire. Where they ask for an address, there are usually two called for—permanent and temporary. Give an address where you are living or from where mail will be forwarded. The telephone number should also be one where you'll be readily reached.

Position Desired. You will usually have a job in mind, but don't be hasty in downgrading yourself—don't say "clerical work" when you want to be a typist or secretary, or "general work" when you want to drive a car or be a lab assistant.

Driver's License. Sometimes important to have.

Health, height, weight. Here it's not optional. If you do have a physical glitch—anything from an allergy to a funny back that might affect the kind of job you might get—it would be wise to put it here. First of all, it would be downright unhealthy for you if they did give you an unsuitable job; second, many companies give physicals to new employees, and if they find you lied, you could be fired; third, there might be other jobs available that they will offer—maybe even something better.

Place of birth, date of birth, religion, age, previous arrest record. It is illegal to ask all of these questions under the Equal Employment Opportunity Law. But don't leave them blank. If you do feel strongly about any one of these questions, try not answering and see what happens. Sometimes the interviewer couldn't care less and is just using old forms. If they make an issue, your own conscience will tell you, in a squeaky little voice, what's more important—money or principles. When they ask for place of birth, they only want city and state.

School Standing. It is definitely in bad taste to say top 100 percent. If your grades were lukewarm, stress your past job experience, any achievements and other activities while in college.

The rest is self-explanatory. The suggestions I made about past employment, hobbies and the rest are the same as for the resume.

Sign your name, look it over, attach a copy of your resume if you have one. You are now ready to embark on one of man's most adventuresome, exciting, pleasant, enjoyable recreations—*The Interview.*

HOW TO WIN INTERVIEWERS AND INFLUENCE BOSSES

Whole books, whole libraries have been written about The Employment Interview. Not to scare you off, it is *the* most crucial part of the job-hunting process. One survey concluded that the interview counts for 85 percent of the decision whether to hire or not. The other 15 percent went to qualifications. Just as there are tricks to interviewing, there are tricks to being interviewed. Once you have the general idea, interviewing can be fun. It's like a game—you mentally check off all the tricks the interviewer is using and parry them to your advantage.

Why does business put through this modern day tribal initiation ceremony? Obviously to make a judgment—they want to see what kind of person you are, if you'll fit in productively with their company. This is no simple task, as you'll see later. Secondarily, the interviewer is also disseminating information, or he should be. After your discussion, you might very well not like what they have to offer and decide they are not for you. Life is a two-way street.

If you are asked for an interview, it means you have already passed some kind of preliminary screening out. The meeting is the last step in the process. Also, it's a step that has been trod countless times before. Everybody has been interviewed, everybody goes through the same nervousness, same feelings of intimidation and inferiority, everybody has blown interviews. Also remember that there will be better applicants than you and worse applications, but you are unique. Something about you might pluck a responsive chord. Twang, employment!

Preparation for an interview is serious business. As soon as you know an interview is coming up, do some homework. Find out a little about the company, if you can. The Better Business Bureau and Chamber of Commerce may help. This knowledge can be craftily woven into the conversation by asking pertinent questions.

Here are a list of things to do if you want the best possible odds in your favor.

Arrive on Time. Nothing will blackball you faster than sauntering in late for an appointment. Allow extra time for a slow train, earthquake or flat tire. Best is five minutes early, it gives you a chance to settle down. Don't get there too early, which is almost as bad as too late. If an emergency does prevent you from showing, an extreme emergency, call immediately. You should be given another appointment. If you are kept waiting, you can review your resume, read the company's annual report, and look like you're having a marvelous time. Don't, repeat, don't complain to the interviewer once you get in the office.

Look sharp. Neatness definitely counts. Unless you're looking for a job in a grease pit or driving a team of oxen, appearance is very important. Taste and cleanliness are the keys. Nothing bizarre in clothes or hairstyle. Even if you're only trying out for a messenger's job, you want to be remembered positively.

Know Thyself. Don't go into an interview without any notion of what you are going to say. Know your qualifications, know what job you are looking for.

Watch your behavior. Your mannerisms are very important. The interviewer is looking to see how you handle yourself. Of course you'll be nervous—everybody is. But don't fall apart. The interviewer really likes people, that's why he's into his job. He's just trying to find the best applicant for the one that's open. And that's you, right? Just don't be overly aggressive, ill-mannered, cynical, over-talkative. They hate that. Pushiness is going to get you nowhere fast.

AN INTERVIEWEE'S CHECKLIST

Be prompt, be neat
Don't chew gum
Wait to be shown a seat
Wait to be offered a handshake

Let the interviewer guide the interview
Look at him straight in the eye
Don't boast, don't talk yourself down, either
Don't mumble
Don't smoke (even if offered)
Expect questions like
   "Why do you want to work for this company?"
   "What are your life's goals?"
   "What kind of salary do you want?" (Ask for the "standard")
   "How did you like your last job?" (Don't knock former employers)
Try to relax
Don't argue
Ask sensible questions about the company and the job
Look interested, alert, enthusiastic even
Listen attentively
Watch for a sign that the interview is over
Thank the interviewer for his time
Express your desire for the job
And when you get home, write a letter thanking the interviewer and expressing your interest. It's a good move.

Recommended Reading: Cash for College, Prentice-Hall, Inc., Englewood Cliffs, N.J. 07632.

Personal Guidelines for Success in Your Career

Edited from material published by
Western Temporary Services, Inc.,
Reprinted with permission.

Job success means different things to different people; it may be a high-paying salary or an impressive title. Whatever it means to you, success comes through hard work, dedication and some common sense principles.

The guidelines presented here for career success which apply to most jobs are based on the collective experiences of over 50,000 persons.

To begin with, it's a good idea to maintain a positive attitude at all times. Try to think in terms of how things *can* be done, not why they *cannot* be done.

Avoidance of office "politics" is one of the wisest decisions you can make. At best, politics can lose your job for you.

This goes hand in hand with the suggestion that you should never discuss your salary with your co-workers. Such discussions can only pollute a good working atmosphere.

Remember that you have two "bosses" to please: your company and your company's customers. Even if you're not directly involved with the customer, your job does affect the quality of your company's product or service.

Getting along with your fellow workers not only makes for a more pleasant atmosphere, but cooperation also leads to a higher quality of product or service. Try to be helpful to your co-workers and customers alike. Courtesy, enthusiasm, and cooperation all are as contagious and beneficial on the job as they are after hours.

A number of basic ways to enhance your job success opportunities should be observed.

Be prompt. Observe company working hours—and this includes lunch hours.

Dress appropriately for your job. While it's true that most companies are more relaxed about dress than in the past, it's important that your clothes don't interfere with your job. For example, the higher heels currently in fashion for men might be dangerous for an industrial worker; jeans and a casual shirt are not right for a receptionist.

Keep a clean "house." This is important for both men and women, and applies to a place on the assembly line as much as a desk in the office or school. It means, simply, that your responsibilities include keeping your area of operation in order—whatever it may be.

When you're at work, work. While this seems simple, many working hours are lost—and therefore much money is lost—by employees socializing on the job or avoiding their responsibilities in other ways. As noted earlier, modern businesses have become far more relaxed than in the past—but they still insist that the employee get his or her work done.

There are several guidelines to remember when trying to improve your job performance and increase your efficiency, which can lead to advancement in your career. If you want to suggest an improvement in the overall company procedure study your idea carefully, and try to look at it from your employer's viewpoint. If you still believe the company would benefit from a change, present your ideas tastefully and tactfully. Initiative tempered with tact is a valued quality in employees.

Learn to face problems on the job—they have a way of growing bigger the longer they're ignored.

Try to avoid making mistakes. Correct those you make and learn from your experience. If your supervisor confronts you with your mistake, don't waste his time and yours with excuses. The best way to handle this situation is simply to admit your error, apologize and correct it.

Get things done. One good way to improve your "get things done" quotient is to set daily goals for yourself: tackle the hardest work first, then go on to easier tasks.

Finish the work you start. It's not good practice to begin work on a project and then leave the finishing to others. It deprives you of the good feeling of accomplishment and is unfair to your co-workers.

Be adaptable. The employee who says, "But we never did it that way before," seems afraid of change and new ideas and limits his own job success.

If your work is confidential in nature, be mature enough to keep it confidential. The need to show off by discussing "the inside dope" or information "straight from the horse's mouth" is childish and has no place in the working world.

Remember to keep calm under pressure. Being able to maintain poise and self-control in difficult situations will help you get a promotion when a new job opens.

These guidelines are offered only as suggestions which can help you succeed on your first job. As you grow in business experience, you will want to adapt these guidelines to your own career situations. An important thing to remember is that most of your adult activities will be spent on the job. It's up to you to make a success of it.

ADVENTURE V

Making Your Education a Lifetime Experience

Let's Talk About You—Your Abilities, Your Goals, and Your Future

BY
O'NEIL HARRIS
Director—Vocational Education
Arlington Public Schools
Arlington, Texas

Will you allow me just a few minutes of your time to chat about you, your abilities, your goals and your job. You will? Great! Let's get along with it.

You are an important person for many reasons, one of the more important being that you are the only one like you in the world. Your particular hereditary characteristics (hair, eyes, height, temperament, abilities, etc.) and experiences (at home, school, with friends, alone, etc.) have been blended to create the only exact model like you in the world. This makes you extra special. Each of us do have many things in common with others which allows us to develop mutual understandings, friendships and agreements as a part of the human race. We need each other but always remember that you are the only one that can make your exact contributions to the world.

Now that we have established how valuable you really are, let's focus a little closer on your abilities which are sometimes called talents. Either indicates a quality in you which implies you are able to do something and usually quite well. An interesting thing about abilities is that some are natural and some are acquired. What are your abilities? What are the things which you do well? Some of these you can identify easily such as the ability to take things apart and put them together (mechanical); to run fast (physical); the talent to put people at ease in your presence (social). Other abilities may be harder for you to identify and will require conferences with skilled people such as your parents, counselors, teachers and friends to get a better understanding of your abilities. As you better understand your abilities, you begin the process of saying to yourself, "These abilities are mine and these are things I would like to do with them." Would you believe that this is known as setting goals?

You are already aware of the fact that you will have many goals in your life. All of them will be important to you or else you would not have them as goals that you are willing to work to achieve. Some of your goals will be short term while others will take months or even years to reach. The long-term goals may even change as you have additional experiences. A few words here for you to think about. You take the time to know yourself and to determine what are the really important things in your life, and then set goals which will help you to do the really important things in your life. Arrange them in your mind as to their importance and then plan and do the things necessary to have the satisfaction of achieving them. Your goals will be in many areas; some will be personal known only to yourself, others will be more general in nature. One goal that you will spend a considerable amount of time exploring will be the choices for selecting your career goal. This career goal should be to select a job that will be satisfying to you. A job that will be one that you look forward to doing because you enjoy doing the things which the job requires. Let's spend the next few minutes looking at jobs.

The basic definition of a job is something which needs to be done and requires some type or types of skills, knowledge, physical strength, etc. in order to perform satisfactorily. It is something which a person can do for themselves or something which the person or company cannot or will not do themselves and wants done to the extent that they are willing to pay someone to do it for them. To say it another way is that an employer is looking for a person to do a job for them which requires certain skills, knowledge or both. Where can you get the skills, knowledge or both necessary to get the job that you are interested in holding? Some jobs require a college degree (four or more years of formal education above high school), such as doctors, teachers, lawyers, F.B.I. agents, dentists, nurses, etc. Other jobs require special technical, paraprofessional, or apprenticeship training (usually one to three years of formal training and/or on-the-job training above high school) which include dental hygienists, electronic technicians, law enforcement, X-ray technologists.

The majority of jobs can be entered with a high school education and offer many opportunities for advancement to those who apply themselves and continue to study and learn more about their job and the business or industry as a whole. Since high school is the last chance that you will have to get a free education, I would urge you to look at the courses available and select the very best ones to help you meet your goals. As you consider your selections let me suggest that you look at the vocational programs available in your school or area.

Before you veto this suggestion let's examine and take that veto apart. The *V* can represent the vocational teacher who is qualified. This person is qualified with years of experience in business, industry or profession that she or he teaches and will help you develop your skills and knowledge for the job you want.

The *E* can represent the experience that you can gain by being in the vocational program you select. When you complete your education and are applying for your first full-time job, you will have the advantage over many applicants your age by being able to list skills, experience, training, and references because of your vocational training.

The *T* can indicate the training you can receive in a vocational program designed to work with you as an individual to develop salable skills in the job that you have chosen to meet your goals. This training begins with basic skills required for your job, but it increases in its specialization as you determine your needs.

The *O* must represent the opportunities available to you to begin to meet the goals that you set for yourself. One opportunity is to begin developing your own potential for the career that you believe you will find pleasure in preparing to do and doing. Another opportunity is being able to find out if the career really is what you believe it to be or if you need to reevaluate your career goals.

I hope that now you feel that instead of a VETO you will see that the same letters can be used to spell VOTE which could represent *V*ocational *O*pportunities for *T*raining *E*xperiences. I would like to encourage you to talk with a vocational teacher in the area of your career goal to get more information, then make a decision that is best for you. It is possible for you, through a vocational program, to develop salable skills for beginning your career immediately after high school. You can also use these skills to partially or completely pay for additional education and training at a technical level or at a college or university. Best of all you can add worthwhile experiences to yourself on the way to developing your goals. Good luck!

Movin' On Up

High School Preparations for College

BY
Whitmer High School Guidance Department
BARBARA STEWART, Director
GERALDINE M. STIEFEL, Counselor

Whitmer High School is one of the largest in the United States. Among the many outstanding Whitmer graduates is Karen Petersen, MISS TEENAGE AMERICA 1975.

We're grateful that the Guidance Department there has agreed to share with you some of the advice they once offered Karen.

Is college in your future? Now that you are in high school, you are faced with making decisions about your future. This is no simple task; it will involve knowing yourself and being aware of career choices, which will determine your course of study in high school. During your high school years, you will need to know more about the college entrance tests, choosing a college, college admissions procedures and financial aid.

What is best for you? Many things must be considered in planning your future. Where do your interests lie? Do your strengths in aptitude with your interest? Are your natural talents being considered? Are you aware of the effort needed to get good grades? What are your financial limitations? Will a two-year or four-year college program best fit your needs?

Career Choice. Many students are overly concerned because they do not know what they want to "be" by the time they are sophomores. It is not necessary to make a final vocational choice at an early age. Students often enter a university and take a variety of courses before choosing a major. However, the sophomore year is a good time to begin thinking of yourself in terms of a career. You might ask yourself:

Do I like working closely with people?
Would I like to deal with data and things?
Do I want to travel?
How many hours am I willing to put into a job?
What salary do I see necessary for the way I want to live?

Will I be happy doing this kind of work?

Am I capable of accomplishing the training for this kind of work?

As you seek answers to these questions, you might talk to people employed in various occupations and visit or tour places that hire workers in your fields of interests. Also, read about occupations—the guidance department has information about most jobs.

College Choice. Perhaps we should pause here to explain that it is acceptable to refer to a university as college, but a university is actually an institution made up of various colleges: College of Education, College of Engineering, College of Medicine, etc. For practical purposes we will use the term college to represent university as well as the singular college institution.

The junior year is a good time to investigate colleges and to make preliminary choices. It is advisable to narrow choices down to three by the beginning of your senior year for two practical reasons: many universities close admissions at an early date because of limited housing, and most colleges require an application fee, often non-refundable.

Just as you ask yourself questions about career choices, you should give serious thought to college selection.

Do I see myself as part of a large university?

Do I want to go to another state or city?

Can I afford a private college?

Does the college offer the curriculum for my career choice?

Do I meet the entrance requirements?

Visits to college campuses are welcomed and may help you make your decision. It is advisable to write to the Director of Admissions in advance to ensure the most benefit from your visit.

High School Courses. In general the academic requirements or recommendations for most colleges include:

- 4 years of English
- 2-4 years of Math
- 2-3 years of Science
- 2 years of Social Studies
- Foreign language may or may not be required

Keep in mind that particular majors may have specific requirements, such as engineering requires four years of math. It is also important that you find out the specific requirements for the college of your choice.

Testing. College testing primarily begins by taking the PSAT/NMSQT (Preliminary Scholastic Aptitude Test/National Merit Scholarship Qualifying Test). This is an important test because it provides experience for taking the required college tests and the PSAT test results are used to determine the National Merit Scholarship winners.

The two most widely used tests for college admissions are the SAT (Scholastic Aptitude Test) and the ACT (American College Test). It is suggested that they be taken in the spring of the junior year. The results of these tests can be used to help you make wise decisions. They may identify your strengths and weaknesses. Colleges use the test scores as an aid in acceptance or placement.

If you have made a specific college selection, you should check the college catalog to be sure which test is needed. If you have not decided on a particular college, you may wish to take both the SAT and ACT.

How to Apply. Write to the Director of Admissions for your college application and catalog.

Financial Aid. Request an application for financial aid at the time you write for an application for admission to the college of your choice. Also, obtain the PCS (Parent's Confidential Statement), FFS (Family Financial Statement), BEOG (Basic Educational Opportunity Grants, a federal program application) and a state grant application, if your state has one, from your high school guidance department. Inquire about scholarships that may be offered by your parent's place of employment, or organizations they may be affiliated with. Your church may also offer financial aid. Generally, however, most financial aid will come from the college in the form of scholarships, grants, loans and work-study arrangements, which will be determined on the basis of the PCS or FFS.

CHECK LIST

SOPHOMORE YEAR

_____Get acquainted with your counselor

_____Discuss your thoughts and plans for the future, your interests, abilities and achievement with your parents and counselor.

_____Read the occupational and vocational information found in the guidance department.

_____Take those courses which are a part of the basic requirements for college.

JUNIOR YEAR

Fall

_____Begin making preliminary college selections. Consider location, size, cost, requirements, etc. Send for or read the catalogs.

_____Attend the conferences of college representatives when they visit your school if you are interested in that particular college.

_____Take the PSAT/NMSQT (Preliminary Scholastic Aptitude Test/National Merit Scholarship Qualifying Test) given in October.

Winter

_____Attend any college night programs offered.

Spring

_____Take the SAT and/or ACT tests (if need for your college choice). This (SAT) early testing allows you to retake the test in the senior year if necessary.

_____Make plans to visit college campuses during the summer.

SENIOR YEAR

Fall

_____Write for applications for admission and for financial aid (if desired) to the colleges of your choice. Write to Director of Admissions and Director of Financial Aid.

_____Prepare the application received (write for them in early fall). Check deadlines and application fees.

_____Give the completed application form to your counselor for forwarding to the college.

_____Check test dates and take the ACT or SAT if necessary.

Winter

_____Concentrate on your studies while waiting for college decisions.

Spring

_____Notifications of college acceptance or non-acceptance should arrive. Withdraw other applications when you make your final decision.

_____Notify your counselor of your decisions.

College Prospecting

BY
UNIVERSITY OF ROCHESTER,
Admissions Office
Rochester, New York

Despite the increase in gas prices, the trend toward combining the annual family vacation trip with a spot of college prospecting is expected to continue apace this summer. If you plan to join this season's campus-bound tourist, the tips suggested by the University of Rochester Admission Office may be helpful.

Before deciding on your college-tour itinerary, ask one of your school's guidance counselors for suggestions. The counselor's recommendations will help to guide you to the kind of college that best meets your needs and interests.

Remember that summer is a busy season at the Admission Office. That means it's wise to make an advance appointment. Occasionally, colleges can provide low-cost accommodations in the dorms during the summer, so be sure to inquire about the possibility of arranging an overnight stay on campus when making your appointment for an interview.

Dress comfortably. Admission officers are human; they recognize that it's hard to look spic and span after a long, hot auto trip with the family small fry in tow.

Don't hesitate to bring your parents. It's important for them to get a realistic impression of each college, too.

Don't be afraid to ask an admission counselor whether your qualifications are such as to make it worthwhile to file a formal application. It's important, of course, that you provide reasonably accurate information on your high school performance to date and on any aptitude or achievement test scores your school may provide. (The more information you bring, the more realistic an admission officer can be about your chances for admission.)

If you're a high school freshman or sophomore, you may find it helpful to tour campuses and pick up general admission and financial aid information this summer. However, it's better to wait until later in your high school career to schedule a formal admission interview. Admission officers find that it is a little early for a high school sophomore to provide objective data—such as College Board scores, comprehensive high school records, class rank—that enable the counselor to give the prospective student an estimate of his or her chances of acceptance.

Remember that on many campuses the summertime student body is different in composition from the regular student roster. For example, universities run a number of workshops, institutes, and special summer programs that are attended by teachers and other professional people as well as by undergraduate and graduate students from other colleges.

Don't try to cover too many colleges during a single trip. You'll be too rushed to get more than a fuzzy idea of each campus—and you and your family certainly won't have much of a vacation!

If you have time, take in some of the special events on campus. With many colleges operating full-steam-ahead throughout most of the summer, you're likely to find summer theatres, library and art exhibits, concerts, special lectures, and sports events listed on the campus calendar. You and your family will enjoy them—and they'll help to give you a more complete picture of college life.

After each visit, make some notes on your reactions to the college. These can be extremely useful when you talk over your college plans with your school guidance counselor next fall.

Follow up your trip by talking with students in your area who attend the colleges you've visited. Summer is a good time to find some of them at home and to get their firsthand reactions to campus life. Alumni in your area will be glad to answer your questions, too.

If your tour raises some additional questions, don't hesitate to write for additional information. But it's wise to check first to see whether such information may be provided in the catalogs and other literature which you received at each admission office during your visit.

MAKING THE MOST OF YOUR CAMPUS VISIT

Visiting prospective colleges can be a big help in selecting the right college. Its value is in providing a firsthand impression for you and your family: about people, programs, facilities for living and learning.

The admissions interview, which is usually a part of the campus visit, deserves a few special comments. Although the importance of an interview varies from college to college, it is probably fair to say that the interview does not count as much in making admissions decisions as most applicants and their parents and counselors think.

Your presence on the campus—and your readiness to talk about yourself and your college plans and to seek information about the "rightness" of the college for you—are important indications of your serious interest in the college. Then, too, the exchange of information and the impressions gained on both sides—yours and the college's—during the interview should be meaningful. It is doubtful, however, that the decision on your admission will turn on what takes places during an interview. So, take the interview seriously but don't overrate its importance.

Before you start thinking about visiting *any* college, some "homework" is in order. The first step is to begin looking through your school's collection of college reference materials. You'll want to become acquainted with *Lovejoy's College Guide* and the *College Board Handbook*, for example. Perhaps you'll want to buy a paperback copy of one of these reference works for home browsing. And you'll certainly want to start thinking about the *kind* of institution that interests you: large or small, four-year or two-year, coeducational or otherwise.

Talk over your preliminary ideas about college with your family and your school guidance counselor. Your counselor will be glad to suggest some colleges for your consideration.

Write to several colleges that seem to meet your general needs, interests, and pocketbook. You'll find that a college's general catalog usually contains information on its programs, admissions requirements, finances, and so forth. But if you're writing to a large university (one that has several schools and colleges), better specify the particular college that interests you.

Be sure and study the catalogs. Try to evaluate each institution in terms of your own interests and aptitudes.

Narrow your list of prospective colleges to a half-dozen. Write to your three or four top choices and ask for an appointment to visit each of them. Because thousands of prospective students are touring the nation's campuses these days, requests for interviews mount up. As a result, it is usually important to write for an appointment well in advance (two or three weeks is none too early) of your proposed visit. A thoughtful and helpful step is to suggest a couple of acceptable dates and times. By so doing you will increase your chances for landing a mutually convenient spot in the schedule. You may find that some colleges are using group discussions rather than individual discussions in order to meet the heavy demand for appointments. In some cases, colleges do not make specific appointments; students are seen as time permits.

To save time and money, you'll probably try to include colleges in the same geographic area on the same trip. If an overnight stay is involved, be sure to make reservations considerably in advance (colleges can usually recommend reasonable accommodations in their areas).

Just before your visit re-read the catalog, especially the sections on admission requirements, tuition and scholarship data, and programs of study.

Also look back over your high school record so that you can answer general questions about your academic performance in high school, and your scores on standardized tests such as the Scholastic Aptitude Tests.

Several tips to keep in mind once you make your visit to campus are to always be prompt, allow enough time to get the "feel" of the campus, pick up the forms that you will need (application form, scholarship blank and a map). Don't hesitate to ask questions—this includes discussing finances, scholarship possibilities, work opportunities, and even estimates of your chances for admission.

Some musts to include in your campus tour are the college library, academic facilities, living quarters, and the students you will be in association with.

In the library, even a ten-minute visit can tell you something about the size and scope of its collections, study facilities, and specialized areas such as "listening rooms," etc.

To get an idea of the academic facilities try to sit in on a class or seminar. If you're a future science or engineering major, try to visit a typical undergraduate laboratory; if languages are your specialty, you may be interested in seeing the language labs.

Living quarters available on campus will be of prime concern to you as an incoming student. Try to visit a typical campus residence, dining hall, student lounge and recreation area. If there are fraternity or sorority houses on campus, you may want to see one of these, too.

It's very important to get some idea of the kind of people you'll live and work with on campus. If a student guide accompanies you on your tour, feel free to ask him or her about any aspect of college life. Your guide will welcome some clues about your interests—sports, dramatics, debate, and so forth—and may include a visit to the headquarters for such activities if time permits.

Evaluation of your visitation is necessary after you leave the campus or when you return home.

Make some notes on your reactions to the college; they'll be useful later on when you're trying to evaluate various institutions, and they may suggest some additional points for discussion with your guidance counselors or parents.

If you're definitely interested in the college, follow through by filing your formal application as soon as possible. If you're not interested, don't consider your visit a waste of time; chances are you'll have learned a lot—about the kind of college you *do* want, and about what other colleges are likely to expect of *you*.

In summary we can say to you that visiting a campus can be a valuable guide for the college bound. By doing some "homework" ahead of time—and some realistic evaluation afterward—you can make the most of this experience.

Good luck!

"I Wish I'd Known That Before I Came to College"

Some Tips for Tomorrow's College Students

From Freshmen
at the University of Rochester
Rochester, New York

College admissions experts say that today's college freshmen are better prepared for campus life than their predecessors, that guidance counselors in secondary schools across the nation are doing an increasingly effective job of advising the college bound. Nevertheless, the jump from high school to college will always be a big one, and many a freshman will still be saying, "I wish I'd known *that* before I came to college" sometime during the first year on campus.

With this in mind, some University of Rochester freshmen were asked what—if anything—they "wish they'd known" before coming to Rochester. Their off-the-cuff comments on topics ranging from academics to social life offer some helpful hints for prospective college students. Incidentally, most of the group interviewed hold scholarships and were high-ranking students in high school; better than four out of five of the University's freshmen come from the top fifth of their high school graduating classes. Here's what they said:

Overwhelmingly, the major "wish I'd known" was followed by the words "how to study" or "how to organize my time." Even those who said they personally had had little difficulty along such lines rated poor study habits or lack of organization as the main problem for freshmen.

Said a pretty blonde Texan, a national science scholarship winner: "At home I didn't have to study to get good marks, so there wasn't much incentive to put forth my best. Here you have the incentive because there are so many bright kids."

Along with a number of other students she confessed to initial bewilderment with the typical college lectures, commenting, "I wish I'd had more experience with lecture-type classes before I came to college. At first, everything seemed to happen so fast during the lectures and, of course, I wasn't able to interrupt to ask questions if I missed something. Even in the smaller classes, I was afraid to ask questions—afraid of sounding silly—with all those geniuses around me."

Her advice to upcoming frosh: "Try to set up a schedule (but be sure to leave some time to relax). Remember that your class and study schedule at college won't be as rigid as in high school—we don't actually have to go to class, for example, so long as we do our work. Also, we get assignments in large batches instead of having to turn in work every day or so, as in high school. As a result, there's a tendency at first to let things slide until the last minute—and then you find you can't possibly get everything done in time. Making and sticking to a schedule seems to be the best answer for me."

To the wish-I'd-learned-how-to-study theme, an upstate New York coed added: "I wish I'd learned how to read for a college course. For the first quarter of the year, I didn't know what I was looking for in my reading. I thought I had to know every fact I read, which was impossible. Then I got a feeling for what was important."

A Pennsylvania girl put it even more bluntly: "I wish I hadn't thought I'd worked in high school—I never knew what studying really was before I left home. And I wish I'd had some high school experience with lecture-type classes—this business of note-taking is really an art."

Her advice: "Learn to budget your time. Be prepared for the fact that it may take a while to learn what you can and can't fit in. Don't panic—after a while you'll find your own way of balancing your activities—but it does take time and effort—and some willpower.

Another student mused: "You have to remember that you're not just learning facts; you're learning how to analyze, how to be intelligently critical. You learn that knowledge is an unending process . . . that you'll never know all there is to know about everything!"

Only a few of the students interviewed felt that their high school had been seriously lacking in preparing them for college. A boy from a small New England town said he wished he'd had "both better teachers and better courses in high school." His advice to other small town youngsters: "Get used to reading a lot on your own, and train yourself to read quickly. Learn to analyze and constantly try to put your reading in perspective and to seek answers for yourself."

And, for other small town or rural students who may be leaving home for the first time, he urged: "Be prepared for the impact of difference—different ideas, different kinds of people." Admitting that he still found some of his "big city" classmates "overly sophisticated," he advised youngsters from small homogeneous communities to try to get away from cliques in high school because "you're going to have to get used to a lot of different people in college." Observing that small town life can have a "repressive influence," he pointed out that "at college, you're freer to be yourself. Being able to develop your talents freely brings a greater understanding of your capacities and with it a greater stimulus to do more and better."

Again on the topic of "meeting people with different ideas," a coed from a small city remarked: "I wasn't so much upset by the diversity of views I encountered at college as by the bluntness with which they often are expressed."

Another boy—from a rural area—commented that even the so-called "accelerated" courses at his high school had not been particularly effective, and that he had had to learn to "look at the forest instead of the trees" in his college studies. For him, the biggest change at college was "from the conservative ideal of a small town to a more liberal attitude," which, he noted, "could be adopted just as unthinkingly as a more conservative one." His advice: "Define your personal and moral values, but keep your ideas open to intelligent change."

On the other hand, a boy from metropolitan New Jersey found college "a more protected environment than big city life, a much more homogeneous community than the city high school I came from. In my school, many of the kids weren't going on to college, a lot of them didn't have any idea what they really wanted to do when they got out of school—here everyone seems to have a goal."

The problem of going from the "top of the heap" in high school to a community where "most of the kids are at least as good as I am and a great many are better" was frankly discussed by a number of students. Commented a scholarship holder from Wilmington, Delaware: "I wish I'd realized how tough the competition was going to be. Even though I knew the University of Rochester is a highly rated college, I didn't have any idea of what I'd be up against academically. Fortunately, I'd taken a how-to-study course in high school. I don't mean it worked miracles, but it helped me to organize my time and gave me confidence in my ability to study efficiently."

His advice: "Take advantage of any courses that will help you to acquire effective study habits. The course I took gave me some ground rules that tided me over until I learned to pace myself in handling the work load at college."

Another boy admitted, that "It's hard to realize you're not in the top group. At home, I was in the top tenth of my class; here I'm in the top two-fifths—maybe!"

Unlike earlier college generations, many of these students had had opportunities to take "enriched" or "accelerated" or "advanced standing" courses in high school. Unanimously, those who had taken such courses urged prospective freshmen to do likewise. Those for whom special courses were not available felt they had missed out on a valuable experience. One girl whose older sister and brother also had attended the University of Rochester said she believed the emphasis on "acceleration and enrichment" courses in her high school had given her a big advantage over her older siblings, who had had far less opportunity for such work before college.

One coed, who had taken an "enrichment" course for advanced high school pupils given by students at a nearby college, said that "such experiences, if they did nothing more, helped to prepare you for being in a group of your intellectual equals—or superiors!"

Her advice: "Try to have some college type of experience—either at one of the summer institutes held at various colleges around the country, or by enrolling in an evening or summer course at a local college, if you can."

All of the students stressed the importance of avoiding an "all work and no play" schedule. ("You need time to let down," "Social life is part of the total campus experience," etc.) But all urged great selectivity—especially during the freshman year—in choosing extracurricular activities. ("Don't lose sight of why you're at college. Choose your activities on the basis of what's important to you—then make and keep a schedule so you won't get swamped.")

Said another: "Remember that you have to take the initiative in joining an organization; people won't keep coming after *you*. It's a good idea to go out for at least one activity in order to meet a nucleus of people with similar interests."

Warned one coed: "At college the atmosphere is much more intellectual than social—extracurricular activities are less important than in high school. Concentrate on one or two activities in your freshman year—you can always join other organizations later."

The group was unanimous in recommending that high school pupils visit their prospective campuses before making a final choice. One student suggested: "Try to have a student guide take you around the campus when you're visiting—you'll feel freer to ask personal questions about finances, social life, fraternities, and so on."

Asked whether they felt any "pressure to conform" at college, most of the students said they felt free to make individual decisions and that they did not have to follow a specific "pattern." ("You can set your own standards in terms of your social behavior; for example, you don't *have* to drink or smoke if you don't want to." "The only people who seem to feel they have to 'conform' to something-or-other are the kind of kids who've always felt they had to do what everyone else was doing—and they're the kind of people who will always behave that way.")

Most of the students felt they had a clear picture of college finances before they came. The only exceptions were boys who had not originally planned to join fraternities in their freshman year, but who decided to do so after they arrived on campus.

Other comments:

On professors: "I wish I'd known from the start that it was all right to go to see my professors—not just when I was having trouble, but simply to talk things over." Advice: "Take advantage of every opportunity to know your professors—they're wonderful people. You'll have some contact with them at coffee hours and discussion groups and such, but if you want to talk to them individually, *you'll* have to take the initiative."

On working-your-way through: "Don't depend on working your way through your freshman year; you'll have all you can cope with. Later on you may find you can handle studies plus a part-time job; usually there are a number of such jobs available."

On personal responsibility: "The biggest change from high school is that you're not supervised, you don't get daily quizzes to check up on you, you don't *have* to see a professor to discuss something you don't understand—it's your responsibility to keep up your work. This doesn't mean that people aren't interested in you—it's part of the whole process of growing up and learning to become independent and assume responsibility."

On group living: "Learning the give-and-take of living with other people is hard for some students. You have to learn to get used to living with some people you don't care for, of disapproving of their actions, yet being able to tolerate them." "You have to learn to be aware of the needs of others, for example, for privacy." "You're much more 'bound up with' the kids you live with than you were with your high school friends."

On fraternities: "It's a good idea to evaluate the whole sorority-fraternity business before you arrive on campus. On some campuses sororities and fraternities are very important; on others, they're not. Better find out what the situation is at your prospective college and have some general idea of how you feel about it."

Only one student confessed to homesickness, although most of the freshmen admitted to occasional feelings of "frustration" or "freshman slump." These were variously attributed to "work pressure," "feeling overtired," "trying to do too much," and so on. A few girls said that letters from friends who had married instead of going on to college occasionally brought a few blue moments. ("If you're just bogged down with work and everything looks grim, a letter like that can make you wonder for a few minutes if it's all worthwhile.")

Their advice to future freshmen and their parents: "Be prepared for periods of feeling overwhelmed or thinking you're not getting anywhere; everybody occasionally feels that way during the frosh year when so much is new and different."

Hopefully, their advice and that of their classmates may help to prepare future freshmen for the exciting, challenging, and ultimately rewarding experience of college life.

To the Class of 1979

WHAT A COLLEGE EDUCATION WILL AND WON'T DO FOR YOU

BY
JACOB NEUSNER
Professor of Religious Studies
Brown University

You come to take your places in an on-going enterprise, a university. It was here before you came. It probably will be here after you leave. But you can and will make your mark upon it. You can enhance its life or blight its future.

Each generation of professors, students, and administrators has that power. For universities are fragile. They rise and fall, go through times of excellence and mediocrity. You will apply to many universities and colleges, and choose the best for you; you realize that significant differences separate one university from the next.

We have no "truth-in-merchandising" law to cover universities; they all call themselves by the same name. But the differences are there, and in the next four years, you are one of the givens, one of the data, that will characterize and distinguish this university.

But your first impression must be otherwise. You must perceive yourselves as the last and least in a long procession of men and women. You see buildings you did not build, a great library you did not create, a faculty you did not assemble, a community you did not form. Everything seems so well established, so permanent. But that impression is illusory. Just a few years ago students in other universities burned and ravaged the buildings built for their use, closed the libraries, shut down the classrooms. So it is clear that students have the power to destroy. By their excellence they also have the power to build.

Professors want to teach the best students they can find; high salaries and pleasant working conditions alone do not suffice to keep talented men and women in universities composed of bored and sullen students. If you are purposeful, if you are mindful, if you show yourselves to be critical, thoughtful, interested students, you will give the university the good name of a place where important things take place, where the life of the mind is fully and richly lived. Within my experience, the university's richest asset is its students.

What happens in a university? First, let me say what does not happen. The problems of the world are not going to be solved by you. You are not coming here to make a better world, to improve the condition of man, or to solve the problem of poverty. Indeed, the money that society (not to mention your parents) spends on you here is diverted from other worthwhile projects. The endowment of this university could purchase better housing for the poor or raise the welfare benefits for the needy; it could go for many worthwhile social purposes. But it is set aside so that you mature men and women, perfectly capable of working at some useful and remunerative task, may remain idle. You are kept unemployed, others have to pay for your keep, so that you may read books, work in labs, listen and talk, write and think.

A university is an ideal expression of a highly aristocratic, anti-egalitarian ideal; it stands for the opposite of the equality of all men and women—rather, their inequalities in matters of the mind and spirit. A great many people past and present have set aside their wealth and their energies for that aristocratic ideal, that excellent minds have the opportunity for growth and improvement, that the intellect be cultivated.

Your four years could likewise go to socially more relevant purposes. You could, after all, take a job and earn a living for yourselves. But you sacrifice that income. Your four years of idleness represent a joint decision, made both by you and your family and by "society," that is better for now to think, so later on you may do; it is wiser now to hold back, so later on you may go much further.

Yet this thing which will not happen here—your immediate engagement with the great tasks of society—imposes on you an extraordinary struggle; the struggle to postpone easy accomplishment and quick distinction. True achievement depends on depth of learning, on capacity for clear thinking, on ability to pursue knowledge where curiosity leads, above all in implacable criticism of all givens. True achievement depends on these things, rather than on the premature acceptance of public responsibility. Young men and women want to go forth, to do great things. We keep you here to study, to think about things.

You come full of energy. You would find it natural to take on great tasks. You want nothing less than to sit long hours in the discipline of the mind. To read and write, to argue and expound, to confront the various claims to truth in a sophisticated, critical spirit—these represent stern tests for men and women at your age (or any other). You are called to an unnatural expression of yourselves: to overcome the natural instincts of your age.

Nothing is so hard as to see your contemporaries at their life's work and to postpone your own. Remember, you represent only a small part of your age group. The majority will not be with you this fall. Nothing is so inviting as to pick up the burdens of the world and enter the workaday life, nor so demanding of self-discipline as to deny them. You come to learn, not with the curious but empty minds of pre-teens, but with the strength of maturing, able men and women. But the conquest of the self, by overcoming ambition, distraction, and sheer laziness, and by pledging your best ability to the service of the mind, will prove most satisfying for those of you who win it.

Above all, if you succeed in acquiring the critical mode of thought which is our ware, you will have the one thing you will need to become important people: the capacity to stand firm in what you think right, in what you propose to accomplish in life. Today you have to postpone the quest for wordly success. Later on it may not come: you may have to walk quite by yourself. When the world is against you, you will have to rely for strength only upon your own convictions. I speak from experience: the world is not going to give you many satisfactions, especially if you propose to change it. For if you do, you thereby claim things are not yet perfect. What everybody thinks is true really is not so. What everybody wants to do, thinks is right and best to do, is not the best way at all. Great men and women achieve that greatness above the mob, not within it. And they cannot be loved on that account. The world will love its own, those who tell and do the things reassuring to the mediocre.

I have said what will not happen in the university. What then does happen here? Only one thing that makes worthwhile the years and money you devote to your university education: that you should learn to ask questions and to find the answers to them. Everything else is frivolous, peripheral, for the shouters and the headline-chasers. And a great many of the questions you will ask and learn to answer are irrelevant to shouting and to headlines.

Now what are these questions? They are not the generalities but the specifics, not the abstractions but the concrete and detailed matters that delimit the frontiers of knowledge. Do not ask what is man, what is truth, what is history, or what is biology. Your teachers may give you answers to these great questions, but these are rote and routine. And your teachers cannot tell you what good is the answer. What we want is only to know: not necessarily how to harness atomic energy and matter, not necessarily how to "cure cancer," but about the nature of living matter.

Your teachers do not propose to tell what is generally agreed upon as "the truth" about this or that. In this regard you must not assume they are like your teachers in high school, whose job it was to communicate established knowledge, to teach you what is already agreed upon. Your teachers here are different because they are actively engaged in the disciplined study and questioning of the given. They are trying to find out new things, trying to reassess the truth of the old.

The high school teacher tends to take for granted the correctness of what he tells you. The university teacher is probably going to ask whether what he tells you is so, how he claims to know it, and above all, how he himself has found it out. He is an active participant in learning, not a passive recipient and transmitter of other people's facts. How he thinks, how he analyzes a problem, therefore, is what you have to learn from him. It is all he has to teach you.

There is a second important process, flowing from the first, in which you must learn to participate: the process of communication. It is not enough to have found ways of thought. One has to express them, as well. As the great Yale historian Edmund S. Morgan has said, "Scholarship begins in curiosity, but it ends in communication." You do not need to justify asking questions. But if you think you have found answers, you do not have the right to remain silent.

I do not guarantee people will listen to you. The greater likelihood is that they will ignore what they do not understand or vilify what they do not like. But you are not free from the task of saying what you think.

This brings me back to where I started: your importance to this university. You are our reason for being, not because you will listen passively and write uncritically, but because without you there is no reason to speak or write.

What happens in the classroom is not the delivery of facts to whom it may concern, but the analysis of possibilities and probabilities by concerned people, teacher and student alike. Learning is not a passive process. A shy person cannot learn. An impatient person cannot teach. Learning is a shared experience. Without students, who is a teacher? More than the calf wants to suck the mother's milk, the cow wants to suckle that calf. I do not mean you have nothing to do but sit back, hear what a teacher has to say, and announce why he is wrong, or why you do not agree with him. That childish conception bears slight resemblance to what is to be done. I mean you have got to learn things for your part, and ask questions about your own perceptions, as much as of your teacher's: it is a shared quest, a collective skepticism.

What is the measure of success? How will you know, in June of 1979, whether you have wisely spent these four beautiful years?

First, you should have a good grasp of some specific field of learning, not solely the data of such a field, although they are important, but the way the field works, how people think within it, and why. You should know some specific thing—indeed, a great many specific things.

Second, you should have mastered three skills that mark the educated man and woman: how to listen attentively, and to think clearly, and to write accurately. No matter what you study, you should learn these three things. To be sure, the modes of thought and the means of writing or other expression are going to differ from one field to the next. But in common they will exhibit concern for accuracy, clarity, precision, order, and lucid argumentation.

Third, you should feel slightly discontented: discontented with yourselves, therefore capable of continued growth; discontented with your field or work, therefore capable of critical judgment and improvement; discontented with the world at large, therefore capable of taking up the world's tasks as a personal and individual challenge.

You come not merely to spend four years in a world you have not made and for which you therefore do not bear responsibility. You come to join and build a community, a community of scholars. If the experience of community is meaningful to you, you will, wherever you may be, never really leave it. You will continue to participate in the scholarly enterprise: asking questions, finding answers, telling people about them.

Reprinted with permission from the *Chronicle of Higher Education*, September 15, 1975. Copyright © 1975 by Editorial Projects for Education, Inc.

Excerpts from Financial Aids for Higher Education 76-77 Catalog

BY
DR. OREON KEESLAR

Reprinted by permission of
Wm. C. Brown Company Publishers,
Dubuque, Iowa 52001

Dr. Keeslar is a respected authority on the subject of financial aid for college students. His book Financial Aids for Higher Education *contains, along with much reliable advice, over 2,500 sources for funds for college and is updated annually. We are pleased to recommend the book to you and are grateful to Mr. Keeslar for his permission to reprint some of the valuable information it includes.*

To win a scholarship, you must show up favorably among many other young people of your age. You have to be good at something, and prove it in competition with others who are also good in the same field. Therefore, it pays to start early in your high school career in developing your skills and capabilities.

During Your Sophomore Year in High School. Try seriously to decide what your life's work is going to be. You'll probably change your mind many times in the years ahead. However, the decision you make now will give much-needed direction and purpose to your life. Everyone needs a star to steer by and it may well save you from making expensive, time-consuming false starts.

Go all out in your efforts to build up a record of good grades and outstanding achievements throughout the last three years of high school. Beginning with your sophomore year, every grade you earn is going to count heavily on your high school record.

Make sure (with the help of your counselor) that the program of studies you've outlined for the rest of your high school career includes all the necessary college-entrance subjects.

During Your Junior Year. Keep up the highest scholastic standards possible in your school work.

Decide which college or university you would like to attend. If you can't pinpoint it, at least narrow the field down to two or three.

Take the PSAT/NMSQT (Preliminary Scholastic Aptitude Test/National Merit Scholarship Qualifying Test) in the fall of your junior year. Ask your high school principal or guidance counselor for instructions as to how and when to take this important test.

You might enter a contest or two as a junior or senior. Contest prizes (scholarships, cash awards, special educational opportunities) may help to subsidize your college career.

During Your Senior Year. Pick out the college best suited to prepare you for your life's work. (An alternate or second choice is advisable, too.) Write to the Director of Admissions for the proper application forms—both for admission and for the financial aid. Do this before the end of October.

Arrange to have three letters of recommendation written for you. Some colleges require them; others do not. The application forms will tell you whether they're necessary. If required, have the personal references mailed directly to the proper official at the college well ahead of the deadline date.

The person writing a letter of recommendation should be someone who (a) is not a relative of yours, (b) is personally acquainted with you, and (c) is a person of some standing in the community, if possible.

Important—The one writing a recommendation will be grateful for the following:

Name and address of the person or institution to which the recommendation is to be sent. Such a letter should never be addressed "To Whom It May Concern:."

A list of your qualifications, extracurricular activities, hobbies and interests, and special skills and achievements, as an aid in composing the letter.

A stamped envelope, addressed to the person or official to whom the letter is to be mailed directly by the writer. (The writer of the recommendation should not hand the letter to you for mailing.)

Take the PSAT/NMSQT (CEEB Preliminary Scholastic Aptitude Test/National Merit Scholarship Qualifying Test) along with the juniors in October if you haven't already taken it. You may need the score from this test on your record.

Register to take the CEEB-SAT and/or Achievement Tests at least one month prior to the testing date selected. They are given at monthly intervals from October to June inclusive with the exception of March.

For details and instructions, see your high school counselor, or write to the College Entrance Examination Board at:

Box 2815; Princeton, New Jersey 08540

WHAT TO DO IF YOU DO NOT GET A SCHOLARSHIP

Don't be one bit discouraged!

The scholarship of former years is being supplanted by the financial aids package. On each campus there's a Financial Aids Officer who knows all the possibilities and angles by which a student can work out a financial plan for his college career. You should look him up, even before you enter your freshman year, and seek his help.

Scholarships aren't the only form of aid available. A cash credit to your account at the college, or a waiver of tuition may be forthcoming under special circumstances. Educational loans (with low interest rate, deferred repayment, and many fringe benefits) are now widely subsidized by state and federal agencies. In addition, part-time jobs and work-study programs are becoming more and more plentiful.

The spirit of the times is growing clearer and clearer. No student capable of benefiting from college training must be deprived of that opportunity because of inadequate financial resources. In other words, if you're able to do college work, you should go on, whether you have the ready cash to do it or not. The money can be found. All you need is the ability and the driving motivation to get a higher education.

Many (though not all) colleges and universities throughout the nation use the CEEB Scholastic Aptitude Test and the Achievement Tests for checking the intellectual and academic qualifications of students who apply for admission, and for selecting those who are to be awarded scholarships. Since these tests are so widely used, and often required of entering freshmen, you might be wise to take one or two of them as a matter of course, just in case such test scores might be needed later on.

The SAT and Achievement scores are sent to colleges on the student's request, as well as reported to secondary schools as a matter of course. The scores on the Preliminary Scholastic Aptitude Test (PSAT), however, are not ordinarily sent to colleges. They are reported to the student's secondary schools for guidance purposes.

PRELIMINARY SCHOLASTIC APTITUDE TEST/ NATIONAL MERIT SCHOLARSHIP QUALIFYING TEST

This test, often referred to as the PSAT/NMSQT, is a one-hour-and-forty-minute test designed for early guidance of high school students.

BASIC FACTS

- The first step in establishing eligibility for National Merit Scholarships and all other scholarships administered by the National Merit Scholarship Corporation.
- A similar but shorter version of the SAT, it can be used to estimate the SAT scores students are likely to obtain.
- A good source of information in helping you to estimate your chances of admission to (as well as your probability of succeeding in) specific colleges. Such information is often provided by colleges in the *CEEB College Handbook*.
- The verbal sections measure your ability to read with understanding, use words correctly, and reason with them.
- The mathematical sections measure the ability to use and reason with numbers and other mathematical abstractions.
- Uses multiple-choice questions, and the scores are reported on a scale ranging from 20 to 80 (paralleling the 200-800 range of the SAT test). SAT scores can be estimated directly from PSAT/NMSQT scores.
- Can be taken by juniors, and some seniors, who are seeking to qualify for scholarships offered by sponsors who specifically require a PSAT/NMSQT score for each candidate.

Procedure for taking the PSAT/NMSQT:

1. Tell your counselor and/or your principal that you want to take the PSAT/NMSQT if it is given in your high school, and be sure that you are notified of the date. The PSAT/NMSQT is usually administered on one of two specific dates which are set by the CEEB. These customarily fall on a Tuesday and the following Saturday in late October of each year.

Your school may choose to give the test on either of these dates. A different form (edition) of the test is used on each date as a means of maintaining the security of the test.

2. The test fee for the PSAT/NMSQT is $2.50 per student which is collected by the school. Schools may charge an additional fee, when necessary, to cover test administration costs incurred by the school.

The test fee and answer sheets are forwarded to the CEEB ready for scoring.

3. At the time the test is administered, you will be asked to indicate on the answer sheet if you wish to be referred to the National Merit Scholarship Corporation, the National Scholarship Service Fund for Negro Students and other scholarship sponsors.

4. The results of your test will be reported to your high school counselor who will relay and explain the report to you. With this report, you and your counselor will receive certain materials to help you understand and interpret your scores and to begin planning for college selection.

SCHOLASTIC APTITUDE TEST

This three-hour test (the one with which most students are familiar) is designed to provide reliable indications of your ability to do college work.

Like the PSAT, it uses multiple-choice questions scored on a scale which has standard range from a low of 200 to a high of 800. This scale is the same for all editions of the test, wherever and whenever they are given. This provides college admissions officers and high school counselors with a common gauge which measures the same degree of ability in Maine as it does in California, whether the test is taken in December or in May, whether the student comes from a small rural high school or a large urban one.

It measures the basic verbal/mathematical abilities that you have acquired over many years, both in and out of school (general educational development). It tests your ability to reason rather than to remember facts, and does not require special preparation. In fact, seven research studies of the effects of intensive coaching and drill preparatory to taking the College Board tests have shown that such practices, at best, are likely to yield insignificant gains in scores! In other words, you cannot "cram" for these tests, you have simply been growing and getting ready for them all your life.

The verbal sections emphasize the ability to read with understanding and to reason with verbal material.

The mathematical sections (which contain various kinds of problems to be solved) stress reasoning ability, rather than a knowledge of specific courses you may have taken in high school mathematics.

Procedure for taking the SAT:

1. If the *Student Bulletin* is not available in your high school

counselor's office, write for a copy from the College Board Publication Orders: Box 2815, Princeton, New Jersey 08540

2. Register for an early date on which to take the SAT (and whatever CEEB Achievement Tests you require), sending in the examination fee ($6.50) with your application. (The fee for the Achievement Tests is $11.00.)

The SAT (and the Achievement Tests) are given in some 4,000 centers throughout the United States and in 90 foreign countries. Additional special centers are established for the convenience of students who otherwise have to travel more than 75 miles from home.

The dates for the tests that are given during the school year always fall on a Saturday and are spaced through the year to avoid certain holidays and the end-of-semester examination periods in high schools.

3. If the scholarship program for which you wish to qualify requires an SAT score, be sure to register the proper code number for it on the Registration Form.

THE ACHIEVEMENT TESTS

Each test requires one hour to complete, and measures your knowledge of a specific subject, and your ability to solve problems related to that subject. Tests are offered in:

Biology	Spanish
Chemistry	English Composition
Physics	Literature
French	Mathematics—Level I (Standard)
German	Mathematics—Level II (Intensive)
Hebrew	American History and Social Studies
Latin	European History and World Cultures
Russian	

There are also seven Supplementary Achievement Tests available to schools for administering on the first Tuesday in February.

There are no passing or failing scores for these Achievement Tests. They merely provide a means of comparing the performance of many students in specific subjects.

Procedure for taking the Achievement Tests:

1. Same as for taking the SAT
2. At the time you send your registration for your CEEB-Testing appointment, include the required fee ($11.00). Your fee entitles you to take any one, two, or three of the 15 tests listed above.

The American College Testing Program (ACT), founded in 1959, is a non-profit educational trust providing counseling, guidance, and information services each year for approximately one million students, over 22,000 secondary schools, and more than 2,400 institutions of higher education in the United States and overseas.

The ACT Assessment Program, one of the best-known services provided by ACT, is administered five times each academic year on five national testing dates at approximately 2,900 test centers in the United States and overseas. The test date schedule for each year is printed in the registration materials and on the poster sent to all high schools.

More than 2,000 institutions of higher education use the ACT Assessment Program for counseling, admission, and planning purposes.

The ACT Assessment consists of four tests:

English Usage—a seventy-five-item, forty-minute test that measures your understanding and use of the basic elements in correct and effective writing (punctuation, capitalization, usage, phraseology, style, and organization).

Mathematics Usage—a forty-item, fifty-minute test of your mathematical reasoning ability (sampling of mathematical techniques covered in high school, plus practical quantitative problems you might encounter in many college curricula).

Social Studies Reading—a fifty-two-item, thirty-five minute test to measure the evaluative reasoning and problem-solving skills required in the social studies (reading comprehension, understanding of basic studies concepts, knowledge of sources of information, special study skills).

Natural Sciences Readings—a fifty-two-item, thirty-five-minute test measuring critical reasoning and problem-solving skills in natural sciences (interpretation and evaluation of scientific materials, understanding of purposes of experiments, logical relations between experimental hypotheses, and generalizations which can be drawn from results of experiments).

You are also required to complete a Student Profile Section, which systematically collects and reports the biographical information often requested in college application forms (aspirations, goals, background, anticipated personal needs, and nonclassroom achievements), and an ACT

Interest Inventory, which measures your interests in six basic areas (Social Service, Business Contact, Business Detail, Technical, Science, and Creative Arts).

Registration materials are routinely mailed in late July to counselors in secondary schools. If your school did not receive materials or wishes additional materials, write to:

ACT Registration Department
P.O. Box 414
Iowa City, Iowa 52240

Registration fee for this service is $7.00 per student, which pays for the testing materials, scoring and reporting to the high school or individual and up to three college choices.

Recognizing the need for a national agency to provide cooperative planning and assessment of student financial need among colleges and universities, the College Entrance Examination Board established the College Scholarship Service in 1954.

The CSS program, emphasizing the equitable distribution of funds on the basis of need, is offered to college candidates and their families, to secondary schools, to noncollegiate sponsors of financial aid programs, and to all institutions of higher education. The CSS controls no scholarship funds and does not recommend any particular action on scholarship applications. Its purpose is to provide information and services for those who offer financial aid to needy college students.

The College Scholarship Service and its participating colleges, universities, and agencies recognize the importance of granting aid on the basis of a student's financial need in order that aid funds can be awarded to more students. In this matter, competition among colleges is minimized, and a more equitable distribution of funds to individuals is assured. CSS is designed to help the college applicant report to colleges the financial circumstances of his family and to help colleges determine the student's need for financial assistance. The Parents' Confidential Statement (PCS) is the instrument of this purpose, and about 1 million students use it each year.

PARENTS' CONFIDENTIAL FINANCIAL STATEMENT

The Parents' Confidential Statement (PCS), specifically designed for dependent students, is the most widely used CSS service for determining a student's financial need for institutional, federal, state, and other student aid funds. PCS booklets are distributed by high schools, postsecondary institutions, and community agencies. The PCS collects complete information about parents' income, expenses, assets, and liabilities, and gives an opportunity for the parents to explain any unusual circumstances that may limit their ability to meet college costs. To improve the reliability of data reported, the 1975-76 PCS contains an authorization to enable CSS to request the parents' federal income tax return. The PCS booklet has clearly written instructions and a completed sample of the PCS to assist parents in filling in the needed information.

When the PCS is sent to the CSS for central processing, it goes through a series of computer checks and in many cases is individually reviewed. If information is needed to complete the analysis, the CSS sends a request to the parents for the missing data. Institutions are alerted by the CSS if parents fail to submit the missing information within 15 days through a "Delayed Processing Report."

After the CSS analyzes the PCS, a copy of it and a comprehensive report of the analysis are sent to postsecondary institutions and agencies listed by the family. The PCS and its analysis, the "Financial Need Analysis Report" (FNAR), provide aid administrators with thorough and reliable information about the family's ability to pay for college costs. Data from previous years is provided for renewal PCS filers. If student budget data are filed with the CSS, the report will also provide financial need figures.

The CSS need analysis method employs standards developed by the United States Bureau of Labor Statistics and is based on Social Security Administration and Consumer Price Index information and data collected over a 20-year period by the CSS and its users. In its continual evaluation and improvement of the PCS service, the CSS relies on the experience and knowledge of aid administrators, economists, and other experts in the financing of higher education. Changes approved for 1975-76 included projecting cost-of-living increases through December 1974, which will result in lowering the expected contribution from parents.

FEES

The PCS processing fee is paid by the parents. The charge is $4.00 for the first institution or agency listed to receive the PCS and FNAR. For each additional recipient listed on the PCS, the charge is $2.25. When the CSS receives the PCS, parents are sent an acknowledgment listing those institutions and agencies they designated to receive copies of the PCS and FNAR. A section of the acknowledgment can also be used to add other institutions or agencies to receive the PCS at a charge of $3.25 for the first institution and $2.25 for each additional one.

STUDENT'S FINANCIAL STATEMENT (SFS)

The "Student's Financial Statement" (SFS) can be used for partially or completely self-supporting, undergraduate, graduate, and professional students, and also for dependent students. The SFS is especially appropriate for those students who are already enrolled and are applying for financial aid. The SFS collects complete information about the income and expenses of the student (and husband or wife) and also provides for the collection of parental information. SFSs are distributed to students by the institutions or agencies that use the form for determining financial need.

Students send the SFS to the CSS for central processing. The institutions designated by the student receive from the CSS a copy of the SFS accompanied by a "Student's Financial Need Analysis Report" (SFNAR). This report provides a comprehensive analysis of both the student's and parents' income and asset information. The SFNAR, like the FNAR, also includes an estimate of student expenses and financial need based on up to four budgets as well as data on that student's eligibility for a "Basic Educational Opportunity Grant."

FEES

Students or parents pay the processing fee. The charge is $3.75 for the first postsecondary institution or agency listed to receive the SFS and the SFNAR; $2.25 for each additional recipient.

FINANCIAL AID STATEMENT (FAS)

The newest CSS need analysis service is the "Financial Aid Statement" (FAS). FAS is a low-cost, quick, and efficient way of evaluating a dependent or self-supporting student's need for financial aid. Central processing by the CSS averages five days and the analysis sent to institutions provides complete information that is consistent with federal program regulations for making awards under any of the campus-based programs. The FAS is easy for parents and students to understand and fill in. Furthermore, it reduces the workload of the aid administrator by calculating the family's financial resources and then sending the institution only a one-page analysis. An added feature that may save time for institutions that award aid other than on a nine-month academic year basis is that the family contribution is given for five different time periods. The FAS is processed during the year the student is in attendance and therefore is especially useful to institutions that frequently make financial aid awards throughout the year.

FEES

Students or parents pay the processing fee of $2.50. As with the PCS and the SFS, postsecondary institutions and agencies may choose to pay the processing fee.

On the basis of one or more of these three fact-finding "Statements" (the PCS, the SFS, and the FAS), the Financial Aids Officer of a college or university can get a fairly clear and accurate picture of a family's financial situation. By applying the principles and procedures outlined in the "CSS Need Analysis: Theory and Computation Procedures," a publication of the College Scholarship Service, the Financial Aid Officer can then compute the amount that the parents of an applicant might reasonably be expected to contribute toward the costs of the student's college education in his particular institution, based on the "financial strength" of the family. The student himself figures in this, too, since he is expected to help pay for part of his own education by employment or savings.

HELPING STUDENTS DETERMINE COLLEGE COSTS

In their investigation into paying for college, students and parents should consider the sources of aid available and the total costs of attending the colleges they are interested in. The best source of this information is usually each college's catalog, although some colleges have additional and more detailed information available in other publications. The expenses listed in the catalog should include each component of a student's college budget. Miscellaneous personal expenses—for laundry, recreation, and so on—are sometimes not mentioned and should then be estimated. The latest edition of *The College Handbook,* published by the College Board in fall 1972, is a source of information on college costs and student budgets at more than 2000 colleges in the United States. A complimentary copy of this book is sent to every high school in the country.

College costs vary greatly according to whether the college is publicly or privately supported, and they also vary within these two classifications. Individual students' budgets differ also, depending on whether the student lives on the college campus or commutes from home, attends college outside his home state, and so on.

Therefore when determining the amount of a student's financial need at a particular college all factors must be taken into consideration; the college's budget, the student's budget, and his parents' expected contributions.

Excerpts From Cash for College

BY
S. ROBERT FREEDE

S. Robert Freede has generously given us permission to reprint parts of his excellent book, Cash for College. *Obviously, it is impossible to cover all of the information the book has to offer here, but we have tried to give you a generous sampling. If you are interested in further information on this subject, we recommend that you read his entire book, published by Prentice-Hall, Inc.* Cash for College *also contains a complete description of Mr. Freede's Scholarship Search Program.*

THE SCHOLARSHIP GOLDMINE

As we all know, a scholarship is an outright gift to undergraduate students (graduates get fellowships) for which no repayment is required. They usually run for a year, which means you have to go through the application hassle whenever a good opportunity presents itself. Sometimes, prior scholarship holders get preferential treatment and hooray for that. But, sadly, some four-year awards are subject to annual review, so if you get one of those, keep your nose clean, your grades up and your need visible.

The requirements for scholarships vary tremendously with the sponsoring organization.

To help sort out your personal possibilities, keep in mind that scholarships may be classified into several broad categories: there are local, national and regional grants; general (open to anybody) and specified (with limiting criteria). When you go out there banging on college money doors, start with the national and general awards. Most of these are open to anyone, and everybody and his brother and sister will be in there competing with you. Your odds for success go up when your competition thins out in the more specified categories.

UNCLE SAM CAN HELP

The largest source of education dollars today is the federal government. In fact, without money from Washington, higher education as we know it probably couldn't exist.

More than one-half billion federal dollars is being given to students in the annual education grant program. In addition, more billions go to educational institutions as contributions for buildings, facilities, research and salaries. Also, there are military, social security and other educational programs as well as tax write-offs for contributions. While prophets of doom cry in their root beer over the uncertainties of federal money for higher education, each year the contributions increase, each year the programs become a little more institutionalized. In reality, government support of education is a fact of life and an accepted and expected part of our society.

Uncle Sam has five major programs to distribute all those tax dollars the government is gathering. Two dispense outright grants, two provide for loans and one is a work/study program. There are also numerous special interest federal and state programs.

SPECIAL GRANTS

In addition to money for the masses Uncle Sam also hands out loot to special groups he has taken under his wing. Chances are good that you are in one of those special groups. Is there any connection between you or your family and the military? Are you a refugee, an American Indian, Eskimo, Aleut? Are you handicapped, deaf or blind? Do you want to be a policeman? A nurse? An officer in the armed services? Is your father a railroader? Is he disabled, retired, deceased?

If any of the above apply, you are in a special group and there is money earmarked for you in some government office somewhere. But you've got to apply for and go after it.

SECURITY BLANKET

One of the best kept secrets is that it is fairly easy to get social security money for college. Sons and daughters of retired, disabled or deceased workers can collect funds with no hassle until the age of twenty-two, if they are unmarried and full-time students. Benefits are as high as $2,400 per year. There are more than a half million students eligible for this money. More Social Security funds are available to this group of students than the combined financial aid from all the colleges and universities in the country. Payments are based on financial need, but the average sum is between 50 percent and 75 percent of the benefits received by the parent.

Furthermore, if you were receiving benefits from your parents' Social Security account, and these payments ceased when you reached eighteen years of age (because of the old law), you might now be eligible for a huge lump sum pack payment.

Under Social Security, you can work during the year, but there is a limit to the amount you can earn before your benefits are reduced or withheld.

These benefits, while generous, are not automatic. You must apply for them at the local Social Security office. Such aid is rightfully yours by law and should not be ignored.

The Railroad Retirement Act provides similar benefits for offspring of railroad workers. There is a further stipulation that payments to a retired railroad worker may be increased if he has children who are full-time students. The local Railroad Retirement Board office is the place to go for further information.

AND THEN THERE'S HOME TOWN, YOUR STATE, U.S.A.

Almost every state in the union provides some sort of educational financial aid. State aid is generally based on need, though many states reward academic excellence or high scores on competitive exams. States without such programs usually provide help for veterans or their families, nursing students, teachers, members of minority groups and the handicapped. The stipends awarded generally vary according to need. In some cases fee waivers at state schools are the only award, which is some benefit at least.

The one almost universal requirement is that you must be a resident of the state.

Because of the variety and constant changes in state aid programs, you should write directly to your own State Board of Education, or to the state administering agency which handles financial aid programs. By contacting the right organizations within your own state, you'll get detailed, up-to-the-minute listings of locally provided educational opportunities. The information on the different kinds and amounts of available state aid is listed under a variety of names.

THE WEIRDOS

Colleges also have most of the responsibility of administering the freaks of the college scholarship world, the weirdo funds that might just make the difference between whether you go to school or not.

For example, just your name can get you scholarship money. Yale might pay you $1,000 if your name is Leavenworth or DeForest. Harvard has funds for people named Anderson, Baxendale, Borden, Downer, Haven, Murphy or Pennoyer; Barnard will finance a Stuyvesant or Van Loon.

Your family ancestry can help, too. Students of Armenian descent are eligible for $1,000 from the Armenian General Benevolent Union of America. Greeks can apply for a grant from the Daughters of Penelope. The same goes for Danes, Poles, Syrians, and Japanese, among others. If you can establish Roman ancestry, you may get a scholarship from Vassar. And the Russian Student Fund has money reserved for non-Communist youth of Russian blood or descent.

Okay, so these are a few oddballs. And, there are a lot more of them, too numerous to list here. But so what? That's the reason the money is available and within reach. You might just as well get some of it as the next Pennoyer.

TRADE UNIONS

Unions not only compete with private business over the bargaining table, but in the scholarship sweepstakes as well. They operate somewhat the same way business and industry programs do. Some funds are donated directly to colleges and universities, but the vast majority are self-administered.

Union awards are divided into two major categories—those given nationally by the national and international unions, and regional stipends offered by local councils, districts and unions. Usually awards are intended for union members and their children, but this is not universal.

PROFESSIONAL ASSOCIATION SCHOLARSHIPS

From biophysics to the graphic arts, if you have special talents or career interests, you will find some ready money from a host of trade and professional associations. If you are into social work, the coal industry, turkey production, insurance, math or funeral science (among others), you will find scores of groups anxious to share the wealth of their professions and stimulate you to enter their special fields. Nurses, scientists, architects and truckers are all giving money for the right students. Many of these trade associations have scholarships for their members' children.

SCHOLARSHIPS FROM ORGANIZATIONS

It would be impossible to list all of the organizations handing out college money. It's doubtful if anything short of a computer could handle it, but a few names sprinkled like salt and pepper will give you some idea of the vast variety.

Youth clubs are pretty generous with such programs—the Scouts, 4-H clubs, Explorers, American Legion Junior Auxiliary, Junior Achievement, the Y, the Future Farmers of America, and the Future Homemakers of America.

Almost every major and minor religious denomination is represented as well as purely local church groups. They vary in their programs—some will grant you outright gifts, some no-interest bearing loans, some hold competitions. Many churches sponsor colleges with reduced fees.

Church related scholarships are almost always restricted to true believers (or at least admitted members) of the denomination. Often, you will be required to attend a church-connected school.

In addition to general scholarship awards, there are a number of organizations which either grant, administer or disseminate information on educational aid for minorities.

SCHOLARSHIP SEARCH

We've also given you some idea of the monumental and frustrating job it is to fully research all of the important sources of aid we've discussed. There is the government, private sources and the colleges themselves, to say nothing of the bewildering array of financial aid types that are open to you—outright grants, loans, cooperative job efforts. Loan write-offs. Whether or not you might or might not be eligible for them is another matter.

There's a lot of cash around. Just how much nobody knows, but you can bet on the data in the information banks of Scholarship Search of New York City. Scholarship Search has the largest repository of such information—more than 250,000 scholarships and financial aid source-items valued at over $500 million—from foundations, corporations, private individuals, unions, organizations of all types, colleges, state and federal government, etc. In fact, all of the college financial aids from anywhere and everywhere you've been reading about, cover only a tiny fraction of the goodies in the data banks of this one-of-a-kind nationwide computerized research and matching system.

Some awards are unusual or unique—some are so weird and far-out that practically nobody qualifies. But the point is that somebody does. Somebody is an American Indian who wants to study farming at Cornell, somebody named Baxendale wants to go to Harvard, somebody wants to make his or her life's work turkey production. The trick is knowing where to look and knowing how to determine what a student is qualified for and eligible to receive.

How are you going to unearth these treasures? Without computerized information banks, it could take you months of full-time intensive research to come up with just a small percentage of the quarter-million source-items that are instantly available through the computer. And although there are several dozen books and directories in libraries on college scholarships, many of their listings are outdated and incomplete.

And even if you dug out some of the sources by yourself, there is the complex task of determining what you're really qualified for and eligible to receive. The job of matching the criteria of all the awards to your individual qualifications is so time-consuming and complicated, that it is virtually impossible for you to accomplish successfully. And think of the ones that got away. You may be qualified for financial aid and never know it. You may take on a loan you didn't need, go to a college you don't like, or worse, not go to college at all.

Scholarship Search helps high school and college students find thousands of dollars in sources of scholarships, grants or other aid which a student may be eligible to receive. It does the frustrating, time-consuming research and matches a student's own particular qualifications to the special donor requirements in the awards themselves. It tells a student how and where to apply for college funds by pinpointing a student's own individual qualifications to those specific sources of money for college, for which the student is eligible. Scholarship Search has already assisted thousands of students all over the United States to successfully locate substantial sums of money for college.

EDITOR'S NOTE: Our readers can obtain complete Scholarship Search information packets (include literature, photos of students who received awards, a student-profile application form, etc.) by sending $1.00 to cover postage and handling to: Scholarship Search MTA Information, 1775 Broadway, New York, N.Y. 10019.

COLLEGE LOANS

You should first exhaust all possible financial aid sources before you decide to go into debt. The very best way of paying for school is by planning ahead, using savings, scholarship money and current income. If this is impossible, and if your Financial Aid Officer gives you no other alternative, it's time to shop around for the best loan deal you can get.

You don't buy a head of lettuce without first asking the price. You don't rush blindly into a debt. You approach a loan slowly, methodically and clinically with a wary eye and a knowing smirk. To protect you from rip-off artists and loan sharks in sheepskins, we offer these suggestions, in descending order of preference, for the kind of loans you should consider.

The first place to apply for a loan is your own school. Quite a few colleges and universities offer very attractive long-term loan programs that they finance and administer themselves. Policies vary, and much depends on the condition of the school's treasury. An institution with limited grant money will try to help its students with a loan program, often packaging the loan with other types of financial aid.

Repayment of college loans is made as painless as possible—low interest rates and long repayment schedules. You don't have to start paying until you graduate and some schools even defer repayment and accrual of interest if you go on to graduate work or military service.

File this handy dandy tip away for a rainy day. Some schools have provision for emergency loans. If you qualify, this allows you to borrow a reasonable sum of money for a short time, from a week to a semester. Such a loan has little or no interest and may be just the thing to keep you fed and/or clothed until you can sell your car or something.

Warning: Extreme caution should be taken when shopping for a college loan. There are many commercial loan companies offering tuition plans that appear to be administered by the college; some will even have the school name printed on their brochures. These high interest plans, while legitimate, are not as highly recommended as bona fide school loans. Read the fine print, ask your Financial Aid Officer, and do some arithmetic.

NATIONAL DIRECT STUDENT LOAN PROGRAM

They once called it the National Defense Student Loan Program (probably to help it through Congress), but it has been pacified into the National Direct Student Loan Program. In its time, the NDSL was a revolutionary advance in college funding—it helped spread more money around to more students and more colleges than anything before, and it popularized the concept of borrowing for an education.

If you're enrolled a minimum of half-time and can show financial need, you can borrow a total of $5,000 toward a bachelor's degree and

$10,000 for graduate study—or a combination of both. However, you can't get more than $2,500 during your first two years.

Money you borrow comes back to haunt you when you least expect it. That's because the government doesn't ask for repayment until nine months after graduation. This gestation period allows you to get settled in a paying job, hopefully. You then begin the long road back at a ridiculous 3 percent per year interest rate with up to ten years to pay off. Even at this rate, you don't have to worry about interest until you actually start the payments, and there are no interest charges during the time you serve in the armed forces, Peace Corps, VISTA, or if you go back to school full-time or half-time.

Your loan can be written off entirely, at the rate of 15 percent a year, if you teach in a designated low income area elementary or secondary school, if you are a staff member of specific preschool programs or in a recognized school for the handicapped. The loan can also be written off at the rate of 12 percent for each consecutive year of service in the armed forces. Funds for the NDSL program are administered by the schools. They also collect the payments.

GUARANTEED STUDENT LOAN PROGRAM

In the 60s, things began getting a bit rough for middle income students applying for financial assistance. You know the problem—too much income on paper to warrant a scholarship and too little of the real stuff to pay all the bills. The only way out was a fat commercial loan with large payments due from day one.

So what the government did was start up the Guaranteed Student Loan Program. As long as you are in school, Uncle Sam pays the interest on your loan. You don't have to start worrying about the principal until you graduate or drop out. Then, the government still picks up the tab for half the interest.

The Guaranteed Student Loan Program has had a substantial effect on student financing. It made it easier to get a loan from a bank, it equalized the financial aid opportunities open to all students, and it initiated the major involvement of individual states in educational loan programs. The guarantee makes it easier and cheaper for you to borrow money. It is a cooperative effort—the federal government working with state agencies, non-profit funding groups and commercial lenders like banks, savings and loan associations and credit unions.

Remember that these loans are made through private institutions, and the burden is on you to find one willing to lend you the money. Approval may be automatic, but availability of funds is not. The money market in recent years has been exceedingly tight, but public spirited institutions aided by the guarantee that the government will pay your loan in case of death or default has at least kept the program alive if not flourishing.

Students can borrow up to $2,500 a year (less in certain states) or a total of $7,500 toward a bachelor's degree. For graduate school or a combination of both, a student can borrow a total of $10,000.

A guaranteed loan works like an NDSL—you don't have to make payments while you serve in the armed forces, Peace Corps, VISTA, or if you return to full-time study (for up to three years).

Bear in mind that many graduating college seniors leave college having accumulated federal and state loans totaling $4,000 to $6,000. If students decide to marry each other, as many do, they are confronted with meeting financial obligations of as much as $12,000. That's quite a burden for a young couple.

QUESTIONS TO ASK COMMERCIAL LENDERS

Commercial lenders must make a profit; therefore, such loans often include not only various additional charges and penalties, but also a number of restrictions. The student or his family should look into the terms of commercial loans and attempt to obtain clear-cut answers to the following questions:

1. What is the "true" interest rate?
2. What are the extra features? How much do they cost?
3. How much may a family borrow annually?
4. How much may a family borrow for each child?
5. What is the total a family may borrow for all its children?
6. Is it possible for the company to terminate the plan before the student's contract ends? If so, under what conditions can the company do this and how much notice must it give prior to cancellation?
7. Is it possible for the borrower to terminate the plan before the contract ends? If so, what are the penalties and how much notice is required?
8. What happens to the debt or the money accumulated if the student dies?
9. Under what conditions, if any, does the note become payable in full and at once?
10. What time periods are possible to repay a loan? What time periods are possible in prepaying (creating savings)?

11. Is it possible to increase the frequency or the amount of loan repayments?

12. Is life insurance on the borrower provided? If so, is a medical examination ever necessary?

13. Does the life insurance, if provided, continue throughout the life of the plan? If so, does the amount remain constant or does it decrease?

14. Is disability insurance on the borrower provided?

15. Is there an age limit above which a parent cannot qualify for the program?

16. Is there any investigation of parents' finances?

17. Are there restrictions of the wage earner changing jobs?

18. How long does it take to complete loan arrangements?

For further reading: *Cash for College,* Prentice-Hall, Inc., Englewood Cliffs, N.J. 07632.

The MISS TEENAGE AMERICA Scholarship Program

BY
CATHY DURDEN
MISS TEENAGE AMERICA 1976

If you're searching for scholarships, don't overlook the MISS TEENAGE AMERICA Scholarship Program. I didn't think it would happen to me, either, but, here I am—the proud owner of a $10,000 scholarship to any college or university of my choice.

MISS TEENAGE AMERICA has been in the scholarship business for fifteen years now. The major goal of the whole program is to increase the number of scholarship awards and the amounts of each award every year.

For instance, my successor, MISS TEENAGE AMERICA 1977 will receive a $12,000 scholarship. (And I was thrilled with $10,000!)

Each of the Alternates and the Semi-Finalists on the national level receive scholarships and there are even special scholarship awards for high scoring girls who do not qualify for the Semi-Finals.

So far, MISS TEENAGE AMERICA has awarded over a quarter of a million dollars in scholarships during the organization's fifteen years of existence. (Pretty good for a teenager, don't you think?) A minimum of thirty thousand scholarship dollars will be awarded at the 1977 National Pageant Finals. Some MISS TEENAGE AMERICA Local Pageants also award scholarships. A new MISS TEENAGE AMERICA Scholarship Foundation is now in the process of being formed, making additional scholarship awards possible.

Thanks to many companies and organizations who believe in the MISS TEENAGE AMERICA Program, like the Dr Pepper Company, The World Book Encyclopedia, and Who's Who Among American High School Students, the scholarship program is growing every year. There is more information on the program in the MISS TEENAGE AMERICA chapter of this book.

Whether or not you win a scholarship, there are so many ways you will come home from the MISS TEENAGE AMERICA Pageant a real winner. Believe me, I know!

How to Be a Super Student

BY
Dr. WILLIAM NAULT
Executive Vice President
and Editorial Director
Field Enterprises Educational Corporation
Publishers of the *World Book Encyclopedia*

The World Book Encyclopedia knows just about everything there is to know about learning and studying. It's their business. In addition to their excellent and well-known encyclopedias, the company also publishes dictionaries, yearbooks, and other reference books.

The written test for MISS TEENAGE AMERICA, *on both the local and national levels, is researched and prepared by World Book. As a National Associate of* MISS TEENAGE AMERICA, *they also award a scholarship for scholastic achievement each year at the National Finals.*

Study means to apply the mind to any subject in order to learn about it. Study is accomplished mostly by means of reading, observation, questioning, listening, and reflection. It is an important part of the process of learning. The purpose of study is the discovery and understanding of information. A good student obtains facts and learns skills by which he can organize and express his thoughts and talents.

Effective or successful study consists of much more than merely memorizing facts. It calls for knowing where and how to obtain facts, and the ability to make intelligent use of them. It means that the student must be able to organize, classify, and arrange facts in their proper relationship to the subject being studied. A student must decide what is important information and then form opinions concerning it. All these things must be done to the best of his ability in the shortest possible amount of time. Because knowledge is important to every person, it is wise to learn how to study in the most effective way.

The mind works best when the body is in good physical condition. Good health demands that we eat properly and get enough rest, sleep, exercise, and recreation. Certain physical defects make study especially difficult. Poor eyesight, for example, can be a great hindrance to study and should be corrected. But many physical handicaps need not prevent one from learning to study efficiently. A crippled child, for example, may learn to study as well as anyone.

Favorable surroundings are also very important when it comes to effective study. Everyone needs a place where he can study regularly without interruption. He must have a desk or table and a chair. Both must be of the proper height to fit his body. Good light, either daylight or artificial light, is necessary to prevent eyestrain. The desk or table should be located so that the light will fall over the left shoulder on the reading matter. The amount of light should be enough to read by easily but not so much as to cause glare, which results in eye fatigue. Noise and other distractions should be eliminated. Some people feel that they can study better with soft music in the background. But most people find the radio or television a distraction. The room temperature should be neither too hot nor too cold.

The art of studying effectively can be acquired only with regular practice. If we neglect to study one day, it is easy to neglect to study the next day. Every human being is subject to habits, and the sum of his habits determines his character. The body and mind perform various functions more easily when they are taught to do so at regular intervals. For example, if we are accustomed to eating dinner at a certain hour, we normally become hungry at that time. Likewise, if a definite period of the day is set aside for study, the mind is more likely to be ready for study.

Effective study depends more than anything else on the ability to make the best use of the printed word. Rapid reading is essential in order to cover as much ground as possible without wasting time. The art of reading rapidly, and with understanding, can be developed with practice. Every student should try to improve his reading by improving his vocabulary, his speed, and his comprehension.

The student cannot always determine immediately how helpful a book may be to the subject being studied. In that case, it is better to skim through the book quickly at first, instead of reading it word by word. In this way, the main points and general meaning are quickly grasped. If the material proves to be helpful, a second and more careful reading can follow. Some students find it helpful to underline key ideas or summary sentences in their textbooks if the book belongs to them. A review of this material refreshes the memory of important ideas, principles, and concepts.

Too many students fail to understand all that they have read because they do not know the meaning of some words. If a word is unfamiliar, it is a good habit to take time to look it up in the dictionary and learn its meaning. By analyzing the organization of material, a picture of what has been read can be formed in the mind. Try to grasp essential facts and sort these out in some kind of order. The important thing is to remember the idea, rather than the author's exact words.

Read critically in order to compare the statements of one author with those of another. A subject can often be presented from different points of view. The student should not form an opinion until the subject has been considered from more than one angle. Nor should he believe everything he sees in print.

If there are questions at the end of a lesson or chapter, it is a good idea to try answering the questions first, on the basis of what you know. The actual reading of the lesson then becomes a process of checking and making certain the answers are correct.

Students sometimes find study time much more enjoyable if they are able to study with a friend. Two or three students can often get good results and save a great deal of time by studying together. One interesting and effective method is for each student to prepare each day's lesson not by "studying" it, but by going through it rapidly in order to prepare a test or examination for the others. Each one then takes the test prepared by the others. The whole group scores its papers together.

Text and reference books are invaluable tools that should be employed to increase efficiency in study. The table of contents in the front of a textbook lists the chapters and may provide a brief description of what each contains. An index at the back of the book gives an alphabetical list of names and subjects referred to in the book, with the pages where the topics may be found.

Both encyclopedias and dictionaries contain many cross references and related subjects. These aids lead the reader from the article he is reading to other articles that will provide additional information.

Many general encyclopedias have a separate index volume. This volume helps the student extend his interest in a subject by showing the interrelationships of a variety of articles.

Many encyclopedias and textbooks include bibliographies. A bibliography is a list of books on a subject for further reading. Reference books also have charts, diagrams, and outlines. These should be studied because they are the author's means of summarizing information. Other aids to study include vocabulary lists, pronunciation guides, photographs and maps.

Cultivate the habit of using all aids to locate material quickly. Learn how to use such basic reference materials as an atlas, an almanac, an encyclopedia yearbook, and the card catalog in the library.

All the study aids available will be of no use to the student if he has not understood the assignment. No subject can be studied effectively unless the student has a clear understanding of the work he is supposed to do. Write out each day's assignment and make a note of what is to be read, the problems to be worked out, and what must be prepared in writing. Ask the teacher to explain any points that are not clear. Take advantage of any directions or suggestions that are offered.

Planning your work can sometimes save a great deal of time or wasted efforts. Plan carefully how to use your time to best advantage. Some students take a few minutes each morning to plan a schedule of their day's activities. Many students find it helpful to make a weekly schedule allowing adequate time for study. A study program should be kept flexible so that adjustments can be made as they are needed.

Schedule your study for a time when you are least tired. Study your most difficult subject first when you are freshest mentally and physically. The easiest subjects should ordinarily be left to do last, unless you become inclined to pass over them too lightly because they are too easy. Plan to keep study periods short and take a few minutes of rest between subjects.

Another practice which is a good one to make a habit is that of taking notes in routine form both while reading and during classroom work. Notes provide a ready source of reference, and they also help you to fix a subject in mind. Do not attempt to write down every word you read or hear. Instead, learn to select essential facts and sum them up in the fewest possible words, using key phrases and abbreviations. To do this efficiently requires considerable practice. But a few well-chosen words can serve as pegs on which to hang ideas. After class, look over your notes and fill in any material you may have missed. The process of reducing a subject to outline form will help in learning how to take effective notes. The outline should be well organized and clear. A good outline is brief enough to allow the student to learn the concepts easily.

Keeping work up to date is also important in gaining the most possible from study time. Nothing can be gained by putting off work from one day to another. You cannot study twice as hard in one day to make up for time lost during another. Each day's lesson must be prepared regularly for rapid progress. But sometimes you may miss work because of illness or for some other unavoidable reason. In that case, extra study time must often be allowed in order to bring the work up to date. Special assistance from your teachers or parents may be needed if you have missed a number of lessons.

Concentration is essential to effective study. This can be accomplished only by mental discipline. The mind is often tempted to wander, sometimes even from an interesting subject. Mental discipline is a habit that can be cultivated only through constant effort. Concentration means that you must think only about the work at hand. If part of the mind is waiting for a telephone call or listening to the radio or television, the rest of the mind cannot concentrate on study.

Some subjects stimulate us naturally, and we enjoy studying them. Others may require a real effort of the will. But no subject need be dull if it is approached with a determination to master it. A subject sometimes seems dull only because we do not understand the reasons for studying it. After its purpose is explained, it may become interesting.

Many reference books contain material other than that about the subject being studied. Sometimes such material may seem so interesting that we are distracted from the work at hand. This temptation must be vigorously resisted until the necessary tasks are accomplished. After the assignment is finished, it may be profitable to turn our attention to any subject we care to pursue. Investigation of this kind can be stimulating to the mind. But to indulge in it before our work is as unwise a practice as eating candy before dinner.

Frequent review is another key concept to getting the most out of study time. Each day's study should begin with a quick review of the previous lesson. This helps to fix in mind the points already learned and to form a bridge to the next assignment. All the work covered during a semester should be reviewed at frequent intervals. Well-kept notes are helpful for this purpose. Never wait until the day before an examination to review the work for an entire period. "Cramming" is the most inefficient method of study, and what is learned in this way is usually soon forgotten. Remember that passing examinations is not the most important purpose of study.

Not all study should be done from books. Everything about us is material study. We can learn much about nature by reading books. But we can learn even more by observation. It is not enough merely to look. We may look without actually seeing. Instead, we must look carefully and think about what we see. Then we begin to wonder and to ask ourselves questions. The answers may be found in books, or we may discover them for ourselves. Knowledge found in this way becomes a permanent part of us.

Museums offer rich sources of material for study. Some of them are mines of information about the past. History comes to life when we see actual examples of furniture, clothing, painting, or sculpture that were used or made by people in other times.

We can learn more about animals by studying live ones in zoos than by looking at pictures in books. And natural history museums present realistic exhibitions of stuffed animals in their natural settings, which most zoos cannot do.

Application of what you have learned is where real benefit can be seen from good study habits. Study has much more meaning if what has been learned is applied to a practical purpose. For example, you might put arithmetic to use by offering to add and check the family grocery bill. A student of home economics may be able to suggest improvements in the family's diet. All recreational activities offer opportunities to put into use something that has been learned in the classroom.

We also gain better understanding of a subject when we learn to express our ideas about it in our own words. This should be done both in writing and orally. Oral discussion stimulates quick thinking, and a written analysis aids careful thinking. You should test your knowledge of a subject by asking yourself questions and then checking the answers with what you have already studied.

Discussions may take place in class. But they also may be continued outside of class with fellow students, members of the family, or older friends.

Finally, a worthwhile thought to remember when you study is that your mental attitude comes into play. A happy outlook of mind helps you to study better. Worries or fear prevent concentration. The cause of a worry may exist only in your mind. Many such worries can be overcome by discussing them with friends, parents, or teachers. Fear of failing in your lessons can sometimes actually prevent effective study. But common sense and reason can help get rid of such fears. Seek the advice of parents and teachers or of someone in whom you have confidence. Your counselor or school adviser will often be able to help you understand your problems more clearly. Having faith in yourself is important to successful study.

Studying Abroad

BY

Council on International
Educational Exchange

A private, non-profit organization, Council on International Educational Exchange has a membership of 196 North American colleges, universities, secondary schools and youth serving organizations which sponsor educational exchange programs. Since its founding in 1947, CIEE has been involved in all aspects of student travel, serving its member organizations and individual students and teachers in the areas of transportation, orientation, information and program development.

Like everything else, studying abroad means different things to different people. To one student it may mean a three-week course in French culture on the Riviera during July, while for another it may mean a year of research on a doctoral thesis in the stacks of a German library. Both of these students are studying abroad, but obviously their needs and expectations are very different.

First you'll have to decide what kind of study experience you want and where, so let's take a look at the options available.

Your choice will depend to a large extent on your capabilities (particularly language skills, if you plan to enroll at a foreign university), your field of interest, how long you want to spend abroad, whether you want academic credit, and how much money you can afford to spend. An alternative to enrolling in a foreign university is to participate in a special study program sponsored by a U.S. institution.

You should realize that university systems and teaching methods in other countries are very different from those in the United States. Some foreign universities require U.S. students seeking admission for degree purposes to have completed two years of college; in some cases they are admitted only when they have completed their undergraduate work. Sometimes qualified undergraduates can make arrangements with their college or university to study independently for a semester or academic year at a foreign university.

If you do decide to apply on your own for study at a foreign university and can meet its admission requirements, be sure to get written approval of your plans from your school, making it clear that you will receive credit for satisfactory completion of the work you do abroad. Instead of enrolling in regular university courses, you may find it easier to enroll in some of the special courses in the history and culture of the country. Some of these courses are taught during the academic year and there are many during the summer when foreign universities usually suspend their regular classes.

If your prefer to join a program rather than study abroad on your own, first check to see whether your own school sponsors an overseas program or is a member of a consortium (an association of colleges and universities) that sponsors a program. Going abroad with your own university will ease the problems of transferring academic credit, securing credit in your major field for overseas courses and maintaining your scholarships or loans. In state schools, tuition charges will usually be less in your home state. It's possible, though, that your college may not sponsor programs in a country where you have language competence or may not offer courses that you can use to satisfy course requirements for your major or for professional preparation.

If this is the case, don't be discouraged: over seven hundred colleges and universities sponsor overseas study programs and most of them accept students from other campuses. Your best bet is to start by consulting the office in your own campus that advises students in foreign study or administers your school's foreign study programs.

When it comes time to consider the various programs, you'll eliminate many of them because of their language requirements, cost, academic focus, or because your own school won't grant academic credit for them. To help you make a decision about the programs that remain, consider what type of courses are provided as well as how much the living arrangements involve you in the social life of the students of the host country.

Does the program provide American-style courses or does it utilize the regular course of the foreign universities? Some programs, at one extreme, export U.S. professors to teach the same courses they would teach at home (in English, of course); others enroll their students in the large lecture classes so typical of a foreign university. In between are a range of compromises: American-style courses taught by foreign professors (in English or in the foreign language); special courses set up by the foreign university for all of their foreign students (occasionally in English); regular courses with tutorial assistance provided by foreign graduate students. Some programs will offer several of these options.

The U.S. student with language competence and good academic skills may profit most by enrollment in the regular courses where he will meet students of the host country and experience its university system firsthand. Students with more limited language skills or academic backgrounds may be wise to avoid direct enrollment. The special courses set up by U.S. programs are sometimes easier to translate into U.S. academic credits, and it's been our experience that most U.S. students find foreign university courses more difficult than expected.

Since a great deal of your learning experience will come from the people you meet and associate with you should concern yourself with student and social involvement. In this area, too, U.S.-sponsored programs provide a range of possibilities. Some programs arrange for all U.S. students to live together in leased or rented hotels or dormitories; others house participants in university dormitories with other students from the host country. Still others provide housing in rented rooms in private homes or apartments; or sometimes students will find living conditions in foreign university dormitories or local homes more austere than those at home. However, in adapting to this austerity and to foreign customs in general, they will acquire greater understanding of the host country and may be helped in learning the language.

The next question to ask yourself is for how long a period will you study abroad? A summer, a semester or a full academic year? Or for one month during the winter term break if you attend a school on the 4-1-4 system?

A semester or academic year of study abroad will give you enough time to become involved in the student life of the country. It can also give you enough time to get miserably homesick. After all, being away from home and friends for six months or a year and having to cope with the pressure of another academic system doesn't appeal to everyone.

If you can't or don't want to interrupt your regular course of studies and go abroad for a semester or year, a summer program might be best for you. An extraordinary variety of opportunities is available to choose from. You can study photography in Germany or archaeology in Peru, landscape architecture in Britain or martial arts in Japan. Taking a summer course might also be a good way to find out whether you would like to study abroad for a longer period of time.

More and more colleges and universities are switching from a two-semester system to what is called a 4-1-4 system. What 4-1-4 means is that students attend classes from September to December and February to May, spending the month studying abroad and joining programs arranged either by their own or another school. The open month of January gives the student an opportunity to participate in interim courses.

It's become more and more common for students to take off the year between high school and college to do something "different" for a while before settling down to more school routine. The alternatives are many for those who want to spend this interim year in another country.

Students who want to work, study or travel abroad for the whole "in-between year," or a part of it, can find many programs that may interest them and for which they are eligible. One possibility for anyone over thirteen is to work with the Club de Vieux Manoir, which is involved in rstoration work on historical sites throughout France. Another is to work on a kibbutz in Israel.

This would also be a good time to take a course in a subject that has always interested you that you never had time to study before. The Institute of International Education is a good source of information on courses that are sponsored by foreign schools and offered to non-matriculated U.S. students. Write to IIE for information.

One study program that has been set up specifically for young people between high school and college is the 13th Year Study Abroad Program sponsored by Youth for Understanding, 2015 Washtenaw Avenue, Ann Arbor, Michigan 48104. YFU's program operates all over the world; participants in the program live with a family and go to school in the host country for approximately fourteen months.

Anyone thinking about taking a year off—whether here in the U.S. or abroad—should order a reprint of an excellent article that appeared in the Summer 1971 edition of the *College Board Review*, "Postponing College: Alternatives for an Interim Year," by Edward F. Babbott. A subsequent *Review* article dealing with the same topic, "Stop-out" by A. Mitchell, might also be of interest, especially to counselors. It's interesting to note that the phrase "stop-out" seems to have been chosen to replace "drop-out"—the change suggests that the idea is gaining in acceptability. Positive proof of this was uncovered by the authors of the above articles, who reported that most institutions questioned said that a student who had been accepted at their school could postpone matriculation for one year without causing any real difficulty. Reprints of both articles are available from the College Board, Publications Order Office, Box 2815, Princeton, New Jersey 08540.

Once you've decided to join a study-abroad program, you will discover how many there are to choose from. At first they will all sound good to you and probably most of them are. But there are some that will not suit your purposes or are not worth the money you will have to spend on them. Unfortunately, there have been several incidents in which students have enrolled in programs only to find, on the eve of their trip, that the organization has disbanded and there is no program. The Department of State often receives complaints from people who have found themselves taking courses offering little or no academic credit when they had been led to believe that substantial credit would be given, or by students who discovered, when it's too late, that they have paid fees far exceeding the value of the services they received.

Often, if the right question had been asked before the students committed their time and money to the program, the disappointments would have been avoided.

Remember there are several places to go for information on study abroad. You can start on your campus at the placement office, office of the academic dean or the international programs office. If you've decided in what country you want to study, you can get information from the consulate, tourist office or information service of that country.

Adapted by permission from the *Whole World Handbook: A Student Guide to Work, Study and Travel Abroad*, 1976-77 Edition. © Council on International Education Exchange. Written by Marjorie A. Cohen; edited by Margaret E. Sherman. Published by CIEE and the Frommer/Pasmantier Publishing Corporation. Copies available for $2.95 from CIEE, 70 Fifth Avenue, New York, New York 10011.

ADVENTURE VI

Making the Experiences of Others a Bridge Over Troubled Waters

A purpose as well as a major objective of this book is to deal candidly and honestly with those subjects which are of major concern to teenage women.

The editors have discussed at length the advisability of including controversial subjects. It was concluded that to ignore or omit such subject matter would be a denial of intent and a failure to acknowledge current issues.

Since research has proven that the intimate subjects are often clouded with misinformation which is the result of hearsay rather than fact, the contents of this section are intended to replace myth with knowledge.

Let it then be clearly understood that MISS TEENAGE AMERICA *states no position on these subjects or issues discussed in the following chapters, but believes that a light cast in the shadows can and will serve the best interests of all who seek knowledge.*

How to Be a Winner When You Feel Like a Loser

(Teens vs Alcohol and Drugs)

BY
MARY SWENSEN

>Lifestyles Unlimited, *to be published this year by the Texas Alcohol and Narcotics Education, Inc. (TANE), is the most recent of Mary Swensen's publications. It is part of an alcohol education program for teenagers which emphasizes value development and individual decision making as the basis for creating a personal lifestyle. Other drug education programs include* Milton and His Magic Motorcycle *and* The Adventure of Daredevil Dog, *also published by TANE.*
>
>*Ms. Swensen has also served as a consultant to several drug education projects both in and out of public schools and was recently a member of a task force on responsible decisions about alcohol. The task force was sponsored by the Education Commission of the States in Denver, Colorado and its purpose is to advise governmental agencies (especially state governments) as they determine educational policies and to help those agencies communicate with each other in implementation.*

"Even in a crowd I felt alone."

"My mother was always there to remind me I wasn't doing things quite right."

"When my stepfather looked at me through the keyhole while I was in the bathroom, I thought it was *my* fault and was afraid to tell my mother."

"I was always hurting on the inside because I felt inferior and had a hard time talking to people."

"A relative told me I was illegitimate and didn't have a father because my mother had been promiscuous."

These are just a few happenings in the lives of real teenagers who felt they were losers. All teenagers have had similar feelings at one time or another and felt like losers—at least temporarily. And, sometimes their feelings were so deep, they seemed unmanageable. The losing feeling was not temporary. It wouldn't go away and there didn't appear to be a way to overcome it.

That's what happened to a girl we will call Linda. When she was a teenager, she felt like a loser, and the way she handled her feelings made her even more of a loser.

"My family was so poor, we couldn't afford nice clothes and the other kids laughed at the way I dressed. My stepfather was an alcoholic, my mother was overly strict, and I felt awkward, ugly, shy and just plain bad in spite of the fact that I was almost a straight-A student," said Linda, remembering her frustrating childhood and early teens. Her silky blouse, well-tailored, blue pantsuit accented with stylish bracelets and neck chains, were in perfect harmony with her artfully up-to-date make-up and hairstyle. She was pretty, subtly sexy and had the kind of good looks that come from highlighting good features while camouflaging less flattering ones. Her lively personality and radiant smile gave no hint that she was the girl being described.

"I was a mess," she continued. "I felt inner pain almost all the time. There was no relief. The constant feeling of inferiority and worthlessness never left me, even when I took my first drink at a school dance. The agony continued all through high school and into college, but at college, I was away from my watch-dog mother and free to do as I pleased. Since all the kids drank, so did I. I began to notice how good I felt after a few drinks. I could begin to communicate! I felt pretty! Self-confidence was my middle name! Or at least it *seemed* that way. Soon, I was drinking every day and before long I flunked out because I couldn't concentrate.

"I took a job, met Jake, my first husband, and was suddenly 'Cinderella' and having a 'ball' because Jake was a well-to-do doctor in a small Louisiana city where our social life was centered around the country club and lavish private parties. For me, it seemed a dream come true to have furs, expensive jewelry, a full-time maid and other material advantages after having been so desperately poor. But it was Glittering Hell.

"Until now, I had been able to 'hold' my liquor. I could drink anyone under the table' and appear sober. I felt confident, sexy and pretty and acted that way.

But then something strange happened. I began to feel drunk after just a few drinks. I flirted with men to the point where their wives got mad. Jake stopped going to parties with me because my behavior embarrassed him, so I went by myself. Almost everyone, and especially the men, thought I was cute. But my social acceptance and marriage abruptly ended when I danced on a dinner table and kicked expensive china and crystal all over the room.

"Jake felt I was evil and weak. His father had been an alcoholic who claimed he would 'stop tomorrow,' all the way up 'til the day he died from alcoholic complications. Even though Jake was a medical doctor, he thought my drinking was a moral weakness and it disgusted him. The thought that it was an illness was foreign to him. In fact, *I* didn't realize I was an alcoholic. I agreed with *him.* I thought I was evil and yet—maybe deep down there was a 'nice' me, a winner, someone I could love and respect. But how could I find her and—Anyway, I drank because I had problems. After all, look at all I had been through. *That's* why I drank. Poor misunderstood little me. I deserved some comfort and alcohol gave it to me."

Divorced, barefoot and in cutoffs, she arrived in New Orleans with some clothes and a car. Her new "friends" were thieves, junkies and other assorted losers. She continued drinking as her friends pursued their pleasures. Eventually, one friend relieved her of all belongings and almost her life, the latter as a result of being stripped naked, beaten and having her hair pulled out by the roots.

Covered only with a tattered blanket and dried blood, she waited at the police station to be photographed. "I thought I was going crazy. I was depressed and considering suicide. No matter what I did, I ended up losing," she mused.

"The next stop was my mother's house and for the next six months, she died slowly along with me. At night, I spent most of my time in bars picking up men to buy me drinks. I paid for the drinks with sex but never remembered anything that happened. In fact, when I lost my virginity back in college, I don't even remember who the boy was because I'd had a blackout—that is, I couldn't remember what happened. Since then, I had been having blackouts frequently.

"Now, I was overwhelmed with guilt over my behavior, so I drank even more to ease my guilt. I was nobody. Just a thing—a lowdown loser. There was no hope for me.

"I guess I must have called AA (Alcoholics Anonymous) one time because they called me back the next day knowing I wouldn't remember the night before. But I was too sick to go to an AA meeting. By now, I was never drunk, but never sober either. I just felt awful.

"One day, as I was drinking some vodka out of a jelly glass, I threw up, but took another drink anyway—and threw it up. And then again and—suddenly, I felt sober, and I knew it was the end. I knew I would either die, go crazy or get better."

Linda had finally reached bottom. Like so many other people who drink or use drugs to escape their problems, she had created even more problems and lost the opportunity to face the ones which prompted her to drink in the first place.

"I struggled to the phone and called a friend to take me to the hospital. She wouldn't because she said I was just mixed up and needed a psychiatrist. I called my cousin and asked her to take me to the hospital—a special hospital for alcoholics I'd heard about on TV.

"At the hospital, they helped me through my withdrawal. You see, my body was chemically dependent on alcohol (and had been for years) so that I had to go through a withdrawal stage (which is unbelievably painful) just as if I was a heroin addict.

"After I was physically free of my alcohol dependence, the hospital helped me get over my psychological dependence. AA and group therapy helped me see myself more clearly and gave me the skills to cope with life. And as a added bonus, I met my present husband, who was my counselor and also a recovered alcoholic! We are happily married and feel our lives really began when we decided to live drug-free."

It was time to end the interview because Linda was leaving for New York to attend a seminar on how to help young people cope with their problems. Her eyes sparkled as she talked about the fun she would have along with the challenge of learning new ideas. "Life itself can be the best high. I love my new life as a college counselor. Every day brings pleasure as I grow and learn, and I feel I'm a winner now because I have a positive way to face life. Oh, I still have problems, and sometimes, I fail or make mistakes. I accept that, without guilt or regret and go forward. When I was a loser, I felt guilty or bad and tried to escape. Each time I face a problem instead of running away, I'm a winner."

What were the skills Linda learned which caused her to change from a loser to a winner? They were the same skills which made Kim a winner.

Kim came from a background different from Linda's. Her family had more than enough money to live a comfortable life and her parents tried to understand and support her. She seemed to have everything, but on the inside, she had many troublesome feelings she couldn't handle and which made her feel like a loser. Like Linda, she chose a destructive chemical escape but unlike Linda, she depended on several drugs including alcohol.

"My big brother gave me four little pills when I was in the fourth grade and told me to save them until I started having big trouble with my parents. When I was eleven, it really got bad at home. In fact, I wasn't too happy about my life in general. I felt apart from people, even when we were having fun. There were so many things I wanted to say about my feelings of self-doubt or things which confused me. My friends all seem so self-confident, I was afraid to talk honestly with them. My parents would never have understood and the counselors at school were only interested in helping me decide whether I should be a dental hygienist or something like that," said fourteen-year-old Kim.

"So, I took one of the pills. At first, I didn't feel anything and thought my brother had played a big joke on me. But then, I felt strange and as I caught a look at myself in a mirror I saw my eyes had dilated.

"I looked up my symptoms in a book I had used in a drug project for science class. LSD! I was shocked. LSD was bad stuff, but, well, all of a sudden, the Red Baron's airplane in the poster on my wall began to fly. Ha! It flew around and around and crashed into the rug on the floor. Wow! I ran to pick up the pieces, but there was *nothing*!

"What a trip! I loved it. It was fun, and I wanted more. It kept me from feeling lonely, and I forgot that I was afraid to say how I felt about things. Escape was the answer!

"It wasn't long before I was on speed, pot, booze or anything! I even tried my mother's diet and pain pills. Any high was okay, but mostly I liked acid and pot. When the supply dried up, I switched to alcohol, usually beer. We'd chug it and really freak out.

"By the time I was fourteen, I was turning on in the school parking lot, *especially* at lunch, because it was more fun than my one o'clock history class, and before long, I started shoplifting to pay for my drugs.

"Then, one day, I was called to the principal's office and taken to the police station when they found windowpane in my purse. I thought I had left it at home, but I forgot—I'd been doing that a lot lately.

"For three years, I'd been in and out of every drug around and so had my friends. I wasn't a 'social' or a 'straight' or even a 'freak' at school, I was just doing my thing. And why not? Nobody cared how I felt. My parents gave me everything I wanted, but they wouldn't listen to my feelings which I mostly let out in a burst of screaming. School was a bore because the teachers handed out thirty questions at the end of each chapter and went out in the hall. And besides, turning on was fun! Except when I got depressed, that is. Sometimes, I felt so bad—well, one time I thought about suicide—but, then I'd get a fresh supply and be happy again.

"Since I was still under the influence of the windowpane I had taken earlier, I saw the cop as a big fat rainbow outlined in black!

"After my parents got over their hysterics and moaning over where they went wrong, I was given two choices. The best one was to be sent to a place that was supposed to help me. I would live there for thirty days and get off drugs and best of all, I wouldn't have to go to school! Wow!

"I just knew this drug rehabilitation program would be a bust. I just knew a straight guy in a suit or some lady with teased hair would tell me to straighten out. Ha! I knew how to handle that and have the thirty-day vacation, *too!*

"But my plan was a flop because J.D. was in cutoffs and had a *beard*. He even told me I didn't have to do anything I didn't want to do. And, then, to make it worse, he actually *listened* to my feelings. I didn't know what else to do so I talked—and talked—and he listened—and listened. And *I* listened to me and heard all the self-pity, defeatism and lies which I'd told myself. Suddenly, I realized I was a loser and said so. (I couldn't believe I was saying it.) J.D. asked me if I wanted to be a winner. I said yes and that's how it all started!"

Like Linda, Kim is now vibrant and attractive because of her own effort to make herself that way. Her long blunt cut hair fanned out on her scenic T-shirted shoulders. As she sat cross-legged on the floor, her body moved enthusiastically while she described her new way of life.

"It's so great to wake up in the morning with a clear head! My memory isn't messed up like it used to be, and I don't get depressed anymore. I've got lots of new friends, and we really love each other. We talk out our feelings and laugh and cry together. It's really the best trip of all!"

Although Linda and Kim differ in economic and family background, types of drugs used, length of drug dependence and how they decided they were losers, they do have several things in common: they both needed relief from personal problems and liked to have fun.

They now share another similarity—the method by which they became winners. Linda recovered from alcohol dependence through the twelve-step program of Alcoholics Anonymous. Even though Kim was dependent on drugs including alcohol, her recovery was based on the twelve step AA program, also. The word "alcohol" was simply crossed out and replaced by "chemical."

"The first rule when using the twelve-step program is to take one day at a time. Sometimes, when things get hectic and I'm under pressure, I need to remind myself to just take care of *today*. It's such a relief and somehow everything works out," explained Linda. "I go to weekly AA meetings to strengthen my understanding of the twelve steps. Along the way, I've made some great friends in the group. We understand each other because we've all been through the same kind of agony."

"My twelve-step program is by my bed, and when I wake up in the morning, I read it and consider each step and how I can make it work—today," said Kim. "Sometimes, I go to AA meetings and I also go to the drug rehabilitation center here in Dallas once a month. It's called DCAP (Dallas Chemical Abuse Program) and we get counseling from people like J.D. and whatever other help we need."

What are these magical steps which can turn losers into winners, one day at a time? Here they are:

THE TWELVE STEPS OF DCAP
(Based on the Twelve Steps of Alcoholics Anonymous)

1. We came to believe that mind-changing chemicals had caused at least part of our lives to become unmanageable and found it necessary to stick with winners in order to grow.
2. We came to believe that a power greater than ourselves could restore us to sanity.
3. We made a decision to turn our will and our lives over to the care of God, as we understand Him.
4. We made a searching and fearless moral inventory of ourselves.
5. We admitted to God, to ourselves, and to another human being the exact nature of our wrongs.
6. We were entirely ready to have God remove all these effects of character.
7. We humbly asked Him to remove our shortcomings.
8. We made a list of all persons we had harmed, and became willing to make amends to them all.
9. We made direct amends to such people whenever possible, except when to do so would injure them or others.
10. We continued to take personal inventory, and when we were wrong promptly admitted it.
11. We sought through prayer and meditation to improve our conscious contact with God, as we understand Him, praying only for knowledge of His will for us and the power to carry that out.
12. Having had a spiritual awakening as the result of these steps, we tried to carry this message to others, and to practice these principles in all our affairs.

"I'm growing now and I wasn't when I was on drugs. It's as if three years were cut out of my life, while I was getting high. I didn't take care of myself, didn't have any goals—I just drifted and looked forward to my next high. Now I have friends, fun, self-confidence, and I really care about me," said Kim with a winning grin as she went to join some friends in a card game.

"The only reason I'm even here to talk about this is because I made a decision to win," remarked Linda. "I'm lucky to be alive. For me, living is more than just breathing and going from one thing to the next. It's loving and sharing and even feeling pain and unhappiness at times," she added as she left for the airport.

Yes, my love, whosoever lives, loses, . . . but he also wins.
—Goethe

The Truth Behind the V. D. Scare

BY
KATHY McCOY
Reprinted with permission from
Teen Magazine (October, 1974)

The headlines about VD are increasingly frantic and shocking: "VD epidemic among teenagers!" "VD most prevalent teen disease after common cold." "Viral VD highly contagious and won't go away!"

These headlines and the stories that follow them can be revealing and —sometimes—misleading.

It is true that venereal disease is a national epidemic. The U.S. Center for Disease Control in Atlanta estimates that 2.5 million cases of gonorrhea and 80,000 cases of infectious syphilis occur each year. A recent report prepared by Koba Associates of Washington (under contract to the U.S. Department of Health, Education, and Welfare) notes that the numbers could be much greater, since private doctors report only about 15 percent of the VD patients they treat. Additionally, cases in the 15-19 age group are growing at an alarming rate. It is estimated that 80 percent of reported cases of gonorrhea occur in individuals under twenty-nine years of age, with 60 percent being under twenty-five. VD is becoming—more and more—a young person's disease.

Many young people, however, react to VD scare stories with disbelief, shock or paralyzing fear.

A *Teen* reader in Ohio, for example, wrote to us describing the nature of her vaginal discharge. "If it's VD, I'll kill myself," she wrote. "I don't want to become insane, sterile, or blind and it's probably too late for treatment. Please tell me it isn't VD!"

Only her doctor—if she would only go to one—could tell her "yes" or "no." Many teens shy away from seeking medical care and advice for their symptoms because of fear. They fear finding out that they have a venereal disease. They fear put-downs from the doctor and the possibility of their parents finding out—this despite the fact that most states have legal provisions for the confidential treatment of any VD patient over twelve years of age. They fear the pain of treatment and the pain of knowing—and having others know—that they have become statistics in the VD epidemic.

These fears are largely unfounded, contends Dr. Charles Wibbelsman, an adolescent-medicine specialist who has seen a number of teenagers who have (or fear they may have) VD in the course of his work in hospitals, free clinics and, most recently, as an adolescent-medicine fellow at the University of Southern California Student Health Center.

"Venereal disease is serious and must be treated, but it is *not* the plague," says Dr. Wibbelsman. "It is curable and the earlier you seek treatment, the better. You shouldn't fear being branded as a terrible person because you have a venereal disease. 'Nice' people *do* get VD. Too many people see VD as a lifelong mark of sin, as a punishment for sex. It's simply a category of disease you risk catching when you have sex—especially when you have intercourse with a number of different partners. All types of VD—even the supposedly penicillin-resistant types of gonorrhea or the viral VD that allegedly won't go away—can be treated and cured. So if you have gonorrhea you aren't automatically doomed to sterility or if you have syphilis, blindness and insanity are far from inevitable. Seeking early medical treatment is the key. Don't try to treat yourself at home because you're afraid that the doctor will give you a shot. While penicillin injections are often used in some types of venereal disease treatment, those allergic to penicillin—or to shots in general—can take oral medication."

Dr. Wibbelsman agrees with headlines stating that VD is a very common communicable disease.

"Venereal disease is much more common than mumps or measles and more common than strep throat," he remarks. "Strep throat, for example, can go into severe kidney disease. But most people seek treatment long before it reaches that stage. Yet, with VD, people often aren't seeking early medical help. There are a number of reasons for this, but let's dispense with the 'fear and branded-for-life' reason first. If you think you have symptoms of VD or may have been exposed to VD, seek medical help. Forget about being ashamed. Your health is at stake. Don't play games with the doctor. Game-playing only hurts you."

An untreated case of VD is a prime contributing factor to the epidemic. He or she will expose and infect others and soon the cases multiply alarmingly.

"One of the major problems is that a majority of females—possibly 80 percent of those with gonorrhea—may not have any noticeable symptoms," says Dr. Wibbelsman. "Symptoms for both gonorrhea and syphilis are usually much more obvious in the male. Unless the male partner tells the female about his infection, she can develop future complications—completely unaware, until the disease has become more severe, that she has a venereal disease. Casual sex creates the problem here. Some young people don't know how to—or won't—get in touch with casual sex partners. Others delay seeking treatment out of ignorance. They don't really know what venereal disease is, its symptoms or means of prevention."

What is VD: How do you know if you do—or don't—have it?

"Venereal diseases are those transmitted usually by intimate sexual contact," says Dr. Wibbelsman. "The 'germs' that cause VD—e.g., the gonococcus bacteria that causes gonorrhea—are very fragile and die outside the human body. So you can't get VD from toilet seats and doorknobs. You can't get it from bathtubs or showers—you may get athlete's foot, but not VD! Intimate sexual contact does not always mean penile-vaginal intercourse. I've seen girls who had VD and were bewildered because they were—technically—virgins. The gonococcus bacteria, for example, can thrive in the mucous membranes of the body—the cervix, urethra, anal canal and the moist lining of the mouth and throat. Many teens ask if you can get VD—especially gonorrhea—from kissing. Usually the answer is no. But you *can* get VD from oral sex. I feel it's very important for teens to know this. If the organs are infected with VD, the other partner may catch it."

While syphilis and gonorrhea are the best-known venereal diseases, there are others, like the viral Herpes 2, genital warts and pubic lice (crabs). There are also other infections that may or may not be sexually transmitted.

"I feel that it's important for teenagers to know about all of these diseases, infections and their symptoms," says Dr. Wibbelsman. "The more aware you are, the less fear and terror you'll have and the more likely you are to seek prompt medical treatment."

The following are brief descriptions of common venereal diseases.

GONORRHEA

This is the most common venereal disease today and is caused by a bacteria called the gonococcus. The bacteria can survive outside the human body for only a few seconds, so transmission must be via very close sexual contact, e.g., vaginal or oral-genital sexual intercourse.

Symptoms: Within three to five days after exposure, the male is likely to notice a discharge from his penis. It changes from clear to thick and white or yellow. He is likely to feel a burning sensation while urinating and may also have enlarged lymph glands in the groin area.

Up to an estimated 80 percent of women have no initial gonorrhea symptoms. In women, the infection is usually centered in the cervix, high up in the vagina, so signs of the disease may be hard for the woman herself to detect. Some women—the luckier ones—may have an irritating green or yellow-green vaginal discharge quite unlike the normal white or clear, non-irritating discharge that all women have. Some may also experience pain during urination.

Many women have no early symptoms, though, and by the time gonorrhea becomes noticeable it may have infected the uterus and fallopian tubes, causing Pelvic Inflammatory Disease which can permanently damage pelvic organs and possibly cause sterility. Untreated gonorrhea can also cause possible sterility in the male. Prompt, early treatment, then, is very important. Only a doctor can tell whether you have gonorrhea (via a painless test).

Treatment: Penicillin is the first choice of treatment for gonorrhea. With a sufficiently high dosage, it will cure any case of gonorrhea—even the supposedly "penicillin-resistant" type. Those afraid of injections may take ampicillin orally. Those allergic to penicillin are generally treated with tetracycline. There are several other drugs that may also be used.

SYPHILIS

Syphilis, while not as common as gonorrhea, is the most serious of the venereal diseases. It is caused by a spirochete called *Treponema pallidum* which is transmitted to the body during sex relations and invades body tissues and organs via the lymphatic system and bloodstream. When some people think of syphilis, they think of blindness, insanity, paralysis or death. These can happen in the third stage of untreated syphilis and take some years to develop. Detecting and curing the disease during the highly infectious first and second stages prevents these tragedies.

Symptoms: The first stage, or primary syphilis, appears eight to thirty days after exposure. A painless sore (called a chancre) appears at the site where the spirochete entered the body: the penis, vagina, cervix, mouth, anus, the area around the vagina or a break in the skin. Because it is painless and especially when it is located out of sight in the vagina or cervix, the chancre often goes unnoticed. It will disappear in a few weeks without treatment, but syphilis is still very much present. The secondary stage of syphilis, usually heralded by a skin rash which may cover the whole body, including the palms of the hands and the soles of the feet, will manifest itself two to six months following the infecting sexual contact. There may also be fever, sore throat, loss of hair and aching. These symptoms also disappear without treatment and the disease enters its latent stage. In four or five years, the third stage—with possibilities of damage to the heart, central nervous system, blood vessels and eyes—occurs. At any of the three stages, a baby born to an infected mother may have congenital syphilis. Many of these babies die before or soon after birth. Others survive but have the disease.

The presence of syphilis can be confirmed by a blood test.

Treatment: Penicillin or other antibiotics for those allergic to penicillin are most often used. Early treatment—with lifelong follow-up examinations—may literally be life-saving!

HERPES GENITALIS OR HERPES 2

This is the disease that has been grabbing headlines lately. It has been called "the viral infection that won't go away" and has been known to cause severe—often fatal—infection in newborns whose mothers were infected. Some reported studies also show signs of possible links to increased susceptibility to cervical cancer, but these studies are not yet conclusive.

The recent publicity surrounding this disease has caused a lot of fright among young people, some of it unwarranted, Dr. Wibbelsman contends.

"Herpes is very common and very painful," he says. "It is also somewhat difficult to treat because it may keep coming back, even when the infected person isn't engaging in sex. Herpes is usually transmitted by vaginal or oral-genital sex and is caused by a virus closely related to—but not the same as—those causing cold sores and fever blisters. The incubation period is unknown, but when herpes manifests itself, a blister or several groups of painful blisters appear on the sex organs. They are very painful at first, but gradually begin to heal. Treatment is important to help prevent—hopefully—recurrent infection. Also, it's important that a woman be aware of the nature of her infection, especially if she's pregnant. When a pregnant woman has Herpes 2, we prefer to deliver her baby by Caesarean section. Otherwise, the baby may become infected while passing through her cervix and vagina and suffer an often fatal brain infection. A woman who has had herpes should have regular exams, including a Pap test for cervical cancer, every six months."

PUBIC LICE (CRABS)

This annoying condition is caused by "crab" lice lodged in the pubic hairs. While these are usually transmitted during sexual intercourse, it has been reported that some people become infected after sleeping in a bed used by a person with pubic lice. The symptoms vary. There may be none or there may be intense itching.

The pubic lice and their eggs may be killed easily by application of the drug gamma benzene hexachloride, which is available in non-prescription creams, lotions and a shampoo called "Kwell"—available at most drugstores. Treatment followed by a change of clothing will usually bring relief.

VENEREAL WARTS

These warts—similar to common skin warts—are caused by a virus and appear on the genital organs. It is believed that they are usually transmitted by sexual intercourse and they generally appear one to three months after the infecting sexual contact. Small genital warts can be removed by application of podophyllin. Larger ones must be removed surgically—often under a local anesthetic.

OTHER VENEREAL AND NON-VENEREAL INFECTIONS

There are a number of other infections that may or may not be sexually transmitted. Non-gonococcal or non-specific urethritis is an inflammation of the male urethra. It is not known for certain that this is sexually transmitted, but doctors report that the disease is rare in men who have not had sexual intercourse.

"It is important for girls to know about this infection which is very common in young men since they may be carriers of the organism that causes non-specific urethritis," says Dr. Wibbelsman. "The man will notice—usually in the morning—a slight discharge. Treatment is by oral medication over a seven- to ten-day period. It is advisable for the female to get treatment, too, because even though she may have no symptoms herself, she may be carrying the disease-causing organisms in her vagina."

Vaginitis or inflammation of the vagina is a very common disease that has several forms and may or may not be sexually transmitted.

One form, *Trichomonas vaginalis* vaginitis, is caused by a pear-shaped organism called the trichomonad. Sexual transmission is the most common way to get this. "The woman has the symptoms this time," says Dr. Wibbelsman. "She may have a frothy, greenish-white or yellow, foul-smelling discharge. The male will usually have no symptoms. Again, treatment of both partners by oral medication over a ten-day period is usually indicated."

Candida albicans vaginitis is caused by a microscopic yeastlike fungus. This fungus is generally present in most healthy people and only occasionally causes disease. While sexual intercourse is sometimes implicated in the infection, there are a number of other factors that may help cause it. Diabetes, pregnancy, some high-estrogen birth control pills, fatigue, emotional upset and generally lowered resistance can make a woman more susceptible to *Candida albicans* vaginitis. The symptoms are intense itching in the genital region and a thick, white, curd-like discharge. Treatment is usually by foaming vaginal tablets. Cystitis is a urinary tract infection occurring primarily in women. It is caused by a common organism called the *E. coli* and may or may not be sexually linked. The symptoms are burning pain while urinating coupled with the frequent desire to urinate. The urine may be hazy and tinged with blood. This condition requires prompt medical treatment to prevent the bacteria from spreading to the kidneys.

Cystitis, which can be diagnosed by a urine sample, is usually treated with sulfa drugs.

Although advances are being made in VD treatment and although all cases of VD can be effectively treated and cured, the best VD fighting tactic of all is prevention.

"One of the best ways you can help prevent and stop the spread of VD is to know your sex partner," says Dr. Wibbelsman. "We all realize that some teens' lifestyles include a more casual viewpoint toward sex. These people are more likely to get VD than those who have only one sex partner. If that is your lifestyle, at least get a phone number so you can reach each other even if you have no intention of seeing each other again. It is particularly important for men to alert women to possible infection, since men often have symptoms and women don't. Whatever your lifestyle, human consideration should enter into it. If you once cared enough to be sexually intimate, you must care enough to warn each other of possible venereal disease exposure."

Some health clinics contact your sex partner(s) without giving your name and ask them to come in for tests and/or treatment. Other times, informing them of their exposure may be your responsibility—not an easy task, but a vital one. The recent Koba Report suggests a new system of tracing sexual contacts with a minimum of embarrassment and a maximum of privacy. According to this plan, a VD patient would be given information kits to distribute to his or her sexual partner(s). These, in turn, could speak to a health officer over the phone without giving a name and a receive a number-coded prescription to be filled by a druggist.

"It is important, too, to be aware of help available if you think you may have or have been exposed to a venereal disease," says Dr. Wibbelsman. "Seek help at a local free clinic or youth clinic if you don't go to your family physician. The care you receive will be totally confidential. If you suspect you may have been exposed to VD, go in for testing within a few days, even if you have your period. During the menstrual flow, the gonococcus, for example, may be even easier to detect. Don't try to diagnose or treat yourself for VD. You can't. Prompt, competent medical treatment is a must."

If the VD epidemic is to be conquered, prevention must play an increasingly major role. Many parts of the picture are brightening, despite the shocking statistics. Most states allow minors infected with VD to be treated confidentially without parental consent. More and more VD, youth and free clinics are appearing on the national scene. Medical research is under way to improve existing VD treatment programs and to discover new ones. Educational pamphlets on VD, its treatment and prevention proliferate. A national effort to stem the VD tide is under way, but its success is very dependent on the knowledge, efforts and responsibility of young people across the nation.

Educating themselves and their friends to face the responsibilities of intimacy, to know the symptoms of VD and the availability of medical care is part of the challenge teens today face. Educating themselves to care is another.

Whatever your moral convictions, sexual attitudes and lifestyle, the fact remains that the fight against the VD epidemic depends very much on *you*!

Abortion—Yes, No, And Why?

BY
KATHY McCOY
Reprinted with permission from
Teen Magazine (January, 1973)

Her face is pale and her eyes betray the fright behind her reserved exterior. She speaks in a tightly controlled voice.

"Marriage is out of the question," Laurie K., sixteen, seven weeks pregnant and unwed, tells the sympathetic counselor. "Tom and I just aren't ready for that. He has three more years of college and I have another year of high school—"

She fights back tears and continues, "I just can't go through with the pregnancy. I can't. I know I couldn't care for and support a baby on my own and I couldn't stand giving it up for adoption. And everyone would know. That's why I think abortion is really the only thing I can do, but I feel so bad, so alone. . . ."

The tears, so long held back, are pouring down her cheeks.

If Laurie does choose to have an abortion, she will join thousands of other teens who had abortions—both legal and illegal—in the United States last year. Of an estimated million and a half abortions, approximately one-third were performed on teenagers.

In a one-year period in California alone, 43,100 unmarried teen girls became pregnant. Countless others became married teens as a result of pregnancy. Of the unmarried pregnant teens, 17,800 had legal abortions.

The statistics—and potential statistics—are growing daily. Planned Parenthood officials in Chicago estimate that there are at least 130,000 sexually active teens in their area. The vast majority of these, like their counterparts across the nation, do not use any form of contraception or, at best, rely on the least advisable forms, like rhythm or withdrawal.

More and more teens are taking the risk of an unwanted pregnancy. Statistics are soaring. Controversy is raging around the issues of teenage sexuality, morals, birth control and alternatives to unwanted pregnancies (especially abortion). While impersonal statistics mount and theoretical controversies rage, the individual stories of ignorance, naiveté, ambivalence and personal tragedy are poured out daily to counselors and clergymen across the nation. Laurie is *not* alone.

Some would call Laurie K. a murderer. Others would see her as a desperate teen in a crisis situation who is trying to choose the best possible alternative—for her. If Laurie does opt for an abortion and if she happened to live in a state with restrictive laws, she would have to fly to a distant city, like New York, Washington, D.C., or Los Angeles to have the simple five-minute operation. However, since she lives in California, a state with relatively liberal laws, Laurie will be able to have a safe, legal, low-cost abortion with good pre- and post-abortion counseling.

The waiting room of Planned Parenthood's Clergy Counseling Service in Los Angeles is crowded with those seeking help. Some are teens like Laurie. Some appear shy and vulnerable. Others seem prematurely hardened to life's harsher realities. Some are with parents or boyfriends. Others are alone. Most are scared, and too nervous or preoccupied to read the numerous magazines scattered around.

One tiny, blond teen girl, however, is bent intently over a school textbook. She looks like any other teen cramming for exams until one looks closer. Her face is crumpled with fear and grief. Big tears are splashing down on the book's unread pages.

These teens generally have one thing in common besides pregnancy. Their initiation into this uneasy sisterhood of suffering has been due primarily to non-use of contraceptives. Some seventy percent of them have never used any form of birth control at all. Why?

"I don't know. . . . I just didn't think it could happen to me," says Lynn, fourteen.

"We didn't expect to go all the way. It just happened," whispers June, sixteen, who has flown in from Louisiana to seek help.

"If we used a contraceptive, it would be like we really planned to have sex and that's terrible. It's so calculated and unromantic, you know? I'd feel cheap!" says Jennifer, fifteen, who is unmistakably pregnant.

"It is hard to plan for something you've been taught is dirty and evil," says Elizabeth Canfield, a sex education counselor at California State College at Northridge. "We often see this need to pretend that intercourse will not take place, to pretend that it was unplanned and therefore more easily rationalized. In my counseling, I always stress responsibility. This has many aspects. It may mean not having sex if you don't feel right about it. Or it may mean—if you *do* have sex—taking adequate precautions against an unplanned pregnancy. That's responsibility."

"I feel that if a teen is single, sexually active and is not using a contraceptive, she is being irresponsible," says Rev. Hugh Anwyl, executive director of the Clergy Counseling Service–Planned Parenthood L.A.

California Assemblywoman March Fong (D-Oakland) cites ignorance as a major cause of these unwanted pregnancies and advocates better sex education as well as more readily available birth control information and services for the sexually active. She's critical of what she calls the "head in the sand" attitude toward sexually active teens.

"Just because a girl doesn't know the difference between a maternity dress and a paternity suit doesn't guarantee that she won't be needing both," Assemblywoman Fong insists. She is disturbed, too, by the alleged imbalance of financial priorities in her state. She says that abortions cost California about $15 million a year while only $1 million goes for family planning and education services.

The experts concur that many factors—like ignorance, naiveté, fear, guilt, shame and denial—have combined to bring this current group of women to the waiting room of the Clergy Counseling Service. These are only a small portion of the more than 1000 women who pass through this room in a single month. Most of these (about ninety-five percent) choose to terminate their pregnancies via legal abortions.

"This isn't because we push abortion as the only alternative," says Rev. Anwyl. "It is because women who know that they definitely don't want an abortion are likely to go elsewhere, like a maternity home, for help."

When a woman seeking help calls the Clergy Counseling Service, she can generally get an appointment that same day. If her pregnancy is already confirmed, she brings the certification with her. If not, she is given a pregnancy test at Planned Parenthood's clinic. After filling out a two-page questionnaire covering medical history, age, last menstrual period, method of contraception used or *not* used and why, etc., she has a personal counseling session with one of the Service's trained experts. She is encouraged to bring her boyfriend or a parent along and many do. Some experienced counselors have observed that, more and more, the decision concerning an unwanted pregnancy is a couple's decision rather than that of a lonely, abandoned unwed mother.

"We thoroughly explore the scene in terms of boyfriend, parents, ages of those involved and so on," says Rev. Anwyl. "We try to determine why the girl got pregnant in the first place. Why did she take chances? Excepting a few medical instances, there is no such thing as a problem pregnancy. There are problems and there are pregnancies. Often the problems give rise to the pregnancies.

"Delving into her past and helping the girl to determine 'How did I get here?' helps her to make a responsible decision regarding 'Where do I go from here?' If this is done, she is likely to choose the alternative best for her, one she can live with and isn't as likely to regret later. Above all, the decision must be—ultimately—her own."

Rev. Anwyl has witnessed instances where parents or others have tried to force a teen into an alternative unthinkable for her.

Alice, fifteen at the time of her visit, is a particularly memorable case. Her mother, fearful of the family's social position in their small Texas town, had brought her to Los Angeles for an abortion. However, Alice quite honestly felt that abortion was murder and that she could not live with the feeling that she had killed her own baby.

"We always try to be supportive of the pregnant girl," says Rev. Anwyl. "In Alice's case, we respected her feelings. We didn't even try to persuade her to have an abortion. We felt that her mother's social position was far less important than Alice's feelings. Alice returned home and had her baby. We don't try to persuade a girl to change her feelings. We're here to help her—whatever option she elects."

For those who do choose abortion, as most of the women who come to the Clergy Counseling Service do, there is an explanation of costs and procedures.

Pregnancies of less than twelve weeks' duration are generally terminated by the dilatation and suction method. After the woman is given a local or general anesthetic, a small plastic tube is inserted through her cervix and the pregnancy is removed by suction (similar to a vacuum cleaner). Performed by a qualified physician in a hospital or clinic, the procedure is quick, safe and relatively painless. Depending on the type of anesthetic used, the fee ranges from $125 to $150 at Planned Parenthood L.A.

More advanced pregnancies (up to twenty weeks) require the more difficult, painful and expensive ($350) saline infusion abortion. Here a saline solution is injected into the uterus, inducing labor and eventually causing the woman to miscarry within a day or so. While early abortion patients generally spend only a few hours at the hospital, saline infusion patients often spend two to three days.

Both local and out-of-town patients are usually taken to Inglewood Hospital for their abortions. Counselors are present throughout the procedure to give comfort and support. Afterwards, the women are given three packets of pills: a drug to help the uterus contract and reduce possible bleeding, an antibiotic to prevent possible infection and a month's supply of birth control pills to get their monthly cycles started again and to get the women acquainted with contraception. They are also urged to return to the counseling center (or the Planned Parenthood clinic in their locale) for a checkup in two or three weeks.

Recently a group of arriving abortion patients at Inglewood Hospital got an unscheduled variation to the smooth, well-planned procedure. They were met by a band of chanting Student Pro-Life pickets outside the hospital. The group, primarily students and young workers under twenty-five, allegedly chanted phrases like "Don't kill babies" and carried signs proclaiming "Abortion is murder!" Some also allegedly attempted to show grisly full-color photos of aborted fetuses to the prospective patients, urging them to reconsider.

"What some of these people don't realize is that while those abortion pictures aren't pretty, neither are pictures of brutally battered children, starving children, emotionally and psychologically abused children," says Rev. Anwyl. "Insisting on the continuation of an unwanted pregnancy can show a lack of regard for human life. If we have regard for life, we will make sure a baby doesn't arrive without its basic rights—the right to be loved, wanted and cared for properly."

A highly volatile and vocal foe to this point of view is Debbie Wiggins, twenty-one, the executive director of the Student Pro-Life group.

She was very much present at Inglewood Hospital on the fateful day and is now being sued, along with her companions, for $4 million—accused of inflicting intentional emotional stress on women about to have abortions.

Debbie's aggressive dedication to the rights of the unborn has its roots in personal experience: A year ago, she faced an unplanned pregnancy herself.

"Everyone, including my family, thought I was mid-Victorian for not wanting an abortion," she says angrily. "I knew from the beginning that I wanted to have my baby. The pressure to have an abortion was unbelievable. There is great discrimination against the girl who elects to have her baby. Fortunately, I found a hospital that sponsored therapy sessions for unwed mothers. These helped me a lot during that difficult time."

When her healthy son was born, Debbie felt even more convinced that she had done the right thing. "When I saw him for the first time, it really hit me," she says. "He was a separate, distinct human being who lived only because I chose *not* to have an abortion!"

After relinquishing her son for adoption, Debbie plunged into Pro-Life activities, making the Student Pro-Life group more politically active. She has also spent much time doing "undercover work" at various abortion referral services mushrooming all over Los Angeles.

"I'm frankly alarmed at the production-line tactics they use," she says. "One girl I know was hemorrhaging after her abortion and no one would help her. They kept saying 'Oh, you're okay' and she wasn't. Also, there is big money involved in these services. One girl I know who wasn't even pregnant went in and got scheduled immediately for an abortion. I also went into a service—definitely not pregnant, right?—and was told that I was ten weeks pregnant. Let's face it. They're out to make money—all of them. Planned Parenthood gets $20 for every abortion case. Multiply that by at least a thousand a month and you get a nice sum."

Problem pregnancy counselors do concede that as more and more referral services do spring up, some abuses by profiteers are creeping in. For this reason, Elizabeth Canfield refers students seeking abortions only to the service she believes is the most reliable and long-established: Planned Parenthood–Clergy Counseling.

"They've been established a long time and they don't make money off abortions," she says. "Their people are salaried and get paid the same no matter how many or how few abortion referrals they handle."

Rev. Anwyl agrees: "Theoretically, twenty dollars of the total fee comes to us, but out of this we pay for the patient's medication and transportation, and a number of our patients require expensive medication that is three times more costly than the twenty dollars. We generally run at a deficit and if we do have any money left over, it is put back into the organization to open and improve birth control services."

A frantic phone call comes from Inglewood Hospital. An out-of-state patient—a sixteen-year-old girl from Las Vegas who requires a $350 saline infusion abortion—has arrived at the hospital with only $150. Rev. Anwyl looks a little impatient. "I thought we already discussed that," he says. "Send *us* the bill for the additional two hundred dollars and let the girl have her abortion. We'll cover any additional expenses."

Emotional aftershocks of abortions is another area of debate brought up by Pro-Life advocates. Ione Jennings, a registered nurse and dedicated BirthRite volunteer in San Francisco, is concerned about such post-abortion emotional problems. "Our Hot Line Helpers are doing as much post-abortion counseling as problem pregnancy counseling," she says. "One girl who called had had an abortion six months before, but kept feeling a kick—like a baby's in her stomach. Another girl—post-abortion—kept hearing a baby cry. Girls who have had abortions are generally very ambivalent."

"Much is said about the adverse emotional aftereffects of abortion," says Jerome Kummer, a Santa Monica, California, psychiatrist. "One may find a certain amount of guilt in a girl who has just had an abortion. That's natural. In a society that generally disapproves of abortion, the girl, as part of that society, will naturally oblige and feel guilty. But we have guilt about all kinds of things. We haven't found any serious post-abortion mental illness."

Some recent studies concur with his views. A Harvard University psychiatric team has reported that ninety-one percent of the women in a study group obtaining abortions were pleased at the outcome of their decisions. In a report to the American Fertility Society, Dr. Leon A. Falik stated that abortions produce few psychological problems in teens and young adults, the largest age group seeking abortions.

"It depends on the girl," says Rev. Anwyl. "If she was forced into an abortion by her parents or boyfriend or she feels that the abortion was murder, she will have problems. Some of these girls become pregnant again right away—to replace the fetus that was lost."

"If some women do feel bad after an abortion," says Elizabeth Canfield, "they generally feel bad about having been pregnant, about being stupid regarding contraceptives. In counseling, I accent the positive. They may be dumb about contraception, but they're *not* evil."

The question of evil, however, is a vital one in the abortion issue. The basic philosophical debate—Is abortion murder? When does a fetus become a person with rights?—transcends all other considerations.

Pro-Life forces and many other individuals believe that life begins at conception and that the abortion of the fetus, no matter how undeveloped, is murder. Others cite the famous constitutional clause defining "men" as those who have been born.

Some states now permit abortions only when the mother's life is at stake. Others, like California, permit abortions if the mother's mental health and well-being are threatened. About ninety-seven percent of California's abortions are done for that reason. Other states, like New York and Hawaii, require no stated reasons. Abortion is a matter between a woman and her doctor.

Restrictive abortion laws are relatively recent—adopted about a century ago for medical as well as religious reasons. At that time, abortion was an extremely dangerous medical procedure. Today, in the illegal back-alley abortion mills, it can still be dangerous. While fatality estimates run as high as 100 per 100,000, it is impossible to tell exactly how many women lose their lives at the hands of unskilled, criminal abortionists. It is also impossible to determine how many suffer permanent injuries as a result of botched abortions. Statistically, an early legal abortion performed by a skilled doctor in an accredited hospital or clinic is safer than childbirth.

Driven by the sincere conviction that abortion is murder and that the rights of the fetus must be protected, however, Pro-Life forces are battling to repeal liberal laws and to reinforce more restrictive legislation.

"Most women don't have valid reasons for wanting an abortion. Most pro-abortion people say 'We want abortions because we want them!'" says Michael Engler, founder of the Southern California Libertarian Movement.

"Isn't that reason enough?" counters Elizabeth Canfield. "A 1965 study shows that in that year—two years before California passed its most liberal abortion law—there were approximately 100,000 illegal abortions in the state. Last year, we had close to 100,000 legal abortions. We aren't changing the number of abortions here. We're simply changing the status from illegal, dangerous and possibly fatal to the mother to legal, clean and safe."

Most people experienced in problem pregnancy counseling agree, and point out that the fact remains that women will have abortions, in spite of state laws or even the dictates of their religion. The Catholic Church, of course, is the religious group most strenuously opposed to liberalized abortion laws. Ironically, Victor Peterson, Development Director of Chicago Planned Parenthood, reports that about forty percent of their patients sent to New York for legal abortions are Catholics! Even within the Church there is ferment. Recently, the Jesuit publication *America* editorialized that the Catholic Church should engage actively in abortion law reform.

Such reform would make abortion a matter between a woman and her doctor. It would make abortion more readily available to those who need it most.

Although abortion is still illegal in Illinois, about 700 women a month go to Chicago Planned Parenthood for abortion referral to New York clinics. Some of these patients are as young as twelve or thirteen.

"The biggest problem we face is the fact that some of the poorer women and students, those who need abortion services most, can't afford them, especially with air fare thrown in," says Vic Peterson. "Some New York clinics will provide a certain number of low-cost or no-cost abortions. It's the air fare that is the biggest problem." It is, he believes, yet another form of discrimination against the poor.

The poor woman left behind, determined to have an abortion, may resort to a number of means. Margaret, seventeen, tried to abort herself with a knitting needle and almost bled to death. Kim, sixteen, douched with turpentine and crawled into a hospital emergency room incoherent with pain. In this same room not long before, a twenty-year-old woman and mother of two toddlers died—the victim of a self-induced coat-hanger abortion.

Some, like Joan, eighteen, get desperate enough to take what money they have and find an illegal abortionist. Although her abortion took place two years ago, Joan still remembers it vividly. She will never forget the horror of being gagged so her screams could not be heard while the abortionist performed a clumsy D&C abortion. Although the procedure was very painful, Joan was given no anesthetic or pain killers and was left to be picked up by a friend on a prearranged street corner shortly afterwards. In spite of her horrible memories, Joan is lucky. She had no complications or infections. She is still alive to tell her story.

Even at its safe, legal best, abortion is not an easy, pleasant experience.

"Post-abortion teens seem to come back from New York much older," observes Chicago *Teen Scene*'s Jane DeLung. "They are our best advocates of responsibility at our teen rap sessions. They tell new patients, 'It's better to use a contraceptive now and feel a bit guilty than to feel innocent and be pregnant!'"

"You can't lie to people," adds Elizabeth Canfield. "The decision to have an abortion may be a painful one. At best, abortion is a regrettable form of emergency birth control. It's a shame when a woman has to have one, but it helps if she can have a legal, safe abortion. Wht most of us are advocating is *not* abortion per se but freedom of choice. No woman should ever be compelled to have an abortion against her will. And no woman should ever have to continue a pregnancy she doesn't want."

Laurie's hand trembles as she signs the bottom of her counseling questionnaire. She has made her decision. She will have an abortion. The decision has been a difficult one. Practical considerations, exploration of all the alternatives and her own feelings about herself and her situation have played a part. She has made her decision in desperation, not cold-blooded calculation; with tears, not malice. The alternative she has chosen is not easy. None of them are. But this one, she feels, is the best for her.

Caught in the crisis of an unwanted pregnancy, countless other teens across the nation are seeking such freedom of choice. Some counselors and doctors are also fighting for this freedom.

"As a social psychiatrist, I'm appalled by society's neurosis, by the hypocrisy that punishes pregnant, unwed women so severely," says Dr. Kummer.

In her own way, a teen named Bridget is fighting too, for understanding, compassion and keeping an open mind. Bridget is seventeen, unmarried and eight months pregnant. She is looking forward eagerly to the birth of her baby. Her first pregnancy two years ago ended in a legal abortion. She is now facing a group of Los Angeles Pro-Life volunteers.

"Don't be too harsh in your judgments," she says. "The fact that I'm going through with this pregnancy doesn't make me Mother of the Year.

The fact that I had an abortion two years ago doesn't make me a murderer. Stop generalizing about the wrongness of abortion. Its rightness or wrongness depends on the person, the time, the circumstances. Having an abortion is not an easy experience. Neither is having a child out of wedlock. It isn't fair to judge a girl, especially if you haven't experienced the crisis of unwanted pregnanacy. You can't know what it's really like—unless *you've* been there!"

ADVENTURE VII

Making the Most of Your Youth

SPECIAL INTERESTS FOR TEENS

Making the Most of Fun

PERFECT PARTIES AND ENCORE ENTERTAINING

BY
JUDY DUE
Director, Consumer Service
Dr Pepper Company

Everyone enjoys visiting with friends. On special occasions you feel like celebrating and entertaining. Who cares what the special occasion is—it's raining outside, or the sun came up today, or it's holiday time or school is out for the summer.

When you are the host or hostess, it is your responsibility to see that all your guests enjoy themselves and that includes you. The only way to have a really good time for all is plan, plan, plan! Get organized and carry through. Below is a basic checklist for party planning. It will be as helpful for those small pizza parties as it will in planning a big school dance.

BASIC ENTERTAINING PREPARATION

Planning:
    Type of party
    Number of guests and who
    Time of party (hours)
    Decorations
    Types of food (what can be prepared ahead)
    Table settings—traffic flow and conversation groupings
    Invitations—R.S.V.P.
    Shopping list
    Preparation in advance—time and motion plan of attack
    Last-minute details

When you decide you want to have a party, then you want to think about what kind and when. First decide on your date and time. This will influence all other factors. Will you entertain during the week? Consider that your friends may have early morning or evening classes or perhaps they work at odd-hour part-time jobs. Or will you entertain on the weekend when time has no limit.

Now decide what time of morning, noon, or evening. For instance:

An early morning breakfast. Everyone meets at your home for a "Top-o-the-Mornin' " breakfast. From the breakfast table on to the pool or beach, or perhaps a bicycle trail or hiking excursion.

Perhaps you would prefer a more sophisticated party for a Sunday brunch. Your friends would have a chance to socialize, relax, yet experience a higher plane of informality. The change of formality in itself could be fun.

Or those wedding bells are chiming for a very dear friend and you want to help them celebrate their happiness! Rather than the traditional shower, plan it for a Saturday night and have a liberated shower. Invite the friends of both the bride and groom. Their friends can bring gifts of linens, kitchen equipment, or decorator items, as well as the essentials—hammer, nails, wrenches, and pliers. Everyone can join in on the fun and you won't have to discriminate against either the guys and gals in our era of liberation.

And of course during the holiday season everyone wants to party. An open house or a dance can be lots of fun and allows you great flexibility in planning. The foods are easy, decorations as simple or elaborate as you choose, and because the purpose is to "mix and visit" you can invite more people.

Now let's see, we have decided what kind of entertaining we are going to do and when. Now we still have a multitude of things we still have to decide on.

How many guests are you going to invite? If you have decided on a sit-down meal, your table size can limit the number of guests you can accommodate. However, if you choose a buffet, the foods are arranged on the main table to allow the guests to serve themselves, then they can eat on smaller conversation tables.

Whom will you invite? Make a list of names and addresses. You may want to refer to it from time to time before the party. And it will be easy to use when you address the invitations or issue a personal invitation. Before you send out the invitations decide on your decorations. You want to tie everything into your party theme. For instance, a New Orleans brunch, or San Francisco bash would set the theme, with invitations, decorations, table settings and background music to all tie into your theme and set the mood.

The invitations should include:

    Date: _____
    Time: _____
    Place: _____
    Given By: _____
    R.S.V.P. (with your phone number)

The R.S.V.P. is a matter of courtesy. The letters are an abbreviation for the French phrase "Répondez S'il Vous Plaît" meaning, "Respond if you will." This helps the host or hostess know how many guests to actually plan for. Once you have responded you are obligated to hold to your answer unless you notify the host or hostess otherwise.

It is menu-planning time! Decide what you want to serve and write it down. As you plan your menu, it would be a good idea to consider how you will serve the foods. If you plan to serve a food that requires a chafing dish, do you have one or can you borrow it? Or if everything requires long serving trays, will your table hold it all? You may have to alter your menu to suit the serving pieces required.

Also plan for many foods that can be prepared in advance. This will allow you more time to relax the day of the party so that you may enjoy the festivities too.

From your menu plan it's easy to make your market order. Read each recipe to learn how many people it serves and how much of each ingredient the recipe requires. Run a tally of all the ingredients needed and it is time to visit your local grocery store. Just a helpful little reminder, before shopping for the necessary foods, be certain to eat a good meal. Shopping on an empty stomach has destroyed many grocery budgets because of all the deliciously tempting foods you can't resist.

Once the groceries are purchased, the food preparation begins. You have already thought through your menu and are familiar with the recipes. Therefore, you know which foods can be prepared in advance. Collect all the necessary equipment for food preparation and measure all ingredients. Follow the recipe precisely, especially if you've never prepared it before. Store the foods properly to maintain their freshness.

Now you may take care of the last-minute details. Inspect the table linens. You may want to air them first by placing them in your clothes dryer on the air fluff setting. Place a damp terrycloth towel in the dryer also to aid in the removal of wrinkles. Remove the linens from the dryer and allow the remaining wrinkles to hang out. You may place the linens immediately on your table so that you can place your serving containers in place.

Arrange the serving dishes on the table before you fill them with food. Arrange the containers on the table so that you have a continuing traffic flow. The table is the center of the party. Your guests will all gravitate toward the food to create one large conversation area. You may wish to use several smaller tables for serving in order to create several conversational areas.

Decorate your party area to carry out the party theme and then relax in a nice warm bubbly bath before your guests arrive. You'll want to be fresh and vibrant for a warm friendly greeting as you meet your guests at the door.

Former home economist, Alice Martin, who is an admired hostess, uses the "backwards time schedule." Here's how that works.

Begin at the bottom of the page with the time planned for the party to begin and put down beside that, "greet guests." Then go backwards in the day, writing upwards on the page, things you need to do to get ready for the party. The handy thing about making out a schedule like this is that you can put things down that you need to do at whatever time you think would be good to do them. Then, if you see that you are having three things that each take thirty minutes to do scheduled for 5:00 P.M. you will be able to adjust that on paper and change a couple of them to an earlier time slot instead of not realizing it until you are at that time and then begin running late. The first few times you use this method you will probably have several changes as you go along. You will learn by making those changes how to make preparation easiest on yourself and the scheduling will become easier and easier the more times you do it.

Here is a sample "backwards time schedule" for a hamburger party before the first football game of the season that may help you see more clearly what one is.

TWO DAYS BEFORE PARTY

4:00-4:30— Select recipes and make out menu for party.
4:30-5:00— Make grocery list using recipes and menu as a guide. Take grocery list to school tomorrow.

DAY BEFORE PARTY

3:30-4:30— On the way home from school go to the grocery store and buy the food for the party. Put it away.

DAY OF PARTY

9:00–10:30—	Make potato salad
10:30–11:30—	Vacuum and dust house
11:30–12:00—	Eat lunch
12:00–12:30—	Set buffet table
12:30–1:15—	Go to piano lesson
1:15–2:00—	Go buy crushed ice and put soft drinks and ice in chest
2:00–2:15—	Shape hamburger meat into patties and place in refrigerator.
2:15–2:30—	Arrange spices and utensils on tray for cooking out.
2:30–3:00—	Prepare relishes for hamburgers and put them in the refrigerator.
3:00–3:30—	Prepare baked beans and put in oven.
3:30–4:30—	Bathe and dress.
4:30–5:00—	Put hamburger buns in the oven, put ice in the beverage glasses, set food out and generally check to see that everything is as you have planned and want it.
5:00—	Greet guests!
5:30—	Begin cooking hamburgers on grill.

One of the main duties of a hostess at a party is to greet her guests as they arrive and make them feel welcome and comfortable. When people arrive, have some music already playing. It can do a lot to set the party mood you want. Another thing that relaxes people right away is to hand them something to drink and invite them to the snack table.

Another duty of the hostess comes all during the party and that is to see that guests are included and feel comfortable. She should get around to all her guests during the party and at least have a short visit with them, make introductions that have not been made yet, offer more drinks or food, help start conversation between people that you know but don't know each other.

It is good for you to read books and articles on how to give a party, and I am glad that you have read my suggestions; however, the way to really become an expert party giver is to actually plan and have a party, then another and another. The old saying, "Experience is the best teacher." is most applicable here.

Even the First Lady and the most socially aware person you know had to have had a "first party" sometime. Everyone has to begin being a hostess sometime. No one is born with the self-confidence and organization that experience gives. The sooner you get started, the sooner you will experience the pleasure of being a good relaxed hostess providing enjoyment for your friends.

PARTY IDEAS AND RECIPES

What's cookin'? Colette Daiute at the time she held the MISS TEENAGE AMERICA 1966 title.

All recipes from Consumer Service
Dr Pepper Company,
P.O. Box 5086,
Dallas, Texas 75222

Now let's get down to some specific party ideas and some special party recipes.

Have a movie party with all the glamor and sparkle of Hollywood itself. Produce your own movie with your guests as your cast. Begin with an invitation that is made to look like a movie ticket. Get some lights, a home movie camera, a mustache or two and a sombrero—now you're ready for a Mexican Movie Fiesta!

> Avocado Dip with tostadas
> Nachos
> Burritos
> Enchiladas
> Chilled soft drinks
> Empanadas

AVOCADO DIP

1 cup avocado pulp (about 2 avocados)
8 ounces cream cheese (softened)
¼ cup Dr Pepper

¼ cup salad dressing
¼ cup green onions (finely chopped)
⅛ teaspoon garlic salt
½ teaspoon salt
½ teaspoon white pepper
⅛ teaspoon celery salt
Few drops tabasco (optional)

Cream together avocado pulp, cream cheese, Dr Pepper and salad dressing. Add all other ingredients. Blend until smooth and fluffy. Chill in refrigerator 2 to 3 hours. Serve with chips, crackers, carrots, celery, green pepper strips or cauliflower pieces.

Yield: 2¼ cups approximately

Note: Add more tabasco and seasonings if desired.

NACHOS

Tostado chips
Bean dip
Cheddar cheese, grated
Jalapeño peppers, thinly sliced

Top each tostado chip with a spread of bean dip, grated cheese, and Jalapeño pepper slice. Broil until cheese is bubbly; serve immediately.

BURRITOS

Leftover pot roast, cut into pieces
Carrot pieces, cooked (optional)
Potato pieces, cooked (optional)
1 clove garlic, crushed
½ teaspoon cumin seed, crushed
½ teaspoon freshly ground black peppercorns
8 flour tortillas

Heat leftover roast and vegetables in gravy seasoned with garlic, cumin, and pepper. Drain meat and vegetables, roll in flour tortillas, place in lightly greased casserole and bake for ten minutes or until thoroughly heated at 350°F.

Yield: 8 servings

ENCHILADAS

1 cup oil, hot
2 tablespoons flour
2 tablespoons chili powder
2 cans tomato sauce
12-14 flour tortillas
Filling mixture*

Heat oil in skillet. In another skillet, mix flour, chili powder, and tomato sauce; heat well. Quickly dip tortilla in hot oil (do not allow it to fry); then immediately dip it into tomato sauce mixture. Lay tortilla on platter; fill with a meat or cheese misture. Roll up and place in baking dish. Sprinkle with remaining cheese. Heat in oven until cheese melts; 350°F. 10 to 15 minutes.
Yield: 12-14
Note: Make only one enchilada at a time.

EMPANADAS
(Turnovers)

2 cups flour
⅓ cup milk
1 teaspoon baking powder
½ teaspoon salt
½ cup shortening
1 pinch cilantro

Mix and sift dry ingredients. Cut in the shortening, and add the moisture. Roll out to ⅙ inch thickness, and cut into 4-inch circles. Fill with fruit mixture (use any fruit pie filling), moisten edges with cold water, fold one half over the other and press edges together. Fry in deep fat until brown, and drain on brown paper. Empanadas are filled with various mixtures. The imagination may go on forever, making new combinations. Mincemeat makes a very desirable filling.

*Suggested filling mixture: browned meat and chopped onions or grated cheese and chopped onions

PRESTO PARTY

To rock on through the evening nothing can be more fun than a presto party! Everyone is having a good time already and the gang decides to move the party. You volunteer your home or apartment because you are always prepared! There is always a standing supply of refreshments at your place. All you have to do is pull it all together with just a little help from your friends. Get them involved in the simple table setting of:

>Popcorn Balls
>Nature's Nibblers
>Mulled Dr Pepper

POPCORN BALLS

- 5 quarts popped corn
- 2 cups sugar
- 1 ½ cups Dr Pepper
- ½ teaspoon salt
- ¼ cup white corn syrup
- 1 teaspoon vinegar
- 1 teaspoon vanilla

Butter the sides of a saucepan and in it combine sugar, Dr Pepper, salt, corn syrup and vinegar. Cook to hard ball stage—250°F. Remove from heat and add vanilla. Slowly pour syrup over hot popcorn—mix well to coat every kernel. Butter hands and shape into small balls.

Yield: 24 small 2½ or 3' inch balls

NATURE'S NIBBLERS

- Combine in large mixing bowl
- 6 cups puffed wheat cereal
- 2 cups pretzel sticks
- 2 cups salted peanuts
- ⅔ cup toasted sunflower seeds
- ¼ cup wheat germ

Heat in a small saucepan over low gas flame (250°F. dial setting on top controlled burner) until smooth

½ cup honey
¼ cup packed brown sugar
¼ cup margarine

Pour mixture over cereal, tossing to coat evenly. Spread in large shallow roasting pan. Bake in low gas oven (250°F.) for 45 minutes, stirring occasionally. (Cereal may seem soft but will become crisp upon cooling.) Cool, stirring occasionally. Break up mixture to separate. Makes 10 cups.

This snack would be great for children as well as adults. It is not spicy but still flavorful. It is very nutritious. This snack also makes a nice gift. It could be packaged in an attractive basket lined with a bright linen napkin. It could also be packaged in a small (quart size) stoneware crock. Decorate the package with a thick yarn bow and tie in artificial sunflowers or peanuts. The crock could later hold the wooden spoons used in stirring the mixture. (A small wooden spoon could even be tied into the bowl.)

MULLED DR PEPPER

2 quarts Dr Pepper
¼ cup lemon juice
¼ cup brown sugar
¼ teaspoon salt
½ teaspoon whole cloves
1 teaspoon allspice
3 sticks cinnamon
¼ teaspoon nutmeg

Pour Dr Pepper into large saucepan. Add lemon juice, brown sugar and salt. Add spices tied in a cloth bag. Heat to boiling; turn heat low and simmer 10 minutes. Remove spice bag. Stir well. Serve in cups or earthen mugs.

Yield: 10 to 12 servings

Note: Ten 6½-ounce bottles Dr Pepper measure approximately 2 quarts.

WATER VOLLEYBALL

Summer is here and everyone takes to the water like a fish. And where there is a pool a game of water volleyball can't be far behind. You could decorate with an oriental theme using Chinese lanterns, wind chimes, nets and fisherman's weights. Pull out the hibachi, set up the iced tea center and enjoy yourself. The menu could include:

> Grilled hamburgers with curry spread
> Snow peas and Chinese vegetables
> Frozen egg rolls with sweet and sour sauce
> Minted Hawaiian tea

SWEET AND SOUR SAUCE

1 8-ounce jar prepared mustard
1 8-ounce jar red current jelly

Combine the two ingredients in a saucepan over a low heat until the jelly melts and the sauce is smooth. Serve warm in a chafing dish.
  Yield: 2 cups
  Note: Can be saved and reheated.

HAWAIIAN MINT TEA

4 cups boiling water
6 teabags
½ teaspoon mint flakes
¼ cup sugar
⅓ cup lemon juice
¼ cup pineapple juice

Pour boiling water over teabags and mint in teapot. Cover and steam for 5 minutes. Strain; combine with remaining ingredients and mix well. Serve over ice cubes and garnish with skewer of lemon and pineapple.
  Yield: 1 quart

A LACE AND HAMMER SHOWER

We mentioned earlier giving a shower for both him and her. The men you invite could help the groom fill up his workbench, while the gals help the bride. Have the shower outdoors and decorate with burlap and gingham. Play a few games as ice breakers and for prizes. (Remember that whoever wins the prize should then give it to the guest(s) of honor.)

Your inviting table may offer the guest:

> Light and Fluffy Summer Pie
> Assorted mints and nuts
> Crunchy Ginger Nut Dip
> Fiesta Punch
> Coffee

LIGHT AND FLUFFY SUMMER PIE

9-ounce frozen whipped topping, thawed
1 6-ounce can frozen pink lemonade or limeade
1 14-ounce can sweetened condensed milk
Lemon juice to taste
1 9" graham cracker crust

Mix first 4 ingredients together well, pour into graham cracker crust. Chill until firm.

To serve: garnish with strawberries, lemon slices, mint sprigs, etc.

CRUNCHY GINGER NUT DIP

8 ounces cream cheese (softened)
¼ cup Dr Pepper
1 tablespoon crystallized ginger (finely chopped)
1 tablespoon fresh orange rind (grated)
2 tablespoons salted peanuts (coarsely chopped)

Place cheese and Dr Pepper in blender or mixer bowl. Cream until light and fluffy. Fold in chopped ginger, grated orange rind and chopped peanuts.

Yield: 1½ cups

Note: Use with grapes, bananas, pineapple chunks, mandarin orange sections or strawberries as dippers.

FIESTA PUNCH

1½ cups sugar
4 cups water
½ cup lemon juice
4 cups (1 quart) bottled cranberry juice
1 cup pineapple juice
¼ teaspoon salt
4 cups (1 quart) cold Dr Pepper
Dr Pepper ice cubes

Mix sugar with 2 cups of the water. Bring to a boil; cool. Combine this syrup with the remaining 2 cups water, lemon juice, cranberry juice, pineapple juice, and salt. When ready to serve, stir in cold Dr Pepper. Pour over Dr Pepper ice cubes in punch bowl.

Yield: 25 to 30 4-ounce servings (3½ quarts)

Note: Freeze Dr Pepper ice cubes in the refrigerator trays, and use in punch bowl to prevent dilution of the punch.

TRAVELING ABROAD

BY

Council on International Educational Exchange

What's your style? Will you put a knapsack on your back, buy a pair of hiking boots and be off, or will you join a prearranged student tour? Will you be making most of your trip on your own, but join some short-term student tours in cities along the way? Will you spend a few days of your vacation at a student resort or spend some time living with a family in one of the countries you visit? What will it be for you?

To travel alone or with a group is one of the first decisions that you should make. The advantages of traveling on your own are obvious. You are free to do what you want, when you want, with no schedule to follow. For some young people this is the only way to do it, but it doesn't suit everyone. Some students want more structure. They feel that they don't really know what the highlights of a trip abroad should be, so they want someone with experience to pre-plan the highlights. It certainly makes things easier to have someone else arrange your transportation, accommodations, meals and activities while you're away. On a tour you'll always have someone to talk to—traveling can be lonely sometimes.

There are disadvantages to traveling in a group, too. A lot of the adventure is planned out of your trip, and since you have to go along with the group, your individual needs may not always be served. You'll have all the bodily comforts, but your psyche might ache a bit as you rush around from cathedral to cathedral, museum to museum. And then there's always the chance that you won't like the people on the tour and will resent having to spend so much time with them.

And then there's money. Tour programs are often quite costly, since the accommodations, etc., are somewhat more luxurious than the ones you might find for yourself. You will also be paying some kind of administrative fee (built into the cost of the program) to cover the operating costs of the tour.

There are tours sponsored by universities and other academic institutions and there are tours sponsored by private agencies. Some center around an interest that is shared by all group members, e.g., art or music or comparative education. Although some may be purely sightseeing and of the "If It's Tuesday, This Must Be Belgium" variety, those designed to appeal to students usually have some seminars or cultural activities included. It is up to you to decide on the value of any cultural experiences that are built into the tour.

One organization that runs tours that are "different" is the American Youth Hostels Association. AYH tours are for young people who like to travel in small and informal groups. Some of the trips are by bicycle and involve cycling at least forty miles per day.

There are student tour programs sponsored by U.S. schools, colleges or other educationally oriented, private, non-profit groups.

If you want to spend a short time with a family while you travel, there are organizations in many countries, often government tourist offices, that will arrange an afternoon or evening visit for you. Another possibility is SERVAS, an organization that sponsors a worldwide program of exchange hospitality for travelers in fifty countries, with the ultimate aim of helping to build world peace, goodwill and understanding. Here's how SERVAS works: You apply and are interviewed. If accepted, you receive a personal briefing, written instructions, and a list of SERVAS families in the area that you are going to visit and an introductory letter. Using this introductory letter you can arrange by letter to stay with the families who are listed. The average stay with SERVAS hosts is two nights. One CIEE staff member took advantage of SERVAS' program and came back from Italy and France raving about the wonderful families he had met and excited about the possibility of returning this kind of hospitality to others visiting the U.S. A $25 donation is requested if you use their services.

There are other kinds of programs that just won't fit neatly under the categories of work or study or travel. These programs may combine some or all of these activities as well as a period of living with a family in the host country. They are open to high school students or undergraduates and may last for a full school year or for a summer vacation only. Organizations that sponsor these kinds of programs include the American Field Service, The Experiment in International Living, Youth for Understanding and the International Christian Youth Exchange.

The traveler's first question will probably be: how much will it cost for me to travel abroad? It would be great if we could answer that question, but how can we? Could we tell you how much it would cost to live in New York for a month or in San Francisco for a week? There are just too many variables for us to be able to give you a definite answer. Hopefully the following advice will give you some help in estimating your costs.

Your cost for transportation to and from where you are going will be your biggest expense, so in figuring out your budget start with that figure. Do try to get yourself a round-trip ticket (you can get open-dated return tickets that won't limit you to a specific date and time), since you want to be able to get home when you decide you've been away long enough.

Once you get to where you're going, it is reasonable to assume that in most places—with the possible exception of some of the major cities of the world—the cost of living will be less than what you are used to. However, at home you are not used to paying for your accommodation every night and for every meal. Doing this makes it seem as though your money is evaporating.

When you decide what your lifestyle will be while traveling, you will know about how much each day will cost. If you plan to stay in hostels or camp out, you should budget from no money to $5 per day for accommodations. If you are planning to stay in hotels and to share your accommodations with a friend, you will save money, since half the cost of a double room is always lower than the cost of a single room.

Your food will cost practically nothing if you buy it at markets or in local grocery stores and eat it al fresco. If you avoid the tourist places, you will get some excellent restaurant meals for less than the same meal would cost at home.

In order to budget money for your transportation after you arrive overseas, you'll have to decide how you want to travel around. In some places you will prefer to hitchhike and in others you will want to use trains or special student flights. You'll be entitled to student or youth discounts on transportation in many countries so you can keep your travel expenses to a minimum if you plan carefully enough.

There are the unexpected extras, too, which will have to be planned for. This may include such expenses as a doctor or a piece of pre-Columbian sculpture that you just can't resist. If at all possible, allow yourself the luxury of being able to buy some things to bring back with you. After all, you deserve it. And don't forget to include the costs of little things like postcards, stamps, or books in figuring what you'll spend.

If you are going to join a program you will have a pretty good idea of what the whole trip will cost and will pay for it all before you leave. Costs vary from program to program. Remember that even if you are going to be traveling with a group, you will still have some expenses of your own. Before you leave, be sure that you understand just what you are expected to pay for and what is being paid for you.

There are some essentials which need to be taken care of long before you begin your travels. No matter where you are heading, there are certain official documents to be obtained and arrangements to be made. When should you start? As soon as you decide to leave the U.S. is when you should begin getting the formalities out of the way.

You need a U.S. passport to enter into or return from just about every country in the world. Your passport should be kept with you all of the time you travel. One good way to assure this is to put it into a leather pouch that is tied at the neck or worn around the waist like a belt. This pouch can hold traveler's checks, too, and should always be kept inside your clothing. Someone who's been all over Asia advises, "Always keep it on, even when you take a bath!"

Application for a passport should be made, in person, before (1) a passport agent; (2) a clerk of any federal court; (3) a clerk of any state court of record; (4) a judge or clerk of any probate court; or (5) a postal clerk designated by the Postmaster General.

When you apply for a passport, you must present the following items: (1) proof of U.S. citizenship (certified copy of birth certificate signed by the official registrar), naturalization certificate, consular report of birth or certification of birth, or a previous passport; (2) two recent identical photographs (have them taken by a professional photographer who knows the requirements; for instance, profiles are taboo); (3) identification—a document such as a valid driver's license with your signature and your photograph or physical description on it. The fee for a passport is $10, plus $3 for what is called an execution fee. Allow about ten days for the processing of your application, longer if you travel during peak travel periods. Passports are valid for five years from the date of issue and may not be renewed.

Loss of a valid passport is a serious matter and should be reported immediately to the Passport Office, Department of State, Washington, D.C. 20524, or to the nearest U.S. consular office.

A visa is official permission to visit a country granted by the government of that country. Visa requirements change from country to country and are fully described in a booklet called "Visa Requirements of Foreign Countries," which is available at any passport agency. If you plan to study in a country for an extended period of time, you may need to get a special student visa. Be sure to check with that country's embassy or nearest consulate for details before your departure.

Another important aspect to consider before leaving this country is your health condition. Although you do not need a smallpox vaccination to leave the U.S., you will need one to get back in from most countries outside of Western Europe. Play it safe and be vaccinated before you leave, wherever you're going. You will be required to show an official record of your immunization that is no more than three years old at the date of your return.

You can be vaccinated by your own doctor or at a health department center, but no matter where it's done, you must have the vaccination recorded on an International Certificate of Vaccination. A form is available at any passport agency, local or state health department or office of the U.S. Public Health Service. The form must show the approved stamp of the local or state health department following vaccination. If possible, you should get your smallpox vaccination a few weeks before you leave so that any reaction you have will have plenty of time to subside.

There may be other kinds of shots needed, especially if you are traveling to Asian, African or Latin American countries.

Be in good general health. Go to the dentist before you leave on your trip, have an extra pair of eyeglasses made up (or have your doctor write out your prescription), and take along any prescription drugs that you may use regularly. If you are carrying prescription drugs, have the prescription with you in case a customs officer asks for it.

A useful and money-saving item to familiarize yourself with is known as the International Student Identity Card (ISIC). If you are a college or high school student and are planning to go anywhere in the world, you should be sure to have an International Scholar Identity Card (for high school students) before you go. The card is official proof of student status and, written in four languages, is recognized internationally. From here on, we will refer to it as the ISIC.

The card, the creation of the International Student Travel Conference (ISTC), an organization of student travel bureaus in forty countries, entitles its holders to discounts on transportation, accommodations, museum entrance fees and concert tickets, and to assorted other student reductions in much of the world. It also offers an entree to the special travel services offered by these student bureaus. It is true that most of the specific discounts that one can get with the ISIC are to be found in European countries and in other countries such as India, Israel, or Turkey that have national student travel bureaus. But even in the many countries that do not have their own bureaus, the card is still recognized as proof of student status and can be helpful in securing whatever student discounts are around. The best thing to do, no matter where you are, is to show your card first and ask whether there are any discounts available, whether it's for a ride on a subway, entrance to a museum, or a stay in a hotel.

To be eligible for the International Student Identity Card, you must submit proof that you are a full-time college or university student enrolled in an accredited institution currently or within the calendar year of graduation. For the International Scholar Identity Card, you must submit proof that you are a full-time high school or other non-university student attending a recognized educational establishment (secondary school offering full-time educational, vocational, or technical courses for the school year). Both the International Student Identity Card and the International Scholar Identity Card cost $2.50 in the U.S.

If imitation is the sincerest form of flattery, the ISIC has had more than its share of flattery. Forgeries and imitations of the card have appeared and will probably continue to appear from time to time, both in the U.S. and abroad. The ISIC trademark, which is registered by the International Student Travel Conference (ISTC), distinguishes the authentic card from forgeries or imitations.

The ISIC can officially be issued only by memebers of the ISTC or by offices specifically designated by the members of issuing offices. One of these is the Council of International Educational Exchange. CIEE can supply information on other authorized organizations.

The Youth Hostel Membership Card is another money-saver for young travelers. At youth hostels located all over the world you can spend the night for approximately $2. But in order to use these hostels you must first have a membership card issued by the American Youth Hostels (AYH). As a member of the International Youth Hostel Federation, an organization of forty-eight national hostel associations, AYH can issue the official hostel card recognized all over the world. The cost of AYH membership goes according to age: $5 if you are under eighteen (Junior Membership), and $11 if you are eighteen or over (Senior Membership). Cards are valid from October 1 to December 31 of the following year.

The hostels in Europe, as in other parts of the world, are designed primarily for the use of hikers or bikers. Accommodations are dormitory style; you are provided with a bed-mattress and blankets; sheets and sleeping bags are required. Some of the larger hostels rent sheets, but for many you'll need your own. In some hostels a sleeping bag will solve the problem.

Certain regulations are set for youth hostels in each country, and although they vary there are certain similarities from country to country. Hostelers usually are expected to share in the cleanup, to abstain from drinking and/or using drugs in the hostels (and smoking in some areas), to stay no more than three days and to be in the hostel by 10:00 P.M.

Insurance is something you should check into and have in good order before you leave the United States. Check to see whether your medical and accident insurance policies are valid when you are traveling outside the United States. You should also investigate the various plans available for baggage insurance and—something that is relatively new—charter flight insurance. Charter flight insurance covers the cost of your charter fare if for medical reasons you are unable to join or finish the flight you have already paid for. You can get full information on insurance from your family broker or write to CIEE for a description of a plan designed especially for short-term travelers going abroad.

An International Driving Permit is something that you may be interested in obtaining. Although most countries allow American citizens eighteen years of age and over to drive with a valid U.S. driver's license, a few countries require the International Driving Permit as well. The permit, and information on which countries require it, can be obtained from automobile and motor clubs. The International Driving Permit is valid for one year from the date of issue, but you must also carry with you a valid U.S. driver's license. Before you leave the U.S., be sure your driver's license will not expire before you return.

General information on driving regulations and road maps for various countries may be obtained in the U.S. from local automobile clubs and from the motoring services of major oil companies.

If you're going to be gone for any length of time, you will be interested in how the mail system works. When writing to organizations abroad, you should enclose two international postal reply coupons to insure an airmail response. Coupons are available from any U.S. Post Office. When giving your address for the purpose of forwarding mail, be sure to give only addresses at which you will be staying for at least three days. If you do not have a mailing address, you can have mail sent to you in care of Poste Restante (General Delivery) at the central post office in the cities where you will be staying. There is a small charge for each letter received.

Some students have their mail sent to them in care of American Express, but American Express mail service is officially only for clients of American Express (which, if you buy American Express traveler's checks, means you).

Carrying a large sum of cash with you on your travels is not a wise idea. Without a doubt, the best way to carry your money abroad is in traveler's checks.

In deciding what kind of traveler's checks you should buy, try to determine how widely the check is recognized and the number of offices the issuing agency has abroad (in case your checks are lost or stolen). Remember that you won't have to go to an overseas office of the issuing agency if you just want to convert your checks to local currency. Most banks, except in the smallest towns, will cash them readily and you will find the waiting line shorter and the rate of exchange better. Try to avoid changing your money in hotels or restaurants, where the rate of exchange is less favorable. When buying something, be sure to ask whether there is a discount for paying in traveler's checks, which is sometimes the case.

One student wrote to us saying that although she had used traveler's checks and found them invaluable, she also found it helpful to have some American dollar bills with her. Even when a small store refused to accept a traveler's check, the dollar bills were welcomed.

Conversion tables listing rates of exchange for dollars in different currencies are found in most guidebooks. You'll be able to buy foreign currency in an air, ship, or train terminal when you arrive. But, if you are going to arrive late at night or on a holiday, or are just the type that likes to be prepared, you can buy a small amount of money from a commercial bank before you leave the U.S.

If you run short of money, traveler's checks or cash can be cabled to you from the U.S. in care of a bank or an agency, e.g. American Express or Thomas Cook. If your bank has a foreign branch, you can have money transferred to you there. It is best to do this in major cities and to make arrangements as far in advance of destitution as possible. You can get more information on wiring money abroad from the agencies that issue your traveler's checks or from your local Western Union office.

The immigration officers of an increasing number of countries are asking travelers, especially student-type travelers, to tell them how much money they are carrying or to show a round-trip ticket plus a certain amount of funds. Apparently there is no official amount that is considered sufficient funds—the amount can be arbitrarily set on the spot and admission to a country can be refused on the grounds of insufficient funds. Check with the consulate of the country you plan to visit to see what kind of proof of solvency you will be expected to show.

Customs involves a set of rules and regulations that are confusing to some people. Everything that you'll need to know about customs regulations for your return to the U.S. is in *Customs Hints for Returning U.S. Residents*, a pamphlet available at any passport agency. Since customs officers are more thorough than ever in their search of returning Americans, especially young ones, you'd have to be crazy to try to bring drugs into the country.

A well-publicized aspect of youths traveling in Europe is that of the drug arrests and incarcerations. Many young people think that drug laws and their enforcement in other countries are more lenient than at home. This is just not true. While there may be some countries that seem to have a more liberal attitude toward drugs, in most countries prosecution of offenders for both the possession and sale of drugs and narcotics is being intensified.

You should be aware of the serious consequences that can result from the possession or sale of drugs, including marijuana, in many parts of the world. As of June 1969, the number of Americans in foreign jails on drug and narcotics violations was 189, most of them under thirty years old. By July of 1973 this figure was up to 910. The prisons in some countries make our jails look like luxury hotels, and in many places there is no provision for bail.

Remember that when you are traveling abroad you are no longer protected by U.S. law but are subject solely to the laws of the country in which you are traveling. Should you get into some legal difficulty, the U.S. consul can provide you with a list of local attorneys, so that you are not discriminated against, and contact your family at home for you, but he can't get you out of trouble or furnish money for your legal fees.

According to the files of American consulates abroad, Americans have been jailed for possession of as little as three grams of marijuana. In France, police are permitted to stop and search people on the street (including the French). Beware of the pusher who—after making a hefty profit on his sale—may easily decide to double his earnings by turning you in to the authorities for a reward. Be sure that if you are required for medical reasons to take any drug that may be subject to abuse, you have your prescription with you.

The U.S. Bureau of Customs will inspect your baggage upon your return to the United States and it is tightening its enforcement procedures. This applies not only to things carried on your person or in your luggage but to articles mailed in the United States from abroad as well.

Before deciding definitely on one plan of travel abroad look into the many alternatives that are available.

Many campuses have their own student travel offices staffed by students who can give you firsthand information on all aspects of travel. These offices usually arrange charter flights, issue the International Student Identity Card and distribute a variety of publications on work, study, and travel abroad.

Recommended Reading on Student Travel: *Youth Travel Abroad: What to Know Before You Go*, U.S. Department of State.

Adapted by permission from the *Whole World Handbook: A Student Guide to Work, Study and Travel Abroad*, 1976–77 Edition. © Council on International Educational Exchange. Written by Marjorie A. Cohen; edited by Margaret E. Sherman. Published by CIEE and the Frommer/Pasmantier Publishing Corporation. Copies available for $2.95 from CIEE, 70 Fifth Avenue, New York, New York 10011.

Making an Ounce of Prevention Worth a Pound of Cure

AVOIDING DANGEROUS SITUATIONS
Things No One Likes to Talk About

BY
CLARENCE M. KELLEY
Director, Federal Bureau of Investigation
United States Department of Justice

Mr. Clarence Kelley, a public servant of great and determined dedication, has brought to the scene of American government a sense of integrity that inspires all.

His leadership in a critical time has proven once again that the true mark of greatness is to serve above and beyond the desire for personal gain. MISS TEENAGE AMERICA *is exceptionally proud and honored that Mr. Clarence Kelley would lend his splendid name in full measure to our endeavor.*

What an exhilarating time to be a teenager! To be on the threshold of adulthood at approximately the same time that our great Republic closes the chapter on two hundred years of self-rule and turns the page for the third century. To know that this is *your* century—that you and your age group will, to a large extent, inscribe the future story of America on that page—must be as exciting to each of you as the crack and sparkle of Fourth of July fireworks!

You have a tremendous responsibility ahead of you, for the moral climate of the United States in its third century will be set by you. As

Mr. Clarence M. Kelley—Director, Federal Bureau of Investigation.

young American women, you also have a tremendous reputation to uphold.

How many of you, I wonder, have read what Alexis de Tocqueville said about American women more than a century ago? Tocqueville's two-volume study of the new nation and its people, "Democracy in America," was concluded with his chapter on "The Equality of the Sexes," saying, ". . . and if I were asked, now that I am drawing to the close of this work, in which I have spoken of so many important things done by the Americans, to what the singular prosperity and growing strength of that people ought mainly to be attributed, I would reply: To the superiority of their women."

That is a challenge for the teenager beginning America's third century!

What was it about the American woman of 1831 that, in Tocqueville's view, made her superior to her European counterpart?

I think he came closest to the real explanation when he pointed out the role of religion in America. . . ". . . its influence over the mind of woman is supreme, and women are the protectors of morals."

You—the teenage American girl—have a vital role to play. Your thoughts and your conduct unquestionably will do much to shape the behavior patterns of America's third century. What you are and how you expect to be treated will do much to set the standard of treatment you receive from reasonable individuals. But it is a fact that, as America begins its third century, your chances of encountering people who are not reasonable—drunken, drugged, or degenerate individuals—are increasing.

For whatever reasons, unfortunately, times have changed since the 1830s when Tocqueville found that American men held all women in great respect. The conduct of American men, he says, implied that they supposed all women to be virtuous and refined, that it was possible for a young, unmarried woman to undertake a long journey alone and without fear. This was unthinkable for a young European woman to do.

Charles Dickens, who traveled extensively in America, supports this view. He wrote that during all his rambling in the new republic he at no time, on any occasion, anywhere, saw a woman exposed to the slightest act of rudeness, incivility, or inattention.

What of today?

We cannot, regrettably, give the same report that Tocqueville and Dickens did. There are far too many areas in our country where a young girl alone—or, indeed, even a group of girls—not only might be subjected to incivility and rudeness, but also to brutal assault and murder.

Every law enforcement officer encounters cases he doesn't even want to think about, much less talk about, because they are so heinous—so brutal and vicious that he wants to wipe the sickening memory from his mind. But he cannot do so if he has a daughter, for in many cases the victim is a young girl. And in an immense number of these cases the crime might never have occurred had that girl not thrown caution to the wind and taken a chance in the mistaken belief that "It can't happen to me."

Crimes of violence are not unusual in this era. There are, however, two types of cases in this category which give the investigating officer the feeling that he is dealing with a nightmare, and which should be of particular concern to you. These are the crime of rape and the frequently brutal crimes which so often result from the simple act of hitchhiking.

The crime of rape is increasing. The total number of rapes reported in 1974 under the Uniform Crime Reporting Program increased forty-nine percent over those reported in 1969. During 1974, an estimated total of 55,000 forcible rapes occurred. We say "estimated total" because while this number of actual rapes was reported by approximately 12,000 law enforcement agencies, the total number of actual rapes is not known. This is because not all agencies contribute data and because, due to fear and embarrassment on the part of the victim, rape is one of the underreported crimes. Fifty-one out of every 100,000 females in this country were reported rape victims in 1974.

No one can tell you why the streets are not safe. We can only offer theories as to why they are not, and everyone has his own opinion. The causes of crime are many and they are extremely complex. Certainly, a basic one is failure on the part of some parents to instill moral values in their children. The bonds of religion which Tocqueville found to have been a powerful influence on the maintenance of democracy in America, no longer are as all-encompassing as they were in 1831, or in 1931, or even twenty-five years. ago.

Changing times do not necessarily mean changing morals. The great virtues are unchangeable. The problem is that some who transgress have never been taught the moral code in the first place; others who have been taught it, too often choose to ignore it.

These two groups—the amoral and the immoral—are a kind of reservoir from which flows an increasing stream of assaults against common decency and floods of criminal activity.

Is there anything that you can do, in the face of this growing danger, to afford yourself a margin of safety?

I believe there are quite a few things that you can do to increase the margin. I am not thinking here in terms of a whistle, or hatpin, or chemical spray, or even a course in self-defense. I am thinking, rather, in terms of a psychological element which, in subtle ways, can have an effect on your safety. This element is *how you feel about yourself, your sense of personal worth, of self-esteem.*

On the basis of years in law enforcement work, which has included many encounters with juvenile citizens, it seems to me that many young girls just entering their teens feel insecure and unhappy with themselves. Some of them are just beginning to taste their first freedom from parental control, and have not been taught to discern between liberty and license. Everything is new, restraints are irritating, and the temptation to experience everything *now,* in great gulps, is almost overwhelming.

But self-indulgence—yielding to the sensations of the moment—can be disastrous to peace of mind, to long-term happiness in the future, and, in many instances, to life itself.

Don't go too fast. Slow down. Take it easy and don't make mistakes that will mar the one lifetime you have to live.

Only those who are unsure of themselves or who, subconsciously, have a low opinion of themselves, will grab at every new experience and not discriminate between the good and the bad. A lack of confidence and self-esteem can be betrayed in a hundred different ways. Sometimes it is apparent in bizarre and provocative clothes of the too-tight, too-short variety. Sometimes it shows in coarse and profane language. Sometimes it is revealed in bold and vulgar behavior.

Such actions, stemming from insecurity, unfortunately make young girls particularly vulnerable to real phsyical danger from that group who, our statistics indicate, are brutally contemptuous of both decency and women.

Some among you, I feel sure, know of one girl, a little careless in her dress, manner, and behavior, perhaps, who "took a chance" and was victimized. Perhaps it was a blind date, arranged by someone she hardly knew, a chance meeting with an attractive stranger, a solitary stroll away from a picnic group in a park area known to be frequented by degenerates, or—most dangerous of all—hitchhiking a ride.

Did the words, "She asked for it!" enter your mind?

Perhaps that girl had no grasp of the reality of what could happen to her.

Hitchhiking can be a deadly means of transportation—a one-way trip to being brutalized, tortured, or killed. And the hitchhike route to death is incredibly ugly.

In separate instances in a midwestern city, twelve girls, ages five to twenty-two, reportedly were victimized by a single individual who enticed them into his car from which the inner door handle was removed.

If I could, by writing this, get a single message across to every young girl—and boy, too, for that matter—in America, it would be:

Don't make yourself vulnerable to conscienceless sex perverts who view the young hitchhiker—girl or boy—as an easy target.

Don't hitchhike!

Remember, too, that an unescorted visit to a disreputable area of entertainment is potentially as lethal as entering an automobile driven by a stranger.

Despite a determination on your part to take no chances, and in the face of every precaution, you may find yourself in a situation beyond your control. If, for whatever reason, you find yourself alone on a deserted street at night, seek the middle of the sidewalk to avoid a possible assailant hiding in a doorway or a potential attacker lying in wait in a vehicle parked at the curb. Stay on lighted streets. Avoid shortcuts through dark alleys, empty parks, or apparently deserted areas.

If you drive, don't unlock your car until you have checked the floor of both seats to assure yourself that no one is hiding in your vehicle. Lock all doors after you enter, and keep your windows rolled high enough to discourage attempts to reach through when you halt at a stop light. Park in a well-lighted area. And if you believe you are being followed, it may be unwise to drive straight home. It may be safer to drive directly to the nearest precinct house and ask for police assistance.

It must be disheartening for a girl in her teens to realize that her predecessors met with more uniform courtesy than she herself does, and that her earlier counterparts could move about without fear more freely than she can at the present time. Possibly part of the reason for this stemmed from the fact that the American girl of an earlier age had great freedom because she herself set very real limits on her conduct. Tocqueville says of that earlier girl that ". . . her reason never allows the reins of self-guidance to drop . . ."

The "reins of self-guidance" still provide effective controls which lead to responsible adulthood in the majority of instances. Teenage American girls today have a greater opportunity than ever before to take an active and constructive part in the democratic system—a system which provides for rational reform and orderly change. The great majority of young citizens love their country, revere their traditions, and are proud of the fact that the self-control of the citizens has been such that it has enabled them to rule themselves under law for approximately two centuries.

There are a few young Americans, however, who currently challenge the concept of self-rule. They see themselves as revolutionaries creating a brave new world—*now*! But the world they are devoting their efforts to bring into being is a world without law—a world of anarchy.

These young people—and they are few in number—have forgotten that our system permits orderly change. They attempt to bring about change by means of dynamite and machine guns. They think bullets, not ballots. They boast of vicious acts of terrorism and announce that the slaughter of police officers—symbols of law—is one of their primary tactics. They demand change. They demand it now, without regard for the consequences to individuals or to individual freedom. Most of them are so self-obsessed they cannot realize that, through their efforts, their free country could be changed into a despotism ruled by fear.

As we turn the page which marks the opening of our third century—*your century*—let us listen to an English philosopher who profoundly influenced the framers of the Constitution.

John Locke, who has been characterized as ". . . an inspirer of the American constitution . . ." once wrote:

> ". . . the end of law is not to abolish or restrain, but to preserve and enlarge Freedom . . . Where there is no law, there is no Freedom.
>
> "Liberty is to be free from Restraint and Violence from others; which cannot be, where there is no law . . ."

Virtue plus law equals freedom, the heart and soul of our republic. Violence, terrorism, and contempt for the law add up to a vicious despotism.

If, as Tocqueville maintains, "No free communities ever existed without morals," and if he is also correct when he holds that ". . . morals are the work of woman," then the standards you promote, in terms of both morals and citizenship, are vital to America's future.

What a responsibility, yet what a privilege lies before you! The quality of future generations of Americans will be determined, to a very great extent, by you.

You number among you the vital homemakers of tomorrow, as well as those for whom great vistas of achievement are opening in all areas—the arts, sciences—indeed, in all fields of endeavor.

Do not distrust yourself. Accept and like the person you are. Develop the confidence and self-control which give poise and strengthen character, and the world will accept you.

Do your share in making the next hundred years the greatest in America's history of self-rule, and when, a hundred years from now, a youthful visitor from a foreign land seeks to account for the superb record written during the magnificent century, he, like Tocqueville, will give credit where credit is due. He will salute the American woman.

SAFETY ON THE STREETS

BY

Officer GAY FISHER
and her husband
Lieutenant GARY FISHER

Lieutenant Fisher has for the past seven years been charged with the responsibility of the safety and security of all of the National Candidates at the MISS TEENAGE AMERICA *Pageant Finals. His entire career has been in law enforcement, including his service as an undercover agent in the Narcotics Division and the Intelligence Division of the Fort Worth Police Department. Twice nominated Officer of the Year, he has received over fifty letters of commendation.*

His wife, Gay, a patrolwoman, adds a feminine touch along with her insights into the special problems confronting young women in today's society.

Your safety can depend on your personal identity concept. Your regard for yourself can make the difference.

I've noticed that great effort made by parents (ourselves included) and adults in supervisory categories to afford, what they are satisfied to believe is a safe framework for activities involving those under their care. This includes transportation for school, proper escorts to social functions, adequate chaperones, hopefully excellent neighborhoods, and advice and warnings advantageous to their welfare. This seems to give an amazing sense of satisfaction to the adult; and if it carries over to you— watch out!

Our daughter, being fourteen, having beautiful dark hair, innocent brown eyes, a frightening developing torso, and an ever-aware grin, grabs her books, or whatever, and takes off on her adventures. They are precisely that! No matter what lengths we have taken to prepare her (this includes such simplicities as lock the front door and do not ride with strangers), her safety once away from us is basically her responsibility. So keeping in mind that your greatest asset at this point, as a beautiful, developing teenage girl, is your attitude about yourself. The fact that you are intelligent, capable of handling yourself as well or better than the next person in a given situation, and that you have reached a mental maturity usually superior to the male populus at your age, and above all you are the one and only one, capable of doing the job of keeping on top or out of a sticky situation.

Many a wily gal has avoided a dangerous ride in a "would-be racer" vehicle by using a little bit of smile and a lot of brain. If being clever seems like cheating to you then by all means be yourself—that's more than enough cleverness to take charge.

I'll cite some situations that need awareness on your part. Many are so common as to be amusing; but just one may sound enough of an alert to you to cause a hasty evacuation, or encourage you to lay the groundwork, affording you just the measure of safety you need. So hang on, compare our thoughts with yours, adapting them to your own lifestyle, and when we're through, your mind will probably be teased into adding a myriad of situations and alternatives we've yet to think of.

First of all, don't fall into the trap of thinking that someone will always be around—they won't. Mr. Muscle is great to be with, but don't think he can take care of you no matter what—he can't. Don't think that expressing your ideas assertively in touchy situations is unladylike and suspiciously feminist in origin—it's not. It's age-old common sense, and since when hasn't what is termed as an "intelligently arrogant female" not been a challenge and delight to the masculine ego? (We'll admit that the way your stand is expressed is the deciding factor.)

Don't be embarrassed to leave an area abruptly (that does mean run) if a stranger approaches you suddenly. If he is honest, he will appreciate your good sense. If otherwise, who really cares. Don't feel obligated to open your door at home simply because it's the proper thing to do. Have either a window or access by which you can identify the caller. If you are alone or suspicious, state you are not interested, or busy.

Remember that when parking in shopping areas, that friendly man who offers to open your door, or start your malfunctioning car may be the one who disabled it to begin with. Don't be a "Thoreau at large" (wandering alone in the woods), if possible. Alone in your room is fine, but many a dreamer has been caught unaware in secluded spots, blissfully believing in nature when confronted with odds that a smile just won't get her out of. To seek crowds may have been a compromise to naturalists, but a telephone inside a store or mixing in a group of people at just the right moment may discourage a publicity-shy stalker.

A word about defense of oneself in case precautions have not been enough. Be aware of items you carry that can be used in your defense. Clasping keys between your fingers (points protruding, hopefully) and swinging at the region of an offender's eyes is often unexpected and quite effective. At this point, however, don't forget the next step, which is to evacuate the premises quickly (yes, run) while screaming to attract attention. Too embarrassing, you say? Well, we've known some gals who wear those whistles on a lovely sterling silver chain, which, if blown, could attract attention. That's not a bad idea. However, if you want to eliminate all doubt that it's physical help you want, and not aid in directing traffic, there is no substitute for one of your own endowments—a good loud scream.

In law enforcement, the physical defense training given to women incorporates a smashing amount of advice such as "Try this, it should work" and "Use good common sense, and hit where least expected," and uppermost, "Don't try to fight fair, just surprise if possible." Now, not being mental pygmies, women who are sometimes half the size of the men that they are having to defend themselves against, know that they will have to use cleverness and well-placed defensive blows, hopefully that are unexpected. Remember, you want to strike an area that will disable an assailant long enough for you to escape. Therefore, depending on the situation, such as whether you find yourself more able to use feet or hands, blows to vulnerable areas such as eyes, nose, throat, groin, shins (just scraping someone's shins can be excruciatingly painful, sometimes immobilizing momentarily), or ankles, can give you just the time you need. Do remember though when resorting to this type of emergency procedure, do strike with maximum force. There are few things worse than angering one with a butterfly chop.

These points are not meant to suggest you fear every stranger. If you are aware of your surroundings and keep your personal safety in mind, soon it will become natural, and surprisingly enough, create more of a feeling of security in knowing there are courses of action available to you, instead of feeling helpless or trapped. And those last two adjectives, by the way, will be what an attacker will count on.

Let's look at another area—telephone calls.

You might consider the age-old problem of someone getting your phone number and making obscene calls. First of all, don't make the mistake of listing your telephone number by your first name. Some people actually do go through the phone book and stop at each girl's name to give it a whirl for whatever kicks they receive from it. So if you are fortunate enough to have your own phone, list it by initials. Your friends will still be able to contact you, and let's face it, who else needs to?

If by chance you do get this type of phone call, the best thing to do is hang up. The longer you listen the more incentive you give the caller to continue. If this does not work you might try saying, "Just a minute, let me turn on the recorder" or, "There is a policeman here that wants to talk to you" or even, "Go ahead and talk, the telephone company has a tracer on my line." These comments are usually very successful and very seldom result in any return calls except when you have bragged to the wrong person. (Sometimes people you think are your friends make these calls.) Of course, as a last resort you can always have your number changed or unlisted.

Be concerned about these type of calls, but don't show fear over the phone because this alone will often excite the caller. In most cases the caller does not know you and has no intention of hurting you.

As with the obscene caller, the "Peeping Tom" has his own fetishes and you can prevent most problems simply by being aware. Don't stand in front of a window when the curtains or shades are open when changing or preparing for bed. If there is nothing to watch, the "Peeping Tom" will never be interested in your window. Don't forget that mirrors often project your image in areas that you might not be aware can be seen from the outside. Also a very bright light in your room combined with very thin drapes could provide a silhouette of interest to a passerby.

As with the obscene caller, the "Peeping Tom" usually has no intention of hurting you but when noticed he should be reported to your local police immediately. Don't be embarrassed to call the police, they are there to serve and protect you.

Here are some other precautions that the National Safety Council recommends.

AT HOME

1. Report to police any mysterious phone calls. Do not give any information to an unknown telephone caller—even your name.

2. If you receive an obscene call, hang up. If the caller persists, call the police. If necessary, have your number changed. A woman should list only the initials of her given names in the phone book.

3. Close and lock all windows.

4. Close and lock all doors.

5. Close and lock all garage doors and windows.

6. Do not leave a key in the mailbox, under the mat—any hiding place.

7. Carry a flashlight if going out at night.

8. Do not carry valuables or large sums of money. Carry checks, credit cards, charge plates if necessary.

9. Keep a list of credit cards at home.

10. Keep emergency phone numbers with you (numbers of local police, sheriff).

ON THE STREET, WALKING

1. Walk with another person if possible. Avoid walking alone.

2. Avoid narrow walkways between buildings at all times.

3. Avoid walking on the street late at night.

4. If you must walk after dark, note shadows which can alert you to a person some distance away.

5. Walk at a distance from alley entrances or shrubbery.

6. Walk near the curb rather than close to buildings.

7. Do not delay in deserted areas.

8. Avoid parks.

9. Carry your purse close to the body or under your coat. Hold it so that clasp will open toward you, not away.

10. Walk on the side of street facing coming traffic. Facing traffic, you will see a suspicious car more quickly than if it slips up behind you. You are safer, too, when there is no sidewalk and you must walk in the road.

11. Never take a shortcut through poorly lighted areas.

12. Watch for loiterers.

13. Be wary if people in a car stop to ask directions.

14. Never accept a ride from a stranger.

15. If accosted by anyone in a car, run in a direction opposite to the way the car is headed.

16. Do not run to your own home. A pursuer would then know where to find you.

17. Do run to the nearest dwelling or business place and summon help.

18. Avoid using public facilities (such as restrooms at night).

19. Plan your route. Take well-lighted, busy streets, if possible.

ON THE STREET, IN THE CAR

1. Be the best driver possible. Be a defensive driver. Avoid alcohol if driving. Determine your reaction to a medicine or drug before driving.

2. Know your car and its care.

3. Remove trunk, house, and other keys from key case when having car serviced or parked in a public lot or garage. They are easily duplicated.

4. Use an attended parking facility if possible.

5. Always lock the car and keep keys in your possession whenever possible.

6. Make sure that you have ample gasoline, good battery, and safe tires for your trip.

7. Check back seat of your car for intruders before getting in.

8. Lock all car doors and put windows up high enough so that no one can put an arm and hand through any of them. If you must ventilate, roll window up when stopped at intersection or stalled in traffic.

9. Fasten your safety belt.

10. Remove driver's license, credit cards, receipts, I.D. cards from car.

11. Do not carry car license number or your name and address on your keys.

12. Do not leave valuables on the car seat. Put them in the trunk. But do not put them in the trunk after you have parked your car and intend to leave it for some time. Instead, when you are en route, pull off the road and transfer your materials to the trunk, then proceed to your destination.

13. Sound horn in short blasts if anyone tries to enter the car. Continue it until police or others come to your aid.

14. If two cars hem you in with obviously threatening intent, sound horn until help comes.

15. Drive to a police station, fire station, or a gas station and report a suspicious-looking car you think may be following you. If this is impossible, make a curb stop where people are about and let the car pass you. If a car follows you to your driveway at night, stay in the car with

doors locked until you can identify the occupant or know the driver's intent. If necessary, sound the horn to attract the attention of your neighbors. The noise also may scare the pursuer away.

16. Leave space between your car and the cars ahead for maneuvering in the event of attack or for safety from collision.

17. Keep car in gear during brief stops at night. Be ready to move instantly.

18. Never pick up hitchhikers.

19. Keep a flashlight in the passenger compartment, but put flares in the trunk.

20. If you have a flat tire in a questionable area, drive on it until you reach a safe or well-lighted spot.

21. Lift the hood, attach a white handkerchief to the antenna or left door handle as a signal for help in the event of car trouble. Get back in the car promptly and lock the doors. At night leave lights and emergency flasher on. If someone stops, lower your window a crack and ask him to call for assistance. Do not let him get into the car.

22. A woman driving alone should not stop to aid others as long as public safety is as uncertain as it is today. If you stop, keep the doors locked, quickly find out what assistance is needed, and drive on to a well-lighted area (if at night) or service station and notify the police or emergency service.

23. Leave car in a well-lighted area when parking on the street at night.

24. Have keys in hand so that you can quickly unlock garage and house doors.

USING PUBLIC TRANSPORTATION

1. Plan to travel with one or more companions when using mass transit.

2. Sit near the driver, conductor or motorman if possible.

3. Never sleep on public transportation.

4. Do not sit near the door where your purse or other valuables can be snatched just as the vehicle is about to move and the thief can escape before the door closes.

5. Do not place your purse or other valuables loosely on your lap when you sit next to an open window. A thief can reach through a window and grab a purse.

6. Remain on a bus or train until the next stop if you suspect that someone is following you. On a bus you can ask the driver to let you off at a selected place.

7. Take a taxi rather than mass transit if you are going to a dark or questionable neighborhood.

8. Request that taxi doors be locked. It is your privilege.

9. Ask the driver to wait while you enter the building or ask him to walk to the entrance with you.

ON THE STREET, IN OTHER LOCATIONS

1. Be cautious in coin laundries. Vary your schedule. Take a companion with you. Call the police if the need arises.

2. Patronize a cocktail lounge only with a friend or escort.

3. Do not invite trouble by placing your purse or valuables on a store counter, in a grocery cart or baby carriage, or on the floor or empty seat in a theater.

4. Be alert for anyone following you after transacting business in a bank.

5. Be unobtrusive when writing a check or displaying money in a strange place.

6. Be wary of women in washrooms.

7. Sit near the aisle in a theater and avoid dark corners. Do not sit in an area of vacant seats in balcony or at rear of theater.

8. Be wary of giving your name, address, or place of business in restaurants and other public places.

9. Keep a hotel or motel door locked. Use the chain if there is one. Put valuables in the safe. When entering your accommodations, check the room before locking the door and cutting off your escape.

10. Be careful in a store or office at street level. Keep valuable possessions out of sight. Costly purchases too bulky to conceal should be delivered by the store.

SAFE DRIVING

If you don't have a driver's license now, chances are that you will in the next few years. A car can be a lethal weapon. It can be used against others and against yourself. Being a careful, alert driver is not enough. You must be a defensive driver as well. You are bound to run into situations you didn't expect. Will you perform under pressure or panic?

A panic reaction could be disastrous. Your very survival may depend on two things: your ability to stay calm, and your knowledge of the best defensive action to take.

Obviously you can't "practice" an emergency driving situation. So the next best thing is to develop the skill and know-how beforehand, in your mind. You must visualize in advance emergencies that might confront you, and plan mentally the defensive action you will take.

You can do this by studying the advice of the experts. Any of the following emergencies could happen to you, maybe today. Fix in your mind now what you should do if any of them happened to you:

YOUR BRAKES FAIL

You step on the brake and the pedal slaps uselessly on the floor. It's a terrifying experience!

If there is any resistance, pump the pedal. You may be able to work up enough pressure to help some.

If there is no pressure and the way is clear ahead, coast in "drive" gear and use the parking brake. If you need to slow faster, shift into a lower forward gear and let engine compression help.

On a hill or mountain grade, you're in trouble. Look for something to sideswipe—roadside brush, a snowbank, a guardrail, even parked cars. (Dented sheet metal can be repaired.)

Use your horn or lights to warn other drivers and pedestrians that you are out of control.

YOU GO INTO A SKID

Abrupt turns, sudden lane changes, or hard braking can throw you into a dangerous skid, especially on wet or icy roads.

If your rear end starts to slide, take your foot off the gas at once.

Your first instinct may be to turn hard away from the direction of the skid. Don't! That will really spin you into a crash.

Instead, turn your wheels in the same direction the rear of the car is skidding. But be careful about it. Don't oversteer. You'll be able to "feel" when the car regains rolling traction. Then straighten the wheels.

Never hit the brakes during a side skid correction. For the fastest stop with the least chance of causing a side skid, pump your brakes with a hard, rapid jabbing and releasing of the brakes.

YOUR ACCELERATOR STICKS

You let up on the gas pedal and nothing happens. Keep cool. This is one of the easiest of driving emergencies to handle.

If you're on the open highway and there's plenty of room ahead, try to pull the pedal up with the toe of your shoe or have a front seat passenger do it. Don't reach down yourself and take your attention from the road. But on some cars there is no connection between the pedal and throttle linkage; check the type you have.

If there isn't time, simply turn off the ignition and brake to a stop. But remember, with power brakes and steering, turning off the engine will make steering and braking hard work. Be ready for the stiffness and bear down.

If a quick stop or maneuvering is necessary, you can leave the power on and shift into neutral or depress the clutch. But get stopped in a hurry and shut off the engine at once. A motor without load can tear itself to pieces quickly.

YOUR HEADLIGHTS GO OUT

There's only one thing to do if your headlights go out and you're suddenly plunged into darkness. Hold a straight steering course and brake as hard as you can without throwing yourself into a skid. Then ease onto the shoulder as far from a traffic lane as you can get.

The idea is to pull your speed down quickly before a slight steering error takes you off the road.

Once stopped, set out flares or use a flashlight to warn oncoming traffic. Use the four-way flasher if it is operable.

If everything is dead, radio, blower, interior lights, etc., the problem probably is the battery cables. Check the terminals at both ends.

If only the headlamps are out, the circuit breaker has opened. Since it is heat actuated, it should open and close giving you intermittent light to help you to safety.

YOU HAVE A BLOWOUT

Keep a firm and steady grip on the steering wheel—and don't oversteer to correct the swerve or pull. If a front tire goes, there will be a strong pull toward the side with the blowout. A rear blowout tends to cause weaving of the rear end.

Above all, *don't* slam on the brakes! Brake smoothly, but easy does it. Sudden braking may throw you into a spin or out of control.

Get onto the shoulder and limp along until you find a place level enough to change the tire safely. Day or night, set out flares or other warning device and turn on flashers.

YOUR HOOD FLIES UP

Brake smoothly and ease onto the shoulder. You'll have to depend on the view from your left window for steering reference. Or on some cars you may be able to peek through the gap under the hinge edge of the hood.

Make it a habit to check whether the attendant securely latched the hood after a service station stop.

YOU MUST STOP ON A HIGHWAY

On an expressway with paved shoulders, signal and pull off at near traffic speed, then slow down. Where the shoulder is unpaved, signal a right turn and slow down to a safe speed before turning off.

Leave low-beam headlights on in dusk, darkness, or bad weather; turn on interior lights and four-way flashers if you have them.

If you must stop close to a traffic lane, on a curve, over a hill or in any risky location, get everyone out of the car and well away from traffic. By all means, don't obscure taillights at night by standing or working behind car.

Day or night, place a flare or other warning device just behind the car and another at least 300 feet back (that's about 120 paces).

Raise the hood and tie a white handkerchief to the antenna or left door handle as a signal if you need help.

YOUR CAR CATCHES FIRE

Most car fires are caused by a short circuit in the electrical system.

It's almost impossible to disconnect battery terminals without tools. So don't waste time. Get the jack handle from the trunk and rip loose any burning wires. They are a lot less expensive to replace than a burned-out car.

If you don't cárry a fire extinguisher, try to smother burning wires with a large article of clothing. Don't grab burning wires with your bare hands; only twelve volts amperage or current can be relatively high in a malfunction.

If the fire is beyond your control, get away from the car before the gas tank explodes. Try to flag down a trucker—they usually carry efficient extinguishers.

YOU ARE ON A COLLISION COURSE

Suddenly your blood chills! Another car is speeding toward you in your lane—a head-on crash looms!

Brake hard. Every mile you take off your speed reduces the impact force. Head for the right shoulder and give him the entire road. If there's time, lean on the horn and flash your lights.

If he continues toward you, take the ditch or any open ground to the right which is free of solid obstructions. Remember that any alternative, even a roll-over, gives you a better chance than a head-on collision.

Whatever you do, don't try to outguess him and swerve to the left around him. He may recover at the last instant and instinctively veer back into his own lane—to hit you head-on.

YOUR CAR PLUNGES INTO WATER

Submersion is about the most unpredictable of all auto accidents, both in the way the car will perform and the way people will act. Water causes more unreasoning panic than any other emergency.

A few tips have grown out of actual tests:

A car with windows and doors closed will float from three to ten minutes. The best escape route is through a window. It is difficult to open a door against water pressure, but a window can be rolled down easily.

Power windows may short out, so try to open them immediately. Tempered glass in the side and rear windows of today's cars can be broken only with a heavy, hard object.

A front-engine car will sink nose first, and some air may be pushed to the rear near the roof. When pressure inside and out is equalized, it is easier to open a door.

Remember that three to five minutes is a lot of time in an emergency. If your seat belts are fastened so you won't be knocked out, and if you keep your head, there's usually time to escape.

A comment on your concept of yourself and how it relates to what has been presented. I've found that society today accepts and encourages girls to be more expressive concerning their feelings and certainly your feelings are not to be placed second in any circumstance. The more you give yourself permission to love and believe in yourself, the more confidence you'll gain in knowing you are making the right decisions for you. They need not carry over to anyone else. You are the one you are responsible for—that's a full-time job. The decisions you make in reference to your physical, mental, and emotional safety are well within your capabilities. Be decisive and as verbal as necessary when a "no" will erase a possible danger. Please remember also that if you are a victim of a crime—get help! There is always someone interested in your problem and anxious to aid you. Too often crimes are not reported by teenagers due to a guilt factor concerning perhaps being in a location contrary to parents' wishes or a desire to avoid criticism. Remember one primary fact. You are the victim—no matter what the locale or circumstances. Once a crime is perpetrated against you—get professional help. I've seen cases of women relating frightening details of an experience to find comfort and support that continued to be strengthening long after unpleasant memories had subsided.

You are special! You are worth the laughter and tears of a lifetime. Believe in yourself, and when you need help, believe in others. Your safety touches all of us and we share a unique bond. We care.

Making "I CAN" a Part of Being AmerICAN!

Scene from the NBC television network special, the 1976 MISS TEENAGE AMERICA pageant.

WHY YOUNG PEOPLE SHOULD TAKE AN INTEREST IN THE GOVERNMENT

BY
JOHN B. CONNALLY

The Honorable John Connally, at the time of serving as Governor of the state of Texas, appeared on two early National MISS TEENAGE AMERICA *Telecasts to extend a greeting to the* MISS TEENAGE AMERICA *Candidates then assembled. He took time from his always-pressured schedule not simply to extend the Governor's greetings but to express his often announced believe in the young women and men of our nation. He has always been* MISS TEENAGE AMERICA's *friend, and we are privileged indeed that John Connally, a great American and one of the world's great statesmen, continues to express his feelings for the* MISS TEENAGE AMERICA *program by contributing to this book. We shall forever hope to merit his friendship.*

Most of you who read this book already have learned firsthand, and at an early age, that America truly is the land of opportunity. What many of us fail to understand is that our country is one of enormous individual responsibility. Unless we meet our responsibilities—unless the average citizen participates in the political process—our freedom and the opportunities it offers will evaporate and elude the grasp of future generations as surely as would a handful of smoke.

Despite all the other problems which plague our nation from time to time, one has dogged our heels persistently since the birth of the United States: apathy of our citizens toward their government.

That was true back in 1787, when our Constitution was written for the benefit of the four million people then in our country. Sixty delegates were named to the Constitutional Convention which met periodically in Philadelphia for some four months—but only about thirty-five of them showed up for most of the meetings.

Nevertheless, they gave us the fundamental blueprint for what has become the greatest nation on earth. They gave us a Constitution which guarantees previously unheard-of freedoms to all our people. It is a remarkable document, and particularly so, when we realize that *even today* only one in five ($1/5$) of the people on earth live in virtually complete freedom. In the face of the tremendous scientific and technological progress which has been made since it was written, its ancient words still form the bedrock of the finest political system ever devised by man.

But, as with all good things, there is a "catch" to it. And that is simply this: our political system requires constant care by the people. To neglect it is to risk all that we enjoy as a free people.

We require our public officials to take an oath in which they swear to "preserve, protect and defend" the Constitution of the United States. We require a similar oath of those who become U.S. citizens through the naturalization process—people who become citizens by choice, often through great sacrifice.

It seems ironic, then, that where we require no such oath of natural-born American citizens, we even fail to convince them that *participation* of the people is essential for the survival of government "of the people, by the people and for the people." We take their participation for granted while *they* take for granted the preservation of our freedom.

All too often, people who should know better are inclined to say that "politics is a dirty business and I don't want to have anything to do with it." If that is true, much of the dirt is on the hands of the good, honest, conscientious American citizens who refuse to involve themselves in the political system.

A few years ago, we lowered the voting age from twenty-one to eighteen. We did so with the hope that our young people, with their high degree of education and with their alert perception of political matters, would give our system of self-government a badly-needed transfusion of energy and enthusiasm. Unfortunately, their participation has been much less than expected. Time after time, surveys have shown that a smaller percentage of younger voters go to the polls on election day than those in other age brackets.

Apparently, they are oblivious to the fact that every uncast ballot amounts to a silent endorsement of those elected by "someone else." After all, it takes very little time or effort to go to the polls and exercise the right to vote—one of the rights for which countless Americans have died.

Of course, it is easier to depend on someone else to elect our public officials. But then who do you blame if that "someone else" does not elect good ones?

Being a good citizen in this country really is not complicated or difficult. In fact, to me it seems quite simple.

First, a good citizen is a *sensitive* citizen. She cares. She cares about her community, her neighbors, her state, and her country. She is willing to try to help solve community and governmental problems.

She is also a *responsive* citizen. She responds to the problems and needs of her fellow citizens, finding satisfaction in public service even when it requires personal sacrifices without commensurate credit or recognition.

A good citizen is a *progressive* citizen. She views the future with optimism and not despair. She faces her concepts with anticipation and not fear. She is willing to try new ideas while sticking to old-fashioned, tried-and-true principles.

She is also a *reasonable* citizen. She tries to be fair and objective in making up her mind. She respects the views of others. She realizes that today's complex problems seldom have easy answers.

She is a *participating* citizen. She does her share to help preserve our freedom and to make this a better world in which to live. She is a participant in this fascinating game of self-government, not merely a spectator.

Above all, a good citizen is a *responsible* citizen. She realizes that the life we enjoy is not ours by divine right. She knows that we can continue our way of life and its bountiful blessings only if we continue to "preserve, protect and defend" the Constitution and the political system which make them possible.

And she recognizes the great truth in Thomas Jefferson's admonition that "eternal vigilance is the price of liberty."

I AM PROUD TO BE AN AMERICAN

BY
W. W. CLEMENTS
Chairman of the Board and President
Dr Pepper Company

It was Mr. Clements' decision that first associated the Dr Pepper Company with the MISS TEENAGE AMERICA *program. This was fifteen years ago, and Dr Pepper was our major National Sponsor before becoming our Parent Company.*

Through the years, his confidence in the program has been more meaningful than any other single factor in MISS TEENAGE AMERICA's *growth. He not only believes in the responsibilities of citizenship, he lives his life in that fashion. Dedicated to the unshakable belief in the future of America, he challenges the* MISS TEENAGE AMERICA *program to speak eloquently for all that is good, that is true and that is beautiful.*

Down through the ages came a dream so fine, so alluring, so challenging that men would die for it. They languished in prison, died on the gallows, and perished in battle in order that their dream of freedom might not perish from the earth.

Their hopes were realized when that dream came into fruition on American soil in a land called the United States. A land of opportunity where:

——A tenant farmer can someday own a farm;
——A poor clerk can become owner of a store;
——A route salesman can become president of the Dr Pepper Company;*
——A penniless student can become a great lawyer, teacher, outstanding salesman or businessman or president of the United States.

America was a great land when Columbus discovered it. It is now a great nation—the strongest in the world. Average Americans, of whom

---

*Editor's Note: Mr. Clements did! He started out driving the truck and now is President and Chairman of the Board.

Mr. W. W. Clements—President, and Chairman of the Board, Dr Pepper Company.

we are a part, made it what it is and are determining the extent to which freedom and opportunity will endure.

Our country is truly the most blessed place this side of heaven!

Freedom in the world at this time is passing through a hazardous period. It behooves all of us—every American who believes in our system of government and the free enterprise system, to take whatever positive steps necessary to make sure they are preserved. We must establish for ourselves and our people: A greater feeling of loyalty to our country, and a greater sense of pride and identification with our business institutions because the success of the American free enterprise system is dependent upon the success of our businesses.

This country has grown great because of the individual freedom it has afforded. We enjoy the freedom of choice which is either rare or nonexistent in other parts of the world. Our country has grown great on the basis of:

——Respect for individual rights;
——The right to succeed—and the right to fail;
——Protection of diversity of opinion;
——Emphasis on education for responsibility in achievement;
——The opportunity to be responsible.

The values of our system of free choice have been forged over many years, and we cannot afford to let them become static or be taken for granted.

We must assume the responsibilities that come with freedom:

——To our families;
——To our church;
——To our schools;
——To our companies;
——To our country.

Without these and the institutions they represent and our system of government, all built on the free enterprise system, we would not have the great opportunities that are ours.

We have the responsibilities to preserve, protect, and perpetuate this country and all that it represents, not only for ourselves but for our children, grandchildren, and their children. We cannot just take—we must put something back.

We are a nation under God, conceived in liberty and dedicated to the proposition that all men are created equal. Each generation must rededicate itself to this principle.

The key to America's future is its youth. They will inherit these traditions which have been fruitful not just for us but for others throughout the world. They must weigh and assess the principles which govern our American way of life. They cannot afford to depart from the solid, basic fundamental truths which have withstood severe tests through America's 200 years of history. At the same time, they must accept change and adjust, improve, and strengthen the principles which have made our nation what it is today.

Advanced technology, rapid communications and transportation have reduced the world community and made personal involvement an essential way of life. No longer can man be an island unto himself. He is a neighbor and must learn to live in a neighborhood environment.

This means involvement at many levels and young people have unprecedented opportunities to take the lead. They are better educated, more responsible and stronger than their peers of a decade ago. Every community needs good leaders, every community needs young leaders with understanding, enthusiasm, energy and dedication. The opportunities for community involvement at local and national levels are unlimited to young people.

The areas of involvement for young people that offer leadership roles include the church, the school, scouting, Junior Achievement, Future Farmers of America, volunteer services and many others. Business, government and industry has opened new opportunities for young people which, in the past, were reserved for adults.

These and other challenging opportunities welcome young people to become a more viable force in the area of citizenship. Young people today are responsible voters and have a voice in choosing political leaders in government at all levels—another reflection on the maturity of today's youth.

One of the great needs of America today is a renewal of patriotism for our country. Regrettably, thousands of our youth of yesteryear died as patriots of this great nation. The challenge of young people today is to live as patriots and prove to the world through deeds, principles, and actions that the United States is still the greatest nation on earth. This will happen only if young people believe, in their own minds, that America is the greatest and are unswerving in their loyalty to this great country and all that it stands for.

This is the great American opportunity of today. Thanks to the free enterprise system many great American companies have, through the years, provided special opportunities for youth. Dr Pepper Company, second oldest soft drink firm in America, is one of those companies.

Throughout the past, Dr Pepper has been identified as a youth-oriented company. It has invested generously in programs that provide opportunity to young people in many fields. One of the company's major involvements with youth today is through the MISS TEENAGE AMERICA program. The primary goal for this activity is to focus attention on deserving young women and open doors to new opportunities.

The basis for selecting candidates for MISS TEENAGE AMERICA are fundamentally sound, emphasizing such qualities as leadership, citizenship, and scholastic achievement. Character and moral standards are also weighed in selecting Candidates.

The program has been rewarding for all concerned. Dr Pepper is proud to have been a National Sponsor of MISS TEENAGE AMERICA since the program was introduced in 1961. It has enabled the company to demonstrate its faith in the youth of our country and offer incentives that will strengthen the role young people play in our society.

Throughout these remarks, we hope one idea is predominantly clear. America is still beautiful; America is still the land of opportunity; America, conceived under God, is still under God.

I am proud to be an American!

I SPEAK FOR DEMOCRACY

BY
SUSAN HUSKISSON
Miss Teenage Knoxville,
Tennessee 1967

We first heard Elizabeth Ellen Evans' "I Speak for Democracy" at the 1967 MISS TEENAGE AMERICA Pageant, when Susan gave it as her Individual Accomplishment presentation. Millions heard it on our national telecast that year and now, nine years later, we still get requests for it.

Lawrence Welk invited her to make the same presentation on his show and the acceptance was overwhelming. During these past nine years, Susan has traveled all over the country to deliver the speech.

I am an American. Listen to my words and listen well. For my country is a strong country, and my message is a strong message. I am an American, and I speak for democracy.

My ancestors have left their blood on the green at Lexington and the snow at Valley Forge, on the walls of Fort Sumter and the fields at Gettysburg, on the banks of the River Marne and in the shadows of the Argonne Forest, on the beachheads of Salerno and Normandy, the sands of Okinawa, and in the bare, bleak hills called Pork Chop and Old Baldy and Heartbreak Ridge.

A million and more of my countrymen have died for freedom. My country is their eternal monument.

But they live on in the laughter of a small boy as he watches the antics of a circus clown, in the delicious coldness of the first bite of peppermint ice cream on the Fourth of July, in the little tenseness of a baseball crowd as the umpire calls, "Batter up!" And in the high school band's rendition of "Stars and Stripes Forever" in the Memorial Day Parade.

America has offered freedom and opportunity such as no land before it has ever known. To a fish crier down on Maxwell Street with the face of a man terribly glad to be selling fish. It has given him the right to own his pushcart, to sell his herring on Maxwell Street; it has given him an education for his children and a tremendous faith in the nation that has made these things his.

Multiply that fish crier by 200 million doctors and mechanics and coal miners and truck drivers and lawyers and plumbers and priests—all glad, terribly glad, to be what they are. Terribly glad to be free to work and eat and sleep and speak and love and live and pray as they desire, as they believe.

And those 200 million American, those 200 million free Americans, have more roast beef and mashed potatoes, the yield of American labor and land, more telephones and orlon sweaters, the fruits of American initiative and enterprise, more public schools and life insurance policies, symbols of American security and faith in the future, more laughter and song, than any other people on earth.

This is my answer. Show me a country greater than our country. Show me a people more energetic, creative, progressive, bigger-hearted and happier than our people. Not until then will I consider your way of life. For I am an American, and I speak for democracy!

Elizabeth Ellen Evans

Reprinted by permission; copyright © 1957 by United States Jaycees, Tulsa, Oklahoma.

INVOLVEMENT FOR ENVIRONMENT

BY
KAREN PETERSEN
MISS TEENAGE AMERICA 1975

"It's our world, and we can help make it better."

Karen Petersen and Cathy Durden, National Titleholders in 1975 and 1976, both contributed a monthly column in Teen Magazine. *We have selected one of the articles done by each of them as examples of ways you can become involved. Helping others and contributing to a better world help make you a better person.*

One of the primary concerns of every Candidate at the National Pageant was that of ecology. What can we do about it? By working together, we can reduce pollution to a level nature can handle.

I think that we would all have to agree that, unfortunately, our progress, technology and discoveries were accompanied by careless destruction of the environment.

Now we must fight for nature. The worst qualities in humans have created our dangerous situation. The best qualities must attempt to bring pollution back into balance, since we can never hope to eliminate it totally.

The number one cause of air pollution is the automobile spewing out 50 percent to 60 percent of the carbon monoxide in the atmosphere, which attacks the hemoglobin in the blood and prevents it from transporting oxygen to the tissues of the body. This causes headaches, dizziness, brain damage, or death. Almost all of the lead in the air results from auto emissions.

You can help by getting the operations manual for your car and checking the octane rating so you can buy gasoline with the lowest amount of lead and yet the proper amount of octane. This will help to cut down on the amount of unburned gasoline and lead vapor emissions.

Other helpful things you can do for cleaner air would be driving at a moderate speed, minimizing idling, having cars tuned up at least twice a year, and driving only when necessary, using car pools as much as possible.

Most electricity is generated in electrical plants by the burning of oil or coal, both of which release polluting gases. Our present use of electricity is soaring nearly five times as fast as the population. Cutting down on unnecessary electrical use at home is a good way for you to do something about pollution. For example, do not run major appliances for small jobs and turn off lights that aren't being used.

In the fight against pollution in general, particularly pollution of the air, nature provides a good ally—trees. They take carbon monoxide out of the air, put back oxygen and filter out many gases and particles. Trees also decrease noise pollution caused by factories and traffic as they add beauty to our cities and countryside.

Planting new trees and shrubs and taking care of existing plants is something that each individual can do. Doing this will help reduce the oversaturation of pollutants in the air, so nature can eventually balance itself again.

Although the earth is almost three quarters water, only a small fraction is drinkable. Obviously, water conservation is important. You can do little things around the home. Don't let water run needlessly. Use the automatic washer and dishwasher only for full loads.

You can help by using low phosphate detergents (usually 8.7 percent phosphate per box) and pure soaps. Cut back on what goes down the drain and help save our clean water.

One quarter of the earth is land, but only a small fraction is accessible to man. Fifty percent of the earth's population lives on only 7 percent of the land.

The most destructive land pollutants are chemicals in fertilizers, pesticides, and chlorinate hydrocarbons. The "bug bomb" sprays found in your home often contain poisons which persist for years where they are sprayed.

Your contribution would be avoiding excessive use of these sprays and not throwing the aerosol cans into incinerators. An interesting project would be placing ladybugs and praying mantises in your garden. Both are aggressive eaters of pests and other insects and you thus avoid some unnecessary spraying.

Solid waste is another burden to our countryside. Over five pounds of solid waste are collected daily for every person in the nation. What should you do with your trash?

Burning trash in an incinerator pollutes the air, throwing it on a dump pollutes the land, flushing it down the drain pollutes the streams. There does not have to be that much trash! The solution lies in recycling. Seventy percent of the solid waste is in packaging that may be reuseable. Buy returnable bottles, recyclable cans, wash and reuse plastic containers and carry a little bag in your car.

Get your group interested in a solid waste collection program. The Dr Pepper Company has environmental pollution test kits and "Ecology and You" booklets that include experiments that can easily be done in your home, along with instructions for the reduction and elimination of sources of pollution.

If you're a member of a group with an interest in ecology, you should plan to show Dr Pepper's film *The Tender Mansion*. It has many good suggestions for teens. Write to Dr Pepper, Box 5086, Dallas, Texas 75222.

It's our world and we can help make it better. Let's get going!

INVOLVEMENT TO HELP OTHERS

BY
CATHY DURDEN
MISS TEENAGE AMERICA 1976

Among the many responsibilities I have as MISS TEENAGE AMERICA, two of the most personally rewarding and satisfying are acting as the National Teen Chairman for the Cystic Fibrosis Foundation and as National Teen Ambassador for the National Easter Seal Society. As of 1976, these organizations are official charities of MISS TEENAGE AMERICA. Youth plays an important role in both these organizations by helping to insure the success of their programs. You, too, can take an active part by volun-

> "Working for those who are less fortunate is one of the most personally rewarding and satisfying parts of my life."

teering your help and at the same time, discover one of the most exciting and valuable experiences of your life. First, let me give some background information.

MISS TEENAGE AMERICA believes in offering a girl a chance to broaden her horizons and to become an active part of a generation that cares about the future. This philosophy is similar to that of the Cystic Fibrosis Foundation, whose ultimate goal is to enable today's generation to solve for its own, the complex disease of cystic fibrosis and hold promise for brighter futures for all children with the disease.

Cystic fibrosis is the most serious lung-damaging disease, the number-one genetic killer of children. CF can affect not only the lungs but also the digestive system. So far, there is no known cure, but incredible progress has been made in hhe past twenty years. Twelve years ago, children plagued with cystic fibrosis did not expect to live past the preschool age; today, fifty percent are living past the age of eighteen.

Many local CF chapters across the country have openings for teen chairmen or can use much assistance in planning their youth activities. The CFF conducts various programs for fund-raising needed to support the cost of research for the treatment and cure of CF. The Cystic Fibrosis Breath of Life Campaign needs volunteers not only to collect contributions for their programs but to educate the public about the disease. People are always needed to publicize their cause. You could become involved in radio, TV, and newspaper coverage. Bike-a-thons are another popular type of promotion utilized by the Foundation. Volunteers are needed to present the program to school assemblies and other groups. Here you could play a vital role. The CFF also sponsors various special events throughout the year which are not only fun but serve a worthwhile purpose. These range from golf tournaments to fashion shows,

Santa's houses to auctions, dinner dances to carnivals. If you are interested in becoming involved with the Cystic Fibrosis Foundation and would like further information, write your local CF chapter or the national headquarters:

>Cystic Fibrosis Foundation
>3379 Peachtree Road, N.E.
>Atlanta, Georgia 30326

The National Easter Seal Society for Crippled Children and Adults offers another type of involvement for youth. Easter Seal centers treat disabled people due to any cause by providing direct rehabilitation services to both handicapped children and adults. Easter Seal is working to improve the environment of the handicapped, especially in the areas of education, employment, housing, and the removal of architectual and transportational barriers.

The Easter Seal Society believes that only through youth involvement can the future growth of the Society be assured. Through your participation in the National Youth for Easter Seals movement you can gain invaluable training and practical experience. As in CFF, volunteers are needed to educate the public. Some of the most effective ways are through youth rallies, school assemblies, community architectural barrier surveys, recreation programs, safety campaigns, and special fund-raising events.

Young people can also be very effective working with the disabled by helping them to overcome their handicaps and to feel wanted and important. Volunteers are needed to help patients with their therapy and to provide encouragement. There are many exciting and fun activities that can be planned such as camping and field trips, parties, sewing and cooking get-togethers, and craft projects. Involving the handicapped in events like wheelchair basketball games and talent shows could be particularly rewarding experiences.

Maybe you have some ideas of your own that would be effective. There is an Easter Seal unit in every state and there is a great need for your help. If you'd like to take part, write to:

>NYES Coordinator
>National Easter Seal Society
>2023 West Ogden Avenue
>Chicago, Illinois 60612

These are the two charities I know best. There are many other places and ways to help—and so many people who need you. I think one of life's greatest pleasures must be the feeling of having helped another person to find some happiness and gain confidence in himself or herself.

It's up to us, today's youth, to assure a brighter future for all.

ADVENTURE VIII

MISS TEENAGE AMERICA Makes the Good Things Happen

The MISS TEENAGE AMERICA *Experience*

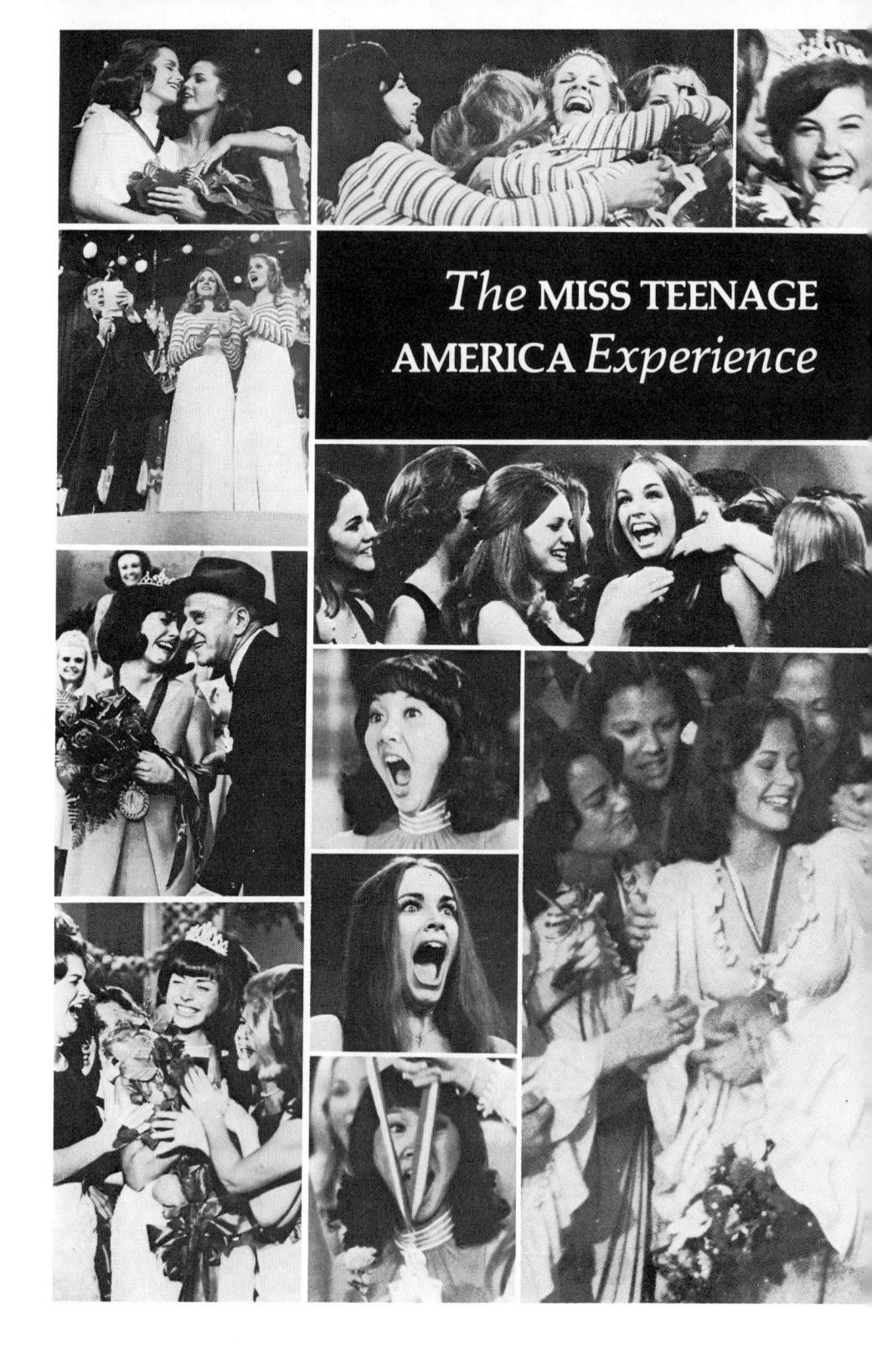

Karen Valentine, Miss Teenage Santa Rosa 1964, was recently asked by a *Family Weekly* reader, "Do you feel pageants are worthwhile?" Karen answered, "Pageants are mocked by many people, which I think is a shame. At sixteen, I was a finalist in the MISS TEENAGE AMERICA Pageant, and that experience changed my life. Not only did I gain confidence, but I also won a scholarship, allowing me to go to college. Also, a talent scout noticed me and this led to an appearance on the *Ed Sullivan Show*. Are the contests worthwhile? Positively!"

The *Sullivan Show* marked the beginning of Karen's career as a television actress. No one could really say whether or not she would have eventually been "discovered" had she not entered the Pageant, but we can say that the purpose of MISS TEENAGE AMERICA, to recognize outstanding young women, was realized in Karen's success.

Even though times are changing, it is still true that young men, through sports and other activities, have more opportunity for recognition, college scholarships, and special encouragement than do their female counterparts. Though we are confident time will provide an improvement on this situation, teenage girls can share these opportunities now, through the MISS TEENAGE AMERICA program.

At National Headquarters we receive many letters from former candidates expressing sentiments like, "Being 'Miss Teenage City' was an important factor in my acceptance at the college of my first choice. It was the one extra advantage that made me more competitive."

Many feel that MISS TEENAGE AMERICA has been helpful to them in getting started in a career. An example is the former candidate who had just landed the public relations job she wanted. She wrote, "The job was between me and one other person and I got it! I really think it was my MISS TEENAGE AMERICA experience that did it. My 'Miss Teenage City' title has really opened doors for me."

Former Candidates will telly you that they gained confidence and poise through this experience, and that it opened their eyes to their own capabilities as well as to the realization that the world offers much to discover.

There may be only one national title holder, but there are certainly no losers in this Pageant. The program is designed to offer something to every girl—lifetime things like knowledge, leadership, friendship, and a belief in her own abilities. It's a very special experience that can, as Karen said, change your life.

NOT A BEAUTY CONTEST

Please don't call us a *beauty* pageant. Nothing could be further from the truth. We have no runways, parading around or swimsuit competitions. As a matter of fact, a swimsuit photo attached to the entry form will result in disqualification.

We *are* a program which recognizes and supports outstanding young women. We are a scholarship award program.* We are a leadership program.

As such, MISS TEENAGE AMERICA embraces the qualities of individual accomplishment, school and community involvement and personal and scholastic achievement. We're one of the few pageants that has no argument with the women's movement. You see, we, too, are primarily concerned with honest opportunity and advancement for young women.

NATIONAL AWARDS

Most girls we have talked to enter the MISS TEENAGE AMERICA Competition for many reasons, but most attractive to them by far is the $12,000 scholarship, to the university or college of *her choice,* that each MISS TEENAGE AMERICA receives.

To some girls, the year of travel is very appealing. The last five MISS TEENAGE AMERICAS have even had the opportunity to visit foreign countries. One or more of them have travelled to South America, Japan, Mexico, the Caribbean, and Europe. They have all shared the experience of knowing their own country better—from New York to California; from the Great Lakes to the Gulf of Mexico—and they have all been impressed with "the wonderful people I've met" from shore to shore and border to border.

MISS TEENAGE AMERICA also receives a minimum cash guarantee of $5,000.00 for personal appearances, but some titleholders have earned over $7,500.00 in appearance fees.

*The MISS TEENAGE AMERICA scholarship program is detailed in the chapter on financial aids for college in this book.

Eight of the first ten MISS TEENAGE AMERICAS got together for a reunion at the 1971 MISS TEENAGE AMERICA Pageant. First row (left to right): Sandy Roberts (1967), Rewa Walsh (1971), Stephanie Crane (1968). Second row (left to right): Jeanine Zavrel (1964), Colette Daiute (1966), Darla Banks (1963). Third row (left to right): Debbie Patton (1970), Melissa Babish (1969).

Any girl would appreciate the other gifts and prizes that go along with MISS TEENAGE AMERICA's title. Among her special awards are a complete wardrobe, a year's supply of cosmetics and skin care products and a complete set of an encyclopedia.

You don't even have to become MISS TEENAGE AMERICA to win scholarships and other awards. National Semi-Finalists and special award winners receive scholarships and prizes, too. Some of MISS TEENAGE AMERICA's local pageants award scholarships, but all of them offer many very attractive prizes and awards.

At MISS TEENAGE AMERICA, award winners come in all sizes and shapes and backgrounds. They have been five foot two, almost six feet tall, fourteen years old, seventeen years old, well-endowed, flat chested, white, oriental, black, American Indian, Jewish, Mormon, Russian Orthodox, Christian, rich, poor, plain, fancy, freckled, and bespeckled, just to name a few.

We invite you to join in the MISS TEENAGE AMERICA experience. Who knows—you could be a future MISS TEENAGE AMERICA. And since there are no losers at MISS TEENAGE AMERICA, even if you don't capture first prize, you're sure to be a winner.

How to Enter the MISS TEENAGE AMERICA *Pageant*

A Day in the Life of MISS TEENAGE AMERICA

The MISS TEENAGE AMERICA Pageant is open to any American girl in the world who meets the requirements of the Official Rules. She may enter one of three ways, depending on her area of residence and whether or not there is a Local Pageant in her area.

I *The Local Pageant*

1. Check to see if there is an official MISS TEENAGE AMERICA preliminary pageant (Miss Teenage "City") in your area of residence.

2. Request an entry form from your Local Sponsor or from the National Headquarters address below.

3. Make sure you meet the qualifications stated in the Official Pageant Rules. Then complete the entry form, attach a recent photograph (swimsuit poses are not acceptable), and return both to your Local Sponsor immediately, or if you don't know whether or not you have a Local Sponsor, to the MISS TEENAGE AMERICA National Headquarters. The MISS TEENAGE AMERICA staff will refer your entry to your sponsor, if there is one. Otherwise, they will enter you in the Candidate-at-Large Competition. Local Pageant deadlines vary from city to city, so make sure your entry is received on time.

4. Your Local Pageant Co-ordinator will contact you.

II *The Candidate-at-Large Program*

1. If there is no Local Preliminary in your city, you may enter through the Candidate-at-Large competition. (If there is a Local Pageant in your area, you are not eligible for the Candidate-at-Large competition.)

2. Request an entry form from National Headquarters. (Address below.) Include a stamped, self-addressed envelope to speed delivery.

3. If you qualify according to Official Pageant Rules, complete the form, attach a photo (no swimsuit poses), and return your entry to the MISS TEENAGE AMERICA National Headquarters office.

4. Unless you are notified to the contrary, you will be automatically entered into the Candidate-at-Large competition. All entrants will receive word from National Headquarters as to whether or not they qualified for the Semi-Finals.

III *The Overseas Candidate-at-Large Program*

At this writing, MISS TEENAGE AMERICA is the only teenage pageant open to American citizens living outside the United States. Overseas entrants should follow the same instructions listed for Candidate-at-Large entrants.

The Overseas Competition is a separate preliminary competition, the winner of which will represent American girls living in foreign countries at the MISS TEENAGE AMERICA National Pageant finals and telecast.

If you're not sure how you should enter or if you need additional information, write the MISS TEENAGE AMERICA *National Headquarters: 1165 Empire Central Place, Suite 101, Dallas, Texas 75247.*

OFFICIAL RULES

1. Candidate must be a female at least thirteen years of age by January 1 of the year in which the Pageant is conducted, but must not have reached her eighteenth birthday on or before December 31 of that year.

2. Candidate must not be under contract to other parties which would limit her services, should she become MISS TEENAGE AMERICA.

3. Candidate, joined by her legal guardian, must consent to a written agreement with MISS TEENAGE AMERICA prior to competing in the National Pageant stating that she will be willing to travel and make personal appearances should she be selected MISS TEENAGE AMERICA.

4. Once a Candidate has participated as a National Candidate in the MISS TEENAGE AMERICA Pageant, she is not eligible to enter the competition again. Candidates who have not participated in the National Pageant may re-enter the local preliminaries, however.

5. Candidate must be a citizen of the United States, of high moral character, must never have been married, divorced, have had a marriage annulled, or committed a felony.

6. Candidate must be enrolled at the time of the National Pageant in grades 8, 9, 10, 11, or 12 in an accredited school and must maintain a passing grade average for the current school year. If selected as a Semi-Finalist, Candidate may be required to support her stated scholastic average with an authentic transcript of her grades.

7. Entry blanks must be received on or before deadline set by Local Sponsor, and each entry must be accompanied by a recent photograph of the Candidate. Swimsuit poses are not acceptable. Photographs will not be returned. All entries become the property of the MISS TEENAGE AMERICA Pageant, Dallas, Texas.

8. The MISS TEENAGE AMERICA Pageant is subject to all state and federal regulations.

9. Participation is not open to employees or the immediate families of MISS TEENAGE AMERICA's National Sponsors, Local Sponsors, their Pageant co-ordinator and staff, affiliates, subsidiaries, or advertising agencies; nor to employees or the immediate families of the Dr Pepper Company, its subsidiaries or advertising agencies.

ABOUT THE JUDGING

Judging in the MISS TEENAGE AMERICA competition is based on the following:

(1) *POISE, APPEARANCE AND EXPRESSION* (45%)

Notice the word, beauty, is missing. This category includes grooming, posture, attitude, sincerity and the way you express yourself. You'll be asked about your school and community involvements and your interests and achievements.

(2) *SCHOLASTIC ACHIEVEMENT* (35%)

You must have passing grades, but A's and B's are better. In this area of the competition the Candidates take a written test to determine general awareness. The test includes some of the basic things you are studying in school and a good assortment of current events.

(3) *INDIVIDUAL ACCOMPLISHMENT* (20%)

This area is largely up to you. What is your special talent? What do you do exceptionally well? What special interest have you worked at and developed? It could be swimming, art, singing, sign language, fashion design, or calf roping. It could be anything. That's up to you.

Your Special Accomplishment must be demonstrated in a two-minute presentation. For those talents (like water skiing) that cannot be presented onstage, films and slides are certainly acceptable.

HOW CAN I PREPARE?

An often asked question.

Before you start running around changing things, remember, *be yourself!* Don't try to be something you aren't or an imitation of a present or former titleholder.

Are you in the habit of being well groomed? MISS TEENAGE AMERICA has to look presentable *every* day. If you've been planning to get that extra ten pounds off, why not go ahead and do it now.

MISS TEENAGE AMERICA writes her own speeches. She will deliver many. Can you express your ideas clearly and sincerely? Do you have a positive attitude toward most things?

The Test: most girls find it helpful to make a habit of reading the newspaper and news magazines. The "Awareness" section covers happenings in the government, movies, books, sports, fashion, science, and world events in general. The "General Knowledge" sections deal with academic subjects like literature, grammar, science, and social studies.

You can start thinking about your Individual Accomplishment. What do you do best? How can you present it most creatively? What can you do to make it more interesting?

STOP! LOOK! LISTEN!

If you decide to enter the MISS TEENAGE AMERICA Pageant, please check and make sure that it definitely is the MISS TEENAGE AMERICA Pageant.

There are many pageants of similar name. The name MISS TEENAGE AMERICA is registered in the United States Patent Office. That is the *only* name we ever use. Other pageant names which use the same words in different order, such as "Miss America Teenage" are not MISS TEENAGE AMERICA. Contests of similar name, such as "Miss American Teenager" are not a part of the MISS TEENAGE AMERICA operation. Don't confuse titles like "Miss National Teenage" with MISS TEENAGE AMERICA's National Pageant finals or MISS TEENAGE AMERICA's National Candidates. If you are required to pay an entry fee, sell programs or solicit a sponsor, it is definitely *not* the MISS TEENAGE AMERICA Pageant. There are *absolutely no financial considerations of any kind* required of any MISS TEENAGE AMERICA entrant. You will not be required or permitted to solicit a personal sponsor to pay such fees for you. You will not be required to sell tickets and programs.

In the MISS TEENAGE AMERICA Competition, those girls who become Local Pageant Winners or one of the Candidates-at-Large receive *all*-expense-paid trips for themselves and their chaperones to the MISS TEENAGE AMERICA National Pageant Finals and National Telecast. They even fly first class! Every cent of expense for this nine-day experience of a lifetime is borne by MISS TEENAGE AMERICA. Even television wardrobe is provided and the Candidates get to keep it.

One National Candidate for the title of MISS TEENAGE AMERICA left her hometown airport with a ten dollar bill. When she returned home eight days later, she still had $9.20. She had spent 80¢ on postcards and stamps!

If you're interested in entering *any* pageant, it would be wise to determine these facts in advance. There is at least one teen pageant (not MISS TEENAGE AMERICA) that claims to charge no entry fee, but if you are chosen as a semifinalist in *that* pageant you must then pay a fee, or find a sponsor to pay your fee, in order to retain that status. Some pageants require you to finance your own trip to the finals, or ask you to solicit a sponsor to pay your own way.

It's also nice to know that the pageant you identify with is one of quality and integrity. We've been notified of instances in which girls attended pageants where prizes were never awarded, where they were given $3.00 a day to cover all meals and where they were roomed four to a room on cots. That's quite a bit different than the private hotel room and the country club banquets, ranch barbecues and specially planned meals the MISS TEENAGE AMERICA Candidates are provided.

At MISS TEENAGE AMERICA all scoring is handled by Certified Public Accountants. There are checks and cross checks to insure honesty and fairness. Even the Policies and Practices Department of the television network verifies all judging and scoring procedures and results to make sure that every girl is treated equally and fairly.

The television show is broadcast via NBC, one of the most prestigious networks, in television's most important time slot in the fall season. Most other pageants are in the summer rerun season. Top-name stars, like Mac Davis and John Davidson, host the show and the girls are supported by some of the finest technical experts in television to give them the same professional quality in sound, lighting, camera work and all of those very important things that famous performing artists receive.

The MISS TEENAGE AMERICA Pageant is a star studded event. Pictured are some of the stars who have appeared on the national telecast with the MISS TEENAGE AMERICA Candidates.

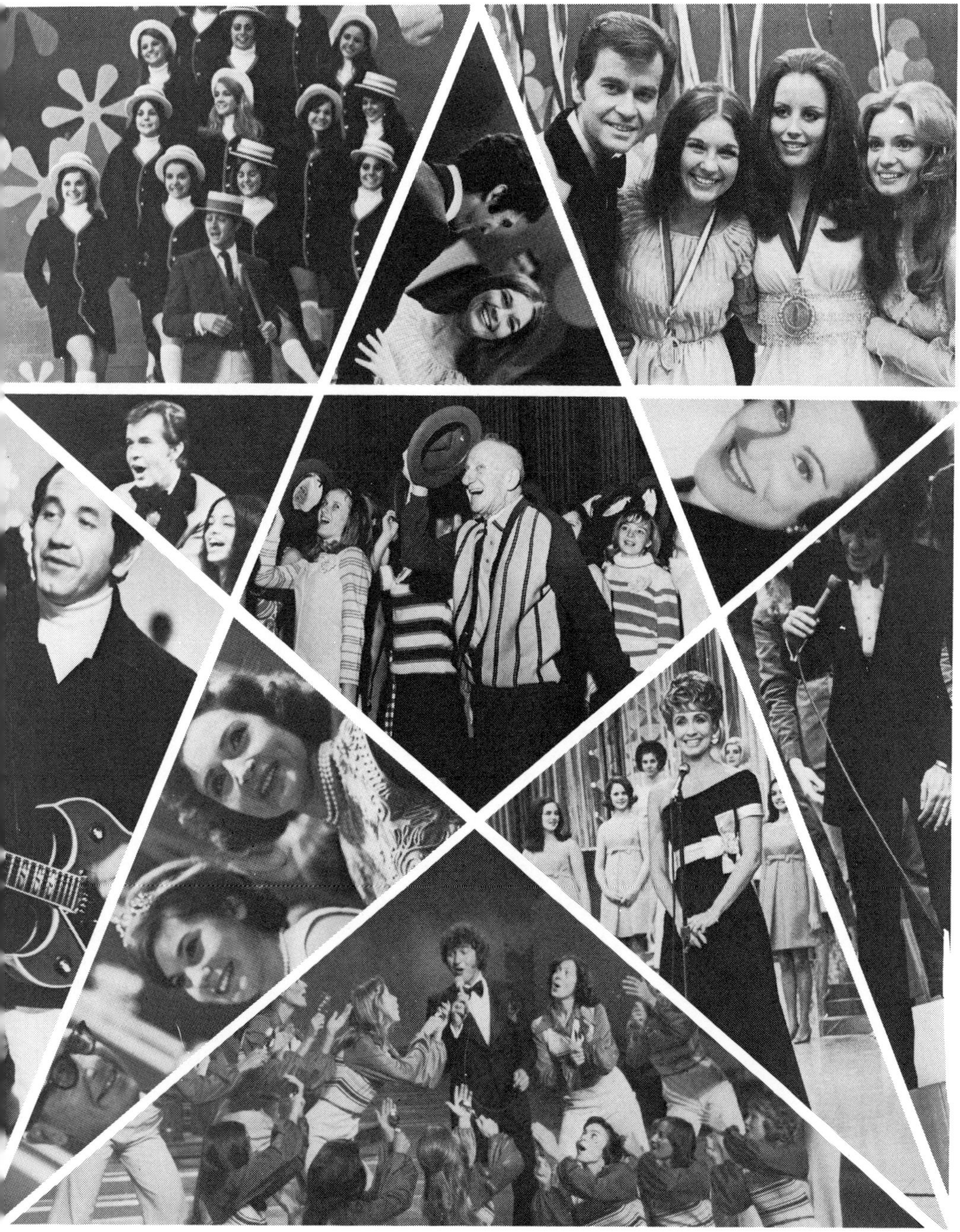

What It's Like to Be MISS TEENAGE AMERICA

BY
COLLEEN FITZPATRICK,
MISS TEENAGE AMERICA 1972
MELISSA GALBRAITH,
MISS TEENAGE AMERICA 1973
LORI MATSUKAWA,
MISS TEENAGE AMERICA 1974

What's it like? Only someone who's been there can answer that, so we presented that question to three lovely people who have the answers.

COLLEEN: It was incredible! Exhilarating! Wonderful! And surely it was fantastic to say the least. It's amazing, and I can describe what it's like and use all the superlatives that I want, but when it comes right down to it, no one will ever *really* know what being MISS TEENAGE AMERICA is like and what it involves, except myself and the other former MISS TEENAGE AMERICAS.

LORI: My year as MISS TEENAGE AMERICA was a Cinderella story come true! I was a small-town girl who suddenly found myself meeting people from all walks of life. I was doing in a year what would normally take me many years to do. It was a year of learning and excitement which I will remember all my life.

MELISSA: The task of describing and condensing an entire year of one's life into a few pages is indeed difficult. I have repeatedly been asked what aspect of my year as MISS TEENAGE AMERICA was most exciting, and still I hesitate to single out any specific event. In retrospect, however, the words "travel" and "people" invariably enter my mind, two words I consider synonymous with that year.

Being the daughter of a career Army officer, travelling was far from a novel experience, but as MISS TEENAGE AMERICA 1973 I easily surpassed the number of miles amassed in my previous sixteen years.

One adjusts quickly to both the thrills and frustrations of air travel as MISS TEENAGE AMERICA since your travels span the entire Western hemisphere. After living in Europe for six years, it was especially exciting for me to travel extensively throughout the United States.

LORI: Some of the questions I was most frequently asked were "Why did you enter?", "How did you prepare?", and "Did you expect to win?" I'll answer those.

I had no knowledge of MISS TEENAGE AMERICA. A friend of mine called and asked if I wanted to enter. My first reaction—"A beauty contest? Are you kidding?" He hurriedly explained that MISS TEENAGE AMERICA was not a beauty contest at all. I was still rather skeptical, so he brought the entry blanks to my home to read. When my eyes lit upon the $10,000 scholarship*, I began to reconsider. "After all," I thought, "there is nothing to lose and everything to gain. Just think of the experience!"

I sent in my entry blank and went through the test and interviews without a serious thought of actually winning. So it was a pleasant surprise when I was named Miss Teenage Honolulu.

There is really no way to be fully prepared for the pageant. A cosmetic consultant taught me how to apply make-up. My friends and I got together and taped the Maori music for my poiball dance. And in less than a month, I was representing Honolulu in the 13th annual MISS TEENAGE AMERICA Pageant.

I entered Pageant Week armed with nothing but my chaperone, Ellie McDaniel, and the attitude that the week would be enjoyable. She and I were determined to make the most of the week and not worry about the competition. Ellie was the key person in my life during this period. She made sure that I was prompt for all events, she gave me tips and advice on my clothing and appearance, she boosted my spirits when they flagged, and all in a loving and a humorous manner! I found no feelings of back-stabbing among the other contestants during the week. Our purpose was to put on the best TV pageant ever. We worked hard and put on a good show!

---

*Since Lori's year as titleholder, the scholarship has been raised from $10,000 to $12,000.

Colleen Fitzpatrick
MISS TEENAGE AMERICA 1972

Melissa Marie Galbraith
MISS TEENAGE AMERICA 1973

Winning the pageant was the shock of my life! Even when there were just the two of us on stage, I never thought I'd win. My parents, who were home in Hawaii, were unable to watch the pageant becuase it wasn't shown there. They found out that I had won when a cousin in Oregon called them. They were flabbergasted!

For the first month upon my return home, I received many cards, letters and telegrams and news clippings from people all over the United States. It was quite overwhelming, but I answered each letter I received. I even received a marriage proposal from eight-year-old Will of Ohio. He had enclosed a stamped, self-addressed envelope for a reply. I wrote back and told him that I wasn't ready for marriage yet and hoped he would understand!

COLLEEN: What do I remember? Getting beyond the adjectives (which are quite sincere) and behind all the obvious facets of the travel, the fun, the glamor, and the people, I remember the responsibility and the adjustment behind it. That word, responsibility, surrounds the title and its duties. I tend to think that most girls believe that MISS TEENAGE AMERICA or any title is a "fluffy" affair—at least I did when I was younger and hadn't experienced a title. However, after I won, I found out soon enough that with the fun comes the responsibility of the job.

Lori Matsukawa
MISS TEENAGE AMERICA 1974

Now this can mean anything from something small—like making sure you catch a plane to an appearance (actually this could turn into a big dilemma!) to really important matters. For example, I had to be always alert to the needs of my sponsors, and I had to remember that at sixteen I had a responsibility to young people, like yourself, that live all over this country. I mean, I was representing you! That's pretty scary!

I went through a difficult transition period in readjusting again after the end of the year. I was once again a typical young girl leading a high school life, worrying about who my next boyfriend would be and whether or not my school had a great football team. I wasn't prepared for it.

MELISSA: I participated in opening ceremonies for several new bottling plants in various states. In addition, I made appearances with Dr Pepper representatives at the Kentucky Derby, the Indianapolis 500, and in the Bahamas, just to mention a few! Trips to South America and Hawaii were fascinating and memorable.

Equally as exciting was the opportunity to meet so many new people, people of every nationality, religion, and lifestyle. I learned so much by talking with and observing people everywhere. In addition, I learned valuable lessons in human nature during my travels and established lifelong friendships which will always provide fond memories.

(Left to right, Colleen Fitzpatrick, Lori Matsukawa, Melissa Galbraith)

Colleen and Melissa were both present to see Lori win her title. Melissa passed on the MISS TEENAGE AMERICA medallion and Colleen was the television hostess that special night in Lori's life.

LORI: I, too, was able to participate in the Cotton Bowl, Orange Bowl, Kentucky Derby and Indianapolis 500 parades, plus the American Academy of Achievement, the Football Hall of Fame, and trips to Japan and Peru! I visted large cities and small towns.

During the year some of the most fun activities were those that popped up unexpectedly, such as making a Dr Pepper commercial for local TV. We had to shoot it ten times to get it perfect—all in all I drank four cans of Dr Pepper before the shooting was done! I received a surprise call while in Arkansas to fly to Los Angeles for the weekend to tape a guest spot on the *Sonny Bono Comedy Revue.* While touring Japan, the Dr Pepper people realized a dream of mine by dressing me in a traditional silk kimono, putting my hair up and taking pictures of the costume under the beautiful cherry blossoms.

Would I call myself a celebrity? I hardly consider myself one! I wanted mine to be a year of learning. People proved to be the most worthwhile and meaningful part of my year. I feel richer, for they have given me, along with their friendship, a part of themselves.

COLLEEN: I was accelerated into learning about the world. During my tenure, I learned by my own experiences and meetings with people what they were all about, how their cultures were, and just about life in general. I also learned how to react to those people and how to relate in a given situation.

LORI: A reporter I met put it very well when she said that I promote America and American teenagers. The events of the year have opened my eyes to the greatness of teenagers. The majority of teenagers are ambitious and intelligent, not lazy or indifferent. At the many conventions I attended, I encountered young people who were talented, accomplished and destined to be part of a great American generation.

I was a bit leery about the way my school friends would accept me. Happily though, when I was in school, everyone regarded me as "plain old Lori." I will always appreciate that! I was still one of the group, not someone out of touch with them. Many people said, "Gee, you don't *act* like a MISS TEENAGE AMERICA! You're still the same!" I considered that a compliment. When I was at home between trips abroad, I did the dishes, cleaned my room and did homework just like everyone else!

My teachers were very understanding and allowed me to read books while I traveled and hand in term papers and reports when I got home.

My dating situation remained much the same as it was before the contest. I dated the same people I had dated before but found out that they felt a little uncomfortable walking with a person who was recognized on the street! The boys had a lot of patience, too! It could become very trying to constantly hear, "I'm sorry. Lori's not home. She's on a trip to_____."

My career plans were altered significantly. Prior to that year I had wanted to become a piano teacher. But after being interviewed by so many radio and TV personalities, I have decided that a career in the field of mass communications is what I want to pursue. My travels have shown me how small my world had been. I now want to be a part of the challenging world of communications.

Was I sad to leave my title? My year was too special to be sad about it. I will look back upon the places I've been and the activities I've done with fond remembrance, yet I also look forward to my college years.

If people asked me for advice for any would-be MISS TEENAGE AMERICA, I'm afraid I wouldn't have too much to give. I'd tell her to be herself and maintain a good, positive attitude.

COLLEEN: When I stop to think about it, each MISS TEENAGE AMERICA must carry around a treasury of personal experiences that she alone can remember, sort through, and relate to for the rest of her life . . .

MELISSA: It was one year of my life that I'll always cherish. Sometimes I found myself exhausted and irritable, but the appreciative smile of a shy, six-year-old girl upon receiving my autograph, or the warm hug of a nine-year-old boy stricken with leukemia in the Children's Hospital, were such wonderful, exhilarating moments that any personal anxieties I felt were totally erased. And it was moments such as these that made me proud to represent my country as MISS TEENAGE AMERICA.

View From Behind the Potted Palm

BY
IRMA PETERSEN
Mother of Karen Petersen
MISS TEENAGE AMERICA 1975

If becoming MISS TEENAGE AMERICA changes a girl's life, imagine how this event affects her family.

All of a sudden your daughter is a celebrity. She's the center of attraction, the object of the camera's eye, the featured speaker of the evening, the special guest that everybody came to see.

As a mother, observing all of this from behind the potted palm, what goes through your mind?

Have you ever watched the MISS TEENAGE AMERICA Pageant and thought for a moment—What would it be like to have your daughter win this coveted title? Well this very thing happened to me. What an awesome and exciting experience—sitting in the audience and hearing your daughter announced as MISS TEENAGE AMERICA!

No one can imagine all the thoughts that run through a mother's mind when this happens: Can she do it? Is she prepared? Is it for real? How will we all adjust to this new "happening"? Can we all accept the responsibility of this new endeavor? Yet I saw my daughter enthusiastically accept the total responsibility of being MISS TEENAGE AMERICA and take each day as it came. Even though her parents were overwhelmed by the year's demand, she never was.

A good feature has been that these many new adventures did not all happen at once; rather they occurred over a one-year period. The experiences of this year have been so wonderfully memorable that they will live in my thoughts the rest of my life.

I must admit though prior to the MISS TEENAGE AMERICA competition I had a great fear of flying. When Karen won, I had to make several important decisions—to forget that fear and accompany her or to allow someone else to take my place and share those great experiences. Needless to say, I made the right decision and was able to travel about eighty percent of the time as Karen's chaperone from coast to coast and border to border.

I was often asked what exactly were the duties of a chaperone of MISS TEENAGE AMERICA. Soon after Karen won, we had a meeting with the staff of MISS TEENAGE AMERICA where the duties were specifically detailed. The mother/chaperone was definitely a "behind-the-scenes observer"; one who only made decisions which had a bearing on Karen's health, welfare, and safety and secondarily, making sure reservations, tickets, flights, and appearances were in order and that we were on time for every commitment. In fact, Karen never missed, was late for, or had to cancel a single appearance—a truly commendable record considering the extent of all the appearances for the year!

After my year's exposure to MISS TEENAGE AMERICA and my observations of Karen at appearances—be it a television show, a speech in a high school, a newspaper interview, or even a parade—it became apparent to me why there was such thorough and intense judging at the Pageant. The judges were able to observe the Finalists in many different circumstances. Many of these potential situations were forerunners for what was expected of MISS TEENAGE AMERICA. I think that Karen's success can be attributed to her winning qualities—her enthusiasm for the concept of MISS TEENAGE AMERICA, her vitality, and her good common sense. In unexpected situations she has been required to meet the press or news media in almost every city she visited. She was always a lady who conducted herself accordingly. Sometimes reporters would try to urge her to speak out on a controversial subject. Karen was always able to "field" those questions and those reporters with ease. I never went into the press conferences with Karen (except for the very first one) because I felt being in the room with Karen would hamper her candor and, perhaps, the interviewer would feel as though I were an intruder. I never ceased to be amazed at how Karen could spontaneously deliver a speech or give just the right comment when called upon. She made all the decisions as far as what she said—she was never coached by me or anyone from the MISS TEENAGE AMERICA staff. From the very beginning of her exciting year Karen was in constant touch with the staff of MISS TEENAGE AMERICA, via her private phone provided by them. All questions, assignments, and information were made directly and only to Karen.

As I look back and reminisce about the past year, I feel probably one of the most important and rewarding features for Karen and me have been the wonderful people we have had the privilege to meet. We traveled extensively throughout the U.S. and have been introduced to hundreds of individuals who I will never forget. By far the most awe-inspiring person that Karen met this year was President Gerald Ford. Can you even imagine the pride and excitement to see your child being honored by the President in the Oval Office, let alone that your meeting was brought about by your own daughter's achievements. No words can adequately express the feelings I have had—to be able to share these great experiences with Karen.

My association with the staff has been a most rewarding experience. They were always concerned and respectful to our family. The man largely responsible for the whole MISS TEENAGE AMERICA concept is the president, Charles Meeker, Jr., one of the finest men I have ever met. My feelings for Mr. Meeker are shared by everyone who has ever been associated with him or the MISS TEENAGE AMERICA Pageant.

The only real hardship for our family during this unforgettable year was for my husband. It was he who had to remain at home while Karen and I had such great experiences. His pride and pleasure, though, came at home when someone would introduce him as "MISS TEENAGE AMERICA'S Father." He did get to visit the President and take part in the exciting Indianapolis "500" activities.

A bit of advice to any mother of a girl entering the MISS TEENAGE AMERICA competition. The desire to enter must be the decision of the daughter and only hers. Once she is convinced that she wants to compete, then the entire family should stand behind her, win or lose. (Karen's first attempt to enter MISS TEENAGE AMERICA was unsuccessful and yet this defeat was a very important part in building her character.) To lose is also a part of life's important hurdles. There is a saying at the MISS TEENAGE AMERICA Pageant—"There are no losers." Even if you are not chosen MISS TEENAGE AMERICA, you are always a winner.

Before Karen entered the MISS TEENAGE AMERICA competition, I wrote a note to her. I would like to share these words of encouragement with you:

Be Yourself.
Like Yourself.
Believe in Yourself.

This great experience of being a participant in MISS TEENAGE AMERICA does change lives in positive ways; new experiences, new opportunities, new friends—all of this I know is true.

Many people asked me during the year, "Isn't Karen going to change?" and "Isn't there going to be a letdown when her year is over?" Yes, Karen changed. She is much more mature and has more confidence than she had one year ago. As far as the letdown—Karen realized from the first day she had one year as MISS TEENAGE AMERICA and enjoyed each experience, at the same time setting her mind to the next new exciting adventure in her life—college, made possible with her wonderful $10,000* MISS TEENAGE AMERICA Scholarship.

MISS TEENAGE AMERICA was one of the greatest things that ever happened to us, and a wonderful experience for Karen. She will have the accomplishments and the happy memories of that year for the rest of her life. As parents, what more can we ask. After all—isn't that our ultimate goal for our children?

---

*Editor's Note: Since Karen held the MISS TEENAGE AMERICA title, the First Place Scholarship Award has been increased to $12,000.

Being a Winner—Even if You Don't Get First Prize

BY
PATTI LARKIN
Miss Teenage San Diego 1974

Oh, Patti was a winner all right. She held the Miss Teenage San Diego Title. But she was also one of the girls who did not hear her name called when the new MISS TEENAGE AMERICA *was announced.*

She's given us permission to use some excerpts from a letter she wrote to MISS TEENAGE AMERICA's *president, Charles R. Meeker, Jr., a year later. In her letter, she expresses her feelings about her* MISS TEENAGE AMERICA *experience.*

It took me by surprise! Despite the fact that I knew preparations for the 1975 Miss Teenage San Diego Pageant were being made, I simply wasn't prepared for the gigantic sign just inside the front entrance of my favorite department store which read, "Enter the 1975 MISS TEENAGE AMERICA Pageant. Applictions Available in the Young California Shop." My heart started beating a little faster. I stopped where I was and looked at my mother, she understood. It was in her eyes as she reached for my hand and squeezed it.

My year as Miss Teenage San Diego over? How could it be? Whoever heard of a two-month year? It couldn't have been a day longer than that since I arrived at the National Pageant and began the most fabulous week of my life.

Although my mother and I didn't say a word, we both knew with that special ESP we share that shopping was out of the question now. We went upstairs, picked up a couple of applications, glanced at the fantastic color shot of Lori and hurried to our car and started driving. Alone in the car, we started talking, memories we shared of our beautiful week at the Pageant flooding out, we babbled and talked, interrupting each other, laughing, remembering. Then, all at once, it hit me, it isn't over! It will never be over. Whoever said "All good things must come to an end" never was a part of the MISS TEENAGE AMERICA Pageant and never knew the lives of the National Contestants are changed forever. Years from now, mother and I will be remembering, sharing, laughing, and enjoying the multitude of new friends we have made this year as a result, direct or indirect, of my participation in the Pageant. I know, in the deepest part of my heart, as long as I live, I will *feel* like Miss Teenage San Diego, and God willing, I will always live in such a way as to reflect the principle and standards of our Pageant, as well as the kindness, good sportsmanship, the meaning and purpose, and, most of all, the love it represents.

James once wrote "The purpose of life is to spend it for something that outlasts it." He must have been thinking of an experience like this when he wrote those beautiful words. My dreams, as well as those of hundreds of other teenage girls, come true!

As far back as I can remember, I wanted to be in the MISS TEENAGE AMERICA Pageant. I can remember watching the Pageant on television and feeling the shivers of excitement as the Pageant progressed. But, of course, every little girl wants to be a part of the MISS TEENAGE AMERICA Pageant, but few of them really believe they ever will be. As I grew older, without realizing it, I discarded the dream with the thought that "I simply wasn't Pageant material." Then, one day last year, I was in a store and there were the applications for the Miss Teenage San Diego Pageant and, all at once, I was a little girl again watching the Pageant on television, feeling the familiar shivers of excitement. I took an application home, showed it to my mother who thought it was a wonderful idea, and encouraged me to enter. After deciding I would "think about it," I put it on my bulletin board and did no more about it. Weeks later, I heard an announcement on the radio informing the public that was the deadline day for getting applications in for the contest. My application was still pinned to my bulletin board. I called my mother at work and we discussed it, both of us finally deciding that it would "really be fun." I filled in the application and the two of us delivered it to the sponsor that evening, just minutes before the deadline.

In the weeks that followed, I found myself thinking more than once, "What on earth am I doing here?" In the scholastic testing, as I sat across from a school friend with a 4.0 average, I silently berated myself as I plodded along on the test (I made the top twenty-five, she didn't). During the poise, appearance, and expression judging, I looked at the beautiful girls with their impeccable grooming and felt very presumptuous being there. Finally, at the individual accomplishment portion of the judging, I peered fearfully at the tiny makeshift stage where I was to perform a twirling routine that required, of all things, space to move in, and looked up to see that the blinding afternoon sun would be directly in my eyes and I again asked myself, "Why, why did you ever get into this?" But, miraculously, it was meant to be. God decided to bless my life beautifully with new friends, new experiences, additional values and lessons, and chose this very special way to do it.

The National Pageant! WOW! Will any of us ever forget it? The excitement of arriving and pinning on the name badges that officially named us National Contestants, the limousine ride to the hotel, the wonderful welcome, meeting Melissa and the other contestants from all over the country. I wonder if all the girls felt as I did, as if they were dreaming and afraid they would wake up and it wouldn't be real. I drifted through each day in such a happy daze, enjoying every single minute to the fullest. So many beautiful memories. . . .

——The welcome banquet at the Country Club.
——The terror of the scholastic testing (only in our minds).
——Meeting the celebrities and guest stars.
——The relief of meeting the Poise and Appearance judges and realizing how nice and comfortable they were.
——The Sandwich Olympics—Wow!
——The talent judging and the devastating moment when my costume split all the way down the back—I wanted to die!
——The fantastic entertainment. The comfort of Carol's words telling me not to worry about the costume.
——The Gary Moore Singers.
——That unbelievably shocking moment when I was announced as a Semi-Finalist on Thanksgiving morning. I couldn't believe it now. I remember feeling a little like an impostor.
——The endless rehearsals, the quiet moments with the other Semi-Finalists, falling totally in love with the staff.
——The endless energy and encouragement and patience toward the contestants as everyone tirelessly worked to make us look good.
——The Pageant!! There will never be another night like that!
——The celebration ball, beautiful, fun, sad.
——The Awards Brunch, the goodbyes and the tears.

Working with MISS TEENAGE AMERICA's charities is one of the lasting gifts of the Pageant. I have become deeply involved and am working very closely with the area director. My mother and I just returned from a visit to the hospital and the desire to help has now turned into love after talking to the doctors there, observing procedures, meeting the tiny patients who depend on the hospital for their very lives. We have so many exciting plans for the future. My career plans are to become a pediatrician, so as you can see, this hospital is doubly precious to me.

I have thought of my MISS TEENAGE AMERICA experience so often since the Pageant. I wonder if you really know what an impact the Pageant made on the lives of all the National Contestants and how much it means to us. I've talked to past National Contestants, current National Contestants, and the opinion is always the same. It means so much to so many people. Thank you.

From the President's File

BY
CHARLES R. MEEKER, Jr., President
MISS TEENAGE AMERICA

Some people collect stamps. Others save coins, match covers, postcards or comic books.

I collect ideas.

I continue to promise myself that time will allow me the opportunity to sort them and organize them. It hasn't happened yet.

Following are a few picked at random from three filing cabinets, all well filled.

If you enjoy them it will bring me pleasure to have had the opportunity to share them with you. If, perchance, one of them might prove to be of value, then the efforts of many have been fully repaid.

For whatever men say in their blindness
In spite of the fancies of youth
There's nothing so kingly as kindness
And nothing so royal as truth.
Alfred Lord Tennyson

We cannot make bargains with blisses
Nor catch them like fishes in nets
Because sometimes that which life misses
Means more than that which life gets
Author Unknown

The best description I have ever heard noting the difference between a professional versus an amateur:

The professional is the one who handles the experience. The amateur is the one who gets handled by the experience.

(As related by Lee J. Cobb in speaking of the character Willie Loman, prior to the opening of *Death of a Salesman*)

SOME MEN ARE LIKE SHIPS

Some men are like ships that
Seek the calm
Of the quiet sheltered cove,
Content to stay where the shallows
Play
With never the will to rove;

And some are like ships that seek
The sea
Where the winds and the tide run high,
Where it's fight for days and the
Loser pays
And nobody questions why;

So some lay to, where the winds
Are few
With their sails all neatly furled,
And some fight home through the
Storm swept foam
With the cargoes of the world.

Author Unknown

A lion and a tiger once drank beside a pool
Please tell me said the tiger
Why you are roaring like a fool.

I am not foolish said the lion,
With a twinkle in his eyes.
They call me king of beasts,
Because it pays to advertise.

A rabbit heard them talking,
And he ran home like a streak.
He thought he'd try the lion's plan,
But his roar was a squeak.

A fox came to investigate;
Had dinner in the woods.
So when you advertise my friends,
Be sure you've got the goods.

Author Unknown

WHY MEN SURVIVE

I do not believe the greatest threat to our future is from bombs or guided missiles. I don't think our civilization will die that way. I think it will die when we no longer care—when the spiritual forces that make us wish to be right and noble die in the hearts of men. Arnold Toynbee has pointed out that nineteen of twenty-one notable civilizations have died from within and not to conquest from without. There were no bands playing and no flags waving when these civilizations decayed; it happened slowly, *in the quiet and the dark when no one was aware.*

If America is to grow great, we must stop gagging at the word "spiritual." Our task is to re-discover and re-assert our faith in the spiritual, non-utilitarian values on which American life has really rested from its beginning.

Lawrence M. Gould

Those who forget history are doomed to repeat it.

Author Unknown

Better never trouble trouble until trouble troubles you,
For you only make your trouble double trouble when you do;
And your trouble, like a bubble that you're troubling about,
May be nothing but a cipher with the rim rubbed out.

*As repeated in a newspaper
column by Dr. Norman Vincent Peale*

I dreamed Death came the other night and Heaven's gate
   swung wide;
With kindly grace an angel ushered me inside.
And there to my astonishment stood folks I'd known on earth,
Some I'd judged and labeled as "Unfit"—of little worth.
Indignant words rose to my lips, but never were set free—
For every face showed stunned surprise—
Not one expected Me.

Author Unknown

Knowledge in itself is not enough.
It can simply make a clever devil
Out of a stupid one.

Bishop Sheen

Half our troubles come from wanting our own way.
The other half comes from getting it.

From an Earl Wison column

HOW TO KEEP TO THE RIGHT IN VERBAL TRAFFIC

I had been warned not to drive alone in Lima, Peru, but I had made it safely to the Gold Museum. Now in the gathering dusk, I was attempting a return to the hotel.

Finally, I had to face the fact that someplace, somewhere, I had made the wrong turn and was now hopelessly lost.

It was definitely not the scenic part of the city and my apprehensions were widening with the settling night. To drive further would only compound the confusion so I finally selected a corner in the middle of nowhere.

A tentative knock on the first shanty-like structure brought a crack in the door and a suspicious eye.

I didn't even know how to say "help" in Spanish so I just said, "I'm lost."

The door closed.

The second door didn't even open, although I could hear muffled voices inside.

By the third door, people from the first and second stops were now outside watching.

The third door produced a ragged boy of about twelve. Again I said, "I'm lost."

He held up a single finger, brushed past me and was off up the narrow street.

By now other doors opened and within ten feet of me stood at least a dozen people all with silent stares.

Finally, after an age had rolled by and the crowd had doubled, my young friend reappeared with a priest at the rear of his pointing finger.

He came quickly with a smile, took my arm, waved the crowd away and we headed for the waiting automobile.

Then in perfect English he said, "Come, I will show you the way."

A few short blocks and crooked turns and I was back on the highway with understandable directions for returning to the hotel.

Refusing offers of money, but hearing every way I knew to express thanks, he hesitated at the curb side.

Then, just before he disappeared in the shadows he turned back to the window and said, "I thank The Father that He has made it possible for me to help people in more than one language."

Of all the sounds of a lifetime none has ever fallen as sweetly on my ears as did the sound of my native tongue spoken in an unfriendly wilderness.

And, as the years roll by, I've become increasingly aware of the unbelievable possibilities that our language offers us to communicate happily with another human being.

That's why I feel acute distress every time I hear it used to offend or disturb.

Says the childhood primer:

> "Hearts, like doors, will open with ease
> With very, very little keys
> Like, 'Thank you, sir'
> And, 'If you please' "

421

The single most admired person I ever knew told me that he never had a conversation with another that he didn't try to say something to brighten his listener's day.

What infinite possibilities are yours and mine if every conversation were begun with the hope that the listener would feel better when it was over.

We could rule the world.

Charles R. Meeker, Jr.

> He drew a circle that cut us out
> Heretic, rebel, a thing to flout
> But love and I had the wit to win
> We drew a circle that took him in.
> *Edwin Markham*

I think that the best way to know God is to love many things.
Author Unknown

> Today, mend a quarrel, seek out
> A forgotten friend, dismiss suspicion
> And replace it with trust. Give a soft
> Answer. Encourage youth. Manifest your
> Loyalty in word and deed. Keep a promise.
> Find the time. Forgo a grudge. Forgive
> An enemy. Listen. Apologize if you were
> Wrong. Try to understand. Flout envy.
> Examine your demands on others. Think
> First of someone else. Appreciate. Be kind.
> Be gentle. Laugh a little. Laugh a little more.
> Deserve confidence. Take up arms against
> Malice. Decry complacency. Express your
> Gratitude. Go to church. Welcome a
> Stranger. Gladden the heart of a child.
> Take pleasure in the beauty and
> Wonders of the earth. Speak your love.
> Speak it again. Speak it still once again.
> *Author Unknown*

To know just where the road does lead
Is more important far than speed
No toilsome journey daunts the soul
When vision sees a worthy goal
    Author Unknown

I'm not allowed to run the train;
The whistle I cannot blow.
I'm not allowed to say how far
The railroad cars can go.
I'm not allowed to blow off steam
Or even clang the bell.
But just you let it jump the track
And see who catches hell!
    Author Unknown

GOSSIP

Gossip is the garbage man
 Collecting from the town,
Seeking rubbish here and there,
 Lugging trash around.

Gossip is a Peeping Tom
 Peering through the blinds,
Squinting through the keyhole,
 Dissecting people's minds.

Gossip is a suicide
 Poisoned from within,
Gossip is a hypocrite,
 Gossip is a sin.
   Betty W. Stoffel

OH, SAY CAN YOU SING IT?

Oh, say, can you sing from the start to the end,
What so proudly you stand for when orchestras play it;
When the whole congregation, in voices that blend,
Strike up the grand tune and then torture and slay it?

How valiant they shout when they're first starting out;
But "the dawn's early light" finds them floundering about.
'Tis "The Star-Spangled Banner" they're trying to sing,
But they don't know the words of the blessed old thing.

Hark, "the twilight's last gleaming" has some of them stopped,
But the valiant survivors press forward serenely to "the ramparts we watched,"
When some others are dropped and the loss of the leaders is manifest keenly.

Then "the rockets' red glare" gives the bravest a scare
And there're few left to face the "bombs bursting in air;"
'Tis a thin line of heroes that manage to save
The last of the verse, and "the home of the brave."

Author Unknown

I walked into my granddaughter's room the other night and said, "What about your prayers?" She said, "I'm saying them." I said, "I don't hear you." She said, "I'm not talking to you."

Author Unknown

The Rev. Dr. Walter L. Underwood, First United Methodist Church, Fort Worth, Texas told about an aerialist who walked a tightrope across Niagara Falls.

Conditions were less than ideal. It was a windy day. The performer was thankful to have made it across.

One of those who congratulated him, after his successful performance, was a man with a wheelbarrow.

"I have faith that you could walk back across pushing this wheelbarrow," the man told him.

The performer shook his head and said he felt fortunate to have accomplished the feat without a wheelbarrow.

The man urged him to try. "I have faith that you can do it," he said.

The performer declined.

But the man kept after him.

Finally the performer said: "You really *do* have faith in me, don't you?"

"Oh, I do," the man assured him.

"Okay," the performer said. "Get in the wheelbarrow."

> I cannot count the stars I see
> Nor can I count your gifts to me
> But Heavenly Father, this I know
> Your gifts are everywhere I go.
>
> *Author Unknown*

Somehow I can't believe there are many heights that can't be scaled by a man who knows the secrets of making dreams come true. This special secret can be summarized in four C's. They are curiosity, confidence, courage, and constancy, and the greatest of these is confidence. When you believe in a thing, believe in it all the way. Have confidence in your ability to do it right. And work hard to do the best possible job.

Walt Disney

THE REAL REASON FOR BEING ALIVE

Ask an American Mother what she wants for her child. The chances are she will reply: "To be happy." But there was a time when what we most wanted, for our children or ourselves, was to *amount* to something.

What is this myth, "Happiness," that has bamboozled so many of us? And what is this idiotic thing, "fun," which so many chase after? Where people once said "Good-by" they now say, "Have fun." They even talk, God help us, of such things as a "fun time," a "fun thing," a "fun book."

I know of nothing more demeaning than the frantic pursuit of "fun." No people are more miserable than those who seek desperate escapes from the self, and none are more impoverished, psychologically, than those who plunge into the strenuous frivolity of night clubs, which I find a form of communal lunacy. The word "fun" comes from the medieval English "fon"—meaning fool.

Where was it ever promised us that life on this earth can ever be easy, free from conflict and uncertainty, devoid of anguish and wonder and pain? Those who seek the folly of unrelieved "happiness"—who fear moods, who shun solitude, who do not know the dignity of occasional depression—can find bliss easily enough: in tranquilizing pills, or in senility.

The purpose of life is not to be happy. The purpose of life is to *matter*, to be productive, to have it make some difference that you lived at all. Happiness, in the ancient, noble sense, means self-fulfillment—and is given to those who use to the fullest whatever talents God or luck or fate bestowed upon them.

Happiness, to me, lies in stretching, to the farthest boundaries of which we are capable, the resources of the mind and heart.

Leo Rosten
in This Week *Magazine*

> One ship drives east, another west
>   While the selfsame breezes blow
> 'Tis the set of the sails and not the gales
>   That bids them where they go
> Like the winds of the sea are the ways of the fates
>   As we journey along through life
> 'Tis the set of the soul that decides the goal
>   And not the storm and the strife.
>
> *Ella Wheeler Wilcox*

FOLLOW ME! WHY? BECAUSE I'M RIGHT! I'M RIGHT BECAUSE... BECAUSE I AGREE WITH MYSELF!

Do something!
Lead! Follow! or Get out of the way!!!!

Author Unknown

ST. LUKE: CHAPTER 10:25–37

25: And, behold a certain lawyer stood up, and tempted him, saying, Master, what shall I do to inherit eternal life?
26: He said unto him, What is written in the law? How readest thou?
27: And he answering said, Thou shalt love the Lord thy God with all thy heart, and with all thy soul, and with all thy strength, and with all thy mind; and thy neighbor as thyself.

28: And he said unto him, Thou has answered right: this do, and thou shalt live.
29: But he, willing to justify himself, said unto Jesus, And who is my neighbor?
30: And Jesus answering said, A certain man went down from Jerusalem to Jericho and fell among thieves, which stripped him of his raiment and wounded him, and departed, leaving him half dead.
31: And by chance there came down a certain priest that way; and when he saw him, he passed by on the other side.
32: And likewise a Levite, when he was at the place, came and looked on him, and passed by on the other side.
33: But a certain Samaritan, as he journeyed, came where he was: and when he saw him, he had compassion on him.
34: And went to him and bound up his wounds, pouring in oil and wine, and set him on his own beast, and brought him to an inn, and took care of him.
35: And on the morrow when he departed, he took out two pence, and gave them to the host, and said unto him, Take care of him; and whatsoever thou spendest more, when I come again, I will repay thee.
36: Which now of these three, thinkest thou, was neighbor unto him that fell among the thieves?
37: And he said, He that shewed mercy on him. Then said Jesus unto him, Go and do thou likewise.

Holy Bible

There are no miracles to those who do not believe in them.

W. G. Benham

Always forgive your enemies—nothing annoys them so much!

Author Unknown

Dear Lady be cautious of Cupid
List well to the lines of this verse
To let a fool kiss you is stupid
To let a kiss fool you is worse

From Executive's Digest, July 1970

Egotism is the anesthetic that deadens the pain of stupidity.
Knute Rockne

OPPORTUNITY

They do me wrong who say I come no more
When once I knock and fail to find you in
For every day I stand outside your door
And bid you wake, and rise to fight and win.

Wait for precious chances passed away
Weep not for golden ages on the wane!
Each night I burn the records of the day
At sunrise every soul is born again.

Laugh like a boy at splendors that have sped,
To vanished joys be blind and deaf and dumb,
My judgments steal the dead past with its dead,
But never find a moment yet to come.

Tho' deep in mire, wring not your hands and weep;
I lend my arm to all who say, "I can!"
No shamefaced outcast ever sank so deep
But yet might rise and be again a man.

Dost thou behold thy lost youth all aghast?
Dost reel from righteous retribution's blow?
Then turn from blotted archives of the past
And find the future's pages white as snow.

Art thou a mourner? Rouse thee from thy spell;
Art thou a sinner? Sins may be forgiven;
Each morning gives thee wings to flee from Hell,
Each night a star to guide thy feet to Heaven.
Walter Malone

The First MISS TEENAGE AMERICA Pageant (1961)

The 1976 MISS TEENAGE AMERICA Pageant

CAPTAINS AND KINGS

Isn't it strange
That Captains and Kings
And clowns that caper in sawdust rings
And just plain folk
Like you and me
Are builders of our destiny.

To each is given
A bag of tools
A shapeless mass and a book of rules
And each must fashion
Ere time has flown
A stumbling block—
Or a stepping stone.

Author Unknown

Since this book is dedicated to young people, it is fitting that we close with a story about young people.

It is a true story which was related to us by Dr. Andrew Edington, a good friend and a tradition at MISS TEENAGE AMERICA as the Special Guest Speaker for the opening festivities each year.

Dr. Edington tells us that in 1886 the President of the United States instructed the Commissioner of Labor to go out and do a complete study of the country and its state of progress.

After two years, the Commissioner reported that America had reached the pinnacle of success, that progress was at the peak and that we should content ourselves with what we had at that time and strive to preserve it.

That year
Thomas Edison was 39
Henry Ford was 23
Charles Steinmetz was 21
Madame Curie was 19
Robert Millikan was 18
Orville Wright was 15
Marconi was 12
Einstein was 7.